113- and

THE STORY OF RELIGIONS
IN AMERICA

A QUAKER EXHORTER IN NEW ENGLAND
From *Harper's Magazine*, July, 1883

✝✝✝✝✝✝✝✝✝✝✝✝✝✝✝✝✝✝✝✝✝✝✝✝✝✝✝✝✝✝✝✝

THE
STORY OF RELIGIONS
IN AMERICA

By WILLIAM WARREN SWEET

University of Chicago

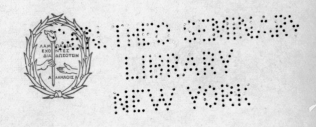

✝

HARPER & BROTHERS PUBLISHERS
New York and London

Table of Contents

{ v }

TABLE OF CONTENTS

Illustrations

THE STORY OF RELIGIONS
IN AMERICA

Chapter I

CREATIVE FORCES IN AMERICAN RELIGION

THE last religious census reveals the fact that there are in the United States two hundred and thirteen denominations of Christians, presenting a more complicated religious pattern than exists among any other people. What are the forces which have been responsible for such seeming confusion? Is there a common thread which runs through the three hundred years of American religious history binding these divergent elements into a whole? It is the purpose of this introductory chapter to point out some of the outstanding factors which have been responsible for the distinctive trends in the history of American religion, and to find, if possible, that magic strand which brings understanding out of confusion.

One element which has contributed to the religious chaos is the fact that American religious history has been written by the denominational historian and in denominational terms. The history of each denomination has been told as a complete story in itself, taking little account of other denominations, or of economic, social and political influences. Too frequently it has been written in a denominational spirit, for the purpose of exalting the denomination or of praising its leaders. But facts relating to one denomination are not enough. Taken by themselves, all the incidents which go to make up the life of a denomination do not mean much in gaining an understanding of the total religious life of the nation. Indeed, the history of one church, taken by itself, may be actually misleading. To gain complete understanding it is needful to take into consideration what all the churches have done, as well as every other influence which has entered into the moral and religious life of the people.

I

The one fact, more than any other, which explains American religion in the period of the colonies is that the colonial churches were largely planted by religious radicals. With hardly an exception, the leaders in the establishment of the American colonies were liberal and even radical in both their religious and political views. Political and religious radicalism naturally went hand in hand. A revolution in politics and religion was in progress at the very time American colonization was under way. The old political faith as well as the old ecclesiastical establishments were under attack from every quarter; the parliamentary party not only opposed the divine right of kings; they likewise contested the divine right of bishops. "Not only were many of the first American colonists dissenters from the established religion, leaving the English shores just as the old political faith was being insistently questioned, but they were in a large majority poor men, dissatisfied with the existing order and easily lured by radical ideas."

"There never was," declared Increase Mather in 1677, "a generation that did so perfectly shake off the dust of Babylon, both as to ecclesiastical and civil constitution, as the first generation of Christians that came to this land for the Gospel's sake." The Puritan colonial leaders from the beginning had visions of a new social order, and they gloried in their escape from the bounds and restrictions of the old. The middle colonies and Rhode Island especially offered asylum for the religious radical. William Penn and his associates were generous in inviting other persecuted radicals, such as Mennonites, Dunkers, Moravians, Schwenkfelders, to come to their colonies, and they came, rejoicing in their escape from the bitter persecutions of the homeland.

The principles of the Baptists and the Quakers struck at the very foundations of the seventeenth century state and ecclesiastical organization, and were considered in the more conservative colonies, such as Virginia and Massachusetts, as dangerously radical. To a certain degree also the Scotch-Irish, swarming to America in the first half of the eighteenth century, to escape their political and religious grievances, were both religious and political radicals and once settled in their new home they were not slow in asserting themselves religiously as well as politically. No group in America were more determined "to find a new heaven and a new earth" than they, and these "bold and indigent strangers" from Ireland, as they were termed by James Logan, the secretary of William Penn, were soon found in every colony in sufficient numbers to make their influence felt.

If many of the colonists were religious radicals on leaving their European homes, their radical tendencies were likely to become even more pronounced after they reached America. In the new world there were few restraining forces. If they had remained in Europe, their radical tendencies would doubtless have been somewhat held in check by tradition, by the presence of high church and civil officials; indeed, conservative forces and influences would have been all about them; but three thousand miles away across the Atlantic—then a much greater barrier than today—these restraining forces were not present, "and men moved forward rapidly, even recklessly, on the path of . . . experiment." All classes in America felt this liberation from the restraint of long established institutions, social, political and religious. Throughout the entire colonial period there was no church official of high rank in America, not an Anglican or Catholic bishop, or any other ecclesiastical official who might have exercised a restraining influence. By the time of the Revolution the people of America possessed a larger degree of freedom in religion than was to be found among any other people. They had carried on the freest debate on all religious questions without regard to bishops, priests, councils or creeds; thus encouraging an individualism in religion such as existed nowhere else.

II

The greatest accomplishment of America is the conquest of the continent, and the greatest achievement of the American churches has been the extension of their work westward across the vast stretches of the continent, keeping abreast with the restless and ever moving population. The first task of the American churches after the Revolution was to follow this westward-moving population over the Alleghanies, thence across the Ohio and Mississippi basins, on over the plains and the western mountains to the Pacific. Throughout this whole period the churches were in continuous contact with frontier conditions and frontier needs, and no single fact is more significant in its influence upon American religion.

The pioneer is always an independent individualist, determined to go his own way in religion as well as in politics, and therefore the frontier was fruitful in the multiplication of new sects. Denominations such as the Dunkers and Mennonites, which were of European origin, when transplanted to America divided and redivided as they moved westward into the undeveloped frontier, and recent studies have shown that the multiplication of the small sect since 1880 has been largely confined to the middle and far West. Good examples of the division of the larger churches caused by frontier conditions are those which resulted in the formation of the Disciples and the Cumberland Presbyterians. In both instances it was frontier liberalism contending against the narrow control of the older settled regions.

The multiplication of small colleges under church control is another result of frontier conditions. Indeed, most of the American colleges have been founded on a frontier. The general poverty of a new country made it impossible to send young men east for their training; therefore, the only alternative was to bring education to the ministerial student on the frontier. The same process of college founding has characterized practically every American frontier, from the founding of Harvard and Dartmouth to the establishment of the newest college in Montana and Wyoming. Besides these far-reaching influences the frontier supplied that challenge to the heroic without which Christianity seems never to have been able to perform its best work. It was the need of the frontier, also, which when brought to the knowledge of the East was largely responsible for the beginning of the modern missionary interest, which has supplied one of the chief influences in the life of the American churches.

III

The most important and far-reaching of the schisms in the American churches were caused by negro slavery, and the effects of that bitter contest in the churches are still with us. This fact has given to the history of American Christianity a peculiarity all its own, and any attempt to understand American church history must of necessity give large attention to the institution of slavery. Apart from its moral and religious aspects, nowhere can there be found a better example of the influence exerted upon organized Christianity by economic conditions than is furnished by a study of the relation of the churches to slavery. Parties in the churches for and against slavery did not begin to form until cotton growing had developed into a vast industry. It was not until church members had become wealthy cotton growers, that the churches ceased to denounce the institution. At the adoption of the Constitution all the churches were unanimous in their opposition to slavery; by the opening of the Civil War the churches had become the chief bulwark of American slavery.

Since the Civil War numerous attempts to heal the slavery schisms have been made, but in most instances in vain. Failure seems to have been largely due to such causes as memories of former bitterness and denominational and sectional pride, while in some instances negro membership in white churches has led to complications. The rapid rise of large negro churches since the Civil War has been a development peculiar to the United States and must be studied in connection with the slavery background.

IV

Up until the third decade of the eighteenth century the lower classes in the American colonies were little influenced by organized religion and only a small percentage of the population were members of the colonial churches. On the other hand, in the nations of western Europe, where state churches commonly existed church membership came about as a matter of course. Even in the Puritan colonies only a comparatively small proportion of the total population were members of the church, while in Virginia at the opening of the eighteenth century not more than one in twenty were church members, and the proportion was undoubtedly smaller in the other southern colonies. Thus there came to be more unchurched people in America, in proportion to the population, than was to be found in any country in

Christendom. It was this situation which made necessary the development of a new technique to win people to the church, and this new method, peculiar to America, was revivalism. The Great Awakening was the first religious movement which made any serious impression upon the common people of the American colonies, and marks the beginning of an aggressive American Christianity.

From that time until the end of the nineteenth century revivalism has manifested itself at frequent intervals in America. In its earlier phases revivalism grew largely out of frontier conditions, and performed its best work in the newer sections of the country, and here also it often produced unfortunate excesses. But whatever may be said in criticism of frontier revivalism, this much must be said in its behalf: it was perhaps the only method by which the frontier could receive any of the benefits of Christianity, warped though it often was, almost beyond recognition. The camp-meeting, one of the by-products of frontier revivalism, served a very large social and religious need and has developed into the present-day community Chautauqua and summer assemblies. This peculiar phase of American Christianity has been gradually passing, just in proportion as frontier conditions have been disappearing, while the more adequate academic training of the ministry has lessened the emotional appeal in modern preaching.

V

In the national period our religious development cannot be understood apart from the economic, social and

{8}

political changes. In other words, the same set of influences has produced similar results in both church and state, and each has exercised a constant influence on the other. The parallels between American political and religious history are both numerous and striking. "The complete separation of church and state in America, and our division into numerous denominations, should not blind us to the fact that there is after all a certain unity in American church history, as well as frequent connection between it and the civil history of the nation."

The American churches were engaged in forming national organizations at the very time our constitutional fathers were formulating the federal constitution. Nationalism was in the air, manifested not alone in the political activities of the nation, but in the religious organizations as well. Between 1784 and 1800 Methodists, Protestant Episcopalians, Presbyterians, Roman Catholics, and the Reformed churches were engaged in nationalizing their ecclesiastical organizations. This same emphasis is likewise indicated in the formation of organizations among the churches to carry on certain phases of philanthropy. Thus in the early years of the nineteenth century the American Bible Society, the American Tract Society and a whole group of similar organizations were formed, which indicate that the churches were viewing their task as one of national scope. "Thus the church and the nation felt themselves called at the same period to grapple with the same problem," that of securing harmonious coöperation among the states and among the churches.

The period of nationalism was followed by the period of the growth of sectionalism. In this era slavery divided the nation, and it also divided the church. Churches began to emphasize their own denominational interests at the expense of interdenominational and national interests. Loyalty to the denomination came now to be the great emphasis, as loyalty to the North or South came to be characteristic in politics. Interdenominational societies gave way to denominational; churches were divided into anti-slavery and pro-slavery groups, while doctrinal schisms added to the confusion.

In the great American wars, the Revolution, the Civil War and the World War, the American churches supported the program of government, and were affected by post-war influences. The new nationalism and the new centralization in government and in business arising after the Civil War found expression in the churches in the formation of the Federal Council, the rise of new inter-denominational organizations, as well as in the emphasis upon centralization and efficiency within the individual churches. During the World War the churches and the nation became internationally minded and built great world programs, to be followed by post-war reaction and a return to a narrow nationalism. Thus has the same set of influences produced similar results in church and state while each has exercised a constant influence on the other.

Chapter II

THE EUROPEAN BACKGROUND

It was long the custom of Protestant ministers in the United States to speak of the discovery and colonization of North America as a providential event. The facts seemed perfectly clear. Just twenty-five years after Columbus made his famous voyage of discovery, Martin Luther nailed his ninety-five theses to the church door at Wittenberg. Thus the beginning of Protestantism and the discovery of America were contemporaneous events. In other words, God appeared to have saved America for Protestantism. To them it seemed that a divine wisdom and a controlling providence had kept the very existence of America a secret until the fullness of time. But whether providential or not, it is a significant fact that these two great historic events, taken together, contain the key which explains to a large degree the establishment of the English colonies in America.

England was more than a century behind Spain and Portugal in founding colonies. At the opening of the period of discovery the majority of Englishmen were little interested in establishing an England beyond the seas, and as late as the opening of Queen Elizabeth's reign (1558) there were, perhaps, not more than a few hundred Englishmen outside the British Isles. But within a hundred years, following the close of that long reign, English trade had gone out in every direction, and English colonies were to be found in America, in Africa, in Asia and in the islands of the sea. England had succeeded Spain as the mistress of the seas and the foundations of the British Empire had been permanently laid. All this was the accomplishment of the sixteenth and seventeenth centuries. The sixteenth was the century of English pioneering on the sea; in the seventeenth every English colony in America was planted except Georgia. These were also the centuries *par excellence* of the English trading companies. But what were the reasons which made these centuries a period of such feverish activity on the part of Englishmen? The economic historian would attempt to explain it by saying that a new set of economic forces were at work, while the political historian would mention the political rivalries between Spain, France, Holland and England as the most important contributing factor. But neither of them, nor both together, can explain adequately the establishment of the majority of the English colonies in America. It is true that economic stress was, very probably, responsible for bringing the majority of colonists to America during the whole period of the colonies, but religion was responsible for the *founding* of more colonies than any other single factor.

To understand this sweeping statement it will be necessary to examine the religious situation in England and also in the several European countries which contributed so largely to the peopling of the English colonies. It is, therefore, the purpose of this chapter to explain the European conditions out of which came the several groups of religionists which migrated to America in the sixteen and seventeen hundreds, and were responsible for laying the foundations of the American churches.

The first English colonies in America were founded by Englishmen, and throughout the whole period of colonization colonists from the British Isles made up the largest part of every colony. We will, therefore, first consider the religious situation in England, Scotland and Ireland, which accounts for the coming of the Puritans, the Caveliers, the Quakers, the Catholics and finally the Scotch-Irish. Out of these groups came Congregationalism, the Established Church, the English Catholic, Baptists, the Friends and the Presbyterians. These were the most important of the colonial churches, though the Dutch and German elements in the middle colonies particularly were not far behind in numbers and influence. From these elements came the Reformed churches, the Dutch and German, and the Lutherans, besides the Mennonites, the Dunkers and the Moravians.

"England passed through the Reformation without a Civil War, yet no country in Europe found greater difficulty in coming to a religious equilibrium after that change." Led by the strong-minded Henry VIII—motivated largely by personal ends—and taking advantage of a strong nationalistic movement already under way against foreign control, the English Church broke away from Rome and formed a national church, with the king as the supreme governor, who appointed the bishops and otherwise controlled the ecclesiastical system. Aiding the king in the government of the church was the English parliament, which embodied in statute law the forms of worship and theological tests, which, however, were framed by the clergy. Though the church thus established was limited by king and parliament, yet it possessed some privileges which tended to offset these restrictions. For instance, the Bishops sat in Parliament while the church received tithes charged upon the land and rates payable by all the people. The national church was the only form of religion possessing legal standing and all the people were required to attend its services.

This national church, as long as Henry VIII lived, was Catholic in forms of worship and in its theology, but just as soon as Henry's son, Edward VI, came to the throne a movement got under way at once to make the English Church Protestant in its forms and theology. Edward at his ascension to the throne was a mere boy, so the government was carried on by a Council of Regency, and this council from the beginning was under the control of the reform party. Immediately radical changes were made in the national church. The result was the publication of the Prayer Books, the first in 1549, the second in 1552, which transformed the worship of the English Church from Catholic to Protestant forms. Latin gave way to English as the language of the service; the sermon was given a place of much larger importance; congregational singing was introduced; while both the bread and wine of the Lord's Supper were henceforth to be administered to all communicants, the term *altar* was to give place to *table* and the term *priest* to *minister*. Thus the English Church became definitely Protestant.

The swing of the English Church toward Protestantism

during Edward's short reign came to a sudden halt with the coming to the throne of the Princess Mary, daughter of the much-wronged Catharine of Aragon. Naturally her consuming desire was to vindicate her mother and restore her mother's faith. To make things worse for the Protestant party she had married the bigoted Philip II of Spain, the archenemy of Protestantism throughout Europe. Immediately a Catholic reaction began, only to stop with the death of the queen five years later. Those who had been chiefly responsible for making the English Church Protestant were driven from office. Some fled the country and found a refuge among the Protestants of Switzerland or in southern Germany, while others were imprisoned. These were years of horrible persecution which have stained indelibly the memory of Mary Tudor and have fastened upon her, justly or unjustly, the name "Bloody Mary." The total number of her victims was about three hundred, a number greater than in Henry VIII's reign of thirty-eight years or of Elizabeth's of forty-five.

The death of the saddened queen—for it is said that Mary died of a broken heart—and the coming to the throne of Elizabeth, the daughter of the sprightly Anne Boleyn, meant the triumph of the Protestant party once more. In 1559 the Act of Supremacy declared the queen the Supreme Governor of the church, and a new revised Prayer Book, following that of 1552, was introduced, while the use of all others was prohibited. At once the Catholic party registered their opposition, not alone to the Acts of Parliament, but to the new queen whose legitimacy they refused to recognize. The results were Catholic plots on the one hand and anti-Catholic legislation on the other, and in the struggle for supremacy which ensued the great majority of the people of England rallied about their queen, and thus Protestantism and patriotism came to mean one and the same thing in sixteenth century England.

The English Protestants who had fled to the continent to escape the wrath of Queen Mary now returned, bringing with them the more extreme Protestant notions which prevailed among the reformed congregations in Switzerland and southern Germany. These and other influences were responsible for increasing the Protestant feeling in the country, and as the sixteenth century wore on, it became evident that the English people were being led farther and farther along the path of reformation. The Thirty-Nine Articles adopted in 1563 expressed the views of Calvin, and in the Convocation of that year the proposal to simplify the rites of the church received strong support, and there was even a petition presented to do away with the use of the surplice. These are but straws which indicate the direction in which the religious winds were blowing, and if it had not been for the queen's liking for stately ceremony, which caused her to prevent these radical changes, it is probable that the English Church might have been purified in the Puritan sense, at this very time, and thus the whole Puritan movement, in both England and America, might have been radically changed. But the old medieval ritual triumphed and was prescribed for all Englishmen. No liberty of worship, whatever, was permitted, and any clergyman who deviated from it was liable to be treated as a criminal, while all non-conformists might be excommunicated and were liable to be imprisoned.

By the death of Queen Elizabeth the Anglican had become the national church in a sense in which it had never been before. At the beginning of her reign the people of England, religiously speaking, were a fluid mass, ready to change from Catholicism to Protestantism and back again, at the bidding of their sovereign. But now a new generation had grown up, which knew no other religion, and the fact that it had the authority of law gave Anglicanism a patriotic sanction which no other church possessed. But in spite of these strong urges toward the national church, it failed to obtain the allegiance and affection of all of the English people. There were, first of all, the Catholics, a small group, it is true, but made up of many wealthy and influential people, the type which generally holds to the old and is slow to take up with the new. Their religion was outlawed, because Catholicism was considered the deadly enemy of the Elizabethan state, although the queen had no antagonism to Roman Catholicism as such, and long lists of anti-Catholic laws were placed upon the statute books by the English Parliament. Such laws were not only passed during the reign of Elizabeth, but even in the reign of James I—from whom the Catholics had expected more lenient treatment—the severity of anti-Catholic legislation was increased, due to the fright the king experienced over the Gunpowder Plot, at the very opening of his reign. During the reign of Charles I the Catholics received better treatment, but from 1640 to 1660, the period of the triumph of extreme Protestantism under the Commonwealth, the Catholics were bitterly persecuted.

All this would seem to indicate that there would be a large Catholic exodus from England, yet few Catholics left England, and no English colony remained Catholic for any length of time. Perhaps the chief reason for this fact has already been suggested. The English Catholics were not of the emigrating class. They represented the nobility and the landed gentry, and the conservative tendency which held them to the old religion would hold them to the old home. Then, being of the higher class, they had a better chance to escape the severity of the laws, and we know that the laws against them were largely unenforced, and they were never so badly treated as the anti-Catholic legislation might indicate. Nor were they ever without hope of a bettering of their condition, while toleration in the colonies was always as uncertain as in the homeland.

Of far greater importance, from the standpoint of English colonization of America, was the second group of Englishmen who were dissatisfied with the newly established Church. These were the Puritans. It has been suggested that if the English government had not interfered, England would have divided naturally into two religious camps—the Catholic on the one hand and the Puritan on the other. The Anglican system was the artificial medium between the two extremes.

Throughout Elizabeth's reign the Puritan party was growing in influence and numbers. During the first two decades, to 1570, they were particularly concerned about purifying the English Church of all its Catholic practices, such as the use of vestments by the clergy, the using of the sign of the cross in baptism, the celebration of saints' days, kneeling to receive the communion, and the use of certain formulas in the service. Failing to accomplish their ends in Convocation, many Puritan ministers began to disregard the law prescribing these formulas and practices, and changed the service to suit their puritanical taste, while some resigned their pastorates. It was at this time that the term *puritan* came into use as a term of opprobrium, signifying those who insisted on an ultra-pure ritual. The next stage in the development of English Puritanism began about 1570, and took the form of agitation to change the government of the church. In 1572, in their "Admonition to Parliament" they declare that "the names archbishops, archdeacons, lord bishops, chancellors, etc., are drawn from the Pope's shop, together with their offices, so the government which they use . . . is anti-Christian and devilish, and contrary to the Scriptures." The system of church government which they advocated was the Presbyterian, which had been introduced from Scotland by the Book of Discipline of 1572. So strong was the movement in this direction that it appeared, for a time, as if the Church of England would be reorganized along Presbyterian lines, but through the stern opposition of the queen and the rigorous administration of the Archbishop of Canterbury, Whitgift, the movement was held in check. Toward the close of Elizabeth's reign the Puritans were emphasizing such matters as strict Sabbath observance, and attacked the immoralities and extravagances of the times.

The great body of the Puritans had no wish to destroy

the Established Church, or to divide it. They were dominated by the ideal of a united national church, a church which would be one in form of worship, organization and doctrine. The queen herself was not more tenacious of this ideal than were the great majority of the Puritan party, but there were a few among them, who might be termed Puritan radicals, who advocated a return to the simplicity of organization of the early New Testament times. They repudiated the idea of a national church, and advocated the plan of church government which they thought was to be found in the Scriptures, namely, the absolute independence of each congregation of believers. This group came to be called Separatists, because they held that there was no chance at purifying the church by their remaining within it, and they looked upon themselves as did the early Christians as "saints, sacred and set apart from a wicked and persecuting world."

The Separatists were never numerous, never numbering more than a few thousand. Their congregations generally met secretly, but some defied the law and met openly. Their attitude toward civil government is well summed up in a contemporary letter: "Nevertheless, this is out of doubte, that the Quenes highnes hath not authoritie to compel anie man to beleeve any thing contrary to God's Word, neither may the subject geve her Grace the obedience. Our bodyes, goodes, and lives be at her commandement, and she shall have them as of true subjects. But the soule of man for religion is bound to none but unto God and his holy word." Naturally the wrath of civil government soon fell upon this little group. Their congregations were broken up; their members were imprisoned; they were deprived of their property, and many of them died under harsh treatment. By the end of the reign of Elizabeth these radicals, or Separatists, had either been driven into exile, or were silenced. We are to hear again of them, when in 1620, discouraged by their ten years of exile in Holland, a little group of them sailed away in the *Mayflower* to found the first Puritan colony in America.

The radical Puritans, however, were relatively unimportant as compared with the great and growing body of Puritans who remained within the Church of England. As this party within the church became more numerous, and their criticisms of the church more outspoken, a self-conscious High Church party arose, defending the church, asserting the divine appointment of episcopacy and upholding the symbolic ceremonials and ritual. Gradually the breach between these two parties widened, as the attitude of each became more and more dogmatic. Besides their original differences they began to develop doctrinal divergences, for the Puritans held to the doctrines of Calvin, while the High Church party more and more came to accept the newly advanced views of the Dutch theologian Arminius.

Such was the situation when James VI of Scotland became James I of England, in 1603. The Puritans, now advocating Presbyterian organization, and denouncing Episcopal, looked to James to favor their position, since he had been trained a Calvinist under Scotch Presbyterianism. Even before he reached England a petition was presented to him signed by several hundred English clergymen, praying for a change in the Prayer Book in the direction of a simpler service. Their hopes, however, were doomed to early disappointment, for at a great conference called to discuss church matters in 1604, known as the Hampton Court conference, King James angered the Puritans by declaring: "Scotch Presbytery—it agreeth as well with monarchy as God and the devil," and he concluded a long speech before the conference with the words: "If this be all your party hath to say, I will make them conform themselves or else I will harrie them out of the land, or else do worse."

When King James began his reign the people had been divided and discontented, and as his reign drew to its close it was clear that discontent and division had increased. The new king, Charles I, unlike his father, was young and full of vigor. But the royal energy instead of being used wisely, only served to widen the breach between the religious parties in England. Charles had married a French princess, the sister of Louis XIII. Before his marriage he had promised to secure toleration for English Catholics; this, together with the tactless methods employed by Archbishop Laud in enforcing uniformity, cost him the favor of the moderates in his own party, and swelled the ranks of the Puritans.

The stronghold of Puritanism was the region in east-central England between the Thames and the Humber. This was the wool-growing district, in close touch with the continent, and especially with the United Netherlands, which had become one of the chief centers of Calvinism. The University of Cambridge was the intellectual center of this region, and many a congregation became

completely Puritan under the influence of clergymen educated at Cambridge. It was from this region also that
Puritan migration to New England began. Here was
located the village of Scrooby, the English home of the
Plymouth colonists. It was in Lincolnshire that the Massachusetts Bay Company was born, formed by wealthy and
influential Puritans of the region. The New England
leaders were Cambridge men. Thus it was but natural
that the first Puritan college in America should be located
in the village which they named Cambridge, since their
infant institution was modeled after one of the colleges at
Cambridge University, and named after a young Puritan
minister, a graduate of Cambridge, John Harvard. It was
mainly from this region that some twenty to thirty thousand of England's strongest and most intelligent citizens
left, between the years 1628 and 1642, to make their homes
in the New England across the sea.

By 1642 Puritanism in England was completely triumphant. Seven years later the king was beheaded, and for
the next decade England was governed without a king
or a House of Lords. The Anglican Church was now
under a cloud. The Puritans in turn became persecutors,
and the Anglicans, who had fought, during the Civil
Wars, on the king's side, began to leave in great numbers
for Virginia, Maryland and the Carolinas. They came to
escape conditions at home just as intolerable as those
which had caused the migration of the Puritans to Plymouth and Massachusetts Bay.

The period of the Commonwealth was one of religious
disintegration in England. The breaking down of the old
organizations and the disappearance of the old authority

presented a glorious opportunity to the individual religious leader, and as a result numerous small religious
bodies began to appear. Among the better known of these
were the Anabaptists, the Millenarians, or Fifth Monarchy men, who went about preaching the millennial
kingdom of Christ on earth' and the Friends, or Quakers.
From the standpoint of their importance in the colonization of America, the Quaker was by far the most interesting and significant of these individualistic religious
movements of the seventeenth century.

Fortunately there have always been mystically-minded
people. Such an individual was George Fox, a weaver's
son and an apprentice to a shoemaker, with little book-
learning beyond the Bible, but blessed with spiritual insight. After years of inner struggle, during which he
wandered about through the Midlands of England, Fox
became by 1647 an apostle of a new reformation. He
rejected all the conventional beliefs and taught that there
was direct illumination from God within every man's
inner being; that there was no need for a priest or minister, since religion is something that begins in the soul of
man, and is not primarily concerned with books, creeds
or institutions. In the propagation of these ideas Fox met
with abuse and violence. Sixty times was he brought before magistrates, and was imprisoned eight times, for
longer or shorter periods. By 1652 others began to join
his movement, especially in the northern counties, where
Swarthmore Hall became the center of their increasing
activities. By 1654 there were sixty people proclaiming
the principles of the Quakers, some of them women, and

by 1659 there were probably thirty thousand Quakers in England.

This rapid increase in numbers, and the enthusiasm with which they preached their peculiar notions, together with their intrusion into the churches, where they denounced the paying of tithes, the taking of oaths, and every other practice which they disapproved, brought down upon them such harsh treatment as only seventeenth century England knew how to impose. They were ridiculed by the clergy, fined and imprisoned by the magistrates and subjected to every indignity by their jailers. Nor did the coming of Charles II to the throne in 1660 relieve their distresses. The Church of England, now once more restored to its place of influence, asserted its despotic power as vigorously as in the time of Laud. By 1662 more than four thousand Quakers were to be found in the jails of England, and in the homeland there seemed no immediate hope for better treatment.

Meanwhile conversions to Quakerism were going on apace. At first the appeal had been largely to people of the lower middle class, but now they began to gain converts from among those of family and fortune. In 1667 William Penn, the son of Admiral William Penn, was "convinced" and soon became one of the most active champions of the persecuted sect. The claim of 16,000 pounds against the king, which was a part of the considerable fortune which Penn inherited from his father, was repaid by Charles II in the shape of a great land grant in America, toward which the tide of Quaker emigration soon set in, and within an incredibly short time a great Quaker commonwealth was created. From 1656 to the end of the colonial period Quakerism was an expanding force in America, for the New World presented favorable opportunities for the carrying out of the Quaker ideals of life which were not to be found in the mother country. There is evidence that America had a prominent part in the thought and plans of George Fox almost from the inception of his movement, for the New World presented to him what seemed a providential field to be won for his truth. By 1750 there were more Quakers in America than in Great Britain and they had played the largest part in the making of three of the thirteen colonies, and a prominent part in the making of three others.

One of the largest single racial elements in the American colonies at the opening of the American Revolution was the Scotch-Irish. Their coming marks the beginning of Presbyterianism in America. What were the causes back of this last great wave of immigration in the colonial period?

The Scotch reformation began somewhat later than did the English, though once under way it swept forward with irresistible force. The Roman Church in Scotland had been largely under the control of the Scottish nobility, who managed to place their younger sons in the highest offices. The lower clergy were generally ignorant, indolent and incapable, but in spite of these handicaps the majority of the Scottish people were faithful to the old church. Gradually, however, Lutheran ideas filtered into the eastern towns along the coast, and by 1535 a reform party was forming in Scotland. Soon Scotland was divided between two religious parties, the Catholic favoring a continuance of the alliance with France, the

Protestant desiring to draw more closely to England. At first the Catholic party was the stronger, and under the able leadership of Cardinal Beaton, archbishop of St. Andrews and primate of Scotland, Protestants were persecuted and several of their leaders burned at the stake. The execution of George Wishart, one of the most famous of the Scotch Protestant preachers, in 1546, was followed by the assassination of the Cardinal by some of Wishart's followers. From this time forward the Protestant party became more aggressive and ten years later were strong enough to take the offensive in a war for their new faith.

The next phase of the Scotch reformation gathers about the name John Knox, Wishart's favorite apostle. Soon after Wishart's execution Knox was taken prisoner by a French fleet, and for almost two years was a French galley slave. Through the instrumentality of the English government he was released in 1549, when he took up his residence in England, where for five years he preached in three English towns, including London. When Mary Tudor came to the throne Knox was one of those who withdrew to the continent, and first at Frankfort and later at Geneva, he preached to Reformed congregations, where he came in contact with the great Calvin, who was then the controlling force in church and state.

Meanwhile affairs were moving rapidly in Scotland. In 1557 Scottish Lords favorable to the Reformation organized themselves into "Lords of the Congregation," and two years later open war began between the two religious parties. In the midst of this war Knox returned from Geneva. The Scottish reformers, up to this time, had favored a system of church government resembling that of the Church of England, but the appearance of John Knox turned the scale in favor of strict Calvinism, and a Presbyterian system was the result.

The next turn in the course of events which accounts for American colonial Presbyterianism is the Scotch colonization of Ireland. From the time of Henry VIII onward the English rulers attempted to extend their control over the whole of Ireland, a policy which was valiantly resisted by the Irish clan leaders. To help in their plan of controlling the country, Irish land was given to English and Scotch landlords, and gradually English and Scotch settlements were formed, especially in the north of Ireland. This policy was carried forward most vigorously by James I, and large numbers of Scotch settlers from western Scotland were soon residing in the four northeastern counties of Ulster. Coming largely from Scotland, these settlers were chiefly Presbyterians. They made excellent colonists, and it was not long until their section became the most prosperous part of Ireland, and their chief city, Belfast, the most important Irish port.

Streams of Scotch-Irish emigration to the American colonies began in the first quarter of the eighteenth century, and by the middle of the century they were coming in great waves. This migration was largely due to economic causes. The English government at this time was, with other European nations, under the delusion that in order to bring prosperity to the mother country it was necessary to restrict the economic activities of colonies. The colonies in North Ireland were treated just as were those in America, and Navigation Acts were passed, restraining exports of live stock and woolen manufactories. This legislation

ruined the woolen trade and thousands of weavers left
Ireland for other countries. As the economic distresses
increased a great stream of migration set in toward America. Added to the economic distresses were religious grievances. A strong and aggressive Presbyterian organization
had been built up in North Ireland with the coming of
the Scotch colonists, with an efficient ministry, trained
largely in Scotch universities. These staunch Presbyterians,
supporting their own churches voluntarily, were, in addition, compelled to pay tithes for the support of the Church
of Ireland, an Anglican organization, which represented
only a small minority of the people. By 1750, it has been
estimated that 100,000 people of this racial group had
found homes in America.

So far the English, Scotch and Irish background of the
American religious groups has been traced; it remains to
discuss the Dutch, German and French background.

When the Reformation began, the Low Countries were
linked with Spain, under the rule of Charles, the grandson of Ferdinand and Isabella. Since the Netherlands
were thus united to the most Catholic country in Europe,
it was but natural that vigorous attempts should be made
to keep out Lutheran ideas, from the beginning. Proclamation followed proclamation, edict followed edict, forbidding open or secret meetings, against printing
unlicensed books, against the reading of the Scriptures.
Long lists of prohibited books were posted while the
penalties for the violation of these prohibitions became
increasingly severe. But in spite of all these precautions
the number of heretics rapidly increased. Persecution followed, attended by harrowing atrocities, and it is esti-

mated that 30,000 people had been put to death in the Netherlands when Charles abdicated the throne in favor of his son in 1556.

If Charles V had scourged the reformers of the Netherlands with whips, Philip II lashed them with scorpions. For four years Philip remained in the Netherlands to administer the edicts against the heretics, but heresy continued to spread in spite of all he could do. Even the Catholics of the Netherlands opposed the enforcement of the most severe edicts, or "Placards" as they were termed, and sent a petition to Philip asking for a change of policy allowing a degree of religious freedom. To this the king responded by introducing the Spanish Inquisition (1565), which only served to increase the number of Protestants within the provinces. Finally, two years later, open rebellion broke out. The Duke of Alva, of dreadful memory, came with his veteran troops, his unlimited powers and "Council of Blood," and ten thousand more victims were added to the already long list of martyrs for conscience sake, while Dutch and Walloon refugees, estimated at four hundred thousand, were to be found in England and southern Germany. William Prince of Orange, himself a Catholic, and recognized as their leader by both Dutch Catholics and Protestants, led the revolt against Spanish rule, and one by one the cities drove out their Spanish governors and placed themselves under his banner. In 1576 came the Pacification of Ghent, in which Holland and Zealand and the fifteen southern provinces agreed to unite to expel the Spaniards. Three years later, after the southern, French-speaking provinces had returned to Roman Catholic uniformity, the Union

of Utrecht was formed, uniting the seven northern provinces, which three years later renounced allegiance to the
King of Spain and constituted themselves an independent
republic. Religious toleration was one of the glories of
the new Republic of United Netherlands, for one of the
provisions of their union was that no one should be questioned on the subject of divine worship.

The long bitter struggle against the Spaniard had intensified Dutch Protestantism, and it was in the midst of
their terrible trials that their churches were organized.
Luther, Zwingli and Calvin, all had their followers in the
Netherlands, but in the end the Calvinist influence proved
the stronger, and the Dutch Church became Calvinistic
in discipline and doctrine. Both the Lutheran and Zwing-
lian systems were closely related to the civil government,
but when the Dutch churches were deciding on their
form of government, the Duke of Alva was the ruler
of the Netherlands and thus the favor of government was
entirely out of the question. The Presbyterian system,
therefore, which had been the form of government
adopted by the church in the early centuries, when it was
under the ban of the Roman Empire, seemed the form
best suited for a "Church under the Cross."

The first one hundred years following independence
were the greatest in the history of the Dutch people. In
the long struggle against the Spaniard the *Sea Beggars*
had played a prominent and heroic part. Again and again
they had routed the clumsy Spanish ships, and whenever
the *Beggars* appeared, the Spaniards had learned through
bitter experience that the best thing to be done was to
flee. The terrible struggle through which they had come,

instead of exhausting their energies, seemed but to have awakened them to a more vigorous life. Having achieved independence, they became at once one of the great commercial and maritime powers of Europe, and Dutch ships were soon finding their way into every port. Those were great years in the history of the Dutch people. Rubens was engaged in painting his glorious pictures; Hugo Grotius was writing his matchless treatises on the Freedom of the Seas, laying the foundation for international law; while Dutch trading companies, both east and west, were establishing the foundations of the Dutch colonial empire.

The Dutch colonies, wherever founded, were primarily trading centers. The Dutch people did not migrate in great numbers to their colonies, largely because the population of the mother country was small, having been sorely depleted by the long, bloody wars. But those who did settle in America were of such sturdy stuff and the institutions they established, including their church, were so highly developed that they continued to exercise an influence far larger than their actual numbers would seem to warrant.

It has been estimated by painstaking students that in 1750 at least 100,000 Germans were to be found in the English colonies in America. The largest share of them were in Pennsylvania, where they numbered perhaps 70,-000, though Germans were also to be found in New York, in the western counties of Virginia and the Carolinas and in Georgia.

To account for this large migration of Germans to the New World it will be necessary to recall some of the

effects of the Thirty Years' War (1618-1648). There is
little doubt but that this war was one of the most cruel
and brutal in modern history. Seventy-five per cent of the
population throughout Germany were killed, while the
property loss was even greater, and it is an accepted fact,
based upon carefully gathered statistics, that the war set
back German material development by two hundred
years. Southern Germany, or the Palatinate, was the region which suffered most. But so fertile was the soil and
so great was the recuperative power of the people, because
of their industry and agricultural skill, that soon after
each invasion the country was transformed from a desert
into a garden, only to attract other plunderers. But as
though the sufferings of the Thirty Years' War were not
enough, Louis XIV of France, on three different occasions (1674; 1680; 1688) in the last quarter of the seventeenth century, sent his armies into the Palatinate to burn
and to plunder. The greed and the cruelty of the French,
we are told, exceeded even that of the "Landsknechte" of
the Thirty Years' War, who drove nearly 500,000 Palatines from their burning houses and devastated fields.

Added to the terrible conditions produced by the wars
and invasions were the religious persecutions. The Treaty
of Westphalia (1648), which marked the end of the
Thirty Years' War, provided for some degree of toleration. Catholics, Lutherans and Reformed were to have
equal rights in the Empire, though the individual princes
could still restrict the religious freedom of their subjects.
But neither Catholics, Lutherans nor Reformed respected
the rights of the small sects, such as the Mennonites,
Dunkers and German Quakers. Thus religious persecu-

tion, the tyranny of petty rulers, destructive wars and general economic distress produced the background out of which came German emigration to the American colonies.

In 1671 and again in 1677 William Penn visited the continent and the lower Rhine region. Penn's sympathies were aroused by the distresses of the Palatines, and when he had become the possessor, a few years later, of his great American province, he appointed agents to solicit settlers from among the Palatines. Penn's pamphlet, "Some Account of the Province of Pennsylvania in America" was translated into German in 1681, the first of a series of pamphlets and tracts by which the people of the Palatinate and the regions outside were made acquainted with the "Holy Experiment" which William Penn was fathering in America. And one may well imagine the joy with which these simple people read Penn's essay on "Religious Liberty" which was appended to his advertisements.

Still another group of persecuted Germans, some of whom eventually found their way to the English colonies in America, were the Salzburgers. These were German Lutherans, driven from the Austrian archbishopric of Salzburg by the fanatical zeal of the archbishop in 1731. More than thirty thousand of them were exiled from their native land, and the cruelty of their sufferings soon aroused the indignation of all Protestant Europe. Seventeen thousand of them eventually found homes in Prussia, where they were received by the king, Frederick William I. Just at this time the colony of Georgia was being planned by a group of philanthropic Englishmen, and they, coöperating with the Society for the Promotion of

Christian Knowledge in London, provided a haven for some of the most daring of the Salzburgers on the soil of the new colony of Georgia. Their first settlement in America was called Ebenezer—the stone of help—for, said they, "hitherto hath the Lord helped us" (I Sam. 7: 12).

It only remains, in this chapter, to recount the background which brought to the American colonies the religious exiles driven from France, by the revocation of the famous Edict of Nantes—the French Huguenots. While they did not come to America in great numbers, yet in proportion to their numbers no single group made so rich a contribution to the English colonies.

The period of the Wars of Religion in France was from 1562 to 1598. There were, all told, eight separate wars during these years. They were ferocious wars indeed, for both Protestants and Catholics were imbued with an extreme fanaticism. Both sides drew allies from the outside. Massacres and assassinations characterized the long struggle; the massacre of St. Bartholomew (1572); the assassination of the Guises (1588); and finally the assassination of Henry III (1589) brought Henry of Navarre, the leader of the Protestant forces, to the throne, as Henry IV. As the only means of bringing peace to his distracted kingdom, Henry resolved to become a Roman Catholic. By this act conditions all over the kingdom changed as if by magic. Nobles, provinces and towns now came forward with offers of their allegiance, and the long wars were at last at an end.

The laws against Protestants, however, were still in force, but the king had given his word to his former companions in arms that all would be well with them. The French Protestant Church was now well organized, with a General Assembly, meeting year by year, and they were demanding equal rights with their Roman Catholic fellow subjects. The king was true to his word and out of the negotiations, carried on by delegates representing the Protestant party, there came finally the Edict of Nantes (1598), the charter of French Protestantism. This granted liberty of conscience throughout the kingdom, state payment for their ministers, while they were given equal entry to all schools, universities and hospitals, and all public offices were open to them.

For nearly a hundred years after the issuing of this famous edict the French Protestants lived under its protection and did their part in resuscitating "the corpse of France." Under Louis XIII, by the aid of his crafty minister Richelieu, France became the ascendant nation in western Europe. It was during these years of returning greatness and wealth that France began the establishment of her colonies in the New World. The early attempts to establish colonies as places of refuge for Huguenots, as in Florida and Brazil, were all failures, while the later colonies founded in the valley of the St. Lawrence, under the administration of Richelieu, were all orthodox Roman Catholic.

Finally in 1685 came the revocation of the edict. This was preceded by twenty years of persecution and forced conversion of the Protestants, and the revocation was but the culmination of a policy of suppression and "jesuitical interpretation of the terms of the edict." Such are the causes for the great migration of French Huguenots which set in toward the close of the seventeenth century and continued until France had lost a large proportion of her best people.

The desire of Louis XIV was not to drive the Huguenots away, but to force their conversion, and for this reason emigration was probihited. Soldiers were quartered in their houses, but some of them left their homes in the night, "leaving the soldiers in their beds," and abandoning their homes with the furniture. Every wise government in western Europe was eager to offer them a refuge, for they brought with them an industrial skill which represented the best that Europe had to offer. Thus they introduced manufacturing in north Germany, a suburb of London was filled with them, while the Prince of Orange soon had regiments of soldiers recruited from among them. Many went to the Dutch colony in South Africa, while every colony in America, from Massachusetts to South Carolina, extended them a welcome.

Chapter III

ESTABLISHED CHURCH BEGINNINGS IN AMERICA

In LIEU of cargoes of gold and silver for which the early
Virginia colonists diligently searched, but failed to find in
the bays and inlets of the Chesapeake, the ships of the
Virginia Company were loaded with ship timbers, cedar,
black walnut and clapboards. For Jamestown, the first
permanent English colony in America, was the child of a
commercial company and was established as a commercial
enterprise. Much of the hardship endured by the Jamestown colony was due to the fact that most of the early
colonists were gentlemen, unaccustomed to such hard
labor as was required to obtain such cargoes. Though
primarily concerned with trade the members of the company were from the first interested in promoting religion
among the colonists as well as in the conversion of the
Indians. Undoubtedly the example of Spain was ever before the early promoters of English colonization. Spain,
the chief Roman Catholic nation of the whole world, had
established her great colonial empire in the New World,
and hand in hand with the Spanish conquerors had gone
the Spanish Catholic missionaries, and tens of thousands
of the natives of New Spain and Peru had been won to,
at least, a nominal acceptance of Catholic Christianity.

Should not England, the leading Protestant nation in the whole world, do as much? And thus, by planting colonies in the New World, England herself would not only be benefited but the cause of Protestantism would likewise be advanced, and the power of Spain might also be held in check.

Among the one hundred and five colonists which landed on the low-lying shores of the James in Virginia, on May 13, 1607, was Robert Hunt the chaplain, a "clergyman of preserving fortitude and modest worth," in whose appointment Archbishop Bancroft had been consulted. Hunt seems to have exercised a wholesome influence over the notoriously quarreling members of the council and on more than one occasion, by his "good doctrine and exhortation" allayed the envy and jealousy so that, to quote Captain John Smith, "our factions were oft qualified, our wants and greatest extremities so comforted that they seemed easy in comparison of what we endured after his memorable death." It was on June 21 of that first year that Chaplain Hunt administered the first sacrament to Englishmen in America, under an old sail hung between three or four trees, to keep off the hot sun of that first Virginia summer, while the worshipers were seated on unhewed logs, the chaplain's pulpit being a "bar of wood nailed to two neighboring trees." After this, we are told, there were daily prayers, morning and evening, while on Sunday there were two sermons and every three months the sacrament.

Just how long Chaplain Hunt lived is not known, but there is evidence that he continued his faithful ministrations at least through part of the year 1608, and then probably died, a victim to the famine and pestilence which swept away so many hundreds of the early Virginia colonists. During the first year a rude, barnlike church was erected, which within a few months was destroyed by fire, together with most of the other buildings in the fort and in the general destruction went the chaplain's meager library. But in the midst of all these distresses, the chaplain was never heard to repine.

In 1609 a new charter was granted to the Virginia Company, independent of the Plymouth Company. The stockholders in this new company numbered 765, among them numerous clergymen, including the bishops of London and Lincoln, as well as twenty-one peers and other individuals representing every "rank, profession or trade in England and included the merchant guilds of London." The old charter had placed the government in the hands of two councils, one in London, the other in America; the new charter abolished the council in Virginia and in its place was a governor. Lord de La Warr, or Delaware, was the first Virginia governor under the new charter, but not being able to come out immediately Sir Thomas Gates was sent as his deputy, and with Gates came the second clergyman to Virginia, Master Richard Bucke, successor to the lamented Robert Hunt. Bucke was an Oxford graduate and was recommended for the place by the Bishop of London who termed him "an able and painful preacher."

The increased number of shareholders in the Virginia Company bears testimony to a growing interest in colonization in England. As a result larger expeditions were soon in preparation, and for the first time sermons were preached in the churches of London to those about to leave for the New World. One such sermon was that by William Crawshaw, preacher at the Temple in London, before Governor de La Warr and the council, which has been termed the first missionary sermon ever addressed by a priest of the Church of England to members of that church. Toward the close of his sermon he gives this sound advice: "A Christian may take nothing from a Heathen against his will, but in fair and lawful bargain. Abraham wanted a place to burie in, and liked a piece of land; and being a great man, and therefore feared, a just and meek man and therefore loved of the heathen, they bad him chuse where hee would, and take it. No, saith Abraham, but I will buy it, and so he paid the price of it; so must all the children of Abraham doe." Further on, he says, referring to profits to be obtained by the members of the Company: "If there be any that come in, only or principally for profit, or any that would so come in, I wish the latter may never bee in, and the former out again. If the planting of an English Church in a heathen country; if the conversion of the Heathen, of the propagating of the Gospell, and the inlarging of the kingdome of Jesus Christ, be not inducements strong enough to bring them into this businesse, it is a pity they be in at all. . . . Let us therefore cast aside all cogitation of profit, let us looke at better things; and then I dare say unto you as Christ hath taught us, that if in this action wee seeke first the kingdome of God, all other things shall be added unto us." Wise advice indeed, but the most casual reading of the story of the founding of Virginia will show how poorly that advice was followed.

At the arrival of Deputy Governor Gates conditions in the colony were discouraging in the extreme. In 1609 there had been more than 500 colonists, but by May, 1610, no more than 60 were alive. On landing, the new governor and the colonists who came with him proceeded at once to the church, now rebuilt after the fire, where the bell was rung and "the dispirited and starving people dragged" themselves to the house of God where Chaplain Bucke offered up a "zealous and sorrowful prayer," and at the close of service the governor's commission was read and the deputy assumed office. But conditions were too bad to be long endured, and very soon the governor, after consulting with Captain Newport and others, decided to abandon the colony. But before the ships with the colonists on board could leave the James, they were met by Lord Delaware coming up the river, who ordered the departing colonists to return. So affected was Lord Delaware by the terrible conditions in which he found the colony, that when the emaciated remainder were drawn up to receive him, he fell on his knees and prayed in the presence of all the people.

As long as Lord Delaware's personal administration lasted especial attention was given to the religious condition of the colony. There is evidence that there were several preachers in Virginia during his brief stay. The secretary and recorder of the colony under Delaware states that: "The Captaine Generall hath given order for the repairing of (the Church), and at this instant many hands are about it. It is in length threescore foote, in breadth twenty-foure, and shall have a Chancell in it of Cedar, and a Communion Table of Black Walnut, and all the pews of Cedar, with faire broad windowes, to shut and open, as the weather shall occasion, of the same wood, a Pulpet of the same, with a Font hewen hollow, like a Canoa, with two Bels in the West end. It is so cast as to be very light within, and the Lord Governour and Captain Generall doth cause it to be kept sweete, and trimmed up with divers flowers, with a Sexton belonging to it; and in it every Sunday wee have Sermons twice a day, and every Thursday a Sermon, having true preachers, which take their weekly turnes, each man addresseth himself to prayers, and so at Foure of the clocke before Supper. Every Sunday, when the Lord Governour and Captaine Generall goeth to Church, hee is accompanied with all the Counsailers, Captaines, other officers and all the Gentlemen, with a guard of Holberdiers, in his Lordship's Liverey, faire red cloakes, to the number of fifty both on each side, and behind him: and being in the Church, his Lordship hath his seat in the Quier, in a greene velvet chaire, with a cloath, with a velvet cushion spread on a table before him, on which he kneeleth, and on each side sit the Counsell, Captaines, and Officers, each in his place, and when he returneth home againe, he is waited on to his house in the same manner."

But while the governor, with his regal show and guard in red coats were worshiping in the little church at Jamestown, conditions in the colony remained desperate and sickness and disease continued to take its toll from among the settlers. Lord Delaware was nominal head of the colony until his death in 1618, but the affairs of Virginia after 1611 were administered by a series of deputy governors. Sir Thomas Dale, whose title was High

Marshal of Virginia, during the absence of Deputy Governor Gates, was in charge much of the time from 1611 to 1616, and this period marks the end of "the starving time" and the beginning of happier conditions. With Dale came Rev. Alexander Whitaker, whose zeal in the cause of Christianity won him the title "Apostle to Virginia." About this time the Virginia Council issued a pamphlet containing a declaration of the purpose and end of the colony, in which they state that religion is the "maine and cheefe purpose" of the plantation. They call upon their countrymen for help, asking them to "remember that what was at first but of conveniency, and for honor, is now become a case of necessity and piety." In conclusion they declare that only those of blameless lives and character should go out to the infant colony. But in spite of the expressed desire of the council, numerous "idle and wicked persons" continued to find their way to Virginia and were to prove "to bee poyson to one so tender, feeble and yet unformed" as was the infant colony.

Sir Thomas Dale has left a reputation for cruelty which he does not fully deserve. He ruled with a strong arm, enforcing a code of laws characterized as "lawes, divine, morall and martiall" in which twenty crimes were punishable by death. But he brought order out of chaos, though the severity of the laws regulating the church tended to make it odious in the eyes of the settlers. In estimating Sir Thomas Dale it is but fair to remember that his punishments were no more cruel than were those practiced in Europe at the same time and as a whole he administered these savage laws with moderation. Through his energy new settlements were formed seventy miles up the James; one was given the name Henrico in honor of Prince Henry of Wales, while the other was called New Bermuda. Here churches were formed; Alexander Whitaker was in charge of the New Bermuda church while Henrico seems to have been in charge of a curate, Mr. Wickham, under Whitaker.

Of all the early ministers in Virginia we know most concerning Alexander Whitaker. He was the son of Dr. William Whitaker, Regius Professor of Divinity at Cambridge and one of the best known of the Puritan clergy of his day. Alexander Whitaker left a pleasant parish in the north of England, "without any persuasion (but God's and his own heart)" and "to the wonder of his own kindred, and amazement of all that knew him, undertook this hard but, . . . heroicall resolution to go to Virginia and helpe bear the name of God unto the Gentiles." Seventy miles up the James from Jamestown in the midst of a group of new settlements he built his parsonage, "a faire framed house," and a hundred acres was impaled for a glebe. Thus Whitaker became the first country parson and missionary in Virginia.

In 1613 there was published in London a pamphlet entitled "Good Newes from Virginia, sent to the Counsell and Company of Virginia, resident in England, From Alexander Whitaker, Minister in Henrico in Virginia," which was a part of a sermon which he had preached from the text "Cast thy bread upon the waters: for after many days thou shalt finde it." To this is added a description of the country and the Virginia Indians, and a plea is made for men and money "who may venture their persons hither, and heere not only serve God but helpe these poore Indians." Young men, he states, are "fittest for this country, and we have no need either of ceremonies or bad livers." Some years later in writing to a friend in London Whitaker says: "I much more muse, that so few of our English ministers that were so hot against the Surplis and subscription, come hither where neither are spoken of," a clear indication that Puritan notions prevailed in Virginia. This good man, imbued with an unselfish and tireless zeal for religion, worked faithfully until his death in 1617, which came by drowning in the James.

Through the influence and labors of Whitaker the first Indian convert was won to Christianity in the person of Pocahontas. All are familiar with the story of her rescue of Captain John Smith from death, to which he had been condemned after his capture by the tribes over which her father, Powhatan, was the ruler. Largely through her influence a treaty was made between the Indians and the English, and the princess became a familiar figure about Jamestown. After Smith's departure the Indians again became hostile, but Pocahontas retained her affection for her white friends, although she now was no longer permitted to visit them. In the spring of 1613 she was taken captive by Captain Argall and held as hostage for the release of some English captives which the Indians had taken in the course of the war. The princess was turned over to High Marshal Dale for safe-keeping, who evidently took her to his plantation on the upper James, where she was near Alexander Whitaker and from whom she received religious instruction. Within a few weeks she was willing to renounce her Indian superstitions and accepted Christian baptism, receiving the name Rebecca.

But Whitaker and Dale were not the only Englishmen who were interested in the Indian princess and in her progress in Christianity. John Rolfe, one of the most progressive of the young planters, and the first to produce tobacco for export, and withal a widower, was soon in love with the enchanting maiden and he confesses, that in her "my hartie and best thoughts are so entangled, and enthralled in so intricate a laborinth, that I was even awearied to unwinde myself thereout." Nor did he ever succeed in unwinding himself, for on the first of April, 1614, he and the princess Pocahontas were married at Jamestown, the old chief Powhatan giving his reluctant consent and sending a brother and two sons to witness the ceremony. Two years later, accompanied by her husband, her young son Thomas Rolfe and Sir Thomas Dale, Pocahontas sailed for England, together with some ten or twelve Indian youths who were to be educated in England. Here she was met by her old friend Captain John Smith; was introduced at court to the king and queen where we are told she, "carried herself as a daughter of a King" and was received everywhere with respect by "divers persons of honor." In the early part of 1617 she was about to return to Virginia with her husband who had been appointed secretary and recorder general of Virginia, when, in the language of the chronicler: "At her return towards Virginia she came at Gravesend to her end and grave, having given great demonstration of her Christian sinceritie, as the first fruits of Virginia conversion, leaving here a good memory and the hopes of her resurrection. . . ."

The year following the death of Lord Delaware (1619), Sir George Yeardley became the governor of Virginia and with him a new era began for the colony. The moving spirit in the company was now Sir Edwin Sandys who was a man of liberal and progressive ideas, whose ambition was to make of Virginia a "free and popular state." He was a friend of the Puritans and an opponent of the arbitrary government of James I, and naturally his election to the treasurership of the company was opposed by the king, who advised the company to "chose the devil if you will, but not Sir Edwin Sandys." It was under the guidance of this liberal man, seconded by the wise Yeardley, that the first representative assembly in America was constituted. The old cruel laws were abrogated and provision was made that a General Assembly was to be held once a year, made up of "the Governor and Counsell, with two Burgesses from each Plantation freely to be elected by the inhabitants thereof." At this time there were four boroughs in the colony and a total population of about 1,000. The first assembly met in the "Quire of the Churche" at Jamestown on July 30, and sat for six days. Twenty burgesses were present. In their order of business, first came the prayer by Master Bucke when the assembly proceeded to business, and in the course of the first session passed thirty-four laws, and of this number twelve had to do directly or indirectly with religion.

The enactment of laws regulating activities of the Virginia clergy and prescribing specifically the religious duties of the colonists indicates that the English canon law as well as the civil law was in force. Early acts of the House of Burgesses (1620-1621) provided that the clergymen were to be paid in tobacco and corn, each receiving 1,500 pounds of the former and 16 barrels of the latter, though accompanied with the statement that if the full amount could not be raised, "the minister was to be content with less." The religious enactments were extremely puritanical in character, prescribing church attendance twice each Sunday, while the other acts condemned "gaming, drunkenness and excess in apparel."

The visit of the princess Pocahontas to England, together with the coming of the Indian youths to be educated, evidently aroused a larger interest in the education and Christianization of the Virginia Indians. Even King James displayed interest and at about the time of the death of Pocahontas, sent a letter to the archbishops asking their assistance in raising funds for the erection "of some Churches and Schooles for ye education of ye children of those Barbarians wch cannot but be to them (the colonists) a very great charge." As a result of this appeal some fifteen hundred pounds was subscribed through the several English bishoprics for a college in Virginia and the company instructed the governor to undertake the planting of a university at Henrico, at the same time setting aside ten thousand acres for its endowment. Judged from the number and generosity of other subscriptions, interest in the enterprise was widespread. A London merchant gave 300 pounds for the university besides 24 pounds which was to be distributed to three godly men who would "bring up three of the Infidal's children in the Christian Religion and some good course to live by." The Bishop of London, Dr. John King, manifested a great interest in the affairs of the colony at this time; was chosen a member of the Council for Virginia and the spiritual jurisdiction of the Bishop of London over the church in America seems to date from this period.[1] He collected a thousand pounds for the Henrico university; Sir Edwin Sandys, the company's treasurer, sent five hundred pounds for the education of Indian youth, while gifts of books, Bibles, prayer books, communion plate and linen were contributed for the godly work.

This was a period of great activity in Virginia. During the years 1620 and 1621 seven ministers came to the colony, while new colonists and servants were coming over in increasing numbers. Plans were made for increasing the number of tenants on the lands belonging to the company and "young single women of blameless reputation" were brought over to be the wives of the bachelor planters and tenants. At the same time the practice of sending convicts to Virginia was begun, a policy which was evidently distasteful to the company officials, and for which the king was responsible. About the same time some Virginia planters purchased twenty negro slaves from some Dutch traders and thus were introduced two most unfortunate elements in the population of the colony.

Meanwhile money was pouring in for the establishment of schools which were to be feeders for the new

---

[1] The question of the origin of the Bishop of London's colonial authority is an obscure question, which has never been solved satisfactorily. For a discussion of this point see Arthur Lyon Cross, *The Anglican Episcopate and the American Colonies* (New York, 1902), especially Chapter I.

university at Henrico. One was to be established at Smythe's Hundred with funds sent to Sir Edwin Sandys by an unknown donor. Another was to be founded at Charles City with money raised by the chaplain of an East Indiaman, the Rev. Mr. Copeland, to which the company gave 1,000 acres as an endowment, while books were promised and even a builder and apprentices were secured to erect the building and an usher was appointed. Prosperity at last seemed to have come to Virginia after the many dreary years of failure and suffering. During the year 1621 some twenty vessels had arrived with more than a thousand new colonists and experiments in manufacturing iron, glass, silk and wines were under way with a fair prospect of success. So pleased was the company at the prospects of their colony that they arranged for a thanksgiving service, which was held April 18, 1622, at which the Rev. Mr. Copeland preached the sermon which was later published under the title "Virginia's God be Thanked."

Little did the Company or the preacher realize what havoc had been wrought in Virginia by a terrible massacre of the planters and their families nearly a month before. On the morning of March 22, 1622, the Indians, no longer held in check by Powhatan, fell upon the settlements on the upper James and within a few hours 347 persons had been killed in cold blood, without respect for age or sex. In this remote region the settlements were almost completely wiped out, among the slain being John Rolfe. The destruction was not so general, however, in the older settlements, due to the fact that here the Indians were more friendly and also to the fact that here the settlers had been warned by a young Christian Indian. The plantations on the upper James were now abandoned for the time being, while expeditions were organized to punish the Indians, but while many were driven into the deep forest, few were actually killed. The progress of the colony was only temporarily checked, but the most unfortunate consequence of the massacre was that it completely changed the attitude of the colonists toward the Indians as a whole. The opinion, previously held by only one of the Virginia ministers, that "till their priests and Ancients have their throats cut there is no hope to bring them to conversion," now, according to Captain John Smith, became general. As a result the elaborate plans for the education of Indian youth, which had been so nearly worked out, were now abandoned and it was to be many years before any further attempts were made to revive that interest.

In 1624, on June 16, the Virginia Company came to an end, and the control of the colony passed directly into the hands of the king. The alleged reason for this action was the misconduct of the company in its failure properly to propagate the Christian religion, increase trade and enlarge the Empire. The real reasons, however, were undoubtedly the refusal of the company to appoint the king's nominees to office; the king's dislike of the leaders; and his desire to please the King of Spain, whose daughter Prince Charles was at the time courting. For the next six years there was a rapid succession of royal governors until the arrival of John Harvey in 1630. Under the rule of this tyrant the church suffered greatly and was left largely to care for itself. Up to this time the ministers who had come out to Virginia were generally men of character and sincerely devoted to the advancement of true religion, but from this period forward the type of ministers in the colony changed for the worse.

The fact that the church in Virginia was completely under secular control accounts largely for its weaknesses. The laws for its regulation were passed by the General Assembly: the appointment of ministers in each parish was in the hands of the vestry, while the removal of ministers was obtained on complaint of the vestry to the governor and his council. The vestries, after 1661, were close corporations, empowered to fill their own vacancies, and the tendency was for the church to be controlled by a local aristocracy. These men as a whole, while thinking of the church as a necessary institution, were devoid of deep religious feeling. Each parish was responsible for the payment of its own minister, and after 1662 the ministers were to receive a uniform salary—16,000 pounds of tobacco. This worked a hardship on many of the Virginia clergymen, since the price of tobacco was tending downward through the eighteenth century. Another factor causing discontent was the fact that the varieties of tobacco differed in value. In certain counties where the best grade, the sweet-scented tobacco, was raised, the ministers received in actual value twice the amount received by ministers serving in districts where only the poorer grade, Aranoka tobacco, could be grown. The glebes provided by law for the clergy proved disappointing; in many instances the minister's tenure was so uncertain he was reluctant to spend time or money in keeping up his little plantation; in other cases the land was so poor it was not worth cultivation or placing buildings upon it.

Until the loss of the charter (1624) the Virginia Church was largely under Puritan control, but with the coming of the royal governors Puritan influence came to an end and acts were passed forbidding all non-Episcopal ministers from officiating in the colony. At the beginning of Sir William Berkeley's first administration (1641) seventy-one Virginia colonists signed an appeal asking the General Court of Massachusetts "to send ministers of the gospel into that region, that its inhabitants might be privileged with the preaching and ordinances of Jesus Christ." In response to this appeal three Puritan ministers were sent to Virginia, carrying letters of commendation from Governor Winthrop, but they were soon silenced, though one of them removed to Maryland where he ministered to some of the Virginia Puritans who had migrated to that colony.

During the period of the Civil Wars (1642-1649) and the Commonwealth (1649-1660), Virginia was greatly disturbed. Religion was at a low ebb and at the time of the restoration few of the parishes had ministers. When Governor Berkeley was restored to power in 1660 among the first acts passed by the Virginia Assembly was one providing "for the building and due furnishing of churches, for the canonical performance of the liturgy, for the ministration of God's Word, for a due observance of the Sunday, for the baptism and christian education of the young." It was in 1671 that Governor Berkeley included in his report to the Commissioners of Foreign Plantations the following account of the religious situa-

An Interview Between Sir Edmund Andros and James Blair

Commissary Blair frequently came into conflict with the civil
authorities and especially Governor Andros

From *Harper's Magazine*, April, 1901

tion in the colony: "There are forty-eight parishes, and the ministers well paid. The clergy by my consent would be better if they would pray oftener and preach less. But of all commodities, so of this, the worst are sent us. But I thank God there are no free schools, nor printing, and I hope we shall not have these hundred years."

The picture of the Virginia clergy generally given is perhaps darker than they deserve. A recent historian of the Colonial Church of Virginia states that in a list of some one hundred and twenty Virginia clergy before 1700 hardly more than a dozen had anything recorded derogatory to their moral or religious character. On the other hand, there is much evidence to show that there were entirely too many incompetents and second rate men in charge of the Virginia churches. In 1696 one of the Virginia rectors wrote to the Bishop of London that "Several ministers have caused such scandals of late and have raised such prejudices amongst the people against the clergy, that hardly can they be persuaded to take a clergyman into their parish." One of the principal causes for the prevalence of inefficient clergymen was the practice, which prevailed throughout the entire colonial period, of vestries employing lay-readers from year to year, instead of having their ministers inducted into office by the governor. A minister inducted into office held his place for life, a condition which would not find favor among the vestrymen. The Rev. Morgan Godwyn, a clergyman who had spent some time in Virginia, wrote to Sir William Berkeley in 1681 a brief description of religion there. "The Ministers," he says, "are most miserably handled by their Plebeian Juntos, the Vestries: to whom the hiring . . .

which was soon assigned him. The bad condition of the Virginia Church had been brought to the attention of the Bishop of London by a pamphlet entitled "Virginia's Cure" prepared by one who had fled to Virginia during the period of the Commonwealth and "for the space of ten years" had been an eyewitness of the things he describes. Among the remedies proposed by this writer was the sending of a bishop to the colony, and there seems to have been an attempt to carry out this suggestion and a bishop was nominated for Virginia. When this attempt failed, James Blair was appointed commissary and was the first such official in any of the English colonies. His duty was to inspect churches, deliver charges, and to a limited extent administer discipline, though he could not confirm or ordain. Although greatly limited in authority, Blair performed an invaluable service to the church in Virginia.

The great massacre of 1622 had completely ended the early attempts at founding colleges in Virginia. But in 1661 at the first meeting of the Virginia Assembly after the restoration, an act was passed providing for a "colledge" "for the advance of learning, education of youth, supply of the Ministry, and promotion of piety." But it was more than thirty years before a college was finally established and this was accomplished through the energy and zeal of James Blair. At first he was unable to obtain the assistance of the legislature, but after he had obtained gifts from private givers, amounting to more than 2,000 pounds, he at last secured authority by legislative enactment to proceed to England to seek a charter for a college. King William and Queen Mary were not only cordial to the petition, but the king granted 2,000 pounds due the crown from Virginia quitrents to the project. But all the royal officials were not so cordial, for when Commissary Blair urged the attorney-general, Seymour, to prepare the charter, with the admonition that the Virginians had souls to save as well as Englishmen, the haughty official answered: "Souls! Damn your souls! Make tobacco." But in spite of this contemptuous official the charter was soon forthcoming and was signed, February 8, 1693, and the same year the Virginia Assembly passed an act providing for the erection of a building at the place afterward selected as the site of Williamsburg.

The college was endowed with twenty thousand acres of choice land and was to receive the income from a tobacco tax as well as an export duty on furs and skins. But from the beginning the college encountered difficulties, one being the destruction of the building by fire in 1705 when it was but half completed. At first few students were in attendance and therefore it could not at once supply the demand for clergymen. Blair was the president of the college from its foundation until his death forty-nine years later. He died at the age of eighty-eight, having been commissary for Virginia fifty-three years.

In 1720 Virginia contained twenty-nine counties and forty-four parishes, large and small. In each parish there was a church either of stone, brick or wood, while in the larger parishes there were one or more chapels in addition. At first the churches were made of logs, to be followed in a few years with larger and more pretentious frame buildings accommodating from 150 to 300 worshipers. In most instances, in the more populous parishes, the frame buildings in the course of time gave place to brick churches, following in some instances the cruciform design, though the larger number were plain rectangular buildings, seating from 300 to 500 worshipers. The chancel was uniformly in the east end, the pulpit against the north wall, while the body of the church was filled with square pews, seating from twelve to twenty-five, each pew surrounded by high sides so that the worshipers could not see from one pew into another. The church stood in a yard of never less than two acres, in which there was always a good spring of water, and frequently there was a graveyard attached. Near the church was the vestry house, which was frequently used for the meetings of county officials.

The service of the church was according to the liturgy, though the clerk, being the only person in the congregation supplied with a prayer book, made all the responses alone. The clerk also lined out and led the "Psalms of David in Metre," generally with the aid of a tuning fork. The congregation was seated in order of social rank; the gentry in their own pews in front and others according to their social position. Considerable time was given to the sermon, which was apt to be dry and repetitious. On certain Sundays children and servants were catechized by the minister, as this was a part of the clergyman's duty.

Turning now from Virginia, brief attention will be given to the beginnings of the Established Church in Maryland. The early religious history of Maryland, however, belongs to another part of this story; that which relates to the first experiments in religious liberty in America.

It was not until near the end of the seventeenth century that the Established Church began to emerge in the colony of Maryland. The first official notice of it in that province was due to a letter written in 1676 by the Rev. Mr. Yoe, who seems to have been one of three Episcopal clergymen in Maryland at the time, addressed to the Archbishop of Canterbury. The letter draws a picture of the deplorable religious conditions in the colony and implores the archbishop to provide some means for the better support of the Protestant religion in the province. The archbishop laid the letter before the Bishop of London. From this time forward official attention, to a limited degree, was given to Maryland and the number of Established Church ministers increased, though the quality of those sent out left much to be desired. The great majority of the people were undoubtedly Protestant and an increasing concern for a church and a settled ministry was manifest among the better settlers. The overturn of James II in 1689 in what is known as the Protestant Revolution furnished the Maryland Protestants with the opportunity to rid themselves of Roman Catholic rule, and in 1692 Maryland became a royal colony. One of the first acts of the assembly after this change was "An Act for the Service of Almighty God and the Establishment of the Protestant Religion."

The act divided the ten Maryland counties into thirty-one parishes and a poll tax of forty pounds of tobacco was levied for the building and repairing of churches and the support of the ministry. Two years following the Act of

Establishment, Sir Francis Nicholson became lieutenant governor, a most important event for the Established Church in Maryland. Nicholson was a devoted friend of the church, incongruous as that may seem, for he was profane, arbitrary, conceited and lacking in self-restraint, and yet his interest and liberality were a prime factor in firmly establishing the church in the colony. It is stated on good authority that he did more for "the erection of Episcopal churches than all the other colonial governors combined," and thirty churches in various parts of the colony owed their existence to his efforts. The capital was now moved from St. Mary's to Annapolis where a new brick church was begun. All this activity on the part of the Establishment met with strong opposition from the Roman Catholics and Quakers, who opposed the poll tax for the support of the church and the other measures. This opposition, together with a large immigration of Irish Catholics which now set in, aroused fear on the part of the Protestants, of the reëstablishment of Catholicism and the reinstatement of the old proprietors. The latter was actually accomplished in 1715, only, however, after the fourth Lord Baltimore had become a Protestant. It was during this period of great activity on the part of the Established Church, that agitation began for the appointment of a commissary for Maryland, a movement which was supported both by the governor and the assembly, and resulted in the fortunate selection of Dr. Thomas Bray who received the appointment from the Bishop of London in April, 1696.

Dr. Bray was a successful rector of a parish in Warwickshire, and is described as one of the first of the "working clergy." Four years elapsed after his appointment before he sailed for America, but these were years filled with plans and work for the American Church. He knew well the difficulty of securing suitable ministers for America, and also the handicaps under which they worked after reaching their distant parishes. Accordingly he exerted himself in securing missionaries and before he sailed for Maryland the number of clergymen in that province had been increased to sixteen. He likewise began the work of collecting libraries for the missionaries, and succeeded in establishing thirty-nine of these, the funds for which he collected, heartily assisted by many of the English bishops and others. This activity eventually resulted in the formation of the "Society for the Promotion of Christian Knowledge" (1698) which took form before he left England for America.

Commissary Bray reached Maryland March 12, 1700, and was warmly welcomed by Governor Nicholson. His first concern was to secure the passage of a law requiring every minister within the colony to use the Book of Common Prayer, which proved a most unwise measure as it aroused the bitter enmity of Catholics and the dissenting groups who now became a unit in opposing the Establishment. His next concern was to reform the clergy within the colony and bring to bear upon them effective discipline. At his own expense he visited all the parishes within the colony to observe the work and manner of life of the clergy. Two of the most flagrant clerical offenders against morals and decency were disciplined, though the Commissary's energetic attempts to better conditions frightened and offended the clergy and people as most of them would have preferred to have been let alone. The hot-tempered governor was likewise offended for he was jealous of his authority in appointing the incumbents.

At this juncture Dr. Bray returned to England, having heard that there was active opposition to the Act of Establishment in the English Parliament. The act was disapproved by the attorney-general, though Bray succeeded in having another act presented, and passed which established the church in Maryland, but at the same time extended to the dissenters and Quakers the English Act of Toleration of 1689, though denying it to the Roman Catholics. This has been termed one of the sarcasms of history. Maryland, which had been founded for the sake of religious freedom by the toil and treasure of Roman Catholics, was now open to all who call themselves Christians save Roman Catholics.

During the agitation over this measure Dr. Bray published a "Memorial upon the State of Religion in America," which aroused great public interest. He declared there was need at once for forty missionaries in America and that the "refuse of the clergy in England would not do for American missionaries," and he submitted a scheme whereby young, learned, strong and able clergymen were to be obtained for America. The plan itself failed, but it soon resulted in the foundation of the "Society for the Propagation of the Gospel in Foreign Parts." Dr. Bray never returned to America. For a while he continued to hold the office of commissary, but soon resigned in order that another might be sent, but his zeal for and interest in America never lagged and until his death in 1734 he continued to labor for the good of the Colonial Church.

The founding of the "Society for the Propagation of the Gospel in Foreign Parts" in 1701 was an event of prime importance for the future of the Established Church not alone in the American colonies, but throughout the world. At the time of its organization the Established Church had hardly made a beginning in the colonies outside Virginia and Maryland. King's Chapel in Boston, begun in 1688 through the influence of the royal governor of Massachusetts, was the only Episcopal church in the Puritan colonies; in North Carolina there were two church settlements but no minister; South Carolina had several congregations, but here also there was a dearth of clergymen; Pennsylvania had one Church of England minister; the Jerseys none; New York one only; while Rhode Island had a church but no minister. The work of planting and fostering the Established Church in these colonies was to be the great task of the venerable society in America during the first half of the eighteenth century.

✠✠

Chapter IV

THE PURITAN COLONIES: THE BEGINNINGS OF AMERICAN CONGREGATIONALISM

FOR about ten years the Pilgrims, as the Plymouth colonists came to be called, lived in Holland. Here they had failed to prosper economically as they had hoped, and there seemed to be no prospect of bettering their condition. Renewal of war was also threatening between Spain and Holland, but the chief reason which determined them to leave Leyden and to seek a new place of refuge was the painful realization that their children were being "drawne awaye by evill examples into extravagante & dangerous courses, getting ye raines off their neks, & departing from their parents . . . so that they saw their posterietie would be in danger to degenerate & be corrupted."

By the end of Queen Elizabeth's reign all of the Separatists or radical Puritans in England had either been driven underground or had gone into exile. It was the Scrooby congregation under the leadership of John Robinson, their pastor, that fled to Leyden, attracted by the liberal government of the Dutch. These radicals were no more acceptable to the great Puritan party within the Church of England than to the conservative Anglicans, for the great body of English Puritans were firm believers in the national church and looked upon the Separatists as schismatics, self-righteous and exclusive. But it was this little band of radicals, despised by all parties among their own countrymen, which was destined to lay the foundations of New England, and to furnish the model of church government which was afterwards to be accepted and developed by the far more numerous and influential Puritans, the founders of Massachusetts Bay.

After considerable negotiation with the Virginia Company, they having been invited to the Virginia colony by Sir Edwin Sandys, the Puritan treasurer, an agreement was finally reached, granting the Leyden congregation land in what was termed the "northern parts of Virginia." The hired *Mayflower*, upon which the one hundred and two Pilgrims embarked for their new home, instead of bringing them to the territory for which they had negotiated, brought them, on November 11, 1620, to the barren shores of Cape Cod, a region belonging to the Plymouth Company. Here they were compelled to land without charter or grant of any kind, from any government, and the settlement which they were about to establish would therefore have no legal basis. Because of this, certain of their party began to talk of doing as they pleased, when they had landed, and it was to ward off this threatened rupture in their ranks that they gathered in the cabin of the *Mayflower* and there drew up the famous *Mayflower Compact*. This instrument, modeled after the agreement by which they had constituted the church at Scrooby, sixteen years before, was to serve as a model for other groups of New England colonists in the years to come. The *Compact* remained the basis of the Plymouth government until 1691, when the colony was united with Massachusetts.

For nine years the Pilgrims at Plymouth were without a pastor, for John Robinson had died before he could join them, but during these years they were led in their worship by William Brewster, the ruling elder. Brewster had been advised by Robinson not to administer the sacraments, but twice every Sabbath he "taught to ye great contentment of ye hearers, and their comfortable edification" and we are told that he had a "singular gift in prayer, both public and private . . . and he always thought it were better for ministers to pray oftener, and divide their prayers, than to be long and tedious in the same." It was not, indeed, until 1629 that the Plymouth church secured a satisfactory minister, in the person of Ralph Smith, who had come first to Salem. It is true that their partners in England had sent over John Lyford to be their minister in 1624, but he proved entirely unworthy and was expelled from the colony.

The Plymouth colonists had been too poor to pay for their transportation to America, nor were they able to meet the expense of maintaining themselves while building the colony. They were, therefore, forced to form a partnership with some London merchants, who advanced them £7,000. The merchants, of course, were primarily interested in profits, and wished to send over active young men who would make good fishermen and fur gatherers, while the colonists were anxious to bring over the remainder of the Leyden Pilgrims, and above everything else, desired to maintain their congregational institutions.

The returns to the London merchants on their invest-
ment, were very small, and after the colony had rejected
Lyford as their minister, the merchants became distrustful
of the enterprise and after some negotiations the colony
bought itself free from their unsympathetic partners,
agreeing to pay £1,800 in nine annual installments. Soon
after this the remainder of the Leyden colonists were
brought out, and by skillful trading and hard work they
were able within a few years to pay off their debt.

The colony, however, grew very slowly, due, no doubt,
partly to the poorness of the soil, but especially because
the Separatists were few in number, while their strictness
and exclusiveness was not attractive to outsiders. By 1630,
however, the permanence of the colony seemed assured.
In that year there were 300 inhabitants at Plymouth while
in the years following new settlements were established,
so that by 1643 there were ten towns and about 2,500
people.

The heart and center of the Pilgrim colony at Plymouth
was their church. A Dutch merchant of New Amsterdam,
who visited Plymouth in 1627, thus describes the meeting-
house, with the order in which the people gathered for
worship: "Upon the hill they have a large square meeting
house, with a flat roof, made of thick sawn planks, stayed
with oak beams, upon the top of which they have six
cannons, which shoot iron balls of four and five pounds,
and command the surrounding country. The lower part
they use for their church, where they preach on Sundays
and the usual holidays. They assemble by beat of drum,
each with his musket or firelock, in front of the captain's
[Myles Standish's] door; they have their cloaks on, and

place themselves in order, three abreast, and are led by a sergeant without beat of drum. Behind comes the Governor [William Bradford] in a long robe; beside him, on the right hand, comes the preacher [Elder Brewster], with his cloak on, and on the left hand the captain, with his side arms and cloak on, and with a small cane in his hand; and so they march in good order, and each sets his arms down near him." Here they were free to carry out the type of church government in which they believed, and to worship according as their consciences dictated. To gain this was to them sufficient reward for all the untold sufferings through which they had come, and the "windswept graveyard" on the hill and the "rude street of hewn-plank houses bore mute witness" as to how much it had cost.

Of far greater importance historically than the Pilgrim colony at Plymouth were the settlements about Massachusetts Bay. A sober historian has stated that: "Probably no colony in the history of European emigration was superior to that of Massachusetts in wealth, station or capacity." In this respect it was in great contrast with the humble and poor people who settled Plymouth.

The first step in the great migration of English Puritans was undertaken through the influence of the Rev. John White, a Puritan minister at Dorchester, England. It was his idea to form a Fishing Company and found a settlement on the Massachusetts coast, part of whose purpose was to care for the moral and religious welfare of the many transient English fishermen who came to that region year by year during the fishing season. This enterprise proved a failure, but it served to arouse White's

EARLY PICTURE OF HARVARD

Reproduced from a picture in possession of the Massachusetts Historical Society

interest in the founding of a Puritan colony. Securing help from a group of Puritan capitalists, a company was formed and a grant of land obtained from the Council for New England. In September, 1628, the vanguard of the great Puritan migration arrived at what is now Salem. Here they found a few remnants of White's fishing colony, and it was after some differences between the two groups had been peacefully settled that they named the place *Salem* (peace). John Endicott, a rigid Puritan and a member of the company, was named governor and by the next year some three hundred people were living under his authority. This was the beginning of Massachusetts.

The next year (1629) twenty-six Englishmen secured a charter for the *Massachusetts Bay Company*. Although the original purpose of this corporation was primarily commercial, control soon passed from the hands of those chiefly interested in business to those whose interests were primarily religious. Just why King Charles I was willing to grant a charter to such a group has never been found out, but it is quite probable that he was not unwilling to have some of the more pestiferous Puritans leave England for his own peace of mind. In August, 1629, still another change took place in the corporation, when all those withdrew who did not intend to go to America. Thus the governing body of the company was removed to American soil, while at the same time they rid themselves of the absentee stockholder, thus minimizing the possibility of governmental interference from England. Such was the business arrangement of the great Massachusetts Bay colony.

At once the full tide of Puritan migration to America set in. In 1629 about nine hundred colonists arrived; in 1630 two thousand, and by 1640, it has been estimated that twenty thousand had found their way across the Atlantic to take up their abode in New England. But we must not suppose that all the colonists were Puritans, nor were they all "gentlemen." It has been found that hardly a fifth of the Massachusetts Bay colonists were even professed Christians, though all the ministers were Puritans, as were the leading laymen. The majority were middle class people, small tradesmen, farmers or artisans.

The Puritans of the Massachusetts Bay colony had, at the beginning, no intention of separating from the Church of England. One of the first two ministers to set foot on Massachusetts soil, Francis Higginson, is reported to have said, as the ship was bearing him out of sight of the shores of England: "We will not say as the separatists were wont to say at their leaving England, 'Farewel, Babylon! Farewel, Rome!' but we will say 'Farewel, dear England, Farewel the Church of God in England and all the Christian friends there!' We do not go to New England as Separatists from the Church of England, though we cannot but separate from the corruptions in it; but we go to practice the positive part of church reformation, and propagate the gospel in America." And doubtless many, if not most, of the Puritans leaders on leaving England felt as did Winthrop and others who esteemed it an "honour to call the Church of England, from whom wee rise, our dear Mother. . . ."

How then did the churches of the powerful Massachusetts Bay colony come to be Congregational? This is

one of the most important developments in the history of
New England and marks a turning point of vast significance. The first influence which led in the direction
of Congregationalism was exerted by Dr. Samuel Fuller,
a deacon in the church at Plymouth. During the first
winter, Endicott's colony at Salem was soon in great
distress because so many settlers fell ill and there was no
doctor among them to care for the sick. The only physician then on the whole coast of New England was the
deacon-doctor at Plymouth, Samuel Fuller. In despera-
tion Endicott wrote to Plymouth asking that the doctor
come to their aid. Fuller gladly responded and in spite of
the lack of proper medicines did what he could to stay
the ravages of disease. As Governor Endicott, who formerly had regarded the Separatists at Plymouth with suspicion, conversed with Dr. Fuller and saw him so
faithfully laboring among the sick, his prejudices melted
away and he is soon writing to Governor Bradford at
Plymouth—in May, 1629—as follows:

Right Worthy Sir: It is a thing not usual that servants to
one Master and of the same household should be strangers. I
assure you I desire it not; nay to speak more plainly I cannot
be so to you. God's people are marked with one and the same
mark, and sealed with one and the same seal, and have for the
main, one and the same heart, guided by one and the same
spirit of truth: and where this is there can be no discord—
nay here must needs be sweet harmony. The same request
with you I make unto the Lord, that we may as Christian
brethren be united by a heavenly and unfeigned love, bending
all our hearts and forces to furthering a work beyond our

strength, with reverence and fear fastening our eyes always on him that only is able to direct and prosper all our ways.

I acknowledge myself much bound to you for your kind love and care in sending Mr. Fuller among us, and I rejoice much that I am by him satisfied touching your judgments of the outward form of God's worship. It is as far as I can yet gather, no other than is warranted by the evidence of truth, and the same which I have professed and maintained ever since the Lord in mercy revealed himself to me, being very far different from the common report that hath been spread of you touching that particular. But God's children must not look for less here below, and it is the great mercy of God that he strengthens them to go through with it.

I shall not need at this time to be tedious unto you, for, God willing, I purpose to see your face shortly. In the meantime I humbly take leave of you, committing you to the Lord's blessed protection, and rest

Your assured loving friend and servant,

John Endicott.

Meanwhile several ordained clergymen of the Church of England arrived in Massachusetts, and July 20, 1629, was set aside as the day for choosing a pastor and teacher for the Salem congregation. A church had already been formed at Salem, at least its first members had united into a covenant in the early spring. After prayer and preaching the two ministers under consideration, Francis Higginson and Samuel Skelton, were asked as to their views concerning a proper call to the ministry, and both stated that an inward sense of fitness and election by male members of "a company of believers . . . joined together in covenant" constituted such a call. Then they proceeded to take a vote by ballot, which resulted in the choice of

Skelton as pastor and Higginson as teacher. Ther
cepting ye choyce, Mr. Higginson, with 3. or 4.
gravest members of ye church, laid their hands o
Skelton, using prayer therwith. This being don
was imposission of hands on Mr. Higginson also.
was the congregational principle, that every C
congregation has the right to choose and ordain
officers, inaugurated in Massachusetts Bay colony
time also a ruling elder and deacons were elected
they were not ordained until later.

In June of the next year (1630) John Winthr
with 840 colonists and a large number of cattle a
and new settlements were forming at Charlesto
and Newtowne. By the end of the year there
settlements, each marking the beginning of
July two churches were formed, one at Wat
other at Charlestown. Both drew up covenar
elected their pastors and teachers and ordain
imposition of hands." In May the next year (
action of the Massachusetts General Court
was limited to church members, and thus (
alism became the state church and the g
Massachusetts semi-theocratic. But the no
pressed, that the ministers in early New
practically in control of the government i
in fact. It is true that they were highly res
usually consulted by the civil authorities,
ment kept them from holding public off
ultimate control of the churches was in
civil officials. The great political importa
ters in Massachusetts and New Haven

to the fact that no one was likely to be admitted to ch[urch] membership without their consent and as the suf[frage] was limited to church members they thus had ind[irect] control over the voting members.

Massachusetts was far from being a democracy. [The] General Court was made up of Governor Winthrop a[nd] twelve freemen, with full legal authority. Govern[or] Winthrop could find no basis in Scripture for democrac[y,] stating that "Among nations it has always been accounte[d] the meanest and worst of all forms of government," an[d] in this opinion he was supported by leaders in bot[h] church and state. Nor was there religious toleration. I[t] must be remembered that the Massachusetts leaders were Church of England men, nor were they opposed to a state church. They never thought of establishing religious toleration, nor did they think of it as in the least desirable. "'Tis Satan's policy, to plead for an indefinite and bound-less toleration," declared one of their preachers in an election sermon, while another stated "All familists, Anti-nomians, Anabaptists, and others Enthusiasts shall have free liberty to keepe away from us." It is true that others besides Puritans were welcomed into the colony, but with the full understanding that they were to accept what they found, and refrain from disturbance. It was not toleration which the Puritan sought, but rather the freedom to carry out his own religious notions, undisturbed.

Year by year, as the stream of immigration continued, new towns were established and new churches formed, following the Congregational practice established by Salem, Watertown and Charlestown. Thus in the course

HINGHAM MEETING HOUSE, BUILT 1681
The oldest New England Meeting House now standing
From Bryant and Gay, *Popular History of the United States*, Vol. II

of about ten years the churches in New England had grown to thirty-three in number, all having adopted Congregational polity, though one or two of the pastors were somewhat inclined toward Presbyterianism.

The disturbers who arose among them were expelled. This practice was begun in 1629 at Salem, when two brothers, John and Samuel Browne, who had objected to the Congregationalizing of the Salem church, began to hold service, using the prayer book of the Established Church. This led to their expulsion from the colony. The most famous of those who were exiled from the Massachusetts Bay colony because they did not harmonize with the ruling element were, of course, Roger Williams and Anne Hutchinson whose story belongs to the establishment of Rhode Island and will be related in the following chapter.

Hardly had the first Puritan colonies been established before the restless spirit and land hunger, which was to prove so largely responsible for the ultimate conquest of the American continent, began to appear. The leader of the first movement westward was the Rev. Thomas Hooker. He had come to Boston in 1633 and soon became the minister at Newtowne. Almost at once he was irked by the autocracy of the government and protested against the limitation of the suffrage, but it was to no avail. In his controversy with Governor Winthrop he states that "in matters that concern the common good, a general council, chosen by all, to transact business which concerns all, I conceive most suitable to rule and most safe for the relief of the whole people." But autocracy was too firmly intrenched to be shaken, and very soon we find a petition before the magistrates, presented by Hooker's congregation, asking permission to migrate to the valley of the Connecticut. At first refused, permission was finally granted, providing they agree to continue under the government of Massachusetts. By 1636 three towns had been founded on the Connecticut River, Weathersfield, Hartford and Windsor, by colonists chiefly from Newtowne, Dorchester and Watertown. The Newtowne church, under the leadership of Hooker the pastor and Stone the teacher, made up the nucleus of the settlement at Hartford, while the minister at Dorchester, John Warham, with his congregation migrated to Windsor. Thus it was that two of the Massachusetts churches were practically transplanted to the Connecticut.

For a few years these Connecticut towns continued under the Massachusetts government, but in 1638 a constitution was adopted, called the "Fundamental Orders," which was based upon the popular consent. The government was somewhat less theocratic than was that of Massachusetts, as only the governor was required to be a church member, while the suffrage was granted to all who had taken the oath, and had been admitted to citizenship by the township. It seems quite probable, however, that in the elections to citizenship care was taken that only church members or those directly in sympathy with the religious aims of the constitution became "freemen."

At the very time the Connecticut settlements were taking shape, a new Puritan colony was being established directly from England. The chief instigators in this enterprise were the Rev. John Davenport, who had been vicar of a London church until Archbishop's Laud's regulations had driven him to Holland, and one of his London parishioners, Theophilus Eaton, a wealthy and influential merchant. Their plan included both religion and trade, and attracted several other English Puritan ministers and their congregations. Accordingly a considerable group sailed for Massachusetts in the spring of 1637. The Massachusetts authorities would have been glad to have had them remain under their jurisdiction, but Davenport and Eaton had an independent colony in mind, and after some exploring they decided to locate in what is now the southern part of Connecticut, to which they gave the name New Haven. They had neither charter nor patent for the land, but after obtaining lands by treaty from the Quinnipiack Indians whom they protected from the Mohawks, they proceeded during the years 1638 to 1640 to the founding of several towns. In June, 1639, a government was framed, based on the Bible, and it was voted that "Scripturs doe holde forth a perfect rule for the direction and governmt of all men in all duet[ies]. . . ."

In this Bible commonwealth the suffrage was restricted, as in Massachusetts, to church members. Annual elections were ordered and the first governor chosen was Theophilus Eaton, and year by year, for nearly twenty years, until his death, he was reëlected to that office. The other towns founded in the vicinity, Milford, Guilford and Stamford, were at first independent of New Haven, but in 1643, at the formation of the New England Confederation, a central government was organized and the four towns were united. Twenty years later (1664) Connecticut and New Haven were united, and with this union the chief characteristics of New Haven disappeared, such as the limitation of the suffrage to church members and the Scriptural constitution.

With the large number of educated clergymen in the Puritan colonies, most of them graduates of Cambridge, it was but natural that there should be early agitation looking toward the founding of a college. Indeed, before 1647 one hundred and thirty ministers had arrived in New England and it is stated on good authority that "such a concentration of educated men in a new settlement, in proportion to the population, has never occurred before or since." Accordingly, on September 8, 1636, the General Court of Massachusetts advanced "four hundred pounds by way of essay towards the building of something to begin a Colledge." But, to quote the opinion of Cotton Mather, "that which laid the most significant stone in the foundation, was the last will of Mr. John Harvard, a reverend, and most excellent minister of the gospel, who dying at Charlestown, of a consumption, quickly after his arrival, bequeathed the sum of seven hundred, seventy nine pounds, seventeen shillings and two pence, toward the pious work of building a Colledge, which was now set on foot." Soon a society of scholars were lodged in the "New Nests," under the direction of Mr. Nathaniel Eaton, who proved such a tyrant, however, beating a young gentleman unmercifully with a cudgel, that he was fined by the court, and was dismissed. Under Eaton's direction Harvard was little more than a school, so that Henry Dunster who became the president in 1640, soon after his arrival in America, was really the first president of the college. In *New England's First*

Fruits (1643) Dunster is described as "a learned, considerable and industrious man, who had so trained up his pupils in the tongues and arts, and so seasoned them with the principles of Divinity and Christianity, that we have, to our great comfort, and in truth beyond our hopes, beheld their progress in learning and godliness also." Dunster remained the president until his adoption of Baptist views caused his resignation in 1654.

In 1642 the first class had graduated, and by the end of the century a large majority of the ministers in both Massachusetts and Connecticut were her graduates; seventy-six of the eighty-seven in Massachusetts; and thirty-one of the thirty-five in Connecticut. Thus Harvard most admirably served its primary purpose, that of training young men for the ministry.

By the middle of the seventeenth century four Puritan colonies were firmly rooted in New England soil, in each of which the Congregational church was the dominating influence. During these years of the rapid development of American Congregationalism, the Puritan party in England began to express concern as to their dangerous tendencies in the direction of separatism. This concern led to questioning, and in the answering of these questions the leading New England ministers formulated the Congregational system of church polity. The ministers particularly responsible for the exposition of the New England Congregational system were John Cotton of Boston, Richard Mather of Dorchester, John Davenport of New Haven and Thomas Hooker of Connecticut. This activity in defending the Congregational system against its English critics led finally to the calling of the *Cam-*

bridge Synod (September 1, 1646) by the General Court
of Massachusetts, at which the churches of Massachusetts,
Plymouth, New Haven and Connecticut were invited to
send their ministers and their representatives, "there to
discuss, dispute, & cleare up, by the word of God, such
questions of church government & discipline . . .
as they shall thinke needfull & meete." This synod adopted
the Westminster Confession as an expression of the Congregational belief, and drew up what came to be known
as the *Cambridge Platform,* which constitutes the Congregational constitution.

The *Cambridge Platform* is simply the gathering up of
the administrative experience of the New England Congregational fathers. Each church was considered as
autonomous, though dependent upon other churches for
council and fellowship. A church was constituted by a
group of Christians uniting into a voluntary agreement,
known as a covenant. At first the forming of a church
was more or less of a private matter, but later, in Massachusetts and Connecticut, the consent of the government
and the neighboring churches was required. The early
covenants were simply promises to worship together, following the divine commandments and promising faithful-
ness to each other, and were largely free of doctrinal
statements. This absence of doctrinal matter in the covenants was largely due to the creedal uniformity prevailing,
rather than to any lack of concern in the matter of doctrine. The officials of a Congregational church were
pastor, teacher, elders and deacons, but by the end of the
seventeenth century, in most instances, the teacher and
elders had disappeared, leaving the pastor and deacons as

THE TRIAL OF A WITCH
From *Harper's Magazine*, December, 1892

the sole officers. At first the officers were selected by the adult male members, and this continued to be the practice in choosing deacons, but later, all the voters in the township, since they were taxed to support the minister, obtained the right to a voice in his selection, whether they were members of the church or not.

At first the minister was ordained by the officers of the congregation, but as fellowship between the churches developed, it became the custom to call in neighboring ministers to perform this service. According to the *Cambridge Platform* Congregationalists do not attach as much significance to ordination as do other Protestant churches, considering it simply "the solemn putting of a man into his place & office . . . wherunto he had right before by election, being like the installing of a magistrat in the common wealth." Nor did a minister without a church continue to hold his ministerial character. At first the ministers were supported by voluntary contributions, but within a few years laws were passed compelling all who had not given voluntarily to be assessed by the constables, and later in Massachusetts the county courts were directed to fix ministers' salaries and collect them. During the early eighteenth century, after other religious groups began to gain a foothold in New England, laws were passed allowing members of other churches to pay their assessments to their own clergymen, in towns where there were such ministers. Otherwise their assessments went to the Congregational minister.

Throughout the whole period of the colonies the meeting-house was not only the place of worship, but it was likewise the social center for every New England community, as well as a meeting place for political discussion. The typical New England meeting-house was a plain, rectangular, frame structure, sometimes with a tower and a bell if the congregation could afford it, with a pulpit at one end opposite the main door. In the early churches there were two pews, somewhat raised above the others, facing the congregation, for the elders and deacons. The sexes were divided in the seating, men on one side, women and the smaller children on the other, while the boys and young men occupied the gallery or the back seats where they were under the watchful eye of the tithing man. This functionary was a township official who assisted the constable in watching over the morals of the community. There was one such official for every ten families, who besides keeping order at the services, was on the lookout for sabbath breaking, tippling, gaming and idleness. Frequently the worshipers were seated according to their social rank, which remained true of a number of New England churches until well on in the nineteenth century. Except for little foot stoves, which were used for women and children, the churches were without means for heating.

The main service of worship of a New England congregation began at nine o'clock on a Sabbath morning. The people were summoned in the larger communities by the church bell, or in the smaller and poorer towns by a drum or conch-shell. Services were opened by a long prayer in which the minister brought the immediate needs of the members and of the community to the Divine attention, and no matter how long the prayer, the congregation stood. Next came the Bible reading, the pastor expounding as he read, for "dumb reading," as reading without comment was called, seemed to smack of the ritualistic service of the Church of England. The sermon was the main element in Puritan worship, but contrary to the usually accepted notion, the sermons were generally not more than an hour in length, though there are instances of sermons two and three hours long. The sermon completed, a shorter prayer closed the service.

The musical part of New England worship consisted of Psalm singing, in which the Psalm was lined out by the ruling elder, or by one designated by the minister. The people knew few tunes and as late as the beginning of the eighteenth century New England congregations were rarely able to sing more than three or four. Even the few melodies commonly known became so corrupted that no two individuals sang them alike, so that a congregation singing sounded "like five hundred different tunes roared out at the same time" often one or two words apart. An eighteenth century New England minister states: "I myself have twice in one note paused to take breath." The story is told of a New England deacon who, because of failing eyesight, found difficulty in reading the first line of the psalm and he apologized by observing:

"My eyes, indeed, are very blind."

The choir thinking this the first line of a common-meter hymn immediately sang it; whereupon the deacon exclaimed:

"I cannot see at all."

This the choir also sang. Astonished, the deacon cried out:

"I really believe you are bewitched"

and the choir responded, "I really believe you are bewitched" whereupon the deacon added "The mischief's in you all" and after the choir had sung that, the deacon sat down in disgust.

The Plymouth colonists brought with them a Psalm book which had been prepared for their use in Holland by Henry Ainsworth in 1612. This the churches of the Plymouth colony used until they were merged with Massachusetts Bay in 1692. The more famous Bay Psalm Book, a new American book, was first published at Cambridge in 1640 and was many times reprinted.

A question of great importance, which arose in the last third of the seventeenth century, and which continued to agitate the New England churches for more than a decade, was that known as the *Half-Way Covenant*. It was a question which had to do with church membership. The early New England Congregationalists maintained that only adult persons of Christian experience should be admitted to full membership in the church, but they also held that children shared in the covenant taken by their parents and were therefore members of the church on that ground. Because of this latter provision, there came gradually to be numerous people, belonging to the second generation, who were members of the church but who made no profession of an experience, but were living good lives, and of course desired that their children receive baptism. The stricter element among the ministers held that only the immediate offspring of believing parents could be admitted to baptism, while there arose a more liberal group contending that children of non-regenerate members, who owned the covenant, might receive baptism, but that they might not receive the Lord's Supper, nor were they to be allowed to vote in church affairs.

As the question became more and more agitated, the General Court of Connecticut proposed to settle the matter through a convention of ministers, representing the four Congregational colonies. Such a convention was called to meet in 1657, but only Massachusetts and Connecticut sent delegates. It went on record, however, as supporting the "Half-Way Covenant." Their decision had little effect in allaying the discussion, and finally the Massachusetts General Court decided to try its hand in settling the matter, by calling a General Synod of all the Massachusetts churches, to meet in Boston in March, 1662. Here, after warm discussion, the Half-Way Covenant again won the day. Still the strife continued and pamphlets for and against were multiplied, while churches were split over the issue, as was the case of the churches in Hartford, Stratford and Windsor in Connecticut, while even the First Church, Boston, was torn asunder, and a congregation from the old New Haven colony migrated to northern New Jersey where they founded *New Ark*, in order that they might be free from such abomination as that established by this innovation, and where the old strictness might be maintained.

The adoption of the Half-Way Covenant marks the passing of the founders of New England and the beginning of the domination of the second generation. Among the ministers of the first generation John Cotton is the outstanding figure. Coming to Massachusetts in 1633, after twenty years as vicar of the church in Boston, England, he at once took first rank among the leaders of

Massachusetts, and was chosen teacher of the First Church in Boston. His grandson, Cotton Mather, characterized him as "a most universal scholar, and a living system of liberal arts, and a walking library," and such confidence was reposed in him that many "believed that God would not suffer Mr. Cotton to err." While hating heresy, and an avowed enemy of democracy, he was likewise suspicious of all hereditary power, and, contradictory as it may seem, he at the same time "was verging toward progress in truth and in religious freedom." Cotton's ambition was to found a theocratic state modeled after that of the Hebrews, "in which political rights should be subordinated to religious conformity," with magistrates to be chosen from a narrow group, whose authority was to be beyond the reach of the popular will, and "with the ministers serving as a court of last resort to interpret the divine law to the subject-citizens of Jehovah." In his philosophy there is no trace of the doctrine of natural rights; but freedom and righteousness were to go hand in hand, while the sinner was to "remain subject to the saint."

Standing out almost, if not quite, as prominently in the second generation, as did John Cotton in the first, is Increase Mather. Born in the Dorchester parsonage, the son of Richard Mather, he graduated from Harvard at seventeen in 1656, and at once sailed for Ireland, where he matriculated at Trinity College, then under Puritan control, for the master's degree. He undoubtedly intended to remain a pastor in England, but the ending of the Commonwealth drove him back to New England, where he became the teacher in the Second Church of Boston, remaining there until his death in 1723. After the division of the First Church, which we have noted, this was the most influential pulpit in Massachusetts, as well as perhaps in the whole of New England. At this influential post, Increase Mather became the staunch defender of the old order of things, both in state and in church. The last thirty years of his life his influence was foremost as an ecclesiastical leader, and well-nigh as great in politics and in education. From 1685 to 1701 he was the acting president of Harvard College, driving back and forth from his Boston parsonage to Cambridge every day in his carriage. In 1688, after the loss of the charter, he was sent to England, as the best prepared man in Massachusetts, to plead the cause of the colony against Governor Andros. And so successful was he in this important mission that the new charter of 1691 was secured and Mather was granted the right to nominate those who should first bear office under it.

Increase Mather was the prime mover in securing the calling by the General Court of Massachusetts of the Reforming Synod of 1679. A series of disasters, such as the two fires in Boston, in 1676 and 1679, a smallpox scourge, King Philip's War, together with the threats against self-government, which finally resulted in the loss of the charter in 1684, seemed to indicate clearly to Mather that God's wrath was turned against New England for their sins. The purpose of the synod was to consider the condition of the New England churches and to adopt such measures as would remedy conditions which were considered the cause of the divine anger. Under Increase Mather's presidency the synod adopted a series of recommendations looking toward a more faithful administration of church discipline and calling for a strict execution of the laws. It also adopted a confession of faith, modeled after the Savoy Confession of the English Congregationalists, which had been formulated in 1658 and which remains the fullest and clearest statement of the faith of seventeenth century Congregationalists.

The disaster which came to Massachusetts in October, 1684, when she was deprived of her liberal charter has already been noted. It was the plan of King James II to unite the American colonies into one royal jurisdiction, and in December, 1686, Sir Edmund Andros came to Boston, first as governor of Massachusetts, Maine, New Hampshire and Plymouth, while later his jurisdiction covered Connecticut, Rhode Island, New Jersey and New York in addition. All popular rights were lost, and with them the freedom of the press and the power of taxation. Not the least of the accusations lodged against Andros was that he had introduced the Established Church among them. The governor had asked for the use of one of the meeting-houses at such a time when it would not interfere with the services of the owners. When this was refused Old South meeting-house was taken by force and Anglican services were held on Good Friday and Easter, 1687. The next year King's Chapel was begun, the first Anglican church in Massachusetts. The danger from Anglicanism soon passed, for when the news arrived in New England that James II had vacated the throne, the beating of drums on Boston Common summoned the militia; a town meeting was held, and Governor Andros and two other royal officials were soon in prison. A provisional government was at once formed which was to carry on until the new charter was obtained. The new charter, though distasteful to Increase Mather because of its limitations on the old privileges, nevertheless retained much that was dear to the New England Puritan. It put an end, however, to Puritan theocracy, by sweeping away all religious qualifications for the suffrage, substituting in its stead property qualifications. Local government was left unchanged, though the governor hereafter was to be an appointee of the crown, while only the lower house of the legislature was to be chosen by the direct vote of the people.

That the hanging of twenty witches at Salem and the execution of ten others at different places, in 1692, was the direct effect of the political and religious disturbances through which New England was passing at this time is perhaps an unwarranted conclusion. There is no doubt, however, but that the public mind was in a most feverish and disturbed state. It is quite the mode in these days to heap wholesale condemnation upon New England Puritanism, and such condemnation usually begins or ends with a description of the Salem witchcraft delusion. As a matter of fact and fairness, it needs to be said that witchcraft delusions were common all over Europe from the fourteenth to the eighteenth century, and during these years the European witch fires were responsible for the death of at least five hundred thousand victims. Between 1645 and 1647 in England one notorious witch-finder alone was responsible for sending three hundred condemned witches to the gallows. This, however, is not a justification for the happenings at Salem, but rather an explanation of them.

The theory concerning witches, usually accepted, was that the witch had sold herself to the devil, to be used as his special instrument and agent, to carry out his evil purposes. Concern over strange apparitions and witches had been expressed previously by the New England ministers and in 1684 Increase Mather had written a book entitled *An Essay for the Recording of Illustrious Providences*, in which he describes several cases of witchcraft. The craze at Salem began in March, 1692, when several children through their strange actions, were thought to be bewitched, and finally they named three old women who they said had bewitched them. These miserable old women were brought to trial in a court held in the Salem church, with the children as the chief witnesses, and all were convicted and condemned. The jails were now filled with accused witches. The royal governor, himself of New England birth, appointed a special court to try the cases, and by January, 1693, twenty-two persons had been condemned, two of whom died in prison and the remainder were hanged. Among the judges who sat in the special court was the high-minded Samuel Sewall.

The delusion passed almost as quickly as it had come, though belief in witches by no means disappeared. Soon critics of the proceedings began to make themselves heard, among them Increase Mather, who contended that other evidence should be required, since "a Daemon may, by God's permission, appear even to ill purposes, in the Shape of an innocent, yea, and a virtuous Man." The trials were stopped by Governor Phipps in October, 1692, and five years later the Massachusetts Court publicly repented and set apart a special day of fasting and prayer, that prayers might be offered asking for forgiveness for "the late Tragedy raised amongst us by Satan," while the twelve jurors published a declaration of sorrow for accepting insufficient evidence against the accused, while Judge Sewall rose in his pew in the South Church and made public confession of his sense of guilt.

Toward the close of the seventeenth century liberal tendencies began to make their appearance in some of the New England churches. Especially was liberalism noticeable at Harvard and in Cambridge where the tutors, William Brattle and William Leverett, began to advocate certain changes in the church. They contended that all baptized persons should have a part in selecting the minister; that no longer should admission to church membership depend upon the relation of a religious experience before the congregation; while they also wished to bring about certain changes in the conduct of the public services. This agitation finally led to the formation of Brattle Church, which was organized without the consent of the other churches, where these innovations were put into practice. This particular incident, which marked the waning influence of Increase Mather at Harvard, was also largely responsible for an attempt on the part of the conservatives, led by the Mathers, Increase and his son Cotton, to create new ecclesiastical machinery which would hold in check this growing radicalism. This led to what is known as the *Massachusetts Proposals* of 1705.

Ministerial associations had gradually come into existence toward the end of the sixteen hundreds, the first having been formed in 1690, made up of the ministers of Boston and the surrounding towns. It met regularly in the college buildings at Cambridge. It was purely a voluntary affair, but it seemed to meet a real need, for it was not long until there were five such associations in Massachusetts. The next step was the *Ministerial Convention*, made up of delegates from the several associations, which met once a year during the spring meeting of the General Court. In 1705, the convention, through a circular letter to the churches, began to advocate reforms in church administration. This led to the gathering of nine ministers, representing the associations of Massachusetts, at which a series of recommendations were formulated, the most important being that ministerial associations were to be formed where they did not now exist, and that these associations have the power to examine and license ministerial candidates, while churches without ministers were to apply to the associations for candidates. The second proposal was that there should be a "standing Council" in each association whose decisions were to be final. The first part of the recommendations were put into operation, but the second proposal, due to the strong opposition which arose, was never carried out.

Out of the welter of discussion which arose over the proposed changes in church government, there appeared an able defender of Congregational polity in the person of John Wise, the pastor at Ipswich, who "possessed the keenest mind and the most trenchant pen of his generation." In two brilliant little books, *The Churches Quarrel Espoused* (1710) and *A Vindication of the Government of the New England Churches* (1717), Wise defended the democracy of the old system, in which the democratic element was emphasized, not alone by an appeal to the Scripture, but also on the ground of natural rights. His books stirred the mind of New England profoundly, and so convincing was his argument that it was accepted as authoritative. He asserted that "Democracy is Christ's government in Church and State"; that "Power is originally in the people"; and further that "by natural right all men are born free." This philosophy of democracy was not alone to influence the affairs of the church, but fifty years later (1772) Wise's books appeared in a new edition, and played their part in the political discussion of the time.

Though partially defeated in Massachusetts, the Massachusetts Proposals were three years later (1708) embodied in the *Saybrook Platform* of the Connecticut churches, and were by them accepted. Thus, the Congregationalism of Connecticut and Massachusetts entered upon divergent courses, the Connecticut churches becoming more and more Presbyterian in their system of church polity. This made fellowship and coöperation with the growing Presbyterianism of the middle colonies natural, a fact which later was to have far-reaching influences in the adoption of the Plan of Union of 1801. The Massachusetts churches, on the other hand, continued to follow the old plan of independent Congregationalism.

The tendency of Connecticut Congregationalism to go its own way, more or less independently of the Massachusetts churches, is further evidenced by the founding of Yale College in 1701. The reason given for the establishment of Yale was that the Connecticut churches desired "a nearer and less expensive seat of learning," though undoubtedly the enterprise met the hearty approval of the more conservative ministers, who hoped that the new seat of learning might offset the more liberal and less orthodox tendencies which were developing at Harvard. At first the new college was located at Saybrook, but in 1716 it was permanently removed to New Haven, and two years later it received the name Yale in recognition of the gifts of Elihu Yale, who though a son of one of the founders of New Haven, had amassed wealth in India where for a number of years he was governor of Madras under the East India Company. His interest in the college had been aroused by the London agent of the New Haven colony, and through a letter written him by Cotton Mather.

New England Congregationalism has now been traced through its first one hundred years and the changes which had gradually come about with the second and third generations have been noted. During the last years of the seventeenth century the question of church polity had occupied the chief attention of the New England ministers, an indication in itself that vital religion was at a low ebb. The religion of the Puritans had become unemotional, with a type of preaching unconducive to revivals and conversion. Out of this general situation had come the necessity for the Half-Way Covenant. The Puritan fathers had held that conversion was solely the work of God, but with the second and third generations, as the number of conversions decreased, gradually the idea began to emerge that there were certain "means" which might be used in putting the soul in a position to receive the regenerating influence of the Spirit of God. Such "means" were owning the covenant, attending divine worship, leading a moral life, reading the Scriptures and prayer. Thus there came to be more and more reliance upon the use of "means" and less and less upon the miraculous power of God, which led to a cold and unemotional religion. Such was the general religious situation in New England when through the preaching and personality of Jonathan Edwards a new and highly emotional reaction set in which we know as the Great Awakening.

Chapter V

THE FIRST EXPERIMENTS IN RELIGIOUS LIBERTY: RHODE ISLAND AND MARYLAND: BAPTIST AND ROMAN CATHOLIC BEGINNINGS

IT MAY appear to students of American history as un-scientific to bring together in one chapter two such divergent themes as Rhode Island and Maryland; one a New England and the other a southern colony; one founded by liberal Puritans and the other by Roman Catholics. But the thing which brings them together and makes it appropriate to discuss them in relation to each other is the fact that in each of these colonies, at about the same period, the principle of religious liberty was put into practice. The beginning of each colony centers about the name of an individual, each of great historic interest and importance, Roger Williams and the first Lord Baltimore, and to understand how the first experiments in religious liberty began in America it will be necessary to tell the story of each of these men.

Roger Williams and his wife embarked in the ship *Lyon* from the port of Bristol in the year 1630 bound for New England and on the fifth of February, 1631, after a tempestuous voyage landed at Boston. At this time Williams was about thirty years of age and is described as "a young minister, godly and zealous, having precious gifts." There is much uncertainty as to his life before coming to America, but he was probably educated at Cambridge, and he first began the study of law, but soon forsook it to enter the ministry. Before coming to America he had already adopted liberal views in regard to both civil government and the church and was an avowed separatist, and possessed that type of mind which would not allow him to keep his views to himself. Indeed, he had hardly landed in the New World before he was in trouble with the authorities for advancing views out of harmony with the principles upon which the Massachusetts colony was established. He refused to join the congregation of the Boston church, for he considered that it had not yet completely separated itself from the corruptions of the English Church, a church which bore on its skirts the blood of saints and martyrs. Accordingly, when a few weeks later he received an invitation to become the pastor of the more liberal church at Salem, he accepted, but on the very day he was to begin his ministry there, the General Court of the colony interfered—a flagrant violation of the Congregational principle of the independence of each congregation—and this interference, on the part of the General Court, led Williams to depart for Plymouth. Here for two years he was the minister of the Pilgrim's Church "where," says Governor Bradford, "he was freely entertained, according to our poor ability, and exercised his gifts among us; and after some time was admitted a member of the church among us and his teaching well approved."

During his pastorate at Plymouth Williams became interested in the Indians living in the vicinity, and began a study of Indian languages, and gained an acquaintance with the Narragansett chiefs which was to prove so useful to him when finally he was banished from Massachusetts.

Again in September, 1634, the church in Salem invited Williams to be their pastor, their first minister Mr. Skelton having died the previous month. Here, it seems, he preached for two years and during this time won a number of adherents to his views, especially in reference to separation of civil and religious authority. It is difficult for us in this day to understand the controversy which now ensued between Roger Williams and the authorities of Massachusetts. Williams' chief opponent was John Cotton. Though a recent arrival in Boston, Cotton's advice was at once given great weight in arranging the civil and religious affairs of the colony. The charges against Williams were thus summed up by John Cotton, and acknowledged as correct by Roger Williams. He held:

First, That we have not our land by patent from the king, but that the natives are the true owners of it, and that we ought to repent of such a receiving it by patent.

Secondly, That it is not lawful to call a wicked person to swear, (or) pray, as being actions of God's worship.

Thirdly, That is is not lawful to hear any of the ministers of the Parish assemblies in England.

Fourthly, That the civil magistrate's power extends only to the bodies, and goods, and outward state of men.

Williams' position seemed particularly dangerous to the Massachusetts officials, for if the state had nothing to do with religion then, of course, the whole Massachusetts government was founded on a false basis. It is, therefore, clear why the Massachusetts authorities now proceeded against Williams and drove him into exile.

Called before the General Court in July, 1635, to answer to the charge against him, his opinions were declared to be "erroneous and dangerous," and the calling of him to Salem "was judged a great contempt of authority." Williams and the Salem church were given until the next session of the court to consider the matter. In the October session Roger Williams was sentenced to "depart out of our jurisdiction within six weeks." Meanwhile, Williams' health was declining, evidently brought on by his troubles, and it seems that on this account the court relented to the extent of granting him until spring to leave the colony. Williams withdrew at once from the Salem church, but his friends and followers gathered at his house, where he preached "even of such points as he had been censured for." This was too much for the magistrates, who took steps to have him sent out of the colony at once on a ship then at anchor in Boston bay. A pinnace was sent to Salem to bring him to Boston, "but when they came at his house, they found he had been gone three days before; but whither they could not learn." His wife and two children were left behind, while a mortgage had been placed on his property to raise money for his exile. He then plunged into the forest; being "denied the common air to breathe in, and a civil cohabitation upon the same common earth; yea and also without mercy and human compassion, exposed to winter miseries in a howling wilderness."

{ 101 }

After fourteen weeks of wandering, during which he says he did not know "what bread or bed did mean," Williams found hospitality among the Indians and in the late summer of 1636 purchased from them a plot of ground at the mouth of the Mohassuck River where he founded the town of Providence. Shortly afterward these lands were reconveyed to his companions, for it was not long until a considerable number of his followers had found their way thither. In a deed of 1661 Williams thus states his purpose in establishing his colony: "I desired it might be for a shelter for persons distressed for conscience. I then considering the condition of divers of my distressed countrymen, I communicated my said purchase unto my loving friends . . . who then desired to take shelter here with me." Williams and his associates adopted a "plantation covenant" in which they agreed to abide by the will of the majority but "only in civil things." The new colony, however, was without legal standing, for they had as yet no charter from any English authority.

One of the accusations which had been lodged against Roger Williams at Salem was that he was inclined toward Anabaptist views, but there is no evidence that he was a Baptist at this time. In 1638 a church was formed at Providence, made up of rebaptized members. A Mr. Holliman who had been a member of the Salem church was selected to rebaptize Williams, and then Williams rebaptized Holliman and ten others. Thus was formed the first Baptist church in America.[1] Williams became

[1] The usual contention that the members of the first Baptist church were baptized by immersion in 1638 is challenged by Professor R. E. E. Harkness in an article in the *Crozer Quarterly* (Vol. V, 1928, pp.

TRIAL OF MRS. HUTCHINSON
From Bryant and Gay, *Popular History of the United States*, Vol. I

pastor of the newly formed church, though only for a few months. He soon became disturbed as to his right to administer the ordinances of the church, conceiving that a true ministry must derive its authority from apostolic succession and, therefore, he could not assume the office of pastor. He, however, continued to hold Baptist views, though he finally came to the conclusion that the church was so corrupt that there could "be no recovery out of that apostacy till Christ shall send forth new apostles to plant churches anew."

A recent interpreter of New England thought has stated that "Roger Williams was the most provocative figure thrown upon the Massachusetts shores by the upheaval in England, the one original thinker among a number of capable social architects." His great contribution, however, was made in the realm of political philosophy rather than as a theologian and his was the first great blow struck at the theory of divine right, for which he substituted the "compact" theory of government. Government to Roger Williams was man-made and rested upon common consent of equal subjects. His idea of the position of religion in the state is thus clearly stated in the preface of his *The Bloudy Tenent of Persecution*:[1]

(1) *God* requireth not an *uniformity* of *Religion* to be *inacted* and *inforced* in any *civill state*; which inforced *uniformity* (sooner or later) is the greatest occasion of *civill Warre, ravishing of conscience, persecution of Jesus Christ* in

440-460) entitled "Principles of the Early Baptists of England and America," in which he contends that the rebaptizing which took place in 1638 was not by immersion and that Williams opposed the new manner of dipping when it was first introduced some years later.

[1] Vol. III, p. 76.

his servants, and of the *hypocrisie* and destruction of millions of souls. (2) It is the will and command of *God*, that . . . a *permission* of the most *Paganish, Jewish, Turkish, or Antichristian consciences* and *worships*, bee granted to *all* men in all *Nations* and *Countries*: and they are only to be fought against with the *Sword* which is onely (in *Soule matters*) *able* to *conquer*, to wit, the *Sword* of *Gods Spirit*, the *Word of God*. (3) True *civility* and *Chirstianity* may both flourish in a *state* or *Kingdome*, notwithstanding the *permission* of divers and contrary consciences, either of Jew or *Gentile*.

How different is our opinion of Roger Williams today from that of Cotton Mather who compared him to a certain Windmill in the Low Countries, which

whirling with such extraordinary violence, by reason of a violent storm then blowing; the stone at length by its rapid motion became so intensely hot, as to fire the mill, from whence the flames, being dispersed by the high winds, did set the whole town on fire. But I can tell my reader, about twenty-five years before this, there was a whole country in America like to be set on fire by the rapid motion of a windmill, in the head of one particular man. Know then that about the year 1630, arrived here one Roger Williams, who being a preacher that had less *light* than *fire* in him, hath by his own sad example, preached unto us the danger of that evil which the apostle mentions in *Rom.* 10-2. *They have a zeal, but not according to knowledge.*

The colony of Rhode Island was eventually made up of three elements: The first being Roger Williams' Providence plantation. A second element was made up of another group of religious exiles from Massachusetts—Anne Hutchinson, with her husband, her brother-in-law

Mr. Wheelwright, and their followers—who settled what is now Portsmouth and Newport; while a third group, led by a well-educated but combative individual, Samuel Groton, founded a colony on the west shore of Narragansett Bay to which was given the name Warwick. In 1644 Roger Williams was sent to England to secure authorization from the Puritan authorities for the Narragansett settlers to form a government. Three years later (1647) it was organized—embodying the principles advocated by Roger Williams—separation of church and state —no church membership qualification required for voters, while every man was to be protected in the "peaceful and quiet enjoyment of lawful right and liberty," "not withstanding our different consciences touching the truth as it is in Jesus."

Mrs. Anne Hutchinson, like Williams, was born out of due time. In England she and her husband had been parishioners of John Cotton, and according to Winthrop was "a woman of ready wit and a bold spirit," who "brought over with her two dangerous errors." Some time after her arrival in Boston she began the practice of holding meetings at her house where the sermons preached the Sunday previous were discussed and the ministers criticized, and finally she seems to have evolved a doctrine of her own in which she professed a direct divine inspiration. All the ministers in Boston, she contended, were preaching a covenant of works, except John Cotton and her brother-in-law, Mr. Wheelwright, who was at the time preaching as a supply minister in a branch of one of the Boston churches. Over against the covenant of works she set the covenant of grace, by which she meant that every man had direct communication between himself and his Maker, while the covenant of works meant conformity to a prescribed order as laid down by the minister.

At first Mrs. Hutchinson found powerful supporters in John Cotton and Sir Henry Vane, the governor, and the majority of the Boston church members were on her side. As long as Vane was governor Mrs. Hutchinson was safe, but in the midst of the excitement of the controversy an election resulted in victory for the conservatives and Winthrop once more became governor, though the three representatives from Boston to the General Court were favorable to Mrs. Hutchinson. Wheelwright was first brought before the court in March, but his case was deferred until November when he was declared guilty of sedition and contempt and was banished from the colony. Mrs. Hutchinson was next tried, and her conviction was a foregone conclusion. She too was banished from the colony and excommunicated from the church. The words of excommunication pronounced upon Mrs. Hutchinson by the Rev. John Wilson reveal the enormity of her offense in the eyes of the Massachusetts' theocrats:

Forasmuch as you, Mrs. Hutchinson, have highly transgressed and offended and forasmuch as you have so many ways troubled the church with your errors and have drawn away many a poor soul, and have upheld your revelations; and forasmuch as you have made a lie, etc. Therefore in the name of our Lord Jesus Christ and in the name of the Church I do not only pronounce you worthy to be cast out, but I do cast you out and in the name of Christ I do deliver you up to Satan, that you may learn no more to blaspheme, to seduce and to lie, and I do account you from this time forth to be a Heathen and a Publican and so to be held of all the brethren and sisters of this congregation and of all others; therefore I command you in the name of Christ Jesus and of his Church as a Leper to withdraw yourself out of the Congregation; that as formerly you have despised and contemned the Holy Ordinances of God, and turned back on them, so may you now have no part in them nor benefit from them.

With Mrs. Hutchinson into exile went numerous of her followers and others who were out of sympathy with the intolerance of the Massachusetts authorities. Most important of those who now went to Rhode Island and established Portsmouth and Newport was Dr. John Clarke. We know very little about the early history of this talented and interesting man, but he arrived in Boston in 1637 just at the time the excitement was at its height over Mrs. Anne Hutchinson. The year Newport was founded (1638) a church was established with Clarke as teaching elder. Whether this was a Baptist church from the first cannot be determined, though by 1648 it is known that there was a Baptist church at Newport with fifteen members. In 1651 Clarke was sent to England by the colonists to secure a new charter, and there for twelve years he remained, finding it impossible to gain the charter under the Protectorate. Finally in 1663, under Charles II, a new charter was obtained which declared that no person should be "anywise molested, punished, disquieted or called in question for any differences of opinion in matters of religion" provided he did not disturb the "civil peace." Roger Williams was still living when the new charter was secured, embodying his great principle of "soul liberty." On Clarke's return to Rhode Island he served two terms as deputy governor, retiring to private life in 1676. During his long residence in England he wrote *Ill News from New England* in which he advocated liberty of conscience, a book which deserves to take rank with Roger Williams' *"The Bloudy Tenent of Persecution."* His services to the colony and to the cause of religious liberty were quite as great, though less known, as were those of Roger Williams.

With the establishment of the first Baptist churches in Rhode Island, Baptist views began to make their appearance in the older Puritan colonies, and among the members of the Congregational churches. Cases of parents withholding their children from infant baptism became increasingly common so that in 1644 the General Court of Massachusetts enacted a statute providing that whosoever "shall either openly condemn or oppose the baptizing of infants, or go about secretly to seduce others from the approbation or use thereof, or shall purposely depart the congregation at the ministration of the ordinances, etc. . . . shall be sentenced to banishment." The most conspicuous case of this kind was that of Henry Dunster, the president of Harvard College from 1641 to 1654.

About 1650 Dunster had become convinced that infant baptism was wrong, and in 1653 when his fourth child was born he failed to present it at the proper time for baptism. His new views he now set forth in several sermons, which naturally caused much excitement. Dunster had been so successful in conducting the affairs of the college that the assistants were reluctant to proceed against him. In 1654 nine of the leading ministers held a conference with Dunster and a few months later the General Court issued an order commanding the overseers of the college not to permit any to teach "that have manifested themselves unsound in the faith." In June Dunster offered his resignation, but expressed his willingness to continue the work "for some weeks or months" until his successor could be secured. This resignation was not accepted at this time, but in the autumn he interrupted the service in the Cambridge church to make a statement as to his position on infant baptism, which he gathered under five points. This was the last straw. His resignation was now accepted and he was indicted for disturbing worship, was tried and condemned to receive an admonition from the General Court. Dunster spent the last five years of his life as pastor of the church at Scituate in the Plymouth colony and was succeeded at Harvard by Charles Chauncy who had been the minister at Scituate.

The most notable case of persecution of Baptists by Massachusetts authorities occurred in 1651 near Lynn, where John Clarke and Obadiah Holmes had gone to minister to an aged Baptist, William Witter, and also perhaps to encourage others who were inclined toward Baptist principles. Here on a Sabbath they were holding services in Witter's home when two constables broke into the house, arrested Holmes and Clarke, who were haled before the court, where they were fined, and in default of which they were to be whipped. A friend of Clarke's paid his fine and he was set free against his protest. Holmes, however, was "whipped unmercifully" in the streets of Boston. There were numerous other cases of persecution, though it must be said in some justification of the Massachusetts authorities that much of what both Baptists and Quakers did would, if done today, have brought them before the police court. Thus Witter had been before the court in 1643 for saying that infant baptism was a "badge of the whore," and three years later he was again in trouble for saying that "they who stayed while a child is baptized doe worshipp the Dyvell."

The first Baptist church in Massachusetts was formed at Rehoboth in 1663, by John Myles, a Welsh Baptist minister who had been driven to America by the Act of Uniformity of 1662. No attention was given to this church by the authorities until 1667 when Myles and James Brown were hailed before the court "for setting up a public meeting without the knowledge and approbation of the Court, to the disturbance of the peace of the place." They were assessed a fine of five pounds and required to remove their church to a distance from the church of the standing order, so as not to disturb the peace of the church and town. The same year a place was set aside for them by the court near the Rhode Island border, which was called Swansea after their Welsh home. Here the church prospered and has maintained an uninterrupted existence to this day. A Baptist church was formed in Boston in 1665 under the leadership of Thomas Gould, who like his friend President Dunster had refused to present his child for baptism. In the above year a church was formed in his house which almost immediately fell under the wrath of the officials. Three of its members, Gould, Turner and Forman were tried and convicted and sentenced to leave the colony, and if they were found in the colony after a certain time they were to be imprisoned without bail. The church was forbidden to assemble again on pain of imprisonment and banishment. In spite of such harsh measures the number of Baptists increased and in 1678 a Baptist meeting-house was begun in Boston. In answer to this bold step the General Court ordered the marshal to nail up the doors, which he proceeded to do. This proved to be the last serious persecution of Baptists in Boston, and the doors remained closed but one Sunday.

The controversy over the Half-Way Covenant served to further the development of Baptist sentiment in New England, since the question under discussion was the matter of allowing children of unconverted parents to be baptized. Many began to ask what is the use of infant baptism since it confers no special privilege? Why not, therefore, postpone baptism until after a personal confession is possible?

As the eighteenth century neared its close persecution of Baptists gradually died out. The English Congregational ministers protested against the intolerance of Massachusetts, stating that dissenting interests in England were greatly injured by it, and even Charles II rebuked the Massachusetts authorities for their cruel persecutions. By the end of the century the Puritan theocracy had proven to be an impossible form of government and the new charter of 1691, uniting Plymouth and Massachusetts Bay, granted "Liberty of conscience to all Christians, except Papists," but "liberty of conscience was so interpreted as to allow the taxation of dissenters for the support of Congregational ministers." It was not until 1728 that an act was passed exempting Anabaptists and Quakers "from being taxed for and toward the support of" ministers, but in order to secure exemption Baptists were required to obtain certificates signed by "two principal members of that persuasion" which must be presented to the town officials.

The most important Baptist center during the colonial period was not in New England, however, but in the middle colonies and especially in Pennsylvania and New Jersey where a larger degree of religious freedom was allowed from the first. Philadelphia was the center of this group of churches, and in 1707 the first Baptist Association in America met at Philadelphia with five churches represented. In 1742 this body adopted a strong Calvinistic confession of faith which is considered a turning point in the history of the American Baptists. Up to this time the Arminian Baptists had been more numerous, especially in New England, but from this time forward the majority of American Baptists have been Calvinistic in their theology, and the Philadelphia Association became and remained the strongest and most influential Baptist body. In the southern colonies Baptist churches were barely getting started by the middle of the eighteenth century; the rapid extension of the Baptists into the southern colonies, therefore, belongs to a later period in this story.

In 1740 there were but eight Baptist churches in Massachusetts, four in Connecticut and eleven in Rhode Island. In the Philadelphia Association in 1762 were twenty-nine churches, embracing Pennsylvania, New York, Virginia and Maryland; while a Baptist church had been formed in Charleston, South Carolina, in 1684. Most of these churches owed their origin to small groups of men and women who had been Baptists before coming to America, most of whom were either English or Welsh. To term Roger Williams the founder of the Baptist Church in America, and the church he founded "the venerable mother of American Baptist churches" as is often done, is historically incorrect, for after all the part played by Williams in American Baptist history is extremely small, and the church he founded bore no living children. The relation of Roger Williams and the American Baptists to the beginnings of the fight for religious liberty in America, however, has a deep significance, for standing first among the five principles of all American Baptists is "Complete separation of Church and State," and the part they played in the triumph of that great principle is of greatest importance.

It is a strange anomaly that the first colony in America to be established embodying the principle of religious toleration should have been founded by a Roman Catholic. It must be understood, however, that the founding of Maryland was not due in any way whatever to the Roman Catholic Church, but was solely the result of the plan and intention of one Roman Catholic nobleman,—a recent convert,—George Calvert, the first Lord Baltimore.

Lord Baltimore's purpose in establishing a colony embodying the principle of religious liberty was vastly different from that of Roger Williams in the establishment of Rhode Island. Roger Williams was a political philosopher, and based his position on great fundamental truths. To him a great principle was at stake, and for that principle he was willing to and did undergo every danger and hardship. Roger Williams was a prophet of the coming of the new day of religious liberty and the separation of church and state; Lord Baltimore was neither a political philosopher nor a prophet. He was rather a practical and hard-headed investor in a great land venture, in which his whole fortune was at stake. He founded Maryland upon the principle of religious toleration in spite of his religion rather than because of it. He knew well enough that ruin would come speedily to his vast enterprise in Maryland if his colony were planted in the interests solely of his church and his coreligionists. It has already been noted that Catholics in England of his day did not belong to the migrating class, and if Baltimore were to sell his land he must depend upon the non-Catholics, and he evidently did not propose to allow his "religious predilections to interfere with business."

George Calvert, first Lord Baltimore, was a man of importance in the government of England in the reigns of James I and Charles I, and was greatly interested in all colonization and trading enterprises. He was a member of both the London and Plymouth companies as well as the East India Company; was a member of Parliament and one of the Secretaries of State. His political career, however, was closed when he became a Catholic, since the oath taken by officeholders required renunciation of the authority of the Pope. He succeeded, however, in spite of his conversion to Catholicism in retaining the good will and friendship of Charles I who made him an Irish peer as Lord Baltimore.

His first attempt at colonization was in Newfoundland in 1620, which after nine years of hardship and the loss

of thirty thousand pounds he abandoned with the thought
of trying again in Virginia. Here his conversion to Catholicism blocked his way, for in answer to the announcement of his intention to "plant and dwell" among them,
the authorities of Virginia welcomed him on the same
terms with themselves, that is, they presented for his acceptance the oath of supremacy, to which as a true Catholic he could not subscribe. He now sailed back to
England, where his influence at court finally was successful in securing from the king a separate province, granted
as an hereditary possession, and thus this Catholic nobleman became the founder of the first proprietary English
colony, a type of grant which was to become most common by the end of the century. The territory given Baltimore was claimed by Virginia, but the loss of its charter
in 1624 left it no legal grounds for procedure.

Death ended the first Lord Baltimore's colonization
venture, but his eldest son, Cecil Calvert, inherited his
father's title and proceeded with the enterprise. The second Lord Baltimore was even more hard-headed and practical than his father and with high degree of tact carried
out the colonization scheme, and for forty years ruled the
colony at long range with skill and economic success.
By far the largest part of the settlers from the very first
(1634) were Protestants, and in the instructions to his
brother Leonard who came out as the first governor his
religious plans are made clear. Care was to be taken by
the officials "to preserve unity & peace among all the
passangers" while "no scandall nor offence" was "to be
given to any of the Protestants." They were to be careful
not to parade the Roman Catholic religion before the non-

Catholics and as far as practicable their peculiar practices were to be conducted "as privately as possible." From the above instructions it is easy to infer that the Lord Proprietor knew well enough the difficulties he faced and desired to run no unnecessary risk in losing his charter.

Maryland prospered moderately from the first, for Leonard Calvert went about the work in hand in a very orderly way; and he was wise enough also to profit by the mistakes of Virginia. The first year corn and tobacco were planted in some Indian fields which they had purchased, and other land was cleared. The location of the settlement was healthy and well drained and at the end of the first summer they were able to send a shipload of corn to New England in exchange for fish.

The colony was thrown open to all religious groups,— Anglicans, Puritans and Catholics,—the charter stating that "all liege subjects of the king" might freely transport themselves and their families to Maryland, though the government was largely under Catholic control. On the first expedition two earnest Jesuit priests were quietly added "as it passed the Isle of Wight," and for some time were the only representatives of religion in the colony. These priests ministered faithfully to the settlers, and among the neighboring Indians, and soon most of the Protestants in the colony were Roman Catholic, and even converts were won from among the Indians. This surprising success on the part of the Jesuits was soon reported to the English Protestant authorities, which brought a rebuke from the proprietor, who now proceeded to limit the authority of the priests, annulled the grants of land made to the missionaries by the Indian chiefs, and finally had the Jesuits replaced by secular priests; and a few years later (1643) even made overtures to secure Puritan immigration from Massachusetts.

The oath prescribed by Lord Baltimore in 1636, to be taken by the Maryland governors, shows plainly his insistence upon maintaining religious toleration in the colony:[2]

I will not myself or any other, directly or indirectly, trouble, molest, or discountenance any person professing to believe in Jesus Christ, for or in respect to religion: I will make no difference of persons in conferring offices, favors, or rewards, for or in respect of religion: but merely as they shall be found faithful and well deserving, and endued with moral virtues and abilities: my aim shall be public unity, and if any person or officer shall molest any person professing to believe in Jesus Christ, on account of his religion, I will protect the person molested, and punish the offender.

While the religious toleration authorized in Maryland by Cecil Calvert was quite evidently primarily based upon practical and business reasons, yet undoubtedly "it was also the outcome of his convictions and kindly nature."

As the number of Protestants in the colony increased, they naturally tended to become more aggressive, which was especially true of that group of Puritans who had been given refuge in Maryland when they were driven from Virginia. Soon they had become bitter antagonists of the proprietor and all his Catholic subjects. The religious troubles brewing in Maryland were brought to the point of explosion by the breaking out of the Civil Wars in England. With the triumph of the Parliamentary party and the establishment of the protectorate, the Maryland

[2] Tiffany, p. 58.

situation was bound to be profoundly affected. At this juncture, in order to avoid criticism and allay suspicion of his colony, Lord Baltimore appointed a Protestant governor (1649), William Stone, with instructions to continue the policy of religious toleration and urged upon the Maryland Assembly the passage of an Act of Toleration. The assembly passing the measure was composed of both Catholics and Protestants, though the proprietor's wish in the matter was quite probably the deciding factor.

Since the passage of this act marks an important epoch in the history of religious liberty, it is well to consider it in some detail. The act does not go far enough to be accounted ideal, since it provides toleration only for Christians, while those who deny "the Holy Trinity or the Godhead of any of the Three Persons etc. was to be punished with death, and confiscation of lands and goods." The great variety of religious groups in Maryland at the time may be inferred by the third provision of the act, which promises punishment by fine or whipping and imprisonment for any person who "in a reproachful manner" calls any person within the Province a "Heretic, Schismatic, Idolater, Independent, Presbyterian, Popish Priest, Jesuit, Jesuited Papist, Lutheran, Calvinist, Anabaptist, Brownist, Antinomian, Barrowist, Roundhead, Separatist, or any other Name or term, in a reproachful manner." The fifth is the most important provision of the act, which reads:

And whereas the enforcing of the conscience in matter of religion, hath frequently fallen out to be of dangerous consequence in those common wealths where it has been practiced,

WHIPPING OF OBADIAH HOLMES

From Bryant and Gay, *Popular History of the United States*, Vol. II

an
Pr
am
wi
or
Ch
les

l this Province, o......

avens, thereunto belonging, professing to believe in Jesus
ist, shall from henceforth be in any ways troubled, mo-
ted, or discountenanced, for or in respect of his or her Re-
ugion, nor in the free exercise thereof, within this Province,
or the Islands thereunto belonging, nor any way compelled to
the belief or exercise of any other religion, against his or her
consent, so as they be not unfaithful to the Lord Proprietor, or
molest or conspire against the civil government established,
or to be established, in this Province, under him or his heirs.

The punishment for the violation of this act was treble
damages to the wronged party and fine for each offense,
to be divided between the proprietor and the damaged
person, and in default of payment, whipping and
imprisonment.

But unfortunately the passage of this act did not satisfy
the aggressive Puritans, and their dissatisfaction was the
more intensified when, in the absence of the Protestant
governor "his Catholic deputy" issued a proclamation declaring allegiance to King Charles II, then in exile. This
untactful move brought things to an immediate crisis
and a Parliamentary Commission took over the management of Maryland affairs, and when Governor Stone refused to recognize the Parliamentary title to the province,
he was removed and the government placed in the hands
of a committee. The Protestant party were now in complete control in Maryland and proceeded at once to
change the Act of Toleration "excluding from its bene-

{ 119 }

England, and in 1657, when the proprietor once again regained control, the Toleration Act was again put in effect. Thus the Protestants again became the aggrieved party, claiming that although the Act of Toleration was in effect they failed to receive their share of the offices.

The overthrow of James II in the revolution of 1688 brought Maryland affairs to a new crisis. Though the new king and queen, William and Mary, were proclaimed in Maryland by the proprietor's government, yet the whole general situation was favorable to the Protestants, and the trend of events played into their hands. A Protestant Association was now formed under the leadership of a cheap agitator, John Coode, and soon an insurrection was under way which succeeded in seizing the government. Justification for the insurrection was placed on the ground that a Protestant government was needed in view of an impending war with a Catholic nation. A convention made up of members of the insurgent group was held in 1690 in which a committee was appointed to carry on the government until a royal governor could be sent over. For two years Sir Lionel Copley, a member of the Established Church, was governor and two years later (1692) Maryland was declared a royal colony and the same year the English Church was established.

At the time of the establishment of the Anglican Church in Maryland the Protestant element made up more than three-fourths of the population. In 1669 there were but two Catholic priests in the colony to minister to perhaps two thousand communicants. In 1673 two Franciscans founded a mission in Maryland and four years later three other Franciscans and three Jesuits arrived. This increase in the Catholic forces soon led to the establishment of a Jesuit school in the colony, while Catholic work expanded somewhat into Pennsylvania and in the seaboard settlements north of Maryland. These feeble Roman Catholic beginnings give little indication of the vast expansion of Roman Catholicism in America which was to proceed largely from Maryland, in the two centuries to follow.

Chapter VI

RELIGIOUS DIVERSITY IN THE MIDDLE COLONIES: DUTCH REFORMED, AND ENGLISH QUAKERS

THE middle colonies, from the very first, contained a great mixture of people. At the time of the colonization of America, Holland was the most liberal country in the world and became a refuge for persecuted sects. Representatives from almost every country in Europe had taken up their residence in this little free country, as had the English Pilgrims in 1607, and when Holland began to obtain colonies of her own it was but natural that the population of her colonies should resemble that of the mother country. When the English captured New Netherlands in 1664 it was reported that fourteen languages were spoken on Long Island, and ten years later eighteen nationalities were to be found in the colony of New York. William Penn's colony of Pennsylvania and the other Quaker colonies, New Jersey and Delaware, dominated as they were by the liberal ideas of Penn and his associates, likewise attracted a great variety of peoples. The Dutch, the Swedes, the Welsh, English Quakers, and the several German groups, and last of all the Scotch-Irish, were attracted to the middle colonies. Out of this great variety of people came a corresponding variety of religious sects.

The most important of these religious groups were the
Dutch Reformed, which was the state church of the
Netherlands; the English Quakers, the Swedish Luther-
ans, the German Reformed, Mennonites, Dunkers,
Schwenkfelders, Welsh Baptists, German Lutherans,
Moravians and Scotch-Irish Presbyterians. It is the pur-
pose of this and the following chapters to tell of the
beginnings in America of these several religious groups.

The Dutch colony of New Netherlands, like several
of the early English colonies, was established by a trading
company known as the Dutch West India Company. This
company received its charter in 1621 giving it the privilege of trading and founding colonies in America. Two
years later, in spite of the protests of the English against
the Dutch invasion of territory which they claimed, thirty
families of Dutch and Walloon Protestants came out to
America and two posts were established. One near the
present site of Camden, New Jersey, was called Fort
Nassau and the other, where Albany now stands, received
the name Fort Orange. By 1625 there were two hundred
people in the colony and in 1626 Peter Minuit, the first
and the best of the Dutch governors, was sent out as
director general. Soon after his arrival he made the famous purchase of Manhattan Island from the Indians, and
a third fort was built on the southern tip of the island
which was named New Amsterdam.

The Dutch came primarily as traders and the fur trade
with the Indians was their chief interest. For the carrying
on of such trade peace had to be maintained with the
Indians and the Dutch were necessarily scattered over a
large area. Nor did the Dutch come out to America in

great numbers, largely for the reason that the long wars with the Spaniards had depleted the population of the Netherlands and the great East Indian trading and colonizing interests of the Dutch left comparatively few people for their American enterprise. When the Dutch colonies passed into English hands they contained not more than seven thousand inhabitants. Throughout the entire period of Dutch control of New Netherlands trade and commercial interests dominated the colony, to the neglect of education and religion.

It was not until 1628, five years after the coming of the first colonists, that a minister was brought out, though two years before (1626) two comforters of the sick came in response to the plea of a few anxious souls. These two lay workers not only visited among the people, but also held informal services in a large room above the horse mill which had been fitted up by its owner to serve as a place of worship. This building even boasted a tower in which were placed bells captured by the company's fleet in the Spanish colony of Porto Rico.

The Dutch West India Company declared the Reformed religion established in their colonies, and ministers, schoolmasters and sick visitors were maintained at their expense. The ministers sent out from time to time were approved by the Classis, or Presbytery, of Amsterdam and the Classis continued to exercise ecclesiastical authority over the Reformed Church in America throughout most of the period of the colonies.

The first Reformed minister to arrive in New Amsterdam was Rev. Jonas Michaelius (1628), who has left us an interesting account of religious conditions in the colony at the time of his coming. He says:

Our coming here was agreeable to all, and I hope, by the grace of the Lord, that my services will not be unfruitful. The people for the most part, are free, somewhat rough, and loose; but I find in almost all of them both love and respect toward me. . . .

Michaelius organized a church the year of his arrival, with the director of the company, Minuit, and the store-keeper as elders. The minister thus describes the first communion service:

We have had at the first administration of the Lord's Supper full fifty communicants—not without great joy and comfort for so many—Walloons and Dutch; of whom a portion made their first confession of faith before us and others exhibited their church certificates. Others had forgotten to bring their certificates with them, not thinking that a church would be formed and established here; and some who brought them had lost them, unfortunately, in a general conflagration; but they were admitted upon the satisfactory testimony of others to whom they were known, and also upon their daily good deportment, since we cannot observe strictly all the usual formalities in making a beginning under such circumstances.

Michaelius found that the French-speaking Walloons understood very little of the service in Dutch and he accordingly arranged to administer the Lord's Supper to them in the French language using the French mode. He tells us that the discourse preceding the sacrament he had before him in writing for, he says, "I could not trust myself extemporaneously."

Just how long Michaelius remained in New Amsterdam is not known. In 1637 he was in Holland, as the Classis was then discussing sending him back to America. It is probable that he had left New Netherlands previous to the coming out of Everardus Bogardus in 1633, who was the second minister to arrive in the colony, coming in the same ship with the second governor, Van Twiller.

Bogardus remained in the colony under the incompetent and corrupt administrations of the next two governors—Van Twiller (1633-1638) and Kieft (1638-1647)—and it is to his lasting credit that throughout the whole time he was in constant conflict with them both, because of his outspoken denunciation of their corruption and mismanagement. During these years of discord, however, two meeting-houses were built, the first a barnlike structure of wood, while under Kieft (1642) a stone church was erected within the fort. This building was seventy-two feet long by fifty wide and its cost was two thousand five hundred guilders. A contemporary has left us the following account of how the director took subscriptions for this church:

The Director then resolved to build a church, and at the place where it suited him; but he was in want of money and was at a loss how to obtain it. It happened about this time that the minister, Everardus Bogardus gave his stepdaughter in marriage; and the occasion of the wedding the Director considered a good opportunity for his purpose. So after the fourth or fifth round of drinking, he set about the business, and he himself showing a liberal example let the wedding guests subscribe what they were willing to give towards the church. All then with light heads subscribed largely, competing with one another; and although some well repented it when they recovered their senses, they were nevertheless compelled to pay—nothing could avail to prevent it.

A few years after the establishment of New Amsterdam the West India Company, in order to stimulate Dutch settlement of America, issued what was known as the "Charter of Freedoms and Exemptions." This provided that anyone bringing over fifty adult colonists within a space of four years was to become a "patroon" or lord of the manor, and would receive a great landed estate on one of the two great rivers of the colony. Each "patroon" was to support a minister, and several ministers were brought out under this arrangement. The best known of all the patroons was Killian Van Rensselaer, a wealthy Amsterdam jeweler whose patroonship was a vast estate near the present city of Albany. And of all the ministers brought over by the patroons John Van Mekelenburg, better known as Megapolensis, the minister at Rensselaerwyck, is the best and most favorably known. Van Rensselaer agreed to provide the minister with a residence and guaranteed him a salary of one thousand guilders a year for six years and two hundred guilders additional for the three following years, if his services were satisfactory. Megapolensis worked faithfully among the Indians as well as with the settlers. The second year after his arrival a church was built. He learned the Mohawk tongue and was able to preach to the Indians, some of whom joined his church, and the claim is made that he was the first Protestant missionary to the Indians.

During Megapolensis' stay as the minister at Rensselaerwyck he was largely instrumental in saving the life of Father Jogues, a French Jesuit missionary, who had been captured by the Mohawks and brought to Fort Orange. Here the Dutch commander and Megapolensis befriended him and kept him concealed until they could send him to New Amsterdam. We are indebted to Father Jogues' stay at Fort Orange and New Amsterdam for a particularly interesting description of New Netherlands. Concerning the religious situation at New Amsterdam, he says: "No religion is publicly exercised but the Calvinist, and orders are to admit none but Calvinists. But this is not observed, for there are, besides Calvinists, in the colony, Catholics, English Puritans, Lutherans, Anabaptists, —here called Mennonists." Of the colony at Fort Orange Father Jogues says: There is "a colony sent here by this Rensselaer, who is the patroon. This colony is composed of about a hundred persons, who reside in some twenty-five or thirty houses, built along the river. In the principal house resides the patroon's agent; the minister has his part, in which service is performed. . . ."

Under the incompetent administrations of Van Twiller and Kieft the affairs of the West India Company had gone from bad to worse and the company was on the verge of bankruptcy with assets of five millions of florens less than its liabilities. The last governor, Peter Stuyvesant, was of different stripe from his two predecessors, for he was an earnest and capable man and an elder in the Reformed Church, though inclined to be arbitrary in his administration. It was during his administration that the people rose and demanded a share in the government, and the governor was compelled to yield, though much against his will. Under Stuyvesant the affairs of the company began to revive; trade increased and people began to come in from surrounding colonies, some of them driven from New England by the exclusive religious policy there. These new settlers were promised "liberty of conscience according to the custom and manner of Holland," with the result that the religious sects became even more numerous than the racial elements in the colony.

During the latter part of Stuyvesant's administration, probably without the knowledge of the directors of the company, the policy of religious exclusiveness was adopted and there was some persecution, especially of the Dutch Lutherans and the Quakers. In this policy Stuyvesant was supported by the ministers of the Dutch Church, who in 1656 made a formal complaint to the governor against the great increase of sects, which led to the passage of an ordinance forbidding preaching by unqualified persons and the holding of conventicles. The law was enforced by fines and imprisonment, which led to complaints directly to the West India Company and to the States-General. The net result of the whole matter was that the company finally disapproved Stuyvesant's action, though their reason for so doing was based on their desire not to hamper the economic welfare of the colony nor discourage settlers.

The company's rebuke to Stuyvesant was brought about through his attempt to put a stop to Quaker worship at Flushing, Long Island. John Browne, a Friend, had built a new house at Flushing and he and his wife called in their fellow members of the Society of Friends to worship. Browne was arrested and finally banished. He went to Holland and appeared before the directors of the company who were, by Browne, so fully convinced that Stuyvesant's policy was wrong that they wrote a letter to him stating, among other things:

Wherefore it is our opinion that some connivance would be useful; and that the consciences of men, at least ought to remain free and unshackled. Let every one be unmolested as long as he is modest, moderate, his political conduct irreproachable, and as long as he does not offend others or oppose the government. The maxim of moderation has always been the guide of our magistrates in this city, and the consequence has been that people have flocked from every land to this asylum. Tread thus in their steps, and we doubt not you will be blessed.

This put an end to Stuyvesant's policy of persecution, and when two years later (1665) Browne returned to America and met Stuyvesant as a private citizen, the old ex-governor seemed heartily ashamed of what he had done, as well any self-respecting Dutchman might, in the face of the two hundred year record of religious toleration in the Netherlands.

While the Dutch were busy with their American colony on the Hudson, a rival colony appeared on the Delaware, or South, River. These rivals were the Swedes. Like the Dutch, the Swedes proceeded in their colonizing project through the medium of a Commercial Company, which had been chartered in 1626, but due to the participation of the great Swedish king, Gustavus Adolphus, in the Thirty Years' War, and finally his tragic death, they were not able to send out colonists until 1638. Peter Minuit, the first governor of the Dutch colony, offered his services to the Swedes and it was under his leadership that the first expedition of fifty colonists set out. Land was purchased of the Indians, though it was already claimed by the Dutch, and a fort was built near the present site of Wilmington, Delaware, and called Fort Christina. Altogether the Swedes sent out twelve expeditions, but New Sweden never became a numerous or prosperous colony. With the first group of Swedish settlers came the Rev. Reorus Torkillus, who has the distinction of being the first Lutheran minister in North America. Torkillus died in Christina in 1643 of a sickness that swept away great numbers of the settlers.

The Rev. John Campanius came out the year Torkillus died, and he not only ministered faithfully to the settlers, but also undertook the work of Christianizing the Indians in the vicinity. His work among the Indians was probably induced by a regulation of the great Swedish chancellor, Oxenstiern, which stated:

The wild nations, bordering upon all other sides, the Governor shall understand how to treat with all humanity and respect, that no violence or wrong be done to them by Her Royal Majesty or her subjects aforesaid; but he shall rather, at every opportunity, exert himself that the same wild people may gradually be instructed in the truths and worship of the Christian religion, and in other ways brought to civilization and good government, and in this manner, properly guided.

Campanius learned the Delaware tongue and translated Luther's Small Catechism, though it was not printed until 1696 and then at the personal expense of King Charles XI. On Campanius' return to Sweden other ministers came out, and at the time of the Dutch capture of New

Sweden in 1655, at least two Lutheran churches had been established. Nearly thirty years later when William Penn founded his colony of Pennsylvania he found from five to seven hundred Swedes living on the Delaware. They were an honest, industrious and religious people, and to-day two of their churches still stand as monuments to the honorable part they played in the early religious history of America, old Gloria Dei Church in South Philadelphia and Old Swedes Church in Wilmington, Delaware, at the southern end of which lie the remains of the first Lutheran pastor, Torkillus.

The Dutch capture of the Swedish colony was followed a few years later (1664), by the English capture of New Amsterdam, and the complete overthrow of Dutch authority. In March, 1664, King Charles II had granted all the territory which the Dutch claimed in America to his brother the Duke of York, and during the summer the new proprietor sent a fleet to seize the territory from the Dutch. Governor Stuyvesant was completely unprepared to defend the colony, though he vowed he would never surrender, but he finally was persuaded to listen to the advice of the ministers and others, and the colony was turned over to the English without striking a blow. Article VIII of the terms of surrender reads:

The Dutch here shall enjoy the liberty of their consciences in divine worship and in church discipline.

The Dutch minister at New Amsterdam informed the Classis of Amsterdam of the surrender in a letter dated September 15, 1664. Toward the end of his letter he states:

It is stipulated in the articles [of surrender] that the religion and doctrine shall continue as heretofore, and the ministers shall remain. We could not abandon our congregations and hearers. We judged that we must continue with them, for a time at least, and perform our offices, lest they should become entirely scattered and grow wild.

Nor did he forget to add:

The West India Company owes me quite a sum, which I hope and desire will be paid.

At the time of the surrender of the colony there were six Dutch ministers in America and thirteen churches. Altogether thirteen ministers had come out from 1628 to 1664. For many years the Dutch Reformed Church remained the strongest religious group in the colony, though, of course, it no longer received any special recognition from the government. From the time of the surrender until 1696 the status of the Dutch Reformed Church was uncertain. The early English governors seemed to consider the Dutch ministers as entitled to receive support from taxation, and in 1670 the governor guaranteed a salary to any Dutch minister who would come over to assist the Dutch minister, Drisius, at New York, and in response to this promise the first recruit after the surrender arrived from Holland.

The best of all the early English governors of New York was the Irish Roman Catholic, Governor Dongan (1682-1688). He was an honest and broad-minded man and on his arrival announced to the Dutch minister at New York, upon whom he called, that the Duke intended to allow liberty of conscience. During this administration numerous French settlers arrived, driven to America by the revocation of the Edict of Nantes. Several of the Dutch pastors who could preach in French occasionally ministered to the Huguenots, though the French were soon numerous enough to form their own congregations and have their own ministers. It has been stated, with justice, that religious toleration was almost perfect during the administration of Dongan, though instructions were sent out to the governor by James II, who we will remember was himself a Catholic, establishing the Church of England in the colony. The list of instructions contains the following:

You shall permit all persons of what Religion soever quietly to inhabit within your Government without giving them any disturbance or disquiet whatsoever for or by reason of their differing Opinions in matters of Religion, Provided they give no disturbance to ye public peace, nor do molest or disquiet others in ye free Exercise of their Religion.

This liberality of King James was, of course, due to the fact that he was anxious to gain toleration for Catholics.

In 1687 Governor Dongan made a report of conditions in the colony which includes a summary of the general religious situation:

Every town ought to have a minister. New York has first a Chaplain belonging to the Fort of the Church of England; secondly a Dutch Calvinist; thirdly a French Calvinist; fourthly a Dutch Lutheran. Here bee not many of the Church of England; few Roman Catholocks; aboundance of Quaker preachers, men and Women especially; Singling Quakers; Ranting Quakers; Sabbatarians; Anti-Sabbatarians; some Anabaptists; some Jews; in short, of all sorts of opinions there are some, and the most part of none at all. The Great Church which serves both the English and the Dutch within the Fort, which is found to be very inconvenient. Therefore I desire that there may bee an order for their building another; ground being already layd out for that purpose, and they not wanting money in store wherewithall to build it. The most prevailing opinion is that of Dutch Calvinists. It is the endeavor of all persons here to bring up their children and servants in that opinion which themselves profess; but this I observe, that they take no care of the conversion of their slaves.

A notion was prevalent at this period that baptism of slaves would *ipso facto* free them, but to the credit of King James he insisted that they be baptized, and instructions to governors frequently contained such admonitions. In the Dutch churches this seems to have been the practice, as the records of the churches show.

At the overthrow of James II the people of New York rose in revolt and Lieutenant Governor Nicholson fled. A Committee of Safety was chosen to take over the government until the new Dutch king, William III, could appoint a new governor. At the head of the revolutionary government was Colonel Jacob Leisler, who was generally considered as the representative of William and Mary and Protestantism. But, strange to say, the Dutch ministers in New York refused to recognize him or his authority. As a result the people refused to hear the ministers preach, nor would they pay their salaries. Undoubtedly the ministers were wrongly advised in this whole affair, although they no doubt thought Leisler unfit for the position he held, and were also very probably influenced by social reasons.

When the new governor, Sloughter, arrived in the colony, he brought instructions from King William, "to permit a liberty of conscience to all Persons (except Papists), so they be contented with a quiet and Peaceable enjoyment of it, not giving offence or scandall to the Government." The new governor was also instructed to require of the officeholders in the province the oaths and tests required in the Test Act of 1673, which required, besides the oaths of allegiance and supremacy to the king, the taking of the sacrament according to the form of the Church of England, as well as the signing of a declaration against the Roman Catholic doctrine of transsubstantiation. These instructions seemed to favor the establishment of the English Church, and the next step on the part of the governor was to suggest the passage of the *Ministry Act*, providing for the "proper maintenance of a minister in every town where there were forty families or more." Proposed first in 1691, similar bills were introduced in 1692 and again in 1693, though when finally adopted the application of the measure was limited to the City of New York, and the counties of Richmond, Westchester and Queens.

This measure by no sense established the English Church, though Governor Fletcher, who urged it, attempted so to interpret it. The act provides that "there shall be called, inducted, and established, a good sufficient Protestant minister" in the counties indicated. The several dissenting groups claimed equal benefit from the act, and in every place outside New York City the dissenters were

able to maintain their own ministers under the act. When
called upon to interpret the meaning of the act in 1695,
the New York Assembly stated, "Vestrymen and churchwardens have power to call a dissenting Protestant minister, and that he is to be paid and maintained as the law
directs." The governor, on the other hand, refused to
accept this interpretation, stating that "there is no Protestant Church admits of such officers as Church wardens
and Vestrymen but the Church of England." It seems to
have been assumed in later legal documents adopted from
time to time that the Church of England had been established in New York, and many came to believe it. To
hold to this legal fiction may have given satisfaction to
the royal governors, but it had little effect upon the stub-
born Dutchmen, who made up the majority in the
assembly.

The Anglican chaplain of the English troops in New
York wrote a description of conditions in the colony in
1695 for the information of the Bishop of London. He
speaks of the lack of churches and ministers, though, he
says, there are many pretended ministers, Presbyterians
and Independents. He urges the necessity of a bishop for
America, who he suggests might be a suffragan of the
Bishop of London. He adds a table of churches, ministers
and families. In New York City there are six churches
including the chapel at the fort where the chaplain presided. The Dutch Calvinists had 475 families, the French
200, the Dutch Lutherans 30, the Jews—already beginning to appear in some numbers in New York—20, while
the families to whom he ministered numbered but 90.
Summarizing the figures for the whole province, the

Dutch had 1,754 families; the English dissenters, 1,365; the French, 261; the Lutherans, 45; the Anglicans, 90; and the Jews, 20.

The passage of the Ministry Act as described above greatly disturbed the Dutch minister at New York concerning the legal status of his church, for he felt that the privileges which they then enjoyed might very easily be taken away. This led to a petition for a charter. At first unsuccessful, a charter was finally granted May 11, 1696, which was the first church charter granted in New York. After conceding to the church the right to hold property, the charter explains the reasons for granting the same, and then declares:

That our royal will and pleasure is, that no person in communion with the said Reformed Protestant Dutch Church within our city of New York, at any time, hereafter, shall be in any ways molested, punished, disquieted, or called in question for differences of opinion in matters of the Protestant religion, who do not disturb the civil peace of our said province; etc.

With the securing of the charter the Dutch minister in New York City, Domine Selyns, now felt that their position was secure, and in reporting to the Classis of Amsterdam he says referring to the charter: "This is a circumstance which promises much advantage to God's Church, and quiets the formerly existing uneasiness." Other Dutch churches from time to time sought and received charters. The only other churches in New York, however, to receive charters were the Established churches, and the first of these was granted to Trinity Church in 1697.

This charter made Trinity Church the established church in New York City, while the churchwardens and vestrymen instead of being chosen by the freeholders of the city, according to the act of 1694, were now to be chosen by those in communion with the Church of England alone. The explanation of this fact seems to be that the Dutch members of the assembly were so elated over receiving their own charter that they were willing to allow Trinity Church to claim all its charter allowed. For the next century and more the Dutch and the English churches and their ministers lived together in peace and harmony, though the Dutch Church was more or less static until aroused through the activities of Theodore Frelinghuysen, and the Great Awakening.

THE QUAKERS

Within ten years after George Fox had begun his new reformation in England (1647) his disciples made their appearance in America, and by the end of the century they were to be found in every colony under British rule, as they were imbued with a dauntless missionary spirit, for as one of them wrote "the Lord's word was as a fire and a hammer in me."

The first Quakers to appear in America were two women, Mary Fisher and Ann Austin, who landed in Boston in 1656. From the beginning, women had been active as Quaker missionaries and these women were but doing what numerous others were attempting. Already they had conducted a successful mission to the Barbados, where influential converts had been won. In Boston, however, they were to have no opportunity to preach the new gospel. Before they could land, orders were received from the lieutenant governor that they should be kept on shipboard, and their effects searched. Later they were imprisoned for five weeks, the windows of the jail boarded up so they could not see or be seen, and among the indignities heaped upon them, they were stripped and subjected to an examination for "tokens" of witchcraft on their bodies while their books were burned by the common hangman in the market place. The captain of the vessel which had brought them to Boston was now compelled to return them to the Barbados, evidently at his own expense, while the Boston jailer had to content himself with their bedding and their Bibles in lieu of fees. But Boston was not done with the Quakers so easily, for hardly was the vessel bearing Mary Fisher and Ann Austin out of sight before another ship landed eight more Quaker missionaries. After eleven weeks' imprisonment they were also sent out of the colony, so fearful were the Puritan fathers that the new heresy would contaminate their people.

Nor is it at all strange that the New England Puritans should have looked upon the coming of the Quakers as a real peril. The ideals and practices of the Quakers were flatly antagonistic to that of the religious leaders of Massachusetts. "The Quaker aimed at a complete separation between Church and State"; while "the government of Massachusetts was patterned after the ancient Jewish theocracy in which State and church were identified. The Quaker was tolerant of differences in doctrine; the Calvinist regarded such tolerance as a deadly sin." Laws were now passed in Massachusetts against the Quakers—for

Ann Austin and Mary Fisher had been imprisoned before there were laws providing for their punishment—the first passed in 1656 fixing penalties for bringing Quakers into the colony; the second in 1657 increasing the penalties; the third in 1658 forbidding Quakers from holding meetings under heavy fines, while in 1661 a law was passed imposing the death penalty upon Quakers who should return after having been banished. And it needs to be said that these laws were vigorously enforced. But in spite of this cruel array of legislation against them the Quakers continued to come, and gradually their treatment became less and less severe, especially after Charles II (1661) had sent a letter to Governor Endicott forbidding further proceedings against the Quakers and directing that in the future they be sent to England for trial. Twenty years later the laws against Quakers were suspended, though numerous Friends were imprisoned thereafter for their refusal to pay tithes. The Connecticut and New Haven colonies passed laws similar to those of Massachusetts, and even in liberal Rhode Island the aged Roger Williams entered the lists against them, and challenged Fox to debate and later produced a pamphlet called "George Fox digged out of his Burrows" which was characterized by Fox as "a very envious and wicked book."

Quakers appeared in New York about the same time as in New England and at first were well treated by the Dutch, but as we have already noticed, during the administration of Governor Stuyvesant, there was a period of persecution and Quaker missionaries were imprisoned and sent out of the colony. This period of persecution, however, lasted but a short time, and was brought to an end (1663) by the appeal of John Browne to the directors of the Dutch West India Company against the policy of Governor Stuyvesant. In the southern colonies Quaker missionaries early made their appearance; in Virginia as early as 1656, in Maryland in 1657, and in the Carolinas at least as early as 1672. Everywhere they were persecuted, outside the so-called Quaker colonies, except in Rhode Island and the Carolinas.

The first Monthly meetings formed in America were those of Sandwich and Scituate in Massachusetts, both founded before 1660, while the New England Yearly Meeting, established in 1661, is likewise the oldest organization of its kind in America.

Of great importance in the early history of the Quakers in America was the visit of George Fox. Fox landed in Maryland in the spring of 1672, whence after a short period he went to Rhode Island where he was entertained by the governor, Nicholas Easton, who was himself a Quaker, and who traveled with Fox through the colony. Later Fox visited Long Island, where he held a number of meetings, thence into New Jersey, where new meetings were established. In November he visited Virginia and under his preaching the number of Friends in that colony were doubled. Of his trip into the Carolinas he has left us a graphic account in his Journal, where on one occasion he says:

Wee passed all day, & saw neither house nor man through ye woods & swamps, & many cruel boggs & watery places, yt wee was wet to the knees most of us, & at night wee tooke up our Lodginge in ye woods, & made a fire.

MARY DYER LED TO EXECUTION

One of four Quakers to suffer the death penalty in the Colonies. Her offense was returning to Massachusetts the third time after her banishment.

From Bryant and Gay, *Popular History of the United States*, Vol. II

He traveled more than a thousand miles southward from Boston, "all of which wee have traveiled by land & downe bayes & over Rivers and Creeks & boggs & wilderness."

The center of Quaker activity in America, however, was in New Jersey, Delaware and Pennsylvania, which are sometimes called the Quaker colonies.

The great Quaker experiment in America had its beginnings in New Jersey. The early political history of this colony is in great confusion. It was included in the grant made to the Duke of York in 1664, who soon gave it to two of his friends, Sir John Berkeley and Sir George Carteret. The governors of New York, however, claimed jurisdiction over the territory, which claim was resisted by the proprietors, who in the end were upheld by the king. The proprietors were anxious for settlers, and made liberal concessions to induce colonists to come to their province. In response to their invitation a considerable number of Puritans came from New England, and some Quakers were early settled along the Raritan River and by 1670 a meeting was formed at Shrewsbury and a meeting-house built. In 1674 Berkeley sold out his rights to two Quakers, Fenwick and Byllingy, who made an agreement with Carteret to divide the province into East and West Jersey, and it was accordingly in West Jersey, in the region bordering on the Delaware River that the first important Quaker experiment in government began. Later the two Quaker proprietors sold out their rights in West Jersey to a number of Quaker gentlemen, among them being William Penn, which marks the beginning of Penn's personal interest in America. The Quaker proprietors now drew up a liberal constitution and towns and settlements sprang up along the Delaware.

The spirit of the charter of West New Jersey which was drawn up in 1676, and called "Concessions and Agreements," is characterized by this statement of the Quaker proprietors:

> Thus we lay a foundation for after ages to understand their liberty as men and Christians, that they may not be brought into bondage but by their own consent; for we put the power in the people. No person to be called in question or molested for his conscience or for worshipping according to his conscience.

By 1681 more than a thousand emigrants had come to West Jersey, most of them Quakers. Burlington, founded in 1677, became the most important Quaker center. At first, worship was conducted under a tent made of sailcloth, and here in July, 1678, a Monthly Meeting was set up. In May, 1680, the Burlington Quarterly Meeting was established and the next year it was determined to establish a Yearly Meeting. The next turn in the affairs of the Quakers in the Jerseys was brought about by the death of Sir George Carteret, the proprietor of East Jersey, whose heirs sold out their rights to another group of twelve Quakers, among whom also was William Penn. Soon after the number of proprietors was increased to twenty-four, among them being several Scotchmen. Under the influence of the Scotch partners numerous Scotch immigrants came out to East New Jersey, many of whom were Presbyterians. Thus was the Presbyterian element introduced into New Jersey. Other immigrants came from New England as well as numerous Scotch-Irish from North Ireland and later these Calvinistic elements combined to make Presbyterianism the outstanding religious force in the colony.

It was in 1681 that William Penn was granted Pennsylvania in consideration of a debt of £16,000 which was due him from the crown. The beginnings of William Penn's interest in American colonization has already been noticed. The next year the Duke of York gave to Penn what is now Delaware, which was called "the territories." This was governed as a part of Pennsylvania until 1702 when it secured its own assembly and eventually became a separate colony. The long-drawn-out boundary dispute especially between Maryland and Pennsylvania is hardly a part of this story, though it kept Penn in England when he might have been with his people in America.

No single Englishman engaged in colonization made such a success of his enterprise as did William Penn. He termed it "an Holy Experiment" and thus explains his intention in planting the colony: "My God that has given it me through many difficulties, will, I believe, bless and make it the seed of a nation. . . . I have so obtained it and desire to keep it, that I may not be unworthy of His love; but do that which may answer His kind providence and serve His Truth and people; that an example may be set up to the nations. There may be room there, though not here, for such an experiment." In April, 1682, he issued his *Frame of Government*, which soon proved too complicated to be used, but which clearly shows Penn's desire to establish the principles of English liberty. In October of the same year Penn arrived in his colony and by 1701 the government had been greatly simplified and popular freedom increased.

The outstanding reason for the success of Pennsylvania was the religious freedom which the proprietor not only guaranteed but also widely advertised. His guarantee of religious freedom included all law-abiding citizens who "acknowledged one Almighty and Eternal God to be the Creator, Upholder and Ruler of the world," which would include Protestants, Catholics and Jews. Later Catholics were excluded from officeholding through pressure from the home government and officeholding was limited to Christians, which, of course, is a limitation which would not be made today in a country where there is complete religious liberty. In spite of these limitations Pennsylvania proved an attractive haven for numerous religious sects and no colony gave them a larger opportunity of working out their own theories.

The majority of the early colonists were English and Welsh Quakers. By 1683 the population was reported as 4,000 and six years later Delaware and Pennsylvania contained not less than 12,000 people. But this was just the beginning of the great inflow, not only from the British Isles, but from Germany, France and Holland. In 1685 Penn estimated that only about half of the people in the colony were English.

At first the Pennsylvania Quakers held their meetings in the homes of the people, but it was not long until meeting-houses began to be built. The first Monthly Meeting was held in January, 1682, and "within three months nine meetings for worship and three monthly meetings had been set up." In 1683 the Pennsylvania Friends attended the Yearly Meeting at Burlington and the same year a Yearly Meeting was held in Philadelphia. The foolishness of holding two separate Yearly Meetings so close together led in 1685 to an agreement that Yearly Meetings should be held alternately in Burlington and Philadelphia. The number of Friends continued to increase and by 1700 there were forty meetings or congregations in Pennsylvania. By 1760 the number of Quakers, or Friends, in America was near 30,000. The size of some of the Pennsylvania meetings particularly was very large, several numbering as many as 1,500 members each.

But as numbers increased spiritual life seemed to decline. This condition was inevitable with the establishment of what is known as birthright membership. This meant that increasing numbers of Friends became members of the Society through birth rather than through any conviction of their own. The increase of wealth among the Quakers was undoubtedly another reason for their spiritual decline as is pointed out by an aged Friend in 1760, looking back over a period of about sixty years. In the early days, he says:

Friends were a plain lowly-minded people, and that there was much tenderness and contrition in their meetings. That at 20 years from that date, the Society increasing in wealth and in some degree conforming to the fashions of the world, true humility was less apparent, and their meetings in general not so lively and edifying. That at the end of 40 years many of them were grown very rich; and many made a specious appearance in the world, that marks of outward wealth and greatness appeared on some in our meetings of ministers and elders, and as such things became more prevalent so the powerful overshadowings of the Holy Ghost were less manifest in the Society. That there had been a continual increase of such ways of life even until the present time, and that the weakness that had now overspread the Society and the barrenness manifest among us is a matter of much sorrow.

Traveling Friends in the eighteenth century speak of "a dry lifeless state" in many of the meetings, "excessive drinking" on the part of some of the members; some who are living "in open profaneness and are riotous in conversation"; while some of the young Friends take part in shooting matches, games of "hustlecap" and are prone to do much drinking, carousing and fighting. The question of drink caused much concern among the Friends of the eighteenth century. Among the first rules adopted by the Friends was one prohibiting the selling or giving away of strong drink to the Indians. The custom of serving liquor at burials became common which led the Yearly Meeting in 1729 to recommend that "When wine or other strong liquors are served (which many soberminded people think needless) that it be but once."

The Quakers from the beginning were a loosely organized body, and what little organization there was among them in America was brought over from England. George Fox was responsible for the establishment of the Monthly and Quarterly Meetings "for better ordering the affairs of the Church; in taking care of the poor; and exercising a true gospel discipline for a due dealing with any that might walk disorderly under our name; and to see that such as should marry among us did act fairly and clearly in that respect." At the First Yearly Meeting held in London in 1668 there was drawn up what is known as the *Canons and Institutions*, of which Fox was the probable author. Here are listed under nineteen heads, advices and regulations concerning all matters which might arise in the church, and these served as the model for the regulations of the early meetings in America. The first regular Books of Discipline did not appear in America until 1759, and then only in manuscript, but with the appearance of these rules of conduct Quakerism tended more and more to become a matter of observing the outward regulations and less and less that of establishing that vital relationship with God, which characterized the earlier years. It was during these years that the "Birthright membership" arose. This came from the legislation of the London Yearly Meeting in 1737 which stated that "All Friends shall be deemed members of the Quarterly, Monthly and Two-Weekly Meeting within the compass of which they inhabited or dwelt the first day of the Fourth Month, 1737"; and "the wife and children to be deemed members of the Monthly Meeting of which the husband or father is a member, not only during his life but after his decease." This act in the words of a Quaker historian: "changed the Society of Friends from a church of believers, at least in theory, to a corporation or association of persons some of whom would be among the unconverted."

Chapter VII

RELIGIOUS DIVERSITY IN THE MIDDLE COLONIES: GERMAN SECTARIES

THE first German settlement in America was Germantown, ten miles north of Philadelphia, and the first German settlers were Mennonites. After Penn's first visit to Germany (1671) a Frankfort Land Company was formed, which eventually purchased 25,000 acres of land in Pennsylvania. A young lawyer, Francis Daniel Pastorius, became the agent of the company, and under his direction, on October 6, 1683, the ship Concord arrived in Philadelphia bringing thirteen Mennonite families, which marks the beginning of German migration to America. These first arrivals were from Crefeld on the lower Rhine and were a thrifty and industrious people, mostly weavers. Eventually many of them became members of the Society of Friends, though in 1688 a Mennonite congregation was formed, and in 1708 the first Mennonite church erected. Later immigrations brought Mennonite settlers into Bucks, Berks and Northampton counties and by 1712 there were two hundred Mennonites in Pennsylvania and a church membership of at least one hundred. Perhaps the largest Mennonite community in America before the Revolution was in what is now

Lancaster county, which was made up largely of Swiss immigrants. Some of these were Amish Mennonites, which represented the most conservative branch of that body. By the end of the colonial period it has been estimated that there were 2,000 Mennonite families in America, most of them in Pennsylvania.

The Mennonites were the direct descendants of the Anabaptists of the Reformation. They receive their name from Menno Simons, a Dutch Catholic priest, who at forty years of age renounced the Catholic faith and cast in his lot with the humble Anabaptists, and it seems that his followers adopted the name "Mennonites" to escape persecution which was everywhere meted out to Anabaptists. The outstanding features of Mennonite faith correspond to the Baptists as to accepting the Bible as the only rule of faith, and the rejection of infant baptism. They did not, however, always insist upon immersion. They taught that the office of magistrate cannot be held by a Christian, though a Christian must be obedient to his rulers and pray for them and pay taxes to support the government. They also held that a Christian cannot take up the sword; that Christians must live secluded from the world; and that it is wrong to take an oath. In many respects the Mennonites were similar to the Quakers and were well treated as long as the Quakers were the ruling element in the colony. They took up good agricultural lands and their settlements soon became prosperous and even wealthy communities.

Another small German religious sect which made its appearance in Pennsylvania in the early eighteenth century was the Taufers, or Dunkers (German Baptists) as they came to be known in the colonies. The first Dunker immigration to America came from the same locality from which had come the first Mennonite settlers, Crefeld on the lower Rhine, and in response to the same set of influences, namely, the advertisement of Penn's agent and the Frankfort Land Company. Peter Becker, one of the ministers of the Crefeld congregation, led out the first settlers in 1719, numbering about 120 persons. They came to Germantown, but soon scattered into several settlements in the vicinity. It was not, however, until 1723 that their first congregation was formed, though worship was held from the beginning in the homes of some of the leaders. In 1729 a second group from West Friesland, numbering 126 people and under the leadership of Alexander Mack, came to Pennsylvania, while four years later a third company, but smaller than the first two, arrived under the leadership of John Naas. Within a few years these settlers were scattered widely, some migrating into Maryland and Virginia, and by the end of the colonial period some nineteen congregations had been formed, twelve of them numbering 200 members or more.

Among the early Dunker ministers in America is Conrad Beissel who holds particular interest because he became the founder of the Ephrata community in Lancaster county, Pennsylvania. This was a schismatic movement and was not the main Dunker interest in the colonies, as is frequently inferred. Beissel from the beginning of his ministry was an advocate of "strange doctrines," such as the denunciation of the marriage state and the advocacy of the seventh day as the Sabbath. Eventually Beissel and his followers withdrew from the Dunkers and a community was established known as Ephrata where by 1745 a large group of buildings had been erected, and prosperous industries had been established. Here the "brothers" and "sisters" lived in separate houses and practiced a kind of monasticism. Several of the early Dunker congregations went over completely to Ephrata, but it was never entirely Dunker, since it drew Germans from other sects, particularly the Reformed.

Like the Mennonites and Quakers, the Dunkers were fundamentally opposed to war and advocated non-resistance. It is probable that at first they did not wear a distinctive dress as has since come to be the practice, but the influence of the Quaker hat and bonnet made plainness of dress the symbol of the non-resisting people. The Dunkers held strictly to trine immersion, face forward, and for adults only. They were strictly Congregational in their form of church government and it was not until 1742 that their "Great Meeting" was formed, which soon became a vital factor in the expansion of the "Church of the Brethren."

The most important Dunker leader in the colonial period was Christopher Saur who was the first German printer in America, and the first to edit and print a German newspaper. It is true that Benjamin Franklin had done some printing for the Germans, previous to the establishment of the Saur press, but he used Roman type and his attempt to publish a German weekly paper proved a failure. Saur began his publications in 1738 and on his death his son, Christopher Saur, Jr., carried on the work. Of great significance to the religious life of early German settlers in America of all creeds was the Saur German

Bible, the first edition of which appeared in 1743, with other editions in subsequent years. This was the first Bible to be printed in America in a European language. The Saurs were undoubtedly the most influential Germans in the colonies, and Germantown, through their activities, was the cultural center for the colonial Germans.

Another small German sect, which also, about this time found refuge in Pennsylvania, were the Schwenkfelders. Their founder, Kasper Von Schwenkfeld, a German nobleman, was a contemporary of Luther, though he was anti-Lutheran as well as anti-Catholic in his theology, and his followers were persecuted by both Lutherans and Catholics. It was in Silesia that they had their greatest success and here they became, after the death of their founder, a distinct sect. In 1720 a movement to convert them to Catholicism by force was begun, which caused most of them to flee into Saxony, Holland, England and America. Their migration to America took place largely in 1733-1734. Previously a group of them had been received on the Saxony estate of Count Zinzendorf where they remained eight years, but the Saxon government would not allow them to stay longer and from thence they migrated to Pennsylvania, some by way of Denmark and others from Holland. The two groups arrived in Philadelphia in September and October, 1734, and settled mainly in the Pennsylvania German counties of Montgomery, Bucks, Berks and Lehigh. Like the Mennonites and Dunkers, they were a simple and industrious people and made a worthy contribution to colonial Pennsylvania.

Among those connected with the German settlement of

Pennsylvania, none are more interesting than Nicholaus Ludwig Zinzendorf, a Saxon nobleman and a religious and social reformer, who was chiefly responsible for the Moravian migration to America. Zinzendorf had been raised amidst Pietistic influences, his parents being followers of Philipp Jakob Spener, and accordingly he was sent to the University at Halle. His parents planned that he prepare himself for a diplomatic career, but his great interest in religion caused him to abandon this plan and led him to settle down on his great estate at Berthelsdorf as a Christian landlord, and attempt to carry into practice the Pietistic ideas of his godfather Spener. In 1722 he offered an asylum to a number of persecuted wanderers from Bohemia and Moravia known as the *Moravians* and built for them, on a corner of his estate, a village which was called Herrnhut.

The Moravians trace their origin back to the Hussite movement in Bohemia. At first they were an organization within the Bohemian Church, but later they broke away entirely from the papacy and formed a Church of their own which they called *Unitas Fratrum*. The Unitas Fratrum became an episcopal church, consecration of their first bishop being received from the bishop of the Austrian Waldenses, who traced his ordination back to the Roman Catholic bishops at the Council of Basel. Throughout the sixteenth century they grew rapidly and were particularly active in printing and distributing books, among them a translation of the Bible into Bohemian. During the Thirty Years' War the *Unity of the Brethren* were driven from their homes and for almost a hundred years were nearly extinct, but during much of this period their bishop, John Amos Comenius (1592-1672), held a remnant together. The revival of the *Brethren* in the eighteenth century was largely due to a humble carpenter, Christian David, and it was under this new leader, when persecution broke out afresh, that they came as refugees to the estate of Count Zinzendorf in Saxony. Zinzendorf and his wife devoted themselves to these refugees and finally brought order and unity out of confusion and differences. Zinzendorf who was a pietistic Lutheran, at first tried to lead the Moravian refugees to accept the pietistic principles and for a time they attended the parish church at Berthelsdorf and considered themselves as Lutherans. Gradually, however, the Moravian Church began to emerge, and with the approbation of the Count, a bishop was consecrated for the Herrnhut group in 1735 and two years later Zinzendorf himself was consecrated a bishop. The formation of the Herrnhut Moravians into a separate church now brought persecution upon them, which accounts for the beginning of their migration to America.

With the beginning of the Georgia enterprise under the leadership of General Oglethorpe, Count Zinzendorf took steps to obtain a refuge for some of the persecuted people who were living upon his Saxon estate. In 1733 he received a promise from the Georgia trustees, of land and a free passage for the Schwenkfelders. After the Schwenkfelders left Saxony, however, they changed their plans and proceeded to Pennsylvania instead. Zinzendorf now proceeded to secure the Georgia tract for the Moravians, and in April, 1735, a company of nine, under the leadership of Spangenberg who had recently joined the

Moravians, arrived in Georgia. The next year twenty additional colonists arrived. On shipboard with this latter group was John Wesley, coming out as chaplain to General Oglethorpe, who has left us in his *Journal* a memorable account of his impressions of the Moravian Brethren. The Moravian colony in Georgia failed to prosper, due to sickness and death of the settlers and also to misunderstanding with the authorities when they refused to bear arms in the war with Spain. Accordingly, when in 1740, George Whitefield offered them free passage on his sloop to Philadelphia, they accepted, and thus the first American Moravian colony was transplanted to Pennsylvania.

At this time Whitefield had a plan to erect a colony for destitute Englishmen at the forks of the Delaware which he called Nazareth and had negotiated for the purchase of 5,000 acres of land. He now proposed to the Moravians that they come into his employ to erect the buildings for his enterprise. This they agreed to do. All went well until doctrinal disputes arose between Whitefield and Böhler the Moravian leader, and the Moravians were dismissed and ordered to quit the land at once. The next spring, however, Whitefield found himself unable to pay for the land he had purchased, due to the death of the man who had agreed to loan him the money, and Whitefield was now more than willing to sell out his interest to the Moravians whom he had so recently expelled. Thus the Moravians acquired the region which was to become their chief center in America.

The chief interest of the Moravians in coming to America was to carry on missionary work, both among the German settlers and also among the Indians. By this time Herrnhut had become a great foreign missionary center, and Moravian missionaries from 1732 on were going to various parts of the world. The destitute religious situation of the various German settlers of Pennsylvania was well known. Thousands who had flocked to the New World were living without schools and churches, and their children were growing up in ignorance and without spiritual instruction. It was the knowledge of this condition of affairs that led to the sending out of the first Moravian missionaries to Pennsylvania. In December, 1741, Zinzendorf himself arrived in Philadelphia on a great missionary enterprise. Just before Christmas he reached the Moravian settlement at the forks of the Delaware, and on Christmas eve he named the place Bethlehem, "in token of his fervent desire and ardent hope that here the true bread of life might be broken for all who hungered."

The thirteen months of Zinzendorf's stay in America were filled with activity. His first great project was an attempt to bring about unity among the numerous German sects in Pennsylvania. Altogether seven synods were held within six months, to advance this worthy project, and in the first four every German sect in Pennsylvania was represented. But after the fourth synod all withdrew except the Lutherans, the Reformed and the Moravians, and Zinzendorf's dream of union soon came to naught. Later the Lutherans of Philadelphia requested him to become their pastor, which he accepted for a time, but the coming of Henry M. Mühlenberg put a stop to that arrangement, and Zinzendorf, at his own expense, built a stone church for the people who held to him, and this became the first Moravian church of that city.

With the failure of his project to unite the German denominations in America Zinzendorf turned to the work of promoting missions among the Indians, and during the latter half of his stay in America made three missionary tours into the Indian country. In the first of his visits he obtained permission, from the chiefs of the Six Nations, for the Moravian Brethren to pass through their country and to live as friends within their domains. In his second journey Zinzendorf visited the Mohican town of Sheko-meko, between the Housatonic and the Hudson, where a Moravian missionary had been at work since 1740, and here he formed the Christian Indians into a congregation. His third journey, from September 24 to November 9th, was to Shamokin the most important Indian village in the Susquehanna valley. Two months after his return from this latter journey Zinzendorf departed for Europe. The following is a summary of his accomplishments while in America: "he inaugurated the first form of government for the Moravian Church in America," giving to Bishop David Nitschmann the oversight of the Indian missions, while to Peter Böhler was given the oversight of the "itineracy"; seven congregations had been either established or aided in Pennsylvania, and two in New York, while four schools had been founded.

Bethlehem and Nazareth became semi-communistic communities; there was community of labor but the holding of personal property was allowed. Their common labor was for the support of the great missionary activities of the church, and the two communities became veritable hives of industry. By 1747 thirty-two different industries were in operation, besides several farms, and they were supporting about fifty missionaries and itinerants, besides furnishing the necessities for the workers and their children.

Zinzendorf, who during his last years lived in London, was in virtual control of the Moravian activities in both Europe and America until his death, which occurred in 1760. Just before his death, however, a board of directors had been formed, which now took over the control. In 1764 the Zinzendorf heirs were paid $90,000 and the church became the owner of the Zinzendorf estates, assuming all debts which had been contracted for the church by the count, which amounted to $773,162.

Meanwhile the Moravians continued to extend their Indian missions. Under David Zeisberger, their best known missionary leader, a Christian village was established on the north branch of the Susquehanna in 1765 which was called *Friedenshütten*—"tents of peace." Two years later another mission was begun in western Pennsylvania on the left bank of the Alleghany. Persecution drove Zeisberger and his associates farther westward, and in 1770 he accepted a tract on the Tuscarawas River in Ohio and *Schönbrunn* and *Gnadenhütten* were established and later *Salem*. Here for a time all was peaceful and prosperous. Numerous converts were made; hundreds of acres were under cultivation and cattle multiplied into great herds. Tents gave place to log cabins, while the churches were unable to accommodate the great number of Indian worshipers. Such was the situation in the great Moravian Mission when the American Revolution began.

So far only the smaller German religious groups in the colonies have been noted. These sects have attracted much more attention than their actual numbers warrant, due to the fact that they are more picturesque than were the more numerous German Reformed and Lutheran bodies.

In most instances the large number of German immigrants who swarmed into Pennsylvania, especially from 1727 to 1745, came without ministers or schoolmasters, and several of the earliest German Reformed congregations were formed without pastors. The first German Reformed church was that at Germantown, built in 1719, but there was evidently no settled pastor at the time, for the corner stone was laid by a Swedish minister. By 1725 three German Reformed congregations had been established; at Falcner's Swamp, Skippack and White Marsh, and in that year they asked John Philip Boehm, who had been a schoolmaster at Worms and had come to America in 1720, to act as their minister. After some hesitation he consented, though he warned the people that it was a violation of the order of the Reformed Church. Boehm, in spite of his lack of ordination, performed a useful service to the scattered German communities, baptizing hundreds of children and preaching in outlying districts. In 1729 Boehm was ordained. After asking the advice of the Dutch Reformed members of New York, he and his friends communicated with the Classis of Amsterdam, explaining the situation which had led him to undertake the work of a minister before he had received proper ordination. The Classis in its reply wisely stated "under the circumstances all the transactions of the said Boehm—his teachings, even his administration of the Lord's Supper—must be deemed lawful," but that now he must receive ordination. This was the beginning of the close relationship between the German Reformed churches in America and the Dutch Church, which lasted for many years.

From 1725 to the middle of the century several German Reformed ministers came out to the colonies, though the great majority of the Reformed people in America were still without ministers and conditions generally were considered deplorable. Among the most useful of these early ministers were George Michael Weiss who arrived in America in September, 1727, having been sent by the Classis of the Palatinate. Weiss organized a church in Philadelphia, but also preached in the surrounding territory, where he came into contact and conflict with Boehm. Later when Boehm was ordained, Weiss was present and from this time on the two worked in perfect harmony. Between 1730 and 1736 there was a large Swiss immigration, which came largely to the region between the Delaware and Schuylkill rivers. Two young Swiss pastors, John Henry Goetschius and Conrad Wirtz, labored among these people and formed several congregations.

A special interest is attached to the arrival in 1730 of John Peter Miller, who at twenty years of age was sent to America by the Classis of Heidelberg, with special authority to administer the sacraments. Soon after his arrival he was ordained by the Presbyterian Synod of Philadelphia, upon whom he made a most notable

impression. Becoming the pastor of the church at Tulpehocken (Reading), he labored among his people with
great success. But at the end of four years he came under
the influence of Conrad Beissel, who visited Tulpehocken,
with the result that Miller and his elders with several
of the members of his church joined Beissel and removed
to the community at Ephrata. On the death of Beissel,
Miller became the head of the community, where he died
in 1796.

The most important name in the formative period of
the German Reformed Church in America is Michael
Schlatter. Schlatter was a native of the town of St. Gall in
Switzerland and came out to America in 1746 under the
Synods of Holland. The poor German emigrants passing
through the Dutch ports on their way to America had
aroused the sympathy of the leaders of the Dutch Church,
and when an appeal was made to them to take over the
care of the German Reformed congregations in America
they finally consented. Hearing of this, young Schlatter
went to Holland and presented himself as a candidate for
the proposed mission. He was accepted, and set sail for
Boston in June, 1746. Schlatter's chief mission was to
organize the American congregations into a synod. He
was a young man of great energy and zeal and by October
he had visited all the more important German Reformed
centers, and had made plans for the formation of a
synod, or Coetus, which held its first meeting in Philadelphia in September, 1747. In 1751, at the request of the
Coetus, Schlatter went to Europe, and in a short time had
raised £12,000 to be invested for the benefit of the
churches in America, under the condition that the Coetus

was to remain under the Classis of Amsterdam. The next year he returned to America bringing with him six young ministers and seven hundred Bibles for free distribution.

A rather curious result of Schlatter's success in Europe was a kindred movement begun in England to raise money to establish schools for the Germans of Pennsylvania. "A Society for the Promotion of the Knowledge of God among the Germans" was formed in England and a large sum of money raised. Charity schools were now established in the German communities, with this fund, but the management of the enterprise was so untactful that it aroused the resentment of many of the leading Germans, among them Christopher Saur. Schlatter unfortunately consented to become the superintendent of these charity schools which resulted in bringing to him great unpopularity, and he became the main object of attack. Finally, saddened by the attacks upon him, he resigned and went into retirement.

The German Reformed Church was, of course, Presbyterian in its form of organization, though there developed a number of independent Reformed churches in the colonies. In most respects the Lutheran and German Reformed people were much alike in doctrine and worship and lived and worked harmoniously together. Schlatter and Mühlenberg were close friends, and were engaged in similar tasks in America, and in many places the two congregations, Lutheran and Reformed, worshiped in the same church.

Most important, at least from the standpoint of numbers, of all the German religious bodies in the American colonies, were the Lutherans. Lutheranism, however, had its beginning in America in the Dutch colony of New Amsterdam, and among the Swedes along the Delaware. The Lutheran congregation formed at New York, as has already been noted, was greatly retarded by the intolerant policy of Governor Stuyvesant and it was not until near the end of Dutch rule that they secured a regular pastor. From the beginning this congregation was extremely cosmopolitan in its make-up, for the majority of the members were Danes, Swedes, Norwegians or Germans, although the language used was Dutch. The story of the early Swedish Lutheran churches has already been related. While the Dutch and Swedish Lutheran beginnings have considerable interest, yet historically they are more or less unimportant, as compared to the German Lutherans who began to swarm across the Atlantic from 1720 onward.

Like the German Reformed settlers the early German Lutherans generally came without pastors or schoolmasters and they were desperately poor. The story of the exploitation of the poor German immigrants during the eighteenth century, by the *Neulanders*, or immigrant agents, and the ship captains has been well told by Faust in his *German Element in the United States*.[1] Many of them were too poor to pay their passage and when they arrived in America were sold for a period of years to the person who agreed to pay the shipmaster. Thus many of them became serfs for their passage money, and not alone was this true of artisans and tillers of the soil, but students and schoolmasters were not infrequently sold in this labor market. The following is a description of

[1] Chapters IV and V.

what took place when a ship laden with German immigrants arrived in Philadelphia:

Before the ship is allowed to cast anchor in the harbor, the immigrants are all examined, as to whether any contagious disease be among them. The next step is to bring all the new arrivals in a procession before the city hall and there compel them to take the oath of allegiance to the king of Great Britain. After that they are brought back to the ship. Those that have paid their passage are released, and the others are advertised in the newspapers for sale. The ship becomes the market. The buyers make their choice and bargain with the immigrants for a certain number of years and days, depending upon the price demanded by the ship captain or other "merchant" who made the outlay for transportation, etc. Colonial governments recognize the written contract, which is then made binding for the redemptioner. The young unmarried people of both sexes are very quickly sold, and their fortunes are either good or bad, according to the character of the buyer. Old married people, widows, and the feeble, are a drug on the market, but if they have sound children, then their transportation charges are added to those of the children, and the latter must serve the longer. This does not save families from being separated in the various towns or even provinces. Again, the healthiest are taken first, and the sick are frequently detained beyond the period of recovery, when release would frequently have saved them.

This description of the conditions of German immigration will help explain why the German Lutherans, as well as the German Reformed, were slow in organizing churches. Their spiritual destitution was acute, in spite of the fact that a few devoted pastors were active among them. Among the earliest of these ministers were Daniel

Falkner, Anthony Jacob Henkel, the Stoevers, father and son, and John Christian Schulz. Falkner was the "first regular pastor of the first German Lutheran congregation in America." Henkel was active in visiting the German settlements and was probably the founder of the congregations in Philadelphia and Germantown. The Stoevers were earnest missionaries; the elder Stoever worked among the Germans in Virginia while the younger stayed in Pennsylvania, preaching in all the German settlements, but especially in Lancaster and Montgomery counties. The last important name among these earliest German Lutheran pastors is John Christian Schulz, whose chief importance lies in the fact that he ordained the Stoevers and after a brief stay in America, as pastor of the congregations in Philadelphia, the Trappe and New Hanover, of less than a year, returned to Germany with two laymen from his congregations to collect funds and to secure ministers and teachers for America.

At this time (1733) a German king (George II) was on the English throne, and the court chaplain was Dr. Ziegenhagen, a Lutheran pastor. Naturally appeals from the American Germans were made to him, as well as to Lutheran leaders in Germany, especially to Professor Francke at the University of Halle. Both were sympathetic and were anxious to do something for the destitute colonists, and efforts were made to secure funds and pastors, but ten years were to elapse before the proper man was secured in Henry Melchior Mühlenberg. The delay was caused largely by a dispute over the matter of a fixed salary for the pastor. Ziegenhagen and Francke insisted that a definite arrangement be made as to the support of a minister, while the Pennsylvania Lutherans steadily refused to bind themselves.

While this dispute over the matter of a fixed salary was going on between these Pennsylvania Lutherans and their European friends, another group of Lutherans were finding their way to America, and were settling in the new colony of Georgia. These were the Salzburgers, who a few years before had been driven from their homes in Austria by the Archbishop of Salzburg, who had stated in 1728 that "he would drive the heretics out of the country, even though thorns and thistles should grow upon the fields." In 1731 all Protestants were commanded to leave Salzburg and in the midst of winter thousands set out toward Prussia whose king, Frederick William I, had offered them a refuge on his estates. Fourteen thousand passed through Berlin alone, and their sufferings and simple faith aroused the sympathy of every Protestant nation in Europe. The new societies but recently organized in England for "Promoting Christian Knowledge" and for "Propagating the Gospel in Foreign Parts" became interested, and provision was soon made to send some of the Salzburgers to Georgia. Free passage and provisions in Georgia for a full year were provided, and land for themselves and children, free of all quitrent for ten years was promised, as well as freedom of worship and the privileges of native Englishmen.

The first of the Salzburgers arrived in Georgia in March, 1734; the next year others came; in 1736 one hundred and fifty arrived and with them John and Charles Wesley and a group of Moravians. And so year by year others arrived until their new settlement of Ebenezer, twenty-five miles up the Savannah River, contained some twelve hundred colonists. Almost at once the colony prospered, for piety and industry generally go hand in hand.

The Salzburgers were provided with religious leaders from the beginning, for Francke had sent over two young Halle instructors as pastors, John Martin Boltzius and Israel Christian Gronau. Both labored faithfully and harmoniously among the colonists, and Boltzius was not alone the spiritual leader but became the business head of the colony as well. The colony continued to prosper until the outbreak of the Revolution, when the British destroyed the place and the people were scattered to the surrounding settlements, where they joined Lutheran congregations in the other southern states.

The coming of Henry Melchior Mühlenberg in 1742 marks the beginning of a new epoch in the history of American Lutheranism. The Germans were more numerous than any other non-English element in the colonies, but they were widely scattered and disorganized, and were divided into numerous religious sects, though undoubtedly the Lutherans were the most numerous. The coming of Zinzendorf to America in 1741 and his attempt to unite the several German religious sects into one body stirred the Halle authorities to immediate action, and Mühlenberg was sent to America to save American Lutheranism.

When Mühlenberg came to America he was a young man of thirty-one; educated at Göttingen with fifteen months' teaching experience gained at the Halle Orphanage. Urged by Francke to accept the call to America, he consented and in the fall of 1742 landed at

Charleston. After spending some time among the Salz-burgers in Georgia he sailed for Philadelphia, where he arrived November 25. He had come as the pastor of the three congregations of Philadelphia, New Hanover and the Trappe, but he had come unannounced and affairs were in confusion. Zinzendorf was busy with his scheme of union, and the majority of the Philadelphia congregation was favorable to that plan, while the other congregations were presided over by unworthy preachers. It took the energetic Mühlenberg but one month to "gain full possession of his field" and before the year ended was installed as pastor of the three congregations by the Swedish pastor at Wilmington.

Mühlenberg, however, conceived of his task as much larger than merely the care of the three congregations of which he was the pastor. The year of his arrival he took over the care of the Germantown church and later Lancaster, Tulpehocken and then York. Soon calls for help began to reach him from many places, to which he responded whenever possible. During these years Mühlenberg sent regular reports of his activities to the authorities at Halle. These were published from time to time, and served to keep the needs of the American brethren before the people of Germany. As a result men and money were soon forthcoming to aid in the work. In 1745 three helpers arrived from Halle, with funds to help build new churches. Schools were established in each of the churches, and the new helpers enabled Mühlenberg to give more attention to the general field.

By the year 1748 Mühlenberg was ready to form a synod. There were now several strong congregations and able ministers in America; new churches had been erected, and candidates for the ministry were seeking ordination. In response to this necessity six ministers and twenty-four laymen representing ten congregations met in the new St. Michael's Church in Philadelphia and there formed the first Lutheran synod in America which came to be known as the Ministerium of Pennsylvania. At the time of the formation of the synod there were perhaps seventy Lutheran congregations in America, but the synod exerted a strong influence over American Lutherans in general and greatly aided in the growth of the church. At the outbreak of the Revolution it is estimated that there were seventy-five thousand Lutherans in Pennsylvania alone, though no doubt a great majority of these were outside churches.

✠✠✠✠✠✠✠✠✠✠✠✠✠✠✠✠✠✠✠✠✠✠✠✠✠✠✠✠✠✠✠✠✠

Chapter VIII

THE SCOTCH-IRISH PRESBYTERIANS

POLITICAL, economic and religious factors all played their part in bringing Scotch-Irish colonists to America. The people who had colonized North Ireland had come largely from the Lowlands of Scotland and had brought to Ireland with them "the strenuous Protestant spirit of Scotch Presbyterianism." Since their coming there had been little intermarriage with the native Irish, and there-fore their religious and social beliefs and practices had undergone little change and the Presbyterian Church was there well organized with an able and aggressive ministry, largely educated in Scotch universities.

This emigration from North Ireland to the American colonies began in the early eighteenth century, and con-tinued until well past the middle of that century. Between 1714 and 1720 it came largely through the port of Boston, and during these years fifty-four ships landed immigrants at the principal New England port. New England at-tracted them, at first, because of their common Calvinism with the New England Puritans. Settlements were estab-lished in central Massachusetts, in southern New Hamp-shire and what is now Vermont and in Maine. The two villages of Londonderry in both the present states of New

Hampshire and Vermont are living testimonies of that early immigration. The Scotch-Irish soon found, however, that they did not mix well with the New England Puritans, and after 1720 they began to find their way into New York, where they gave the names *Orange* and *Ulster* to two of the counties on the west side of the Hudson. But by far the largest part of this immigration found its way into central Pennsylvania, then the farthest frontier, where they took up land in the valleys of the parallel mountain ranges of the Alleghanies, and gradually moved southward into western Maryland, Virginia, the Carolinas and Georgia.

By the opening of the American Revolution the Scotch-Irish were to be found in every colony in sufficient numbers to make their influence felt. Of all the races which had colonized the American colonies, they were the only one with a uniform religion. In contrast to this uniformity, note the great diversity of the German immigrants. Scotch-Irish distribution through the several colonies at the opening of the Revolution, was as follows: in New England there were seventy communities; in New York from thirty to forty; from fifty to sixty in New Jersey; in Delaware and Pennsylvania one hundred and thirty; in Virginia and Maryland and over the mountains into what is now east Kentucky and Tennessee more than a hundred; in North Carolina fifty; in South Carolina and Georgia near seventy.

To a large degree American Presbyterianism owes its existence to the coming of the Scotch-Irish, though there were feeble beginnings previous to this immigration. Several of the Puritan leaders of Massachusetts Bay colony were Presbyterian in theory, and Presbyterian ideas of church polity were put into operation in several of the New England churches. John Eliot, the apostle to the Indians, was a supporter of Presbyterianism, and as has already been seen, Increase and Cotton Mather were advocates of what was really the Presbyterian system, when at the Ministerial Convention of 1705 they urged the adoption of the Massachusetts Proposals. In this contest Congregationalism won the day in Massachusetts, but in Connecticut the movement was strongly in the direction of Presbyterianism. With the adoption of the Saybrook Platform (1708) the Presbyterian system came into full operation in Connecticut and the names Presbyterian and Congregational came there to be used interchangeably.

With the movement of New England Puritans into the middle colonies, especially into New York, where they came into an atmosphere strongly charged with Presbyterian ideas, their transformation into Presbyterians was but natural. Thus there came to be several Presbyterian congregations on Long Island of New England origin, by the middle of the seventeenth century. The beginning of Scotch migration to East New Jersey in the latter sixteen hundreds has already been mentioned, so that here also was a nucleus for Presbyterian organization. Indeed, in practically all the colonies, by the end of the seventeenth century, there were small bodies of Scotch or Scotch-Irish settlers, and in such localities Presbyterianism would naturally have the right of way.

The father of the Presbyterian Church in America, the one who, more than any other, deserves the honor of

laying the foundations of organized American Presbyterianism, is Francis Makemie. Makemie was an Ulster-
man, a licentiate of the Presbytery of Laggan who had
come to the Island of Barbados in 1683 and from there
had proceeded to Maryland where he established preaching stations among the several Scotch and Scotch-Irish
communities on the eastern shore. In 1684 he formed a
church at Snow Hill, and for the next several years he
journeyed from place to place, preaching in the scattered
settlements in Maryland, Virginia and the Carolinas. Impressed by the great need in America for ministers, he
crossed the Atlantic and made his appeal to the Independent and Presbyterian Ministers' Union of London
and in 1703-1704 John Hamilton and George Macnish
came with him to Maryland with promise of support
from the London Union. By this time the Anglican
Church had been established in Maryland, and in the
very year Hamilton and Macnish arrived, South Carolina
likewise had adopted the Anglican as the state church,
and the progress of Presbyterianism in these colonies as
well as in Virginia was hampered by persecution and
intolerance. By 1705, however, a number of congregations
had been gathered, under the direction of Makemie and
his helpers, and in that year six ministers met in Philadelphia and there formed the first American Presbytery
with Makemie as moderator.

An example of the kind of persecution which the Presbyterian ministers met at this period is that experienced
by Makemie in New York in 1706. After the second
meeting of the presbytery in Philadelphia in October,
Makemie and Hamilton set out for New England to

consult with the Boston ministers, for Cotton Mather was particularly interested in the progress of Presbyterianism. On the way to Boston, Makemie and Hamilton stopped in New York where the Congregationalists invited them to preach. The Dutch church was offered them for this purpose, but the royal governor, Cornbury, refused to permit it. Makemie then preached in a private house, while Hamilton on the same day preached at Newtown, Long Island. The next day they were both arrested on a warrant of the governor on the ground that they had preached without his permission. The charges against Hamilton were dropped, but Makemie was brought to trial the following March. He was defended by three able lawyers and was acquitted on the ground that he had complied with the English Toleration Act in that he had secured a license under that act while in the Barbados which was recognized as valid throughout the queen's dominions. Though he had won his case, Makemie was compelled to pay the cost of his prosecution which amounted to more than £83.

From year to year the number of preaching places increased and by 1716, the year in which the first synod was formed, the number of ministers had grown to seventeen recruited from Scotland, Ireland and New England. In the minutes of 1707 is found this item: let every minister of the Presbytery supply neighbouring desolate places where a minister is wanting, and opportunity of doing good offers.

At each meeting of the presbytery petitions were presented by communities asking that ministers be sent them. Thus in 1708 the minutes record that a letter sent by the people of and about White Clay Creek, in New Castle County, importing their desire and petition to the Presbytery, to have the ordinances of the gospel administered with more convenience and nearness to the place of their abode, for the greater advantage and ease to their several families, promising withall due encouragement to the minister that shall be appointed thus to supply them.

Although such petitions were numerous and the need for ministers great, yet there was no letting down of the educational standards required of ministers. In 1710 information came to the presbytery that a certain David Evan, "a lay person," was preaching and teaching among the Welsh settlers in the Great Valley, and they consider that Evan "had done very ill." But evidently recognizing the need of just such men as David Evan they suggest that "he lay aside all other business for a twelve month, and apply himself closely to learning and study" under the direction of two members of the presbytery. Year by year Evan was examined by the presbytery as to his progress and it was not until 1715 that he was finally ordained.

The presbytery corresponded with the Dublin Presbytery; with Sir Edwin Harrison, an eminent dissenter of London; with the Synod of Glasgow; with Cotton Mather, and with others from whom they hoped to obtain assistance. In a letter addressed to the Presbytery of Dublin in 1710 is this description of American Presbyterianism within the bounds of the Philadelphia Presbytery:

In all Virginia there is but one small congregation at Elizabeth River, and some few families favouring our way in Rappahanock and York. In Maryland only four, in Pennsylvania five, and in the Jerseys two, which bounds with some places of New York makes all the bounds we have any members from, and at present some of these be vacant.

Much of the business of the Philadelphia Presbytery and later of the synod had to do with quarrels between congregations and their ministers and moral offenses, of both ministers and people. Van Vleck, a minister of Dutch extraction, was accused and found guilty of bigamy; there were "unhappy jarrings among the people of Woodbridge" and with their minister, Mr. Wade. In 1720 a minister is brought before the synod for fornication which he confessed "with great seriousness, humility, and signs of true repentence" and his attitude was so satisfactory to the synod that after a suspension for four Sabbaths he was permitted "again to preach the gospel." Another minister "had been diverse times overtaken with drink" and of using "abusive language, and quarrelling and stabbing a man." Still another is charged "with a lie relating to a bargain of a horse," and also with "folly and levity unbecoming a gospel minister," while a Mr. Laing is rebuked and suspended "for violating the Lord's day, by washing himself in a creek." All of which seems to bear out the characterization of the Scotch-Irish settlers made by James Logan, the secretary of William Penn, who termed them "bold and indigent strangers" from Ireland, and who occupied land without legal title on the ground that it was "against the laws of God and Nature, that so much land should be idle while so many Christians wanted it to labour on."

It was the great migration of Scotch-Irish settlers into the middle colonies which so increased the number of

Presbyterians that it became necessary in 1716 to divide the Presbytery of Philadelphia into four presbyteries and organize a synod. The four presbyteries now organized were the Long Island, which included the churches in New York and eastern New Jersey; the Philadelphia, which embraced the churches in eastern Pennsylvania and western New Jersey; the New Castle which at its formation had six ministers and was made up of churches in Delaware, and the Snow Hill Presbytery in Maryland and Virginia. The territory covered was from eastern Long Island to Virginia, and the number of ministers at the formation of the synod was nineteen.

The Presbyterian Church naturally grew in proportion to the migration from North Ireland, and as we know, this was particularly large from 1720 onward. By 1730 the number of ministers had increased to thirty, the largest share coming from New England though Ireland, Scotland, England and Wales contributed a considerable number. Jonathan Dickinson, a graduate of Yale College, destined to play a prominent part in the affairs of the church for forty years came from Massachusetts; Thomas Craighead, the first of a long list of Craigheads, was the son of an Irish minister, who worked first in New England, where Cotton Mather became his loyal friend. But perhaps the most significant name to be added to the list of ministers in these early years was that of William Tennent. Tennent had been a priest of the church in Ireland, but was admitted to membership in the synod in 1718 after he had given six reasons why he dissented from the Established Church in Ireland. Perhaps no single minister in the synod at that time was to have a larger influence upon the Presbyterian Church in America.

During these years of rapid growth in the middle colonies, the few Scotch-Irish who had remained in New England were engaged in forming congregations and in 1729 organized a presbytery, known as the Presbytery of Londonderry, or as it was called by their neighbors, "the Irish Presbytery." In communities where this new migration mingled with the native New Englanders they encountered strong prejudice, and in most cases were compelled to support the Congregational minister. Persecution was particularly severe in Boston and Worcester. In the latter town a small body of Presbyterians attempted to erect a meeting-house, and the building was in process of construction when a mob, some of whom were persons of "consideration and respectability," gathered at night and demolished the structure. In a few places, however, such as Londonderry, New Hampshire, the new settlers were in the great majority and conducted the affairs of their town to suit themselves. In a few instances also an older community was dominated by the new arrivals from Ireland with the result that the Congregational Church became Presbyterian. But as a whole Presbyterianism remained weak in New England throughout the whole colonial period and has since remained so.

Of great importance to American Presbyterianism was the passage by the synod of the Adopting Act of 1729. This provided that all ministers and licentiates must subscribe to the Westminster Confession. This had already been adopted as the practice of the New Castle Presbytery and the purpose of the act was to protect the American Presbyterians against the "many pernicious and dangerous corruptions in doctrine" which have "grown so much in vogue and fashion," such as "Arminianism, Socinianism, Deism, Freethinking, etc." Such a proposal had already split the Presbyterian Church in Ireland and its adoption was much opposed in America, particularly by the New England and Welsh ministers. Jonathan Dickinson stated that it would neither "detect hypocrites, nor keep concealed heretics out of the church," and occurrences which soon followed proved this to be true. Eventually, however, the Adopting Act was passed, though not until a concession had been made allowing ministers and licentiates to express any scruples they felt as to any article in the Confession while the presbytery, or synod, were to judge whether such scruples were "essential and necessary articles of faith." With the great increase in the number of Scotch and Irish ministers, however, the tendency was to override the scruples any minister might have, and to demand strict adherence to the Confession "without the least variation or alteration." Thus the attempt to introduce liberality into the Presbyterian Church in America on the part of the New England group met with prompt and decisive defeat at the hands of the Scotch-Irish.

The feeble attempts to gather Presbyterian churches in Virginia by Makemie and his helpers resulted in no permanent organization. In fact by Makemie's death in 1708 the Presbyterian Church ceased to exist in Virginia. But within a few years from that time Scotch-Irish immigrants were moving into the region west of the Blue Ridge in considerable numbers. Governor Gooch, himself a Scotch-man, began his administration in 1727. He knew the Scotch-Irish and welcomed their coming. Indeed, he insti-tuted the policy of granting patents to all applicants without reference to their religious belief, but only with the provision that within the required time a sufficient number of settlers should be found upon the grants. This generous policy attracted not only the Scotch-Irish but the Germans and English as well, and there soon came to be representatives of numerous religious sects in the Great Valley of Virginia. In 1738 two new counties were formed west of the Ridge, Augusta and Frederick, the former being almost exclusively settled by Scotch-Irish people. At the same time the new counties were formed into parishes of the Established Church and provision made to elect vestries. In Augusta the vestry was com-posed largely of dissenters and when an Established Church minister was sent them, he preached without a surplice, while the congregation received the sacrament standing according to Presbyterian usage, and eventually the congregation dwindled away.

As early as 1719 occasional preachers visited the Valley from the Synod of Philadelphia and several of these visiting ministers organized congregations. Indeed, by 1738 there had come to be four or five congregations in western Virginia, and in that year application was made to the Synod of Philadelphia for aid, with the result that John Craig was sent as the minister over two congrega-tions, Tinkling Spring and Augusta. The same year the synod sent a representative to Governor Gooch of Vir-ginia in the interest of certain Presbyterians who were considering settling on the Virginia frontier. The synod's representative brought with him an address to the governor asking that the settlers be allowed "liberty of consciences and of worshipping God in a way agreeable to the principles of their education." In his reply the governor stated:

And as I have always been inclined to favor the people who have lately removed from the provinces to settle on the western side of our great mountains: so you may be assured that no interruption shall be given to any ministers of your profession who shall come among them, so as they conform themselves to the rules prescribed by the Act of Toleration in England, by taking the oaths enjoined thereby, and registering the place of their meeting, and behave themselves peaceably toward the government.[1]

From this time forward Presbyterianism made rapid progress in western Virginia, though the greatest impetus to southern Presbyterianism came from Hanover county in central Virginia. This, however, is a part of the story of the Great Awakening, and will be told in that connection.

[1] With the coming to the throne of William and Mary, English dissenters for the first time obtained legal recognition and toleration, with the passage of the Toleration Act of 1689. The act suspended the penal laws against those who attended other places of worship besides the Established Church, provided they took the oath of allegiance and supremacy and subscribed to a declaration against transubstantiation. Dissenting ministers, however, had to subscribe to thirty-five of the Thirty-nine Articles and a greater part of two more. Papists and those who did not believe in the Trinity were excluded from the benefits of the act.

Chapter IX

THE GREAT AWAKENING IN NEW ENGLAND

THE latter seventeenth and early eighteenth centuries were crowded with disturbing influences for the New Englander. First of all it was a time of almost continuous warfare. The hundred years' struggle between France and England for the Mississippi Valley began in 1689 with the War of the Palatinate, known in America as King William's War. Within four years after the treaty was signed closing this war, the War of the Spanish Succession, or Queen Ann's War, began (1701), which did not end until 1713 with the signing of the famous Treaty of Utrecht. Then after a considerable period of peace there followed in rapid succession the War of the Austrian Succession (1739-1748) and the Seven Years' War (1756-1763). In all of these intercolonial wars New England bore the brunt of the struggle, and since the Indians played a conspicuous part in them, the New England frontier was never out of danger from Indian forays. Thus the whole atmosphere of the New England frontier, for years together, was filled with alarm. It was also a period of political unrest. From 1660 on to the end of the century the political status of the New England colonies was uncertain, and this served to occupy the attention of the Puritan leaders at the expense of moral and religious affairs.

The intensity of New England religion had considerably cooled by the end of the seventeenth century. The second and third generation Puritan was much less "religious" than had been his father and grandfather. It has been noted that by the adoption of the Half-Way Covenant unawakened persons were permitted to become "half-way" church members, and thus there came to be large numbers of people in every church whose relation to the church was merely formal. It is true that the Calvinistic doctrine of conversion was still theoretically held by the majority of the ministers—that is that conversion was the work of God alone—but it was now recognized by many ministers that there were certain "means" which might be used to put the soul in position to receive the regenerating touch of God's spirit. In other words, a new doctrine of conversion was evolving which laid increasing emphasis upon human responsibility. It was the combination of these two influences—the presence among the people of a "tremendous amount of latent fear" and the doctrine of human responsibility in conversion—that largely accounts for the great revival which began in central Massachusetts in the fourth decade of the eighteenth century.

At the very center of this great religious movement stands Jonathan Edwards, the minister of the church of the standing order at Northampton, at that time the most important inland town in the colony. In many respects Jonathan Edwards is the outstanding intellectual figure of colonial America and has been generally recognized as one of the greatest minds America has produced. "In Edwards there was a rare combination of fervor of feeling, of almost oriental fertility of imagination, and intellectual acumen."

Jonathan Edwards was born in East Windsor, Connecticut, where his father, Timothy Edwards, was the minister. He graduated from Yale in 1720 at seventeen years of age and after several years of further study and some preaching, and teaching at Yale, became the minister at Northampton, where for sixty years his maternal grandfather, Solomon Stoddard, had been the pastor. Soon after coming to Northampton he married Sarah Pierpont, the daughter of the Rev. James Pierpont of New Haven, and throughout her husband's great career her name was intimately associated with his. Indeed, she has been termed the ideal New England minister's wife. Hers was a joyous piety, while she saved her husband from all the troubles of household affairs, training and disciplining the numerous children, maintaining a genial and attractive hospitality until her home became like a sanctuary to multitudes. To understand Jonathan Edwards, Sarah Pierpont must not be left out of the picture. The town of Northampton at the opening of the great revival contained about two hundred families and generally speaking the people were intelligent and religious. During Solomon Stoddard's long ministry there had been five periods of religious awakening, an unusual condition for those years. This better spiritual condition at Northampton was due to the wise, common-sense position of Stoddard, in regard to the birth members. It was his practice to admit them to the sacrament, as a means of leading them to conversion. The standard of regenerate membership was well enough for an age of deep religious emotions, "but it was too exacting in a period when such deep emotions were lacking."

Young Edwards came to Northampton in 1727, at a time "of extraordinary dullness in religion." He thus describes certain conditions in the town just before the revival began:

Licentiousness for some years greatly prevailed among the youth of the town; they were many of them very much addicted to night walking and frequenting the tavern, and lewd practices wherein some by their example exceedingly corrupted others. It was their manner to get together in assemblies of both sexes, for mirth and jollity, which they called frolics; and they would often spend the greater part of the night in them, without regard to order in the families they belonged to: indeed family government did too much fail in the town.

It was not long, however, until a change in the general religious atmosphere began to be manifest under the preaching of this tall, slender, grave young man. Edwards was by no means what might be called a popular preacher. He lived the life of a student, spending thirteen hours daily in his study, writing two sermons each week, one to be preached on Sunday, the other at the weekly lecture. To him sermon preparation and study were far more important than pastoral ministration, for he seldom visited among his people. In the pulpit he was quiet, speaking without gesture, and in a voice not loud, but distinct and penetrating. It was the content of his sermons, filled as they were with fire and life, combined with the remarkable personality and presence of the preacher which accounts for the results which now began to be manifest among his hearers.

The revival began in December, 1734, while Jonathan Edwards was preaching a series of sermons on justification by faith alone. The sermons were intended to meet the growing tendency toward Arminianism which was considered by Calvinists as a matter for alarm. They felt that when men once began to trust in human measures for salvation they would cease to depend on Christ. Indeed, they were sure that Arminianism was a long step in the direction toward popery, and could only end in complete acceptance of a salvation won by good works, such as penance and offerings prescribed by priests. So sure were the Calvinists that Arminianism led to popery that John Wesley, the great advocate of Arminian principles in the eighteenth century, was accussed of being a Jesuit in disguise. In his sermons Edwards denied that any action "however good in itself, done by an unconverted man" could avail in procuring salvation. Salvation was the gift of God alone. With terrible vividness and earnestness Edwards depicted the wrath of God from which his hearers were exhorted to flee. Soon religion became the chief topic of conversation throughout the town among people of all ages.

Again, Jonathan Edwards relates the happenings attendant upon the beginning of the revival:

Presently upon this a great and earnest concern about the great things of religion and eternal world became universal in all parts of the town, and among persons of all degrees and all ages; the noise among the dry bones waxed louder and louder; all other talk but about spiritual and eternal things was soon thrown by; all the conversation in all companies, and upon all occasions, was upon these things only, unless so much as was necessary for people carrying on their ordinary secular business. Other discourse than of the things of religion would scarcely be tolerated in any company.

"Soon," he tells us, "a glorious alteration" was to be noted in the town, "so that in the spring and summer following, anno 1735, the town seemed to be full of the presence of God: it was never so full of love, nor so full of joy, and yet so full of distress as it was then." "There was scarcely a single person in the town, either old or young, that was left unconcerned about the great things of the eternal world."

During the first year of the revival in Northampton more than three hundred professed conversion, among both the aged and the young, though by May, 1735, the excitement began to die down, probably because the "physical power to endure excitement was exhausted." Through the next several years revivals, independent of each other, began to appear in various parts of New England, especially in the Connecticut valley, until by 1740 the movement could be described as general throughout New England. Meanwhile a similar revival was in progress in New Jersey, especially among the Presbyterians, produced by the fervid preaching of the Tennents, particularly Gilbert Tennent. This revival seems to have begun entirely independent of the New England awakening, though the movements were in a sense brought together through the influence of George Whitefield, who began his first extensive evangelistic tour of America in 1740.

In 1737-1738 Jonathan Edwards wrote his *Narrative of the Surprizing Work of God*, which was soon being read on both sides of the Atlantic. At the same time the Methodist revival was just beginning in England, under the preaching of the Wesleys and Whitefield.

The Wesleyan revival may be said to have begun in 1737, when a little group of Oxford students, who had formed at that ancient university a Holy Club, whose members had been nicknamed "Methodists," removed to London and began the work of carrying religion and morality to the masses. "Their voice was soon heard in the wildest and most barbarous corners of the land, among the bleak moors of Northampton, or in the dens of London, or on the long galleries, where in the pauses of their labor the Cornish miners listened to the sobbing of the sea." Never had England heard such preaching; never had England witnessed such results. It was from this little group that the greatest preacher of the century sprang in the person of George Whitefield.

Whitefield was the son of a tavern keeper in Gloucester, and spent his childhood amidst the scenes common in the English public houses of that degraded time. Fortunately in Gloucester there was an endowed school, and here Whitefield was admitted as a pupil. Here he was prepared for Oxford, and in 1732 entered Pembroke College as a "Servitor," where he earned his way waiting on the tables of Fellows and Gentlemen Commoners. When he entered Oxford the "Holy Club" had been organized three years, and the next year he became identified with this one spiritual oasis in the university. His conversion he dated from Easter Week, 1735. Graduating in 1736 he was ordained to the priesthod of the Church of England by the Bishop of Gloucester and began to supply churches in Oxford and London, at the same time offering himself to go to Georgia to take up the work there at which the Wesleys had failed.

Within a year after his graduation, and while he was waiting to set out for Georgia, Whitefield leaped into fame as the greatest preacher of his day. From Gloucester to Bristol, thence to Bath, England's most fashionable resort, thence to London, everywhere pulpits were opened to him and the people flocked to hear him. He could not begin to meet the calls which poured in upon him, though he preached nine times each week. "On Sunday morning," he tells us, "long before day, you might see streets filled with people going to church, with their lanterns in their hands, and hear them conversing about the things of God." So dense were the crowds which filled the churches, that "one might, as it were, walk upon the people's heads," and thousands were turned away, unable to enter even the largest churches.

In 1738 Whitefield made a brief visit to Georgia to look over the ground preparatory to the beginning of his work there and the founding of his orphanage. The next year, in August, he again landed in America at Lewes, Delaware, and this marks the real beginning of his American evangelistic tours. He visited the Tennents, in whose work he took great delight; he was in Philadelphia in November where throngs came to hear him every day in Christ Church. From Philadelphia he went to New York, where he heard Gilbert Tennent preach the most searching sermon he had ever heard; thence back to Philadelphia and then southward to Georgia, passing through Maryland, Virginia and the Carolinas. Returning in April in his own sloop, he again visited Philadelphia, and New Jersey, thence back to Georgia. On September 14, 1740, he landed in Rhode Island and the next month was given to a tour of New England, already filled with religious excitement by the events of the last several years. Everywhere he was received with enthusiasm. Newport and Boston gave him an immense hearing. The students at Harvard heard him and under the spell of his matchless oratory men wept, women fainted and hundreds professed conversion.

Leaving Boston in October, Whitefield journeyed toward Northampton, preaching as he went, drawn by the fame of the great revival that had begun there six years before. Whitefield's four sermons at Northampton greatly moved both Edwards and his congregation, and a new revival broke which was to continue for two years. Whitefield in turn was so favorably impressed with Edwards and especially with Sarah Pierpont that he wrote in his diary "she caused me to renew those prayers which for some months I have put up to God, that He would send me a daughter of Abraham to be my wife."

Whitefield's short visit to New England caused a renewal of evangelistic activity. From December, 1740, to March, 1741, the New England revival reached high tide. A number of the more successful revivalist preachers, among them Jonathan Edwards, Eleazer Wheelock and

Joseph Bellamy, became for the time being itinerant evangelists, and under their preaching physical demonstrations were common in many communities; strong men fell as though shot, and women became hysterical. When Jonathan Edwards preached at Enfield, Connecticut, in July, 1741, taking as his theme "Sinners in the Hands of an Angry God," "there was such a breathing of distress, and weeping, that the preacher was obliged to speak to the people and desire silence, that he might be heard." These bodily exercises were defended, even by such men as Edwards, and it is not strange that some among the ministers went to even greater extremes in their appeal to the emotions, and adopted extravagant methods to arouse the people. Such a minister was James Davenport of Long Island, who "more than any other man . . . embodied in himself and promoted in others, all the unsafe extravagances into which the revival was running," and who declared "that most of the ministers of the town of Boston and of the country are unconverted, and are leading their people blindfold to hell."

During the years from 1740 to 1742 there was a wonderful ingathering of members into the New England churches. Out of a population of 300,000, from twenty-five to fifty thousand were added. The general moral effect of the revival upon New England communities was clearly manifest. Speaking of Northampton in 1743, Jonathan Edwards states: "I suppose the town has never been in no measure so free from vice—for any long time together—for these sixty years, as it has this nine years past." Similar testimony of moral changes in other communities are numerous and there is no doubt but that the whole moral and religious life of New England was raised to a higher plane, and the revival amply deserves the name generally given it—the "Great Awakening."

Out of the New England awakening came several influences of great significance. In the first place, the revival definitely divided the New England ministers into two groups. One heartily supported the revival and its methods, the other condemned it and looked upon its results as but temporary. At the head of the first group stood Jonathan Edwards; the leader of the latter was Charles Chauncy, the liberal pastor of First Church, Boston, who in 1743 published an attack upon the revival called "Seasonable thoughts on the State of Religion in New England." Those favoring the revival were soon known as "New Lights," those opposing it were designated "Old Lights," and it was not long until these two opposing parties were filling New England with controversy. In Connecticut a General Consociation of ministers condemned itinerant ministers and later the legislature passed an act forbidding the practice. Congregations split over the question, the revivalists withdrawing and forming themselves into separate churches and known as "Separatists." For attending a "Separatist" meeting two students were expelled from Yale College in 1744. The Ministerial Convention of Massachusetts likewise condemned the revival, especially "its errors in doctrine, and disorders in practice," though a strong minority gathered in Boston to affirm "that there has been a happy and remarkable revival of Religion in many parts of the land."

Under these conditions it is not strange that the revival

interest passed away almost as quickly as it had arisen. According to Jonathan Edwards' own statement, the church at Northampton from 1744 to 1748 was utterly dead, not a single application for membership being made during those years. When in the fall of 1744 Whitefield began his second tour of New England he met with opposition on every hand. Many pulpits were now closed to him; associations took action against him, while both Harvard and Yale colleges issued declarations opposing his conduct and methods. But thousands flocked to hear him and he still had staunch friends among the ministers who supported him to the last. Altogether he made five tours of New England, the last three in 1754, 1764 and 1770, dying in Newburyport in the latter year, where he lies buried under the pulpit of the Old South Presbyterian Church. Whatever limitations Whitefield may have had, he was undoubtedly one of the chief "human factors in the greatest religious overturning that New England has ever experienced."

It will now be necessary to consider the doctrinal discussion which arose in New England following the Great Awakening, and which resulted in the forming of two distinct doctrinal schools. These ultimately led to the division of Congregationalism into two wings, orthodox and liberal, or Unitarian, though the actual severance did not take place until the opening years of the nineteenth century.

The liberal doctrinal school had its roots in the tendency, already noticed, to emphasize the use of human "means" in salvation. At the same time, there was a rising tide of Arminian views among certain English writers whose works began to be read in America. Two of these writers were the Rev. Daniel Whitby, an Anglican clergyman, and the Rev. John Taylor, a Presbyterian. Both Whitby and Taylor made attacks upon Calvinism, Whitby's discourse upon the five points of Calvinism being considered an unanswerable argument by the Arminians. Taylor inveighed chiefly against the imputation of Adamic sin upon the race and advanced a new theory of the atonement in opposition to the limited atonement held by Calvinists. These views were soon adopted by a few New England ministers who in turn began to write in defense of what was termed the Liberal Theology. Thus Experience Mayhew, in 1744, published a treatise entitled "Grace Defended" in which he advocated the use of means of grace in obtaining pardoning grace, though he affirmed himself essentially a Calvinist. This publication aroused little interest compared to the furor caused by a published sermon of a young minister, Lemuel Briant, in 1749 on "The Absurdity and Blasphemy of Depreciating Moral Virtue." Sermons were preached in reply and tracts were issued attempting "to put a stop to the prevailing contagion of Arminian errors and other loose opinions . . . which threaten to banish vital piety out of the land." Eastern Massachusetts especially was now in the midst of a "general doctrinal ferment" which was to continue with little let-up until the split in the church was consummated two generations later. The churches and ministers holding the liberal views were generally those which had opposed the revival, and this opposition was confined largely to Boston and its immediate vicinity.

At the opposite pole from this liberal school stood

Jonathan Edwards and those associated with him who were responsible for what has come to be known as the New England Theology. In 1750 Edwards was dismissed from Northampton amidst bitterness and slander, after he had announced his change in view regarding the admission of the unconverted to participation in the sacrament. Turned out of his pastorate at the age of forty-seven, with ten living children, it was at once necessary that he find a new field of labor. Finally in December, 1750, he received a call to the frontier village of Stockbridge, in western Massachusetts, where he was to be the missionary to the Housatonic Indians. Here he came in the summer of 1751 and here he remained until January, 1758, when he was called to the presidency of the college at Princeton. He took up that office, however, only to lay it down, for in March of the same year he died of inoculation for smallpox at the age of fifty-five.

The period which Edwards spent at Stockbridge "was the harvest time of his intellectual activity." Altogether twenty-seven publications of Edwards' appeared during his lifetime and nine were published after his death. The most important of his publications, the one on which his fame as an original thinker principally rests, is his treatise on "The Freedom of the Will," which was written during his Stockbridge residence and made its appearance in 1754. Edwards maintained that man had the power to act in accordance with the choice of his mind, but with the origin of the inclination man has nothing to do. This left some room for moral responsibility and for human choice. Four years later he published a book defending the doctrine of Original Sin, against attacks by Charles

Chauncy and the Rev. Samuel Webster and the English liberals. Edwards departed somewhat from historic Calvinism, though his chief aim was to defend it against the Arminian school. He always held staunchly to the sovereignty of God, but was at the same time convinced that larger recognition must be given to man's responsibility. He thus became chiefly responsible for the establishment of what came to be known as the "New Divinity," or the Edwardian school.

Edwards was a man of warm friendships and soon loyal disciples were defending his views from the attacks of the liberals on the one hand and the Old Calvinists on the other. Among the most influential of these Edwardian leaders were Joseph Bellamy and Samuel Hopkins who were companions of Edwards' later life, while in the next generation the chief supporters of the New Divinity were Stephen West, John Smalley, Jonathan Edwards the younger, Nathaniel Emmons and Timothy Dwight. Bellamy and Hopkins were controversialists of great power, and were responsible for adding certain important features to the New Divinity. Among these new features was their assertion of a general atonement, though Edwards himself was inclined to a limited theory of the atonement. Hopkins especially developed Edwards' teachings beyond Edwards and put his own stamp upon them so fully that he often is considered as the founder of a new school of thought called Hopkinsianism.

The development of this ultra-Edwardian school headed by Hopkins and others led to a heated pamphlet warfare between the old Calvinists and the advocates of the New Divinity, while both Old Calvinists and the supporters of the New Divinity united in their attacks upon the liberals in and about Boston, who were inclining more and more toward Universalism and Unitarianism. Thus Charles Chauncy in 1782 came out boldly on the side of Universalism in a tract published anonymously called "Salvation for all Men Illustrated and Vindicated as a Scripture Doctrine" which was ably answered by Edwards the younger. This, however, was a development which came largely after the Revolution.

It is an interesting fact, and one of considerable importance for an understanding of later developments, that the Edwardian school came to be the dominant party in Connecticut and western Massachusetts. The struggle between Old Calvinism and the Edwardian party long continued in these sections, but by the end of the century the New Divinity had won the victory. These views of modified Calvinism also spread among the Presbyterians of the north middle region, a fact which was to have large significance in the Presbyterian Church in the nineteenth century. Though Calvinism in its modified form triumphed in western Massachusetts and Connecticut, the Liberal theology won the day in eastern Massachusetts, especially in and about Boston. The cleavage between the two parties was destined to grow deeper and deeper until a complete separation was to be the result. The account of this separation, however, belongs to a later period in our story.

The fifty years following the Great Awakening may be characterized as one of spiritual deadness, a period of religious and moral indifference throughout New England. The bitter doctrinal controversy was undoubtedly one of the causes, but there were other causes, among them two wars including the American Revolution, and a long period of great political unrest.

Chapter X

THE GREAT AWAKENING IN THE MIDDLE AND
SOUTHERN COLONIES

THE series of great religious awakenings which swept over
the American colonies in the middle of the eighteenth
century were in many respects the most far-reaching
social movements of the whole colonial period. They
influenced all the churches, either directly or indirectly.
In New England, of course, the Congregationalists were
the ones primarily affected, though the indirect influence
upon the Baptists was large. In the middle colonies it was
a movement largely among Presbyterians, though it began among the German sectarians and the Dutch Reformed churches of central New Jersey. In the southern
colonies the revival manifested itself first among the
Presbyterians, especially in Virginia; in its second phase
it was largely a Baptist movement, while it continued in
a third phase as a Methodist movement.

The great variety of racial and religious groups to be
found in colonial Pennsylvania, New Jersey and New
York have been noticed. Many of the German colonists,
though representing several religious sects, were Pietists.
The founder of the Pietists was Philip Jacob Spener who
advocated the establishment of devotional groups within

the Lutheran churches of Germany for the purpose of Bible study and promoting true piety. The new university at Halle became the center of the Pietists and it was to Francke, the successor of Spener at Halle, that the Lutherans in America looked for aid, and the great Lutheran leader Mühlenberg came out to America from this Pietistic center. There were Pietists also among the German Reformed leaders in the colonies, but the Pietistic, or evangelical, influence was particularly strong among the smaller German groups such as the Mennonites, the Dunkers and the Moravians. This Pietistic emphasis among the Pennsylvania Germans was one of the sources of the great revival movement in the middle colonies.

Of much greater importance was the revival among the Dutch Reformed churches begun under the influence of Theodore J. Frelinghuysen, a German Pietist who came out to America in 1720 to be the pastor of some Dutch churches on the New Jersey frontier. From the moment of his landing in America Frelinghuysen began to fight against formality and dead orthodoxy which he found completely permeating the Dutch churches in America. In his first sermon, preached in New York soon after landing, Frelinghuysen struck such an evangelical note that he at once aroused the opposition of some of the Dutch ministers. He became the pastor of four churches in the Raritan valley, and his earnest preaching, in which he laid emphasis upon conversion, so astonished his Dutch congregations that many were outraged, and soon parties began to develop, one opposing, the other accepting the new doctrines. At the end of three years his new gospel had disrupted his churches. The disaffected published their *Complaint* against him in a book of 246 pages, and an answer was soon forthcoming prepared by two of Frelinghuysen's friends, and thus the Dutch ministers were divided into hostile camps.

Meanwhile Frelinghuysen's fervid evangelical preaching was bearing fruit and numerous conversions were taking place. In 1726 the ingathering of new members was particularly large, and invitations to visit other churches began to pour in upon him. Some of these he accepted and soon the revival was spreading beyond the Raritan valley. Of particular importance is the fact that the revival spirit began to manifest itself among some English-speaking Presbyterians scattered through the region, who in 1726 called a young Presbyterian licentiate, Gilbert Tennent, to be their pastor. Frelinghuysen gave every assistance to this young Presbyterian minister, encouraged his own members to subscribe toward his salary, permitted him to use the Dutch meeting-houses, and sometimes held joint services with him. All this was abundantly helpful to the cause of Christianity in central New Jersey, but it brought down increased maledictions upon the head of Domine Frelinghuysen, whose enemies objected to the use of English in Dutch churches.

Gilbert Tennent, the young Presbyterian minister welcomed so heartily by Domine Frelinghuysen, was destined to be the heart and center of a revival movement among the Presbyterians of much greater significance than that among the Dutch Reformed. Gilbert Tennent was the son of William Tennent, whose admission to the synod in 1718 has already been noted. In 1726 the elder Tennent became the Presbyterian minister at Neshaminy, Bucks county, Pennsylvania, and here he established what came to be known as the "Log College."

William Tennent had four sons, Gilbert the eldest having already been trained for the ministry under his father's care. To better facilitate the education of his younger sons a log cabin was built in his yard to serve as a school and here three of his own sons and fifteen other young men received their training for the ministry. The elder Tennent not only drilled his students in the languages, logic and theology, but he imbued them with an evangelical passion which sent them out flaming evangelists. The sons of William Tennent—Gilbert, William Jr., John and Charles—all became ministers of Presbyterian churches in central New Jersey, while Samuel Blair, also a graduate of the "Log College," became the pastor of several small churches centering at Shrewsbury. Thus there came to be a group of ministers, evangelical in sentiment, settled near New Brunswick, and in 1738 the New Brunswick Presbytery was formed of these five evangelical ministers. At their first meeting the presbytery licensed John Rowland, another graduate of the "Log College," and later ordained him. The conservative ministers objected to this action, as they were fearful lest the Presbyterian ministry would be deluged with half-educated enthusiasts. This fear led the synod to pass a regulation permitting presbyteries to examine and ordain only those candidates who were graduates of New England or European colleges. This action, of course, was intended to check the activities of the "Log College" and the admission of its graduates.

Thus the Presbyterian ministers in New Jersey were

soon divided into two parties, but meanwhile a great revival was getting under way induced by the fervid preaching of the evangelicals. Especially was John Rowland's
preaching effective in stirring his people, and religion
became the single topic of conversation in the little rural
communities where he ministered. The revival spirit was
now manifest in many centers. At Newark where Aaron
Burr was the minister the revival attained its height in
1739 and 1740; in the highlands of New York and on
Long Island the revival flame burst forth while a group
of Yale graduates, among them Jonathan Dickinson, now
came over to the aid of the evangelical party and took
their part in the revival. Even some of the conservative
Scotch-Irish congregations in Pennsylvania responded to
the revival preaching of Samuel Blair and a revival broke
out at Fagg's Manor where he had become the pastor in
1739, which soon spread to other places in Pennsylvania.
Here was the very center of the opposition to the revival,
but so strong was the movement among the people that
even unfriendly ministers were constrained to invite the
evangelists to visit their communities.

Such was the general situation among the Presbyterians in the middle colonies when George Whitefield
arrived in America on his first evangelistic tour. Whitefield was one of the most catholic-spirited ministers of his
time, and could coöperate with Quakers, Baptists, Lutherans, Moravians, Presbyterians, Congregationalists and
Dutch Reformed and all others as long as they like himself advocated vital religion and preached conversion. On
one occasion, preaching from the balcony of the courthouse in Philadelphia, Whitefield cried out: "'Father

Abraham, whom have you in Heaven? Any Episcopalians?' 'No.' 'Any Presbyterians?' 'No.' 'Have you any
Independents or Seceders?' 'No.' 'Have you any Methodists?' 'No, no, no!!' 'Whom have you there?' 'We
don't know those names here. All who are here are
Christians—believers in Christ—men who have overcome
by the blood of the Lamb and the word of his testimony.'
'Oh, is this the case? Then God help us, God help us all,
to forget party names, and to become Christians in deed
and in truth.' " On this first tour Whitefield spent several
days in Philadelphia and then passed through central
New Jersey toward New York. He met the aged elder
Tennent in Philadelphia; at New Brunswick he preached
in Gilbert Tennent's meeting-house, and from thence to
New York Gilbert Tennent accompanied him. In New
York he preached in the Presbyterian church, as well as
in the fields where great throngs assembled. Journeying
back to Philadelphia, Whitefield was invited by Jonathan
Dickinson to preach at Elizabethtown, and coming again
to New Brunswick he met Domine Frelinghuysen and
several of the evangelical leaders.

The year 1740-1741 marks the high tide of the revival
in the middle colonies. Whitefield's preaching had stirred
all classes and all the churches. Even the deistic Franklin
became his admirer and lifelong friend, and the revival
became exceedingly popular with the common people.
But from the beginning the revival had aroused criticism,
and unfortunately the revivalists themselves were largely
responsible for it in that they tended to become censorious
and critical of those who did not agree with them. Gilbert
Tennent preached his famous sermon on "Danger of an

Unconverted Ministry" in March, 1740, which did not help allay opposition, while others of the evangelical preachers were ready to indict all ministers who did not support the revival movement.

Opposition to the revival among the Presbyterians came to a head at the meeting of the synod in 1741. At this meeting a protest was presented against the action of the evangelical ministers in intruding uninvited into the bounds of other ministers; for their censorious judgments of those who did not walk with them; for violating the act of the synod in regard to the examination of candidates; for preaching the terrors of the law "in such a manner and dialect as has no precedent in the Word of God"; and for claiming that truly gracious persons are able to judge with certainty both of their own state and that of others. These were the grounds on which the New Side party, or the evangelicals, were now excluded by the Old Side, or conservatives, from membership in the synod. The ministers and elders of the New Brunswick Presbytery and others who were in sympathy with them now withdrew. The evangelical, or the New Side party however, did not form a new synod until efforts had been made to undo the action taken in 1741. This was in vain, however, and in September, 1745, the New Side party formed the New York Synod at Elizabethtown, New Jersey.

From 1745 to 1758 the Presbyterians in the colonies were divided into two main bodies. The New Side body embraced a large proportion of the able and fervent men of the church and grew rapidly in numbers and influence. On the other hand, the Philadelphia, or the Old Side,

Synod made no progress during the years of separation. At the time of the schism the Old Side numbered twenty-five ministers, while the New Side numbered twenty-two. In 1758 at the time of the reunion the Old Side had decreased and numbered but twenty-two, while the New Side had grown by leaps and bounds and numbered seventy-two. "The New Side churches were active, growing and full of young people," while the heroism of their enthusiastic leaders, such as Rowland, Blair and Brainerd, all of whom burned themselves out while still young men, attracted other young and enthusiastic men to take their places. The members of the conservative group, on the other hand, were old men; while their opposition to the popular revival movement rendered them and their churches unpopular with the young people. These years of separation mark the unmistakable triumph of the revival party within the Presbyterian Church.

Fortunately for American Presbyterianism the schism caused by the Great Revival was soon healed. The first steps in the direction of reunion was taken by the New York Synod in 1749. In that year Gilbert Tennent published his *Irenicum* in which he attempted to allay the bitterness caused by his earlier attacks upon those who opposed the revival. At first the Philadelphia Synod spurned these friendly gestures, but the New Side Synod persisted and refused to allow their own temper to be ruffled, while their reunion committee headed by Gilbert Tennent continued their negotiations. Finally in 1758 an agreement was reached. The question of the examination of candidates as to their learning and religious experience was left to the presbyteries, and nothing was said about synodical examination or college degrees. It was provided that ministers should not intrude into the parishes of other ministers uninvited, while the act of 1741 expelling the New Brunswick Presbytery was declared irregular. The reunited church now entered upon a period of great activity and rapid growth which was to continue up to the outbreak of the American Revolution.

It was during the period of the Great Awakening that two other branches of Presbyterianism found their way into the colonies: these were the Reformed and the Associate Reformed, representing the most conservative Scottish and Irish groups known as the "Covenanters." Naturally, representatives of these groups found their way to America in the great migration from North Ireland in the eighteenth century. At first they united with the larger body, but when the schism between the New and Old Side occurred the Covenanter ministers adhered to the New Side, upon whom they urged the necessity of renewing the Covenants. When this was refused an appeal was sent to the Reformed Presbytery of Scotland and eventually helpers were sent to minister to the scattered Covenanters of Pennsylvania. In 1644 a split had occurred among the Covenanters of Scotland and the Associate Reformed Presbytery was formed, while this latter group divided (1746-1747) over the question of the lawfulness of the oath exacted of burgesses, into Burghers and Anti-Burghers.

The educational influence of the great revival in the middle colonies was particularly significant. William Tennent's school, called in derision the "Log College," was the seed of a whole group of similar institutions, some of which have lived to this day. All of its sixteen or eighteen graduates were men of earnestness and zeal, more than half of whom became preachers of extraordinary power, and several became eminent as educators as well. Many of these Log College graduates established log colleges, or private schools, modeled after that of William Tennent at Neshaminy and out of these classical and theological schools came graduates destined to take a notable place in the leadership of American Presbyterianism. One such school founded on the model of the Log College was that established by Samuel Blair at Fagg's Manor in Chester county, Pennsylvania. The first graduate of this school was Samuel Davies, who was to become the leader of the Presbyterian Church in Virginia and finally president of the College of New Jersey. Other students at the Fagg's Manor school were John Rodgers, of New York, James Finley and Robert Smith, all of whom became leaders of distinction. Another such school was that established at Nottingham, Pennsylvania, by Samuel Finley. From this school came other noted leaders in both church and state, among them Dr. Benjamin Rush, while Finley himself succeeded Davies as president of Princeton. Pequea, in Lancaster county, Pennsylvania, was another such school, established by Robert Smith, a graduate of the Fagg's Manor school. From the Pequea school came John McMillan, one of the founders of Jefferson College who in turn conducted a Log College in connection with his work in the Redstone country of western Pennsylvania.

Of greater importance than these academies was the establishment by the New York Synod of the College of

New Jersey. Tennent's Log College ceased with his death in 1746, and the same year a charter was obtained, largely through the efforts of Jonathan Dickinson, for a new college. The trustees selected Dickinson as the president and in May, 1747, the college opened in Dickinson's house at Elizabethtown, New Jersey. Dickinson's death occurred in the fall of the same year, and the trustees turned to Aaron Burr, the minister at Newark, to take up the work of education. The college was now removed to Newark. In 1755 the college was permanently established at Princeton, and on the death of Burr in 1757 his father-in-law, Jonathan Edwards, succeeded to the presidency. The revival leaders in New England had grown suspicious of the New England colleges, especially after their condemnation of the revival, which accounts for Edwards' willingness to accept the presidency, though he hardly lived to enter upon his office. The College of New Jersey, as Princeton was called in its early years, admirably served the purpose of its founding and poured a stream of zealous young men into the ministry of the Presbyterian Church.

The founding of the University of Pennsylvania came indirectly out of the Great Awakening. During Whitefield's several visits to Philadelphia, Benjamin Franklin became his admirer and finally his staunch friend. Franklin states in his biography, "Our friendship was sincere on both sides and lasted to his death." At first the evangelist was permitted to preach in the Established Church in that city, but on his later visits this was denied him, and it became necessary for him to preach in the fields or from the courthouse steps. Finally Whitefield's Philadelphia friends conceived the idea of erecting a building to accommodate the great crowds who wished to hear him. Thus Franklin describes the erection of the building: "Sufficient sums were soon received to procure the ground and erect the building, which was a hundred feet long, and seventy broad. Both house and ground were vested in trustees," of whom Franklin was one, "expressly for the use of any preacher of any religious persuasion, who might desire to say something to the people of Philadelphia." Here Whitefield preached when he visited the city and here his friends, the Tennents, Blair, Rowland and others, occasionally ministered, and here for nine years the Second Presbyterian Church of Philadelphia, of which Gilbert Tennent was pastor, worshiped. In 1751, largely through the efforts of Franklin, the building was used for an academy, and two years later it was chartered as the "College, Academy and Charitable School of Philadelphia," which finally (1791) grew into the University of Pennsylvania. There now stands, appropriately, in one of the quadrangles of the university a life-size statue of George Whitefield, erected by the Methodist students and graduates of the University of Pennsylvania.

Shortly after the establishment of the Academy in Philadelphia steps were taken to found a college in New York. This was accomplished by royal charter in 1754, after Trinity Church had agreed to convey to the institution a part of the queen's farm which Queen Ann had given to Trinity parish. This was done with the express provision that the president of the college should forever be a member of the Established Church and that the liturgy of the church should always be used at the morning and evening service of the college. There was much opposition to these restrictions on the part of the Dutch Reformed, Presbyterian and Lutheran groups, who would have preferred that the college be established by an Act of the Assembly. The new King's college opened in a building belonging to Trinity Church, with President Samuel Johnson the entire faculty. The first advertisement of the college disclaims any intention of imposing "on the scholars the peculiar Tenets of any particular Sect of Christians; but to inculcate upon their tender Minds, the great Principles of Christianity and Morality, in which true Christians of each Denomination are generally agreed."

Since the beginning, the Reformed Church in the colonies had been completely dependent upon the Classis of Amsterdam, but the elder Frelinghuysen began to realize the necessity of training up young men in America for the ministry and was the first to favor some degree of independence for the American churches. This agitation finally culminated in the formation of an American Coetus, or presbytery (1747), subject, however, to the Classis at Amsterdam. Soon after the establishment of King's College certain Dutch Reformed leaders began to advocate the establishment of a Professorship of Theology for the Dutch Church, in the New York College, but this eventually failed. The Dutch Church was now divided into two parties, the one desiring to remain under the complete control of the Holland Classis, and to continue to depend upon Holland for its ministry; the other stood for an American trained ministry and a degree of independence for the American churches. The latter party was made up of the friends of the great revival, who were anxious to establish a college where the young men who had been stirred by the evangelical passion might receive training for the ministry. Eventually the opposers of the revival and of an American trained ministry withdrew from the Coetus and formed a body called the "Conferentie," and thus a schism similar to that in the Presbyterian Church was precipitated in the Dutch Church. The conservatives also insisted upon the use of the Dutch language in the churches while the evangelicals were more and more introducing English, and English preaching became very popular, especially among the young people in New York City. Eventually (1772) the disputes in the Dutch Church came to a happy end through the wisdom and tact of a young minister, John H. Livingston, a native of New York but educated for the ministry at the University of Utrecht, who now was called to a pastorate in New York. He brought with him a plan of union approved by the Classis of Amsterdam, which fully upheld every contention of the Coetus, and led to the establishment of Queen's College at New Brunswick in 1770, of which Livingston eventually became the president. The triumph of the evangelical party and the policies it advocated undoubtedly saved the Dutch Church from final extinction.

Dartmouth College and what is now Brown University grew out of the general educational interest created by the Great Awakening, as did also Liberty Hall, later known as Washington College, and Hampden-Sidney College in Virginia. The story of the beginnings of

PRESIDENT JOHNSON OF KING'S COLLEGE TEACHING HIS FIRST CLASS
From *Harper's Magazine*, October, 1884

these institutions, however, will be related in another connection.

The coming of the Scotch-Irish settlers into the western valleys of Virginia and the suspension of the intolerant ecclesiastical laws in their favor soon led to the formation of several Presbyterian congregations in these new settlements. Itinerant missionaries and then pastors were sent them by the Synod of Philadelphia, so that by 1738 there came to be four or five congregations west of the Blue Ridge. But the greatest expansion of Presbyterianism into the south was to come from another source, namely, Hanover county in central Virginia. The churches and ministers in the Great Valley were generally opposed to the revival, but Hanover county became the revival center of southern Presbyterianism. The revival in Hanover county began as a spontaneous movement among a small group of laymen of whom Samuel Morris was the leader. He and several others became interested in some religious books which fell into their hands, such as Whitefield's sermons and some of Luther's writings, and they met together in one another's houses where these books were read. Finally, the meetings attracted such crowds that their houses became too small to accommodate them, and special houses were built, the first such building being called Morris's Reading House.

In 1742-1743 William Robinson, a graduate of the Log College, was sent out by the New Brunswick Presbytery to visit Presbyterian settlements in western Virginia and North Carolina, and on this tour visited Hanover county. Other revival missionaries followed Robinson, and in 1748 Samuel Davies was sent to Hanover county as the first settled Presbyterian minister in the region. Here Davies, perhaps the most brilliant Presbyterian preacher of the colonial period, was so successful that within a few years the work was greatly extended and a presbytery was formed (1755), called the Hanover Presbytery, destined to become the "Mother" Presbytery of the south and southwest.

Davies succeeded in winning the good will of Governor Gooch by his eloquent support of the cause of the colonies in the French and Indian War and his fame spread far and wide. He obtained concessions from the Virginia government in favor of increasing the number of Presbyterian chapels, winning his cause against the opposition of the attorney-general of Virginia. Soon he was itinerating over seven counties, under a license issued by the colonial authorities, while all of his chapels were legally registered. Davies never proceeded on any new enterprise until he had won the legal right to proceed and thus he gave Presbyterianism a stable legal status in Virginia, such as no other dissenting body had succeeded in gaining. The growing unpopularity of the Established Church, due to the Twopenny Acts (1755, 1758) and the Parson's Cause, aided the growth of Presbyterianism and numerous defections from the Establishment to Presbyterianism took place. Once the status of Virginia Presbyterianism was legally defined their churches entered upon a period of rapid growth and expansion. Revivals were of frequent occurrence and by the year 1758, in which the schism between the Old and New Side was healed, Presbyterianism was firmly established in central Virginia, and from then until the outbreak of the Revolution expanded rapidly both southward and westward.

Samuel Davies left Virginia in 1759 to accept the presidency of the College of New Jersey. He, with Gilbert Tennent, had previously visited England and Scotland to raise money for the support of the college and their mission had proved most successful. After three times refusing the presidency on the death of Edwards, Davies finally was persuaded to accept, though his term of office lasted less than two years, he dying of a fever in February, 1761.

The Presbyterian revival in Virginia has more than a religious significance. Indeed, it was the "first mass movement that was to bring about a social and political upheaval in Virginia—the first breach in the ranks of privilege." But this movement received even greater impetus from the next two phases of the revival, in which Baptists and Methodists were to play the principal rôle.

To understand the Baptist revival and expansion into the South it is necessary first to glance at the influence the Great Awakening in the New England and middle colonies exerted upon them. At first the Baptists took little part in the New England revival, probably due to the fact that they had been so harshly treated by the Congregationalists that they felt little inclination to join them in this movement. But the Baptists reaped great indirect benefit from the revival through the controversies and divisions which soon appeared in many New England Congregational churches. In numerous instances those favoring the revival separated from those who opposed it and formed *Separate* congregations. Many of the Separate congregations became Baptist, though some of them returned to the older congregations, while others, due to internal dissensions, were soon disintegrated. Thus the number of Baptist churches in Massachusetts grew from six to thirty; in Connecticut from four to twelve; in Rhode Island from eleven to thirty-six, while Baptist churches were established in New Hampshire, Vermont and Maine.

While the growth of the Baptists in New England during the period of the Great Awakening was proportionately rapid, in the middle colonies there seems to have been but normal growth. This is accounted for by a Baptist historian with the statement that ground once preoccupied by Presbyterians is relatively irresponsive to Baptist effort. Though there were many schisms in Presbyterian churches in the middle colonies as a result of the revival, yet there seems to have been no Baptist church formed as a result.

The rapid increase of Baptists in New England and especially in Rhode Island, from about 1740 onward, and the appearance of a better educated leadership, led naturally to the establishment of educational institutions, first and chief of which was Rhode Island College. The idea of founding an institution to be controlled by Baptists originated with Morgan Edwards of the Philadelphia Association, though he soon obtained the coöperation of a brilliant young graduate of the College of New Jersey, James Manning. The idea once suggested was immediately taken up by the leading Baptists of Rhode Island and in 1764 a liberal charter was obtained. Baptists were to control the institution, but Quakers, Congregationalists and

Episcopalians were to share in its government, while no religious tests were ever to be required and places on the faculty were to be open to all denominations of Protestants. The founding of the college of Rhode Island, however, had little to do with the expansion of Baptists southward.

While there were Baptist congregations in Virginia as early as 1714, yet they remained unnoticed and unmolested and had little part in Baptist expansion. Those responsible for the Baptist revival in Virginia and North Carolina came directly from New England and were the products of the great New England awakening. The leaders were Shubal Stearns and his brother-in-law, Daniel Marshall, who were Separate Baptists from Connecticut. Stearns was a convert of the Great Revival and was one of those who withdrew to form a Separate congregation. Becoming a Baptist, he began to preach and was ordained in 1751. Three years later he left New England and settled on Opekon Creek, Virginia, where there was already a Baptist church. Here he was joined by his brother-in-law, Daniel Marshall, who had gone through much the same experience as had Stearns, though he had come from Presbyterian ancestry. At first Stearns and Marshall preached as evangelists in Virginia, but here they met opposition from the Baptists as well as others, and they determined to remove to North Carolina where they located in Guilford county, on Sandy Creek, in 1755.

Soon after their arrival in North Carolina a church was organized called the Sandy Creek Church and Stearns became the pastor. Soon Stearns, Marshall and other Baptist evangelists were traveling throughout a wide territory and Sandy Creek Church grew from 16 to 606 members. Other churches were formed, preachers were "raised up," among them James Reed, Dutton Lane and, most important of all, Samuell Harriss, a man of influence and education, who had held several offices, among them burgess of the county and colonel of militia. Five years after the formation of the Sandy Creek Church (1760) the Sandy Creek Association was organized which is called the Mother Association, as Sandy Creek Church became the "mother, grand-mother and great-grand-mother of forty-two churches."

For the next ten years the progress of the Separate Baptists is almost unparalleled in Baptist history. Whole communities were stirred and strong Baptist churches established. The following is a description of the type of work performed by Harriss and Read in Virginia:

In one of their visits, they baptized seventy-five at one time, and in the course of one of their journeys, which generally lasted several weeks, they baptized upwards of two hundred. It was not uncommon at one of their great meetings, for many hundreds to camp on the ground, in order to be present the next day. . . . There were instances of persons travelling more than one hundred miles to one of these meetings; to go forty or fifty was not uncommon.

In these meetings there were many excesses and the preaching of the Baptist evangelists undoubtedly encouraged extravagances. An eyewitness at one of their meetings saw

multitudes, some roaring on the ground, some wringing their hands, some in extacies, some praying, some weeping; and others so outrageously cursing and swearing that it was thought they were really possessed of the devil.

Unlike the Presbyterians in Virginia, the Baptists were little inclined to conform to the letter of the law in securing licenses for their meeting-houses. They were also more open and extreme in their attacks upon the Established Church; and these facts, added to the fear aroused that their rapid increase constituted a menace to society, brought down upon them bitter persecution. The years from 1768 to 1770 are known as the Period of the Great Persecution. Baptist ministers were arrested as disturbers of the peace, and more than thirty, to use the phrase of one of their number, "were honored with the dungeon."

As is usually the case, persecution, instead of retarding, served to promote their cause, and when it became generally known that the Baptists held as one of their principles the separation of church and state many leading men came to favor them. The patient manner in which they bore persecution gave them a reputation for piety and goodness and "every month," to quote their chief historian, "new places were found by the preachers whereon to plant the Redeemer's standard." Although but few, perhaps, became Baptists in each place, yet the majority would be favorable. Such was the Baptist situation in Virginia and in the other southern colonies when the Revolution opened. Though still relatively a small body, the Baptists were strong enough to make it important for either side to gain their influence and support, an advantageous position which the Baptists were not slow in perceiving. More and more the religious issue became associated in men's minds with the political issue, and many came to see that Baptist notions were in harmony with the political philosophy of the American Revolutionary leaders, for was not the paying of taxes to support the Established Church taxation without representation?

Just as the Baptists were becoming well established in Virginia and North Carolina a third phase of the revival began under Devereux Jarratt, an evangelical Anglican minister, who was associated with the early Methodist preachers. Jarratt had been converted under Presbyterian influence and was thoroughly imbued with evangelical ideas. He became rector of the parish of Bath in Dinwiddie county in 1763 and his warm evangelical preaching soon filled his church to overflowing. He got very little sympathy or assistance from his fellow clergymen, however, in his attempt to evangelize the Establishment. Speaking of his isolation he says in his autobiography:

At that time I stood alone not knowing of one clergyman in Virginia like minded with myself; yea I was opposed and reproached by the clergy—called an enthusiast, fanatic, visionary, dissenter, Presbyterian, madman, and whatnot;—yet was I so well convinced of the utility and importance of the truths I declared and the doctrines I preached, that no clamor, opposition, or reproach could daunt my spirit, or move me from my purpose and manner of preaching. . . .

Organized Methodism first appeared in the American colonies in 1766 when Philip Embury began to hold meetings in his house in New York and soon afterward formed a society. Probably two years earlier Robert Strawbridge began to preach in Maryland and likewise formed a society near Sam's Creek where a log meeting-house was erected. Three years later (1769) Mr. Wesley sent out two of his preachers from England, Mr. Boardman and Mr. Pilmoor, to the American colonies. A little later Robert Williams, a local preacher, arrived, having come on his own accord, though Wesley gave him a permit to work under the direction of the missionaries. Boardman and Pilmoor worked in Pennsylvania, New Jersey and New York, while Williams went to Maryland and Virginia. Jarratt states that Williams was the first Methodist preacher he conversed with, and in 1772-1773 Williams was welcomed in Jarratt's parish where he preached several sermons. Williams assured Jarratt that the Methodists were true members of the Church of England and its preachers did not assume to administer baptism or the Lord's Supper, but looked to the parish ministers to perform that service. With this assurance Jarratt welcomed the Methodist itinerants, seeing in them a means of reviving the Established Church in Virginia and the Carolinas.

Jarratt has left us a vivid account of his activities in his *Autobiography*. As Methodist activities increased particularly after 1773 and as the revival spread Jarratt was called upon to travel extensively in meeting his preaching engagements. Often he held open-air meetings and preached on the average five times each week and altogether his work carried him into twenty-nine counties of Virginia and North Carolina. This phase of the Virginia and Carolina revival reached its culmination just as the Revolution was beginning, though the revival continued throughout the war while Jarratt continued to work whole-heartedly with the Methodists until they withdrew from the Established Church at the close of the war.

The rise of these three large bodies of dissenters in Virginia in the years just preceding the Revolution helps to explain the part played by Virginia in that struggle. Their presence also explains why the struggle for the separation of church and state was won in Virginia.

The Presbyterians, with their emphasis upon an educated ministry, established educational institutions in Virginia as soon as they became strong enough to support them. Thus in 1776 Hampden-Sidney College was established in Prince Edward county, while west of the Ridge Liberty Hall Academy was planted the same year. The Baptists, on the other hand, standing as they did for an unpaid and uneducated ministry, were naturally slow in establishing schools. The Methodists were too few before the Revolution to think of schools, though soon after the war steps were taken to establish a college.

✣✣✣✣✣✣✣✣ ✣✣✣✣✣✣✣✣✣✣✣✣✣✣✣✣✣✣✣✣✣✣✣✣✣

Chapter XI

MISSIONS AND BENEVOLENT ENTERPRISES IN THE AMERICAN COLONIES

When the Spaniard began the colonization of America he came with a strong and sincere desire to spread the Catholic faith and in the midst of his many and various activities he never lost sight of his religious purpose. With hardly an exception priests accompanied every colonizing or conquering expedition and no opportunity was ever lost for establishing Christian worship among the natives of America. At the end of the colonial period the religious establishments in the English colonies could not compare with those of Roman Catholicism in the Spanish colonies. When England began colonization the Spanish Colonial Empire in America had been in existence more than a hundred years, and through the efforts of Spanish missionaries thousands of natives had been brought to at least a nominal acceptance of Christianity.

Of all this the English were well aware, and one of the frequent arguments used to advance the cause of English colonization was that it would bring the Christian religion to the savages. Thus Sir George Peckham glowingly describes the great benefits which English colonization would bring to the natives of America; of these benefits

First and chiefly [he says, are those] in respect of the most gladsome and happy tidings of the most glorious gospel of our Saviour Jesus Christ, whereby they may be brought from falsehood to trueth, from darkness to light, from the hie way of death to the path of life, from superstitious idolatrie to sincere Christianity, from the devill to Christ, from hell to heaven. And if in respect of all the commodities thay can yeelde us (were they many more) that they should receive this onely benefit of Christianity, they were more than fully recompenced.

It is undoubtedly true that religion was frequently used as a disguise and a decoy to attract the religiously-minded to the support of colonization, and much of what we read about the desire to convert the natives was but pious fraud, but at the same time there was undoubtedly a real missionary interest on the part of many of the leaders in the colonizing enterprise.

The early interest in the Christianization and education of the Indians in the Virginia colony was destroyed by the great Indian massacre of 1622. The New England Puritans seem to have been genuinely concerned about the conversion of the Indians from the beginning. The charter of the Plymouth colony called for "the conversion of such savages as yet remain wandering in desolation and distress to civil society and the Christian religion." Likewise the Massachusetts Bay charter called upon the colonists to win the savages "to the knowledge and obedience of the only true God and Saviour of mankind," while the seal of the colony was the figure of an

Indian with a label at his mouth representing him as saying "Come over and help us." In the Plymouth colony, even during the hard early years, the Indians in the neighborhood were not neglected by the ministers and in 1636 laws were passed providing for the preaching of the gospel among them.

The work of Indian Christianization in early New England is generally gathered about the name of John Eliot, though the Mayhew family on Martha's Vineyard began their work among the island Indians, off the Massachusetts coast, at about the same time and with much the same degree of success. John Eliot, a graduate of Cambridge, came to Boston in 1631 and the next year became the teacher at the Roxbury Church, where he remained until his death in 1690. From the beginning of his ministry at Roxbury, Eliot began to prepare himself to work among the Indians. Through several years he studied the Indian language, aided by an Indian captured in the Pequot War, who lived with him and accompanied him on his visits to the Indians in the neighborhood.

Finally in 1646 he preached his first sermon in the Indian tongue five miles from Roxbury. These early efforts aroused the general interest of the Massachusetts ministers and a few weeks later, probably incited by what Eliot had already done, the Massachusetts Assembly passed an act ordering the ministers to elect every year two of their number to act as missionaries to the Indians. The work was now carried on with great success, and villages of Christian Indians were erected in the vicinity of Boston which adopted simple regulations, on Eliot's advice, for their civil and religious regulation. Eventually there came to be a number of such Indian towns, all under the care of Eliot and his helpers. One of the most successful of these Indian towns was Natick. It was located on both sides of the Charles River and consisted of three streets, of Indian wigwams and a meeting-house fifty by twenty-five feet, which was used also for a school. Thus is its founding described by Cotton Mather:

Here it was that in the year 1651 those that had heretofore lived like wild beasts in the wilderness now compacted themselves into a town; and they first applied themselves to the forming of their civil government. . . . Mr. Eliot on a solemn fast, made a public vow; that seeing these Indians were not prepossessed with any forms of government, he would instruct them into such a form, as we had written in the word of God, that so they might be a people in all things ruled by the Lord. Accordingly he expounded unto them the eighteenth chapter of Exodus; and then they chose rulers of hundreds, of fifties, of tens. . . .

The little towns of these Indians being pitched upon this foundation, they utterly abandoned that polygamy which had heretofore been common among them; they made severe laws against fornication, drunkenness, and sabbath-breaking, and other immoralities . . .

At length was a church-state settled among them; they entered as our churches do, into an holy covenant, wherein they gave themselves, first unto the Lord, and then unto one another, to attend the rules, and helps, and expect the blessing of the everlasting gospel . . .

England learned of these early successes among the Indians through several pamphlets describing the Indian work. One such tract was that written by Eliot in 1647 entitled "The Day-Breaking if not the Sun Rising of the Gospel with the Indians in New England," while the next year "The Clear Sun-shine of the Gospel Breaking Forth Upon the Indians in New England," by the Rev. Thomas Shepard of Cambridge, appeared. So stirred was Cromwell's Parliament with this cheering information that a corporation was created by their act called "The President and Society for the Propagation of the Gospell in New England," which was given power to hold lands, goods and money. Collections were now ordered to be taken throughout England and by 1661 a sum producing £600 a year had been collected. The administrators of this fund were the commissioners of Massachusetts, Plymouth, Connecticut and New Haven. With the assistance provided by this society the work of Christianizing the Indians went forward more rapidly, while the money furnished by the society was used not only for the salaries of missionaries but also for printing books, and furnishing tools and clothing for the Indians.

When Charles II came to the throne, the Society for Propagation of the Gospel in New England went out of existence, since all the acts of the Long Parliament were now declared illegal. Fortunately, however, those in charge of the interests of the society were successful in catching the king when he was anxious to please all parties and succeeded in securing a royal charter. The society was now reorganized under this charter, with the name "The Company for Propagacion of the Gospell in New England, and the parts adjacent in America." The incorporators numbered forty-five and included both Anglicans and Nonconformists, among them some of the high officials of state.

One of the outstanding achievements of John Eliot was his translation of the Bible into the tongue of the Massachusetts Indians. Cotton Mather points out some of the difficulties in learning the Indian tongue; the strange harshness of pronunciation, the enormous length of many of the words, and its unlikeness to any of the languages of Europe, all of which rendered the task peculiarly difficult. In 1661 the society published at Cambridge Eliot's translation of the New Testament and two years later the whole Bible was issued from the same press. Other translations followed, including treatises by the Mathers and Baxter as well as the Cambridge Platform.

The very year Eliot began his work among the Indians of Massachusetts a similar work was begun among the Indians on the island of Martha's Vineyard by Thomas Mayhew, the minister on the island. Mayhew's father had been given these islands as a grant, they originally not being included in any of the New England governments. On this and the surrounding islands there was a native population of several thousands, and Mayhew, like Eliot, soon after his settlement as minister on the island began the study of the Indian tongue. In 1646 he began to preach to them, and four years later two of the principal *powwows* or medicine men professed conversion. This circumstance so amazed the natives that they began to flock to Mayhew by whole families, and soon two congregations of natives had been formed.

In 1657 Thomas Mayhew, Jr., lost his life while on a voyage to England to procure greater assistance for his

DAVID ZEISBERGER PREACHING TO THE INDIANS

From an engraving in possession of the Pennsylvania Historical Society

Indian work. After this tragic loss, the elder Mayhew, though governor of the island and nearly seventy years of age, took up the work of preaching to the Indians. Two natives were now ordained to work with the elder Mayhew while he continued as an evangelist until his death. Shortly before his death one of his grandsons, John Mayhew, became the settled pastor on the island and he likewise took up the work among the Indians. A few years following his early death, his son, Experience Mayhew, continued the Indian work until his death in 1758. Experience Mayhew was considered especially skillful in the Indian language since he had been familiar with it from childhood, and published translations of the Psalms and the Gospel of John, and much of what we know of the Indian work is due to his account of thirty Indian converts.

The Society for the Propagation of the Gospel in New England also gave some assistance to the Indian work on the islands. By 1674 there were four Indian congregations on the island of Martha's Vineyard made up of some eighteen hundred Indians. In eastern Massachusetts there were at the same time four congregations with more than two thousand Indians. The praying Indians, however, were mostly from the weaker tribes, located between the powerful and warlike rivals, the Narragansetts and the Mohegans. Eventually these Indian churches disappeared due to the almost complete dying off of these weaker tribes or their intermarriage with the negroes which caused the absorption of the Indians in the negro population of New England.

King Philip's War (1675-1676) was a great blow to the

New England Indian missions. Much to the distress of the missionaries a few of the praying Indians went back to their savage kinsmen during this terrible struggle, though most of the converts proved faithful to their Christian profession. When the war ended work among the Indians was again vigorously carried on, though it was now a crippled enterprise. With the death of Eliot in 1690 the first period of New England Indian missions comes to a close, though there continued to be some interest manifested, even though the whole religious life of New England was at low ebb. It was the Great Awakening which aroused new interest in Indian Christianization, as well as in other humanitarian movements.

This reawakened interest in Indian missions is well illustrated by the work among the Housatonic Indians, a small tribe in western Massachusetts, begun in 1734 by the Rev. John Sergeant, a former tutor at Yale. Here Sergeant labored with success until his death in 1749. The Indians were gathered into a new settlement called Stockbridge where a plan was devised for the education and training of the Indian children. To help carry forward this plan for an Indian Charity School a subscription was begun in England, headed by the Prince of Wales, but the sum raised was not sufficient to put the plan into operation. A Baptist minister, however, the Rev. Mr. Hollis, established a small charity school in coöperation with Sergeant. The work of Sergeant resulted in the baptism of 182 Indians, most of whom were living in houses built in the English style at Stockbridge instead of bark wigwams, while a school was conducted with fifty or more children in attendance. On the death of

Sergeant (1749) Jonathan Edwards became the minister at Stockbridge where we are told he labored "with no remarkable success," though his work was satisfactory to both the English and the Indians as well as to the commissioners of the New England Society who had the direction of the mission. Edwards was succeeded at Stockbridge by a Mr. West and he in turn by John Sergeant the son of the founder of the mission. Following the Revolution the Stockbridge Indians, as they came to be called, were removed to the Oneida country, where New Stockbridge was built.

Upon the great seal of Dartmouth College are the words *Vox Clamantis in Deserto,* "the voice of one crying in the wilderness." To explain this motto it is necessary to recount the story of Moor's Indian Charity school conducted at Lebanon, Connecticut, by the Congregational minister, Eleazer Wheelock, who was one of the most active of the revival preachers during the course of the Great Awakening. The first graduate of this school was a Mohegan Indian, Samson Occom. To this school also came several Mohawk youths among them Thayendanegea, known to history as Joseph Brant. This school also welcomed the sons of the colonists, and thus Samuel Kirkland, the son of the minister at Norwich, Connecticut, became a scholar there where he was prepared for the College of New Jersey. In November, 1761, Wheelock sent young Brant and Kirkland into the Mohawk Valley to seek other Indian pupils and in 1767 Samson Occom, who had become a minister after his conversion in the Great Awakening, was sent to England with Nathaniel Whitaker to raise money for the school at Lebanon. Occom caught the popular fancy in England, where he preached over three hundred sermons and raised more than ten thousand pounds. Previous to this Wheelock had received allowances from the Commissioners of the New England Society as well as private gifts from both England and America, while the Scotch Society for Propagating Christian Knowledge also helped his school with appropriations for the support of Indian scholars.

As the school developed Wheelock conceived the plan of making it into a college, the primary purpose of which would be to train young white men for missionary work among the Indians. Accordingly, after having investigated several possible locations, it was finally decided to locate the institution in the province of New Hampshire where Governor Wentworth had made a generous offer of land and endowments. This was thought a proper location because it was near the Indian country and its selection was recommended by Lord Dartmouth who had been made chairman of the trustees of the funds which had been collected in England and Scotland by Occom and Whitaker. It was George Whitefield who was responsible for Lord Dartmouth's interest in the new college, for it was he who had arranged for Occom and Whitaker to meet and dine with him. The college began at Hanover, New Hampshire, in the autumn of 1770. Wheelock had arrived in August to push forward the building operations, but before they were completed his family and twenty or thirty students arrived. His wife and the "females" of his family were placed in one hut, while his sons and students made booths and beds of hemlock boughs, "and in this situation," he says, "we continued about a month, till the 29th day of October, when I removed with my family to my house." The house for the students, eighty by thirty-two feet and two stories high, was finally completed and Dartmouth College thus was started upon its honorable and useful career.

Perhaps the best known of all the Indian missionaries, in the period following the Great Awakening, is David Brainerd. Brainerd was a convert of the Great Revival and, like many others, soon after his conversion (1739) felt the call to preach and entered Yale College to prepare for the ministry. Here he won distinction for his scholarship and was the leader of his class. His sympathy for the revival, to which the college had become opposed, caused him to make a disparaging remark concerning one of the tutors, which was overheard by several students. This, together with the accusation that he had attended a Separatist meeting, caused his expulsion. This act on the part of the college was strongly opposed by some of the ministers, who were led on this account to become greatly interested in Brainerd. In 1742 he was licensed to preach in the Congregational Church, and the same year was sent as a missionary to the Indians under the auspices of the Society in Scotland for Propagating Christian Knowledge. His first mission station was about halfway between Stockbridge and Albany, but here the Indians were few in number and he soon persuaded them to join the settlement at Stockbridge where they could be under the instruction of Sergeant. After receiving ordination by the New Side Presbytery of New York in 1744, he took up his Indian work in New Jersey, where remarkable success attended his efforts. Since his student days Brainerd had suffered from tuberculosis and the terrible exposure which his work entailed soon brought the disease to a crisis. Several times he made long journeys to the Indians on the Susquehanna, which further drained his strength. Early in the year 1747 his health would no longer permit the continuation of his work and he died at the home of Jonathan Edwards at Northampton, to whose daughter Jerusha he was engaged to be married.

Brainerd's saintly character and his absolute obedience to duty in spite of bodily weakness and pain made a profound impression upon his generation. Soon after his death Jonathan Edwards published an account of his life together with his diary, which proved a tremendous stimulus in promoting the cause of missions. For many this little book was a manual of religious guidance and few books have had a larger religious influence. Indeed, David Brainerd dead was a more potent influence for Indian missions and the missionary cause in general than was David Brainerd alive.

In the years following the Great Awakening the Presbyterians began to take great interest in missions to the Six Nations, and succeeded in securing the coöperation of the Society in Scotland for Propagating Christian Knowledge. In 1764 Samuel Kirkland, the former companion of Joseph Brant at Wheelock's school, on his graduation from the College of New Jersey began his work as a missionary, first to the Senecas and later to the Oneidas. Kirkland continued his work with considerable success to the outbreak of the Revolution, and even during the war made frequent visits to the Indian country and when the war was over returned to them. The Presbyterians also worked among the Indians on Long Island where the revivalist, James Davenport, began a remarkable work which was carried on by Simon Horton.

The most successful Protestant missions of the whole colonial period were undoubtedly those conducted by the Moravians. To the Moravian, missionary work was the most important thing in life, and the Moravian industries at Nazareth and Bethlehem, Pennsylvania, were carried on in order to give support to their missionaries.

The first Moravian missionary in America was Christian Henry Rauch who began work among the New York Indians in 1740. He took up his residence at the Mohegan town of Shekomeko and here he was visited by Count Zinzendorf in 1742 when the first Indians were baptized and admitted into the church. The number of missionaries was now increased and the work progressed rapidly. Settlers in the region, however, stirred up by false reports that the Moravians were allies of the French, finally secured the passage of an act prohibiting the missionaries from giving instructions to the Indians. This caused the withdrawal of the missionaries from Shekomeko and finally the Christian Indians were invited to remove from New York and settle in the vicinity of Bethlehem. Land was purchased about thirty miles distant from Bethlehem and here a town was built called *Gnadenhütten*, or Tents of Good will. Here within a few years the Indian congregation grew to about five hundred.

The outbreak of the French and Indian War brought terrible suffering to the Moravian missionaries and their Indian converts. The Indian town of Gnadenhütten was attacked on November 24, 1755, and completely destroyed.

Nitschmann was shot, other missionaries were burned to death, and but four out of fifteen remained to tell of the fate of their brethren. The Indians, however, escaped and fled to Bethlehem, and throughout that anxious winter were cared for by the Brethren. Later another town called *Nain* was built about a mile from Bethlehem, while some of the Indian converts were removed beyond the Blue Ridge where a second town was erected, called *Wechquetank*. This isolated settlement was later destroyed by the infuriated Scotch-Irish settlers, though not until its Indian inhabitants had been removed to Philadelphia, where they were under the care of the English government.

On the return of peace it was determined to remove the Christian Indians to the Indian country since they could not live in the neighborhood of the whites without being continually molested by them. Accordingly in 1765, after a journey of five weeks, they came to the banks of the Susquehanna where *Friedenshütten*, or Tents of Peace, was built, which soon became a prosperous community attracting visitors from many of the Indian tribes, all of whom were given generous hospitality. Under the leadership of David Zeisberger the Indian work now went forward rapidly. Other towns were founded on the Alleghany, but because of persecution of the Christian Indians by the non-Christian members of their tribe they again moved on. Finally in 1770 they accepted an offer of a tract of land in what is now Ohio on the Tuscarawas River and here a group of villages was founded the principal one being Schönbrunn. Here prosperity reigned and all was happiness and peace when the American Revolution began.

The Roman Catholics were active in the propagation of their form of Christianity throughout this whole period. The Spanish missionaries conducted missions in Florida, Texas, New Mexico, Arizona and California; the French in New York, around the Great Lakes and along the rivers flowing into the Gulf of Mexico. These missions were carried on by the several orders; by the Franciscans and Jesuits chiefly. Seventy years after the founding of St. Augustine the Christian Indians in Florida numbered from twenty-five to thirty thousand, distributed among forty-four mission stations. The conquest and Christianization of New Mexico began in 1595 under Don Juan Oñate and after many hardships the Franciscan missionaries carried forward the work at a marvelous rate. In 1609 Santa Fé was founded and by the end of ten years eight thousand baptisms were reported and sixty friars were at work. Eighty years after (1680) the founding of this prosperous mission, however, an Indian uprising swept away, at one blow, all the Spaniards had accomplished and the cause of Catholic Christianity never completely recovered. Father Kino, a Jesuit from the Mexican province of Sonora, established the first mission work in what is now Arizona in 1687, while a Franciscan, Padre Hidalgo, planted the first mission in Texas at San Antonio in 1718. Mission work in California was not begun until 1769 when another Franciscan Junípero Serra founded the mission at San Diego; in 1776 the mission at San Francisco was established and later Padre Serra founded nine other missions on the Pacific coast of what is now the United States.

It is generally agreed that the French exercised a greater influence among the Indians of America than did the English. Their first settlements were primarily based on the fur trade with the Indians, which led to the establishment of trading posts in widely separated regions. They also intermarried more readily with the natives, which gave them some advantages, but at the same time brought them into conflict with other tribes, such as the Iroquois, who served as an effectual check upon French expansion. At the opening of the French and Indian War (1756) the French had established posts down the St. Lawrence, around the Great Lakes, and along the Mississippi and its tributaries. When this vast region became English at the end of the French and Indian War (1763) there was little left of the mission work which had been carried on by the French Jesuits at various places. Successful work had been begun among the Iroquois, first by Father Jogues, and later (1667) by three other Jesuits. In ten years, more than two thousand baptisms had taken place, all among the Iroquois in New York, but by the end of the century this work had practically disappeared, due to the expulsion of the French missionaries. It is interesting to note that the expulsion of the French Jesuits came during the administration of the Catholic Governor Dongan who feared that the French priests were influencing the Iroquois against the English. He was, however, willing that English Jesuits should replace the French.

The Catholic missions about the Great Lakes were more successful than were those among the Iroquois, and their work has lasted until this day. The French Jesuits were intrepid explorers as well as devoted missionaries, and America is in their debt for making known to the world for the first time much of the region which now is included in the states of Michigan, Wisconsin and Minnesota. By 1690 missions had been established at Mackinaw, Green Bay, Sault Ste. Marie, besides new missions on the St. Joseph and St. Croix rivers. In 1701 the mission at Detroit was established which twenty years later included three villages of Christian Indians. During the early eighteenth century French missionaries entered the region of the lower Ohio and Mississippi, following the French traders as they pushed southward, and missions were founded at Kaskaskia and even as far southward as the Tennessee.

The work performed by the great Anglican society, "The Society for the Propagation of the Gospel in Foreign Parts," remains to be noted. The Anglican Church in the American colonies has been judged very largely by the church and ministry of Maryland and Virginia. It is true the Establishment was stronger there than anywhere else in the colonies, but it is hardly just to judge the more than three hundred unselfish S. P. G. missionaries, who labored in the colonies from 1701 to 1785, by the worst class among the clergy to be found in America.

The society met popular approval from the start and received numerous subscriptions. Its incorporators included the noblest names in England, headed by the Archbishop of Canterbury, while its first action was characterized by good sense. The instructions issued to applicants for appointment state that before embarking they shall call upon the Archbishop of Canterbury for instructions; on shipboard they shall conduct themselves so as to be examples of piety and virtue to the ship's company; that they shall try to prevail upon the captain to have morning and evening prayer and special services on Sunday; on arrival in the country where they are sent they shall "be circumspect; not board or lodge in public-houses; game not at all; converse not with lewd persons, save to admonish them; be frugal; keep out of debt; not meddle with politics; keep away from quarrels; say the service every day, when practicable, and always with seriousness and decency; avoid high-flown sermons; preach against such vices as they see to prevail; impress the nature and need of the Sacraments; distribute the Society's tracts; and visit their people." Their salary was to be fifty pounds a year besides ten pounds for outfit.

The first representatives of the society to visit America were the Rev. George Keith and his friend, the Rev. Patrick Gordon who were sent on a tour of inspection in 1702. Keith had previously been in America, where as a Quaker he had quarreled with that society and had separated from them, and was well endowed with energy and was now an enthusiastic churchman. Gordon died soon after landing, but Keith was joined by the ship's chaplain, John Talbot, who became his companion in his journey through the colonies. The tour lasted two years, and covered the territory from Boston to Charleston. "From this time until the War of Independence the History of the Church in America is to be looked for in the records of the Venerable Society."

The following is a summary of the work of the society

in the American colonies from its origin to the opening of the War for Independence:

It had maintained 310 ordained missionaries, had assisted 202 central stations, and had expended £227,454 or nearly a million and a quarter of dollars. It had stimulated and supported missions to the negroes and the Indians, as well as to the white colonists. Its labors were chiefly in those colonies where the church was not established.

The society's most successful mission to the Indians was that conducted by the Rev. Henry Barclay who was appointed catechist to the Mohawks at Fort Hunter on his graduation from Yale College in 1734. Three years later he became rector of the church at Albany, but continued also his work among the Indians. In 1741 he reported to the S. P. G. that he had, besides his Albany congregation, five hundred Indians under his pastoral care, settled in two towns about thirty miles from Albany, and that only two or three out of the whole tribe remained unbaptized. When Barclay became the rector of Trinity Church, New York City, he continued his interest in the Indians, while at this period the society employed sixteen missionaries to work among the Indians and negroes in New York.

Considerable attention was given by the society to negroes and its missionaries received instruction to work for their conversion. In 1741 the society made a special appeal for funds to promote this work and receive a considerable sum for that purpose. These efforts met strong opposition at first among the slave owners, but the policy of the society was very definitely in favor of such work.

Other societies closely allied to the S. P. G., such as the "Society for Promoting Christian Knowledge," the "Associates of Dr. Bray" and the "Society for Promoting Christian Learning," were likewise interested in negro work. Negro schools were established by the Associates of Dr. Bray in New York, Newport, Rhode Island, and Williamsburg, Virginia, while the other two societies maintained missionaries for work among the negroes and sent books and tracts to be distributed to the slaves.

Among the dissenting churches in the American colonies the Quakers were the only one to question the right of church members to hold slaves. But many Quakers, especially in the South held slaves, though the Yearly Meetings generally manifested an interest in their religious welfare. In the New England Yearly Meeting (1769) slave owners were advised to take the slaves to their places of worship and give them instruction; as did also the Yearly Meetings in Virginia and North Carolina. This, however, was not the universal practice even among Quakers, and some refused or completely neglected the negro's religious welfare.

Among the other churches there was no uniformity of practice in regard to their treatment of the slaves. The clergy were frequently slave owners and in some instances slaves were accepted as a form of endowment. Here and there a minister is found who because of his personal opposition to slavery manumitted his slaves, which was true of Freeborn Garrettson. Samuel Davies during his ministry in Virginia gave particular attention to the negroes and frequently preached to them and admitted them as communicants. Samuel Hopkins, the Congregational minister at Newport, was active in his opposition to slavery and the slave trade and fearlessly denounced both on every possible occasion in this most active center of the American slave trade. During the Baptist revival in Virginia and North Carolina many negroes were converted and were frequently admitted with their masters to church membership and there are instances of negroes speaking in their meetings. As a whole the moral and religious condition among negroes in America at the end of the colonial period left much to be desired. Writing of conditions toward the close of the Revolution, a contemporary states: "One thing is very certain, that the negroes of that country, a few only excepted, are to this day as great strangers to Christianity, and as much under the influence of Pagan darkness, idolatry and superstition, as they were at their first arrival from Africa."

Throughout the eighteenth century, especially after the Great Awakening, there were many educational and charitable projects begun in the American colonies, and their agents were frequently sent to England or the continent to solicit funds. Samuel Davies and Gilbert Tennent (1754) collected considerable funds in Scotland, Ireland and England for the College of New Jersey. In London alone they received more than £1,200, while collections were ordered in all the churches in Scotland and Ireland by the General Assembly of the Church of Scotland and by the Synod of Ireland. Some twelve years later Morgan Edwards (1767) went to England to solicit funds for the College of Rhode Island, was dismayed by the amount of begging going on, and despaired of raising any large sum. He secured only about £900 though Samson

Occom, the Mohegan Indian, and Nathaniel Whitaker, the agents of Eleazer Wheelock's Indian School, who were in England at the same time, were successful in securing ten times that amount.

Michael Schlatter, the German Reformed minister, was active in raising funds on the continent for churches and schools among the destitute Germans of America. His appeal to the Synod of North Holland and to the German churches in the Palatinate (1751-1752) soon brought the sum of £12,000. His appeal was translated into English by the English preacher in Amsterdam who was a member of the Classis and was circulated widely in Scotland and England. So profound was the impression made that eventually £20,000 was raised and an English Society formed to manage this fund, known as the "Society for the Promotion of the Knowledge of God among the Germans." A scheme was then drawn up for the forming of Charity Schools which were to be open to Protestant youth of all denominations. Schlatter became the superintendent of these schools, which soon became extremely unpopular among the Germans. Part of the German opposition was due to their injured pride in being represented as ignorant and "proper subjects to be civilized by a foreign charity." In 1760 there were eight of these schools maintained in several of the Pennsylvania German counties with an attendance of some six hundred students.

Perhaps the most widely known of all the American colonial benevolent enterprises and certainly the most widely advertised was George Whitefield's Orphan House in Georgia. While Charles Wesley was serving as secretary to General Oglethorpe, the governor of the colony, he had drawn up a plan for an orphanage at the request of the trustees. Both Charles and John Wesley had written Whitefield about joining the work in Georgia, and when he offered himself to the trustees he was accepted. In preparing for his first visit to the colony (1738), then but six years old, Whitefield collected from his friends more than three hundred pounds to be used for the poor of Georgia, which he used for the purchase of everything which he thought might be needed by the colonist from prayer books and spelling books to clothing, provisions of all kinds of hardware, including gunpowder. This first visit was brief, as it was necessary for him to return to England to obtain priest's orders, but during his stay of four months he had satisfied himself as to the need of an orphanage, and throughout the remainder of his life, it occupied chief place in his thoughts.

Returning to England, Whitefield spent the next nine months in raising funds and making other necessary provisions for the establishment of the Orphan House. The trustees granted him five hundred acres, for its location and support, and by the time he was ready to leave England he had collected about a thousand pounds besides large sums for English charities. Whitefield named the place where the orphanage was located—ten miles from Savannah—Bethesda, "a house of mercy," and here were begun in March, 1740, several brick buildings, which were completed early the next year. By the time the main building was completed forty-nine children had been collected, only twenty-two of them, however, orphans. So indefatigable was Whitefield in gathering children for his orphanage that he brought them from other colonies and in one voyage brought some from England.

The school maintained at the orphanage was at first vocational rather than classical, but within a few years, probably influenced by the founding of the College of Philadelphia and the College of New Jersey in which he had had a part, Whitefield conceived the idea of changing his orphan house into a college. This plan, although it met the hearty approval of the governor and council, failed due to the insistence of the Archbishop of Canterbury that its charter require that the head of the college be a member of the Established Church and that the liturgy of the church be used in its services. Whitefield insisted that "it should be on a broad bottom and no other." The archbishop and the Earl of Dartmouth, President of the Privy Council, held to their position and then the plan was ultimately frustrated.

Whitefield objected to the policy of the trustees in prohibiting the use of slaves in the colony for the first fifteen years, and asserted that "Georgia never can or will be a flourishing province without negroes are allowed." He purchased a plantation and slaves in South Carolina in an attempt to reduce the costs of maintaining the orphanage and justified himself on the ground that the enslavement of negroes made possible their conversion. Later when slavery was permitted in Georgia (1750) the South Carolina property was sold and a plantation near Bethesda was purchased for a similar purpose.

During the thirty years from 1740 to the death of the founder in 1770, there was a total expenditure of £15,000 for the maintenance of the orphanage, a large part of which had been raised by Whitefield—£3,300 had been contributed at various times by Whitefield from his own funds, to meet the debts. The classic example of the great evangelist's success as a money raiser is that related by Benjamin Franklin in his *Autobiography*:

I did not disapprove of the design, [of the orphanage] but as Georgia was then destitute of materials and workmen and it was proposed to send them from Philadelphia at a great expense, I thought it would have been better to have built the house here and brought the children to it. This I advis'd; but he was resolute in his first project, rejected my counsel and I therefore refus'd to contribute. I happened soon after to attend one of his sermons in the course of which I perceived he intended to finish with a collection, and I silently resolved he should get nothing from me. I had in my pocket a handful of copper money, three or four silver dollars, and five pistoles in gold. As he proceeded I began to soften and concluded to give the coppers. Another stroke of his oratory made me asham'd of that and determin'd me to give the silver; and he finish'd so admirably that I empty'd my pocket wholly into the collector's dish, gold and all.

Chapter XII

THE WAR OF INDEPENDENCE AND THE AMERICAN CHURCHES

THE political historian has failed to take adequate account of the influence which came indirectly from the Great Awakening. For the first time the American people found, in the revival, a common intellectual and emotional interest; for the first time intercolonial leaders emerged, which broke over political as well as sectarian lines; "Whitefield, Edwards and Tennent preceded Franklin and Washington as rallying names for Americans irrespective of local distinctions." The leaders in the revival were the advocates of coöperation and union; the whole movement was the foe of denominational and racial prejudice. It was the direct and indirect cause of the movement of population from one colony to another which helped create a common American spirit. One of the ties binding the colonies to the mother country was the Anglican Church; the revival weakened that tie by winning over to the evangelical churches a considerable share of its nominal membership, while the Calvinistic churches—Congregational and Presbyterian—were drawn together in a combination against the Anglican body. In these respects the Great Awakening may be considered one of the important contributing factors in preparing the way for the Revolution.

The most recent attempt to enumerate the religious organizations in the American colonies at the close of the colonial period gives the total at 3,105, with about a thousand each for New England, the middle colonies and the South. Of this total the Congregationalists had 658, most of which were in New England. Ranking next came the Presbyterians with 543, located largely in the middle colonies; then came the Baptists with 498, the Anglicans with 480, Quakers, 295, German and Dutch Reformed, 251, Lutherans, 151, and Catholics, 50. In nine of the colonies there were established churches. In Massachusetts, Connecticut and New Hampshire it was the Congregational that was supported by taxation and established by law, though since the beginning of the century other churches had been tolerated. In six of the colonies the established church was the Anglican, which included all the colonies south from Pennsylvania and New York, though in the latter it was only established in New York City and a few counties surrounding. In none of these colonies was the English Church in the majority, and in none of them did it include even a half of the population, with the possible exception of Virginia.

A recent writer on the period of the American Revolution has stated that "the religious temper of America was one of the prime causes of the Revolution," which is borne out by the statement made by Edmund Burke before Parliament. In America, he said, religious beliefs and practices were in advance of those of all other Protestants in the world. In America the people were accustomed to free and subtle debate on all religious questions, and there was among them little regard for priests, councils or creeds. Their church organizations were simple and democratic, as were those of the Congregationalists and Baptists, or republican as the Presbyterians, and they were accustomed to elect and dismiss their own religious leaders. In short, in America at the end of the colonial era there was a larger degree of religious liberty than was to be found among most of the people of the world, and possession of religious liberty naturally leads to a demand for political liberty.

One of the questions which came up for frequent discussion in the colonies in the two decades previous to the opening of the Revolution was that concerning the establishment in America of an Anglican bishop. John Adams states that this agitation contributed "as much as any other cause, to arouse the attention, not only of the inquiring mind, but of the common people, and urge them to close thinking on the constitutional authority of parliament over the colonies." In the most recent discussion of this whole question, Professor Cross, in his *Anglican Episcopate and the American Colonies,* concludes that if the agitation of this question "did not contribute a lion's share in causing" American hostility to England, it was at least strongly involved and must "be regarded as an important part of it."

The Established Church in the colonies was undoubtedly greatly handicapped because of its complete dependence upon the Bishop of London and "The Society for the Propagation of the Gospel in Foreign Parts." The earnest missionaries of the S. P. G. were particularly con-

cerned for an American bishop and at intervals throughout the first three-quarters of the eighteenth century were
largely responsible for agitating this question. During
Queen Anne's reign, in the early years of the century, the
project came near succeeding, but George I and Robert
Walpole were not interested in the project, though
Thomas Secker, Bishop of Oxford, and Sherlock, Bishop
of London, later revived the issue in the middle of the
century.

Beginning in 1763 a bitter attack was begun on the
S. P. G. by Jonathan Mayhew, the minister at the West
Church, Boston. He declared that the purpose of the
S. P. G. was to "root out Presbyterianism," and he warned
his countrymen that: "People have no security against
being unmercifully priest-ridden but by keeping all im-
perious bishops, and other clergymen who loved to lord it
over God's heritage, from getting their feet into the
stirrup at all." A newspaper and pamphlet warfare now
ensued which involved both sides of the Atlantic. Bishops
were denounced as "Apostolical monarchs," or "right
reverend and holy monarchs," who, once established in
America, would introduce "canon law—a poison, a pollu-
tion." So real did this danger seem to the New England
Congregationalists and the Presbyterians of the middle
colonies that from 1766 to the opening of the Revolution
they united in a series of annual conventions, the primary
purpose of which was "to prevent the establishment of an
Episcopacy in America." The conversion of President
Timothy Cutler and Samuel Whittlesey,—the whole
teaching staff of Yale College—in 1722 to Anglicanism,
together with five respected Congregational ministers,

and the later conversion of others in Connecticut, including Samuel Seabury, Sr., "shook Congregationalism throughout New England like an earthquake, and filled all its friends with terror and apprehension."

Opposition to the S. P. G. and the establishment of an American episcopate were much stronger in those colonies where the S. P. G. missionaries were the most active. Thus opposition was largely confined to the New England and the middle colonies. But in Virginia and Maryland even among churchmen themselves there was no great desire for an American bishop. The Established Church in Virginia was under state control and the Virginia laity did not relish interference from the British government. Even some of the clergymen were fearful that agitation would "infuse jealousies and Fears into the Minds of the Protestant Dissenters," while Arthur Lee regarded the whole idea of an American bishop "as threatening the subversion of both our civil and religious liberties." The question of an American episcopate sharply divided the members of the Established Church in the colonies and when the Revolution came those who had favored an American bishop went largely into the Loyalist party while those who had opposed it generally identified themselves with the patriots.

In the autumn of 1776 the rector of Trinity Church, New York City, reported to the secretary of the S. P. G.:

All the Society's Missionaries, without excepting one, in New Jersey, New York, Connecticut, and, as far as I can learn, in the other New England Colonies, have proved themselves faithful, loyal subjects in these trying times; and have to the utmost of their power, opposed the spirit of disaffection and rebellion which has involved this continent in the greatest calamities.

He further states that the missionaries went about their duties in the midst of the tumult and disorder, preaching the gospel without touching on politics, but everywhere they were threatened and reviled and some of them were seized and confined for several weeks. After the Declaration of Independence the difficulties of the loyal clergy were increased and in many places they were compelled to close their churches. The Rev. Samuel Seabury, Jr., the Anglican minister at Westchester (N. Y.) and later to become the first American bishop, whose father was one of the Congregational ministers in Connecticut to enter the Established Church, was suspected of unpatriotic acts and with the authorship of the *Westchester Farmer*, was seized by a party of armed men and taken to New Haven where he was committed to prison. Later he was released but after the battle of Long Island, Seabury fled to the British lines where he became a chaplain in the British army.

Other prominent loyalist ministers in the Established Church were President Myles Cooper of King's College and Jonathan Boucher of Virginia. The Rev. Jacob Duché, the rector at Christ Church, Philadelphia, at first identified himself with the American cause as also did Jonathan Boucher and preached some notable sermons in its defense, but after the Declaration of Independence he left America because of his loyalty to the crown. He was succeeded by the Rev. William White, the assistant rector, who took the oath of allegiance to the United

States, became chaplain of Congress, and later was to take the leading part in organizing the Protestant Episcopal Church in the United States. Bishop Perry states that two-thirds of the signers of the Declaration of Independence were members of the Established Church and that six of them were either sons or grandsons of Anglican clergymen, while such leaders as George Washington, James Madison, John Marshall, Patrick Henry and Alexander Hamilton were counted among its members. It is incorrect to identify the Established Church in the American Revolution solely with either one side or the other, for they were much divided; in New England both clergy and laity were largely loyalist; in the southern colonies, especially Virginia and Maryland, it was strongly American, while in the middle colonies it was about equally divided. With these facts in mind it will not be surprising to learn that at the end of the War for Independence no American church was in so deplorable a condition as was the Anglican.

No church in the American colonies had so large an influence in bringing on the War for Independence as had the Congregational. Its ministry had been most influential in public affairs from the beginning, and although the political influence of the New England ministers in the eighteenth century was not so great as in the century previous, yet their opinions on all public matters were still of great weight. As a whole the New England clergy at the time of the Revolution were American trained and were graduates of Harvard or Yale. As early as 1633 in Massachusetts and 1674 in Connecticut the practice of preaching election sermons arose. These were delivered before the governor and assembly year by year. Frequently these sermons were printed at government expense and distributed among the towns, and the themes there discussed were rediscussed in the pulpits throughout New England. The first adequate study of these election sermons in their bearing upon the American Revolution has recently been made in a volume by Miss Alice M. Baldwin, entitled *The New England Clergy and the American Revolution*. In these sermons she discovers the whole political philosophy of the American Revolution set forth many years before the opening of the war. They preached the doctrines of Civil Liberty as taught by Sidney, Locke and Milton. Civil government, they claimed, was of divine origin; rulers were God's delegates and derived their power from Him, not directly but through the people. They emphasized fundamental law and its binding quality. God and Christ, they claimed, always governed by fixed rules, by a divine constitution. There are certain great rights given us by nature and nature's God and no ruler may violate these rights and rulers as well as people are strictly limited by law. Thus the Congregational ministers "gave to the cause of the colonies all that they could give of the sanction of religion."

At each crisis in the ten years from 1765—the passage to the Stamp Act—to 1775—the beginning of the war, the New England pulpits "thundered" and dwelt more and more on the rights of resistance. When the news came in 1766 that the hated Stamp Act was repealed Charles Chauncy at First Church, Boston, preached from the text "As cold waters to a thirsty soul, so is good news from a far country." The ministers piously magnified the "Boston Massacre" and John Lathrop preached in Boston on the subject "Innocent Blood Crying to God from the Streets of Boston" while in the same year the Rev. Samuel Cooke in a sermon before Governor Hutchinson and the Massachusetts House of Representatives preached from the text "He that ruleth over men must be just, ruling in the fear of God," etc. The New England ministers, to quote Miss Baldwin, "With a vocabulary enriched by the Bible, . . . made resistance and at last independence and war a holy cause," and through their influence, perhaps more than any other, New England, and the Congregationalists particularly, gave to the Revolution overwhelming support.

When actual fighting began many New England ministers became "fighting parsons." Ministers exerted their influence to raise volunteers and sometimes marched away with them, as did Joseph Willard of Beverly, where two companies were raised largely through his influence. At Windsor, Vermont, David Avery, on hearing the news of Lexington, preached a farewell sermon, then called the people to arms and marched away with twenty men, recruiting others as they went. Many New England ministers became officers of troops raised among their parishioners. The fiery and sharp-tongued John Cleaveland of Ipswich "is said to have preached his whole parish into the army and then to have gone himself." Besides acting as recruiting agents, chaplains, officers and fighters, the New England ministers supported the war with their pens, and gave of their meager salaries to support the cause.

As noted earlier, the Presbyterians in the colonies at the opening of the Revolution were largely Scotch-Irish and represented the most recent immigration, that from North Ireland, and were still burning with hostility to England for the wrongs which had caused their migration. Scotch-Irish settlements everywhere throughout the colonies were strong supporters of the cause of liberty. The famous Mecklenburg Resolves of May 31, 1775, came from the Scotch-Irish of western North Carolina while the battle of King's Mountain was won on October 7, 1780, by bands of Scotch-Irish frontiersmen. Joseph Galloway, a leading loyalist of Pennsylvania, stated before a committee of Parliament in 1779 that about one-half of the American army was made up of Irish, while five years before he had stated that the chief opponents of the British government were "Congregationalists, Presbyterians and Smugglers." A report (1776) to the S. P. G. by the rector of Trinity Church, New York, already referred to, states:

I have it from good authority that the Presbyterian ministers, at a Synod where most of them in the middle colonies were collected, passed a resolve to support the Continental Congress in all their measures. This and this only, can account for the uniformity of their conduct; for I do not know one of them, nor have I been able, after strict inquiry, to hear of any, who did not, by preaching and every effort in their power, promote all the measures of the Congress, however extravagant.

The Presbyterian leader of greatest influence during the Revolution was John Witherspoon, who in 1768 came from Scotland to accept the presidency of the College of

New Jersey. Without delay he entered at once into the spirit of the new country, and soon won recognition as an educational and religious leader. In 1776 he was chosen a member of the New Jersey provincial congress to frame a constitution, and from then until the close of the Revolution Witherspoon "was busy applying the Presbyterian theories of republicanism to the constitution of the new civil governments." He was chosen one of five delegates to represent New Jersey in the Continental Congress and was the only minister to sign the Declaration of Independence. He also signed the Articles of Confederation, and was particularly active and effective in his work on the finance committee of the Congress in which he was associated with Robert and Gouverneur Morris, Elbridge Gerry and Richard Henry Lee.

A Tory Anglican minister, Jonathan Odell, who fled from his parish at Burlington, New Jersey, to the British lines in 1777, where he wrote numerous characterizations of leading patriot Americans, thus pays his respects to Witherspoon:

> Known in the pulpit by sedicious toils,
> Grown into consequence by civil broils,
> Three times he tried, and miserably failed,
> To overset the laws—the fourth prevailed.
> Whether as tool he acted, or as guide,
> Is yet a doubt—his conscience must decide.
> Meanwhile unhappy Jersey mourns her thrall,
> Ordained by the vilest of the vile to fall;
> To fall by Witherspoon!—O name, the curse
> Of sound religion, and disgrace of verse.
> Member of Congress, we must hail him next:

"Come out of babylon," was now his text.
Fierce as the fiercest, foremost of the first,
He'd rail at kings, with venom well-nigh burst,
Not uniformly grand—for some bye-end,
To dirtiest acts of treason he'd decend;
I've known him seek the dungeon dark as night,
Imprisoned Tories to convert, or fright;
Whilst to myself I've hummed, in dismal tune,
I'd rather be a dog than Witherspoon.
Be patient, reader—for the issue trust;
His day will come—remember, Heaven is just.

While John Adams was attending the Continental Congress in Philadelphia in the spring of 1775 he was frequently present at the services of the Third Presbyterian Church of that city where George Duffield was the minister. In his letters to his wife Adams sometimes speaks of the minister's sermons, whom he describes as "a preacher in this city, whose principles and prayers, and sermons more nearly resemble those of our New England clergy than any that I have heard." During the summer of 1776 Duffield joined the patriot army as a chaplain and remained with it throughout the disastrous campaign in which Washington was defeated on Long Island and began his retreat across New Jersey. Returning to his pulpit in the fall, Duffield rebuked his congregation because there were so many men in the house and stated "there 'would be one less tomorrow, and no lecture on Wednesday evening.'" Another Presbyterian minister whose name has lived because of his sturdy support of the cause of independence is that of James Caldwell, pastor of the church at Elizabethtown and chaplain of a New Jersey regiment. During a skirmish at Springfield (N. J.), when wadding for the muskets of the patriots was running low, Caldwell ran to the Presbyterian Church and returned with an armful of Watts' Psalm Books exclaiming "Now, boys, give them Watts!", an incident which Bret Harte thus describes:

> Think of him as you stand
> By the old church today; think of him and that band
> Of militant ploughboys. See the smoke and the heat
> Of that reckless advance, of that straggling retreat!
> . . . . They were left in the lurch
> For the want of more wadding. He ran to the church,
> Broke the door, stripped the pews, and dashed out in the road
> With his arms full of hymn-books, and threw down his load
> At their feet. Then above all the shouting and shots
> Rang his voice; "Put Watts into 'em! Boys, give 'em Watts."

Later both Caldwell and his wife were killed by the British and his church was burned.

At the meeting of the Presbyterian Synod in 1783 the "Pastoral Letter" prepared by a committee of which Witherspoon was a member stated: "We cannot help congratulating you on the general and almost universal attachment of the Presbyterian body to the cause of liberty and the rights of mankind. This has been visible in their conduct, and has been confessed by the complaints and resentment of the common enemy. . . . Our burnt and wasted churches, and our plundered dwellings, in such places as fell under the power of our adversaries, are but an earnest of what we must have suffered, had they finally prevailed. The Synod, therefore, request you to render thanks to Almighty God, for all his mercies, spir-

FATHER HENNEPIN CELEBRATING MASS

Hennepin was one of the Catholic missionaries who continued
the work of Father Marquette

From Parkman's *LaSalle and the Discovery of the Great West.*
Little, Brown & Company

itual and temporal, and in particular manner for establishing the Independence of the United States of America."

The Dutch Church supported the Revolution with almost as great unanimity as did the Presbyterian, although their chief churches were located in that region where the British were most active during the war, in the Hudson valley and in New York. As a result many Dutch congregations were driven from their churches, pastors and flocks separated and much of their property destroyed. One of their churches in New York was used by the British as a riding school while another served as a hospital. John H. Livingston in a sermon reopening one of these churches in 1790, that on Nassau Street, said:

I dare not speak of the wanton cruelty of those who destroyed this temple, nor repeat the various indignities which have been perpetrated. It would be easy to mention facts which would chill your blood! A recollection of the groans of dying prisoners, which pierced this ceiling; or the sacrilegious sports and rough feats of horsemanship exhibited within these walls might raise sentiments in your minds, perhaps, not harmonizing with those religious affections, which I wish, at present, to promote, and always to cherish.

The two largest German churches, the German Reformed and the Lutheran, were on the whole decidedly patriotic. There was some pro-British sentiment among the German Reformed body, as represented by one of the ministers in New York City, the Rev. John Michael Kern, who on the close of the war migrated to Nova Scotia. The most prominent loyalist among the Germans was Dr. John Joachim Zubly, of Savannah, Georgia. Like several of the Anglican ministers, he at first supported the cause of the colonies and wrote and preached in its behalf. He was one of five representatives sent by Georgia to the Continental Congress and no man in that colony had greater influence. But the idea of separation from the mother country completely cooled his ardor for the cause and he was finally banished from Savannah. On the other hand, there was a large number of staunch patriots among the German Reformed ministers and people. At the opening of the war one of their ministers got into trouble for preaching on the text "Better is a poor and wise child, than an old and foolish king, who will no more be admonished," while the Rev. C. D. Weyberg of Philadelphia suffered imprisonment because of his too great activity for the patriot cause. The Reformed minister at Lancaster preached to the Hessian prisoners there, taking for his text, "Ye have sold yourselves for naught; and ye shall be redeemed without money."

The leadership of the Mühlenberg family among the Lutherans in America guaranteed almost unanimous support of that body to the patriot cause. Of the sons of the elder Mühlenberg, John Peter Gabriel Mühlenberg became a brigadier-general in the Continental army, and on the close of the war was breveted major-general. When the war began he was minister of a German Lutheran church at Woodstock, Virginia. Having accepted a commission as colonel of a Virginia regiment, he preached his farewell sermon to his congregation in January, 1776. In his sermon, after describing the situation in the colonies, he concluded by saying, "In the language of Holy Writ, there is a time for all things. There is a time to preach and a time to fight; and now is the time to fight."

After the benediction he stripped from his shoulders his pulpit robe and stood before his congregation in a colonel's uniform, and then with roll of drums stood at the church door and enlisted his frontier parishioners. His brother, Frederick Augustus Conrad Mühlenberg, was a minister of Christ Lutheran Church in New York, but fled on the approach of the British. He later became a member of the Continental Congress, and of the Pennsylvania Assembly; was a member of the state constitutional convention; president of the convention of Pennsylvania which ratified the Federal Constitution, and from 1789 to 1797 was a member of lower house of the National Congress and has the distinction of being chosen the first speaker of that house. In New York City one of the Lutheran ministers was a staunch loyalist and when the city was evacuated by the British fled with a large part of his flock to Nova Scotia, while in Georgia there was also some pro-British sentiment among the Lutherans.

Isaac Bacus, the leader among the New England Baptists in the latter eighteenth and early nineteenth centuries, has left us a detailed account of Baptist activities in the Revolution and in the period immediately following, in his *History of New England Baptists*. He tells us that the Baptists joined the Revolutionary cause because Baptists had suffered most from Episcopalians; because the "worst treatment received by Baptists comes from the same principles and persons that the American war did"; because the Baptists hold to the compact theory of government; because the British claims are unjust, and finally because the deliverance of America might regain for the Baptists their invaded rights. During the whole

{ 265 }

period of the war the Baptists kept up a continual fight for religious liberty. The Warren Association, made up of Baptist churches in New England, furnished the machinery for the assault while Isaac Backus, President Manning of Rhode Island College, John Gano and Morgan Edwards were the leaders in the movement. On every occasion the grievances of the Baptists were presented: first to the Continental Congress; then to the provincial congress of Massachusetts, but at this period their work was in vain for as John Adams is reported to have said, "the Baptists might as well expect a change in the solar system as to expect that the Massachusetts authorities would give up their establishment." The Baptists, however, could not be completely ignored, for their support of the patriot cause was too whole-hearted and too valuable to lose. Accordingly in 1779 the Baptist minister at Boston was invited to preach the election sermon of that year, and in other ways the Baptists were given to understand that their support of the patriot cause was at least appreciated by the "Standing Order," even though they were not yet willing to give them all that they demanded.

Likewise in Virginia the Baptists used the principles of the Revolution to advance the cause of religious liberty and the separation of church and state. In Virginia they were an even more important factor, because of their support of the war, than they were in New England. In 1775 a concession was made in allowing them to hold services for their adherents in the army, while the next year the philosophy of religious liberty was incorporated in the organic law of the state.

Unfortunately for the Methodists in America during

the Revolution, John Wesley, their great founder, was a staunch Tory and a loyal supporter of the policies of George III and his ministers. At the opening of the war Wesley was inclined to be critical of the government measures in regard to America, but the reading of Samuel Johnson's famous tract, "Taxation no Tyranny," completely converted Wesley to the king's side and from that time forward he was most active in his support of the king. Almost immediately Wesley printed under his own name an abridged edition of Johnson's pamphlet under the title, "A Calm Address to the American Colonies," which the English historian Trevelyan estimates as much more influential in shaping British public opinion than was Johnson's original tract. Later Wesley wrote other pamphlets bearing on the American war, and frequently preached on the question, which brought him the gratitude of the English governmental officials, but also brought down upon the head of his followers in America the accusation of Toryism and persecution. Wesley advised his American preachers, when the war began, to remain free of all party, "and say not one word against one or the other side."

Soon all of Wesley's English preachers who were in America returned to England, except Francis Asbury who determined to identify himself with the Americans. Some of the Methodist preachers were non-combatants from principle, as was Jesse Lee, and others refused to take the oath required in some of the states. This was true of Asbury, who on being required to take the oath in Maryland, refused, and on that account was forced to leave the state and seek refuge in Delaware, where the oath was not required of clergymen. Here he was practically in exile for two years, but finally, having become a citizen of Delaware, he was permitted to travel in other states under the protection of his adopted state. In Maryland the Methodists suffered great hardships because of their supposed Toryism. Here "some of the preachers were mulcted and fined, and others imprisoned" for preaching, while others "were bound over in bonds and heavy penalties, and surities not to preach in this or that county." Some were thrown into jail; some were beaten, while others were tarred and feathered. All the native ministers among the Methodists were loyal to the cause of liberty, as were Philip Gatch, Freeborn Garrettson and William Watters. In spite of handicaps, the Methodist revival reached its high point in Virginia at the opening of the Revolution, continued through the war and by 1780 Methodist membership numbered more than 13,000 in the United States as compared to less than four thousand in 1775.

The influence of the wealthy Carroll family of Maryland was largely responsible for determining the course of the small body of American Roman Catholics during the Revolution. Catholics, in recent years, have laid claim to a larger share in winning the Revolution than they deserve, as instanced by a recent book by Michael J. O'Brien entitled *A Hidden Phase of American History: Ireland's Part in America's Struggle for Liberty,* but there is no doubt but that the Catholics of Maryland and Pennsylvania did give practically unanimous support to the cause. Archbishop Carroll, himself an ardent patriot, wrote some years following the war, "They [Catholics] concurred with perhaps greater unanimity than any other body of men in recommending and promoting that government from whose influence America anticipated all the blessings of justice, peace, plenty, good order, and civil and religious liberty. The Catholic regiment, 'Congress Own,' the Catholic Indians from St. John, Maine, under the chief Ambrose Var, the Catholic Penobscots, under the chief Orono, fought side by side with their Protestant fellow colonists. Catholic officers from Catholic lands— Ireland, France, and Poland—came to offer their services to the cause of liberty." The Catholic signers of the Declaration of Independence were Thomas Fitzsimmons; Thomas Sim Lee, the war-governor of Maryland; Daniel Carroll, and Charles Carroll of Carrollton, who at the time of signing pledged his fortune to the cause.

The first diplomatic representative sent to the United States was from France and on July 4, 1779, the French minister plenipotentiary invited the American officials in Philadelphia to attend a *Te Deum* in the new Catholic Chapel in celebration of the independence of the United States of America. The presence of many French Catholic soldiers in America, with their Catholic chaplains, brought Roman Catholicism for the first time into many localities and introduced to the American people the solemn Catholic service of worship.

The effect of the Revolution upon the "Conscientious Objectors" located largely in Pennsylvania—the Quakers, the Mennonites and the Moravians particularly—makes a tragic chapter in the history of the War for Independence. Already a large number of Quakers especially in Philadelphia had adopted the principles of James Logan, the

Penn family agent, who considered a defensive war Christian and justifiable. Many wealthy Quaker merchants in Philadelphia joined the preliminary non-importation measures, for such methods of passive resistance suited their principles. Two Quaker firms were the consignees of the tea sent to Philadelphia in 1773, both of whom agreed to the citizens' decree that the tea should not be landed. The Friends were not only opposed to war, but were also against revolution, the latter position based probably on the advice of George Fox that, "Whatsoever bustlings or troubles or tumults or outrages should rise in the world keep out of them." This seemed to put the Friends not only in opposition to the war but also to the new government, set up for the purpose of independence. Their opposition was not active, however, and many of them undoubtedly sympathized with the American cause, but likewise there were doubtless many loyalists at heart.

During the early years of the war many were expelled from the Monthly Meetings for paying war taxes, or placing guns for protection on their vessels; for paying fines in lieu of military service or in any way aiding in the war on either side. Thomas Mifflin, who later became a general and governor of Pennsylvania, was one of the first to go. Altogether there were four or five hundred Quakers who came out for the American side, and probably not more than a half dozen who joined the British army. Some of the "disowned" Friends formed a society known as the Free Quakers, who followed the old Quaker customs as to worship and business but encouraged its members in the performance of their military duties.

They built a meeting-house on Arch Street in Philadelphia to which both Washington and Franklin subscribed. Among the original members of this society was Betsy Ross, but eventually their numbers dwindled and worship was discontinued (1836).

When the war came to Philadelphia in 1777 and 1778 the Quakers suffered from both sides. A number of leading Quakers accused of being friendly to the British were arrested on the approach of General Howe and sent to Winchester, Virginia, where they were confined during the winter. Nothing was ever proved against them, however, though some of them may have desired the success of the British. When the British army left Philadelphia in the spring of 1778, and the Americans reëntered the city, extreme revolutionists gained control and the Quaker residents were made to suffer. Rufus M. Jones estimates the property loss to Quakers at not less than £50,000, from fines and distraits and foraging parties. Quaker school teachers were imprisoned for refusal to take a test of allegiance; others were arrested and confined to prison for months without trial; Friends were elected to offices which it was known they would not accept and were then fined for non-compliance. As is always the case in time of war, the position of the conscientious objector was misunderstood though the courage required to maintain such a position is far greater and finer than that which sweeps men along with the popular current.

The Mennonites scattered through the Pennsylvania German counties held principles similar to that of the Quakers regarding war. Most of them, no doubt, sympathized with the American side, though there were a few out-and-out Tories among them who at the close of the war migrated to Canada. In 1776 the first split among American Mennonites occurred over the question whether Mennonites should pay the war tax. One group led by Christian Funk contended that the tax should be paid, stating that "Were Christ here, He would say, give to Congress that which belongs to Congress and to God that which belongs to God." The opposition party, however, were in the majority and Funk and his followers were expelled and formed their own congregations. As a whole, the Mennonites were treated leniently by the state authorities, since it was known that most of them were at heart loyal, though some of the horses and wagons of the rich Mennonite farmers were pressed into service by the quartermaster during the Pennsylvania campaigns.

Of all the non-resistant groups the Moravians suffered most in the American Revolution, though directly and indirectly they rendered great service to the American cause. Their buildings at Bethlehem were used as a general hospital for the American army during several years of the war while they cheerfully responded to numerous requisitions for supplies. It was through their Indian missions, however, that they rendered their greatest service. Zeisberger was responsible for keeping the Delawares from taking up the hatchet in the early years of the war, a service that later won generous recognition. Twice during the war Zeisberger and the other Moravian missionaries were taken to Detroit accused of being American spies, but in both instances he and his associates were successful in establishing their innocence. The war bore particularly hard upon the Moravian Indians. Frequently they persuaded Indian war parties to turn back, and on several occasions warned settlements of projected raids. This they did not do because of a preference for one side or the other in the contest, but because of their humanitarian principles. This, of course, was misunderstood by the British as well as the Americans and they were forced into the British lines, where they spent a dreadful winter, almost without food. Later they were allowed to return to their villages on the Tuscarawas in Ohio. Here after hospitably receiving a company of American militiamen, who the Indians thought had come to assist them, they were herded into two buildings and butchered in cold blood, only two boys of the whole number escaping to tell the sad tale. Thus were they rewarded for their loyalty to what they had been taught was the teaching and will of Christ.

✛✛✛✛✛✛✛✛✛✛✛✛✛✛✛✛✛✛✛✛✛✛✛✛✛✛✛✛✛✛✛✛✛✛

Chapter XIII

THE NATIONALIZATION OF THE AMERICAN CHURCHES

IN NINE of the American colonies at the opening of the War for Independence there were established churches. Congregationalism was established in three of the New England colonies, the Anglican in five of the southern colonies and New York. In every case the political connections of these churches were with the colonial governments rather than with the mother country, so that when the colonies became independent states that change did not affect the relationship of the churches to the governments. Nor did the war in itself make any change in the religious situation in any of the colonies, but it was inevitable that "the shock of revolution would necessarily loosen the bonds which bound unwilling multitudes to any church establishment with which they had no sympathy."

Increased agitation for the separation of church and state began with the opening of the war, especially in New England and Virginia. In New England the forces for separation were led by Isaac Backus, the agent of the Baptist churches in Massachusetts and Rhode Island, assisted by several of the other leading Baptists, among

{274}

them President Manning of Rhode Island College. The agitation was continued throughout the war, the Baptists bombarding the Massachusetts assemblies particularly with the memorials and petitions, but Congregationalism was too firmly intrenched with the majority of the people to be endangered at this time. The New England Congregational ministers and church members generally were on the American side, while in most instances the New England political leaders were likewise affiliated with the state church. In the Massachusetts constitution, adopted in the very midst of the Revolution (1779), article three asserts "the right and duty of the legislature to authorize and require the several towns, parishes, precincts, and other bodies politic, or religious societies to make suitable provision at their own expense, for the instruction of the public worship of God." The Baptists protested against this article, but to no immediate avail, and it was not until 1833 that Massachusetts provided for disestablishment. In New Hampshire disestablishment came in 1817 and in Connecticut in 1818.

In most of the colonies where the Episcopal Church was established by law, disestablishment came with more or less ease. In the southernmost colonies, in Maryland and in New York disestablishment came early in the war, but in Virginia the struggle was prolonged and bitter. The rapidity with which the Presbyterians, Baptists and Methodists increased in the southern colonies and especially in Virginia, in the two decades previous to the Revolution, was a determining factor in the struggle. Before the Declaration of Independence, however, the Baptists were alone in demanding the separation of church and state. The Presbyterians were simply demanding their rights under the Act of Toleration and nothing more, while the Methodists were still nominally a part of the Anglican establishment, and seemed at first to favor its continuance. With the close of the Revolution these three dissenting bodies, and especially the Baptists and Presbyterians, united in the fight for complete religious liberty.

In Virginia the dissenting bodies were greatly aided in their struggle by such statesmen as George Mason, James Madison, Patrick Henry and Thomas Jefferson all of whom had become thoroughly convinced of the desirability of religious liberty. In 1776 the Virginia Convention incorporated the philosophy of religious liberty into its organic law as article sixteen, introduced by Mason and amended by Madison, which declared:

That religion, or the duty which we owe our creator, and the manner of discharging it, can be directed only by reason, and conviction, not by force or violence; and therefore, all men are equally entitled to the free exercise of religion according to the dictates of conscience; and that it is the duty of all to practice Christian forbearance, love, and charity towards each other.

But it is one thing to endorse a philosophy and quite another to put that philosophy into practical operation, and the Baptists, especially were not satisfied to let matters rest with simply a declaration; they were soon asking how this philosophy of religious equality was to be applied. Accordingly when the first Virginia legislature met under the new constitution petitions were numerously presented from Baptist associations and churches and also from Presbyterians and Lutherans asking for the disestablishment of the state church. A bill was soon introduced and passed repealing all laws forcing dissenters to contribute to the support of the state church, but this was not enough to satisfy the dissenters; they were now demanding complete religious equality and nothing else would suffice.

For the next three years (1776-1779) petitions flooded the Virginia Assembly, from churches, associations, presbyteries, and conferences urging complete disestablishment, while the Anglicans, now thoroughly aroused to the danger confronting them, were equally active in behalf of their cause. The next step in the process of disestablishment was the passage on December 13, 1779, of an act repealing portions of the "Act for the support of the Clergy and for the regular collecting and paying the Parish Levies," and all and every other act or acts providing salaries for the ministers, and authorizing the vestries to lay the same. Thus were the purse strings of the establishment cut. But even yet there was not equality, for there were certain grievances still existing in the civil laws and these were now subject to the attack of the dissenters led by the Baptists. Laws were still in existence prohibiting dissenting ministers from performing marriage ceremonies, while the Episcopalian vestries in the several Virginia counties were in charge of certain public duties, and these vestries were closed corporations.

The final struggle over the issue came between the years 1779 and 1785. In the former year several bills were offered, among them one prepared by Thomas Jefferson which was finally to be written into the laws of Virginia, as the "Bill for Establishing Religious Freedom." But the road to the passage of this famous measure was long and painful, and for six years it was discussed pro and con both in and out of legislative halls. In 1784 the cause was almost lost through the introduction of a bill providing for a general assessment for the teaching of religion. According to this measure, persons might declare the denomination to which they wished their assessment to go, but if no declaration were made the money would be used to encourage schools in their respective counties. Washington could see nothing wrong with this measure and it was likewise supported by Marshall, Patrick Henry and Richard Henry Lee, but Madison and Jefferson were against it. At first certain of the Presbyterian clergy favored it, but as usual the Baptists saw the flaw in the measure and stood staunchly in opposition. Madison, writing to Monroe concerning the situation, states: "The Episcopal people are generally for it though I think the zeal of some of them has cooled. The laity of the other sects are generally unanimous on the other side. So are all the clergy except the Presbyterians, who seem as ready to set up an establishment which is to take them in as they were to pull down that which shut them out." The Baptists, however, standing firmly by their avowed principle of the complete separation of church and state, declared it "to be repugnant to the spirit of the Gospel for the Legislature thus to proceed in matters of religion, that no human laws ought to be established for this purpose." The Hanover Presbytery now passed strong resolutions opposing the bill which were later approved by the Virginia Presbyterian Convention. This combined opposi-

PIONEERS OF THE OLD WEST
From Howard Pyle, *Book of The American Spirit* (Harper &
Brothers, 1923)

tion finally succeeded in defeating the measure though by a majority of only three votes.

The way was now open for the final victory and on December 17, 1785, Jefferson's measure was passed, and on January 19, 1786, was signed by the Speaker and became law. Section II reads thus:

We the General Assembly of Virginia, do enact that no man shall be compelled to frequent or support any religious worship, place or ministry whatsoever, nor shall be enforced, restrained, molested or burdened in his body or goods, nor shall otherwise suffer on account of his religious opinions or belief; but that all men shall be free to profess, and by argument to maintain, their opinions in matters of religion, and that the same shall in no wise diminish, enlarge or effect their civil capacities.

Religious freedom had triumphed in Virginia and was soon to spread throughout the nation, and a few years later in the form of the first amendment to the Federal Constitution was to become a part of the fundamental law of the land. At the time of the passage of the measure Jefferson, its author, was in France, but so proud was he of his part in the memorable struggle that he asked that it be recorded on his gravestone: "Thomas Jefferson, Author of the Declaration of Independence, of the Statute of Virginia for Religious Freedom, and Father of the University of Virginia." But justice compels the admission that Jefferson's part in this accomplishment was not so great as was that of James Madison, nor were the contributions of either or both as important as was that of the humble people called Baptists.

The years immediately following the close of the War

for Independence was a period of general constitution making, in the nation, among the states and in the ecclesiastical bodies. Several of the American churches had, previous to independence, Old World connections. Thus the Episcopalians had been subject to the Bishop of London; the Roman Catholics to the Vicar Apostolic of London; the Methodists were under the control of John Wesley; the Reformed churches had connections with the Classis of Amsterdam, while the Presbyterians, Quakers, and Lutherans were not so specifically tied to Old World organizations. The Congregationalists and Baptists were, of course, indigenous American churches with each congregation theoretically independent.

The first American religious body to form a national organization was the Methodists and their priority in this respect is due to the fact that their national organization was largely worked out for them by Mr. Wesley. At the close of the Revolution the Methodists in America, as well as those in Great Britain, were still a part of the Anglican body. Francis Asbury and the other American preachers were unordained men and their societies were dependent upon Anglican clergymen for the administration of the sacraments. But during the war the Anglican Church was so disrupted and so many of the clergymen fled that the growing body of Methodists had no way of securing the ordinances of the church. This situation became so serious that a movement was begun in the South under the leadership of William Watters to declare complete independence of Wesley and the English Church and to ordain ministers, to administer the sacraments. In 1779 Asbury, in semi-exile in Delaware, called a small body of preachers together in a conference, to elect him General Assistant for America, and on this basis Asbury claimed authority over the whole body of American Methodists. A much larger group of preachers met in Fluvanna, Virginia, a little later in the same year, took no notice of the northern conference or the selection of Asbury as assistant and proceeded to take steps looking toward ordination of ministers. Schism was threatened, but in the end a peaceful settlement of differences was reached and the southern preachers agreed to delay their action regarding ordination and to recognize Asbury as Wesley's assistant. Such was the situation when the war closed.

On the close of the war, Wesley immediately turned his attention to the American problem. He again assumed control of his American followers and advised that none be received who made any "difficulty of receiving Francis Asbury as the General Assistant." He then proceeded to provide an organization for the American Methodists suitable to their independence. After thorough consideration he decided that under the situation he as a presbyter of the Church of England had the right to ordain ministers for America. This right he based on the precedent of the Alexandrian Church where bishops had been ordained by presbyters. Accordingly he called together two ordained clergymen of the Church of England, who were associated with him, Thomas Coke and James Creighton, and they assisted him in the ordination of Richard Whatcoat and Thomas Vasey as deacons, and the next day as elders. Two days later Creighton and Whatcoat assisted in ordaining Coke as superintendent of the Methodist

Societies in America. Wesley's next step was to remodel the Thirty-nine Articles of the Church of England, reducing them to twenty-four, leaving out all reference to Calvinistic teaching. He also prepared a "Sunday Service" which was an abridged form of the English liturgy and compiled a hymn book "full-freighted with Methodist theology," and these he sent with Coke, Whatcoat and Vasey to America. With them also he sent a letter to "Dr. Coke, Mr. Asbury, and our brethren in North America" in which he explains his action: "I have," he says, "appointed Dr. Coke and Mr. Francis Asbury to be joint superintendents over our brethren in North America; as also Richard Whatcoat and Thomas Vasey to act as elders among them by baptizing and administering the Lord's Supper. I have prepared a liturgy, little differing from that of the Church of England (I think the best constituted national church in the world), which I advise all the travelling preachers to use on Lord's Day in all congregations."

Dr. Coke and his two companions landed in New York, November 3, 1784. A week later they met Asbury in Barrett's Chapel in Delaware where Coke unfolded Wesley's plan for the American Church. It was decided that before the plan could be put into operation it must be accepted by the preachers, and we are told that Freeborn Garrettson was sent out "like an arrow" to summon the preachers to meet in Baltimore, December 24, 1784. On the day assigned the "Christmas" Conference opened; Coke read Wesley's letter, which made a profound impression on the fifty odd preachers present. It was agreed to follow Mr. Wesley's advice and form an Episcopal

Church, the name, Methodist Episcopal being suggested by John Dickins. Asbury refused to accept Wesley's appointment as superintendent and the conference then proceeded to elect both Coke and Asbury to that office. Asbury was now ordained deacon, elder and superintendent, on succeeding days, while twelve other preachers were elected and ordained elders and three to the order of deacons. A form of discipline was drawn up and adopted; the twenty-four articles of religion drawn by Wesley with one additional, making twenty-five, were accepted, together with the Sunday Service and hymns. After enacting some other regulations the Christmas Conference adjourned, having been in session ten days. Jesse Lee the first historian of American Methodism states that "The Methodists were pretty generally pleased at our becoming a Church, and heartily united together in the plan which the Conference had adopted, and from that time religion greatly revived." Though Wesley remained in nominal control of the American Methodists until his death, yet as a matter of fact the work of the Christmas Conference practically severed the connection of the American Methodists with their founder. They accepted most of Wesley's suggestions, it is true, but they did so as free agents, and three years later we find them annulling the agreement to obey Wesley in matters of church government.

Of all the American churches the Episcopalian suffered most as a result of the Revolution. The S. P. G. missionaries left the country almost to a man, at the opening of the war, leaving deserted the country parishes, outside Virginia and Maryland. At the opening of the war, in

Virginia there were 95 parishes, 164 churches and chapels and 91 clergymen. When the war closed 23 of the 95 parishes were either forsaken or extinct and of the remainder only 34 had ministers. Everywhere also the church had suffered in its prestige. It had been the church of the royal officials and this fact alone was a severe blow to its popularity. It is interesting to observe that in the reorganization of the Episcopal Church the strongest leadership came from the states in which there had been no establishment.

The outstanding Anglican leader in America at the close of the Revolution was Dr. William White, the rector of Christ Church in Philadelphia. He was born and educated in America, and began his ministry in 1772 as assistant minister at Christ Church, where he became the rector on the retirement of Mr. Duché to England after the Declaration of Independence. Toward the close of the war (1782) White wrote a pamphlet, published anonymously, called "The Case of the Episcopal Church Considered." This pamphlet outlined an organization for the American Episcopal Church and proposed that since there was no immediate prospect of obtaining an American bishop that, as a temporary expedient, the church be organized without. This pamphlet has particular significance since the form of organization it proposed was that later followed, though it was not necessary to proceed without a bishop. Later White explained that the non-episcopal ordination he proposed was simply to be considered as conditional, though he never gave up his liberal views on the subject, and stated that "a temporary departure from Episcopacy would have been warranted by the Church of England's doctrines and practices." His proposal of lay representation in the annual assemblies and in the national convention indicates the influence of the new American spirit in government.

At about the same time, Dr. William Smith, formerly the provost of the College of Philadelphia but now in Maryland, called a conference of clergymen and laymen of that state (November 9, 1780) to petition the General Assembly for an act empowering the vestries and wardens to raise money to keep in repair the churches which were rapidly falling into ruin. It was in this petition that the name "Protestant Episcopal Church" was first used, probably at the suggestion of Dr. Smith. In August, 1783, a second convention of Maryland clergymen met in Annapolis and adopted a "Declaration of Certain Fundamental Rights and Liberties," in which they declare their independence of the church in any other state, and here also Dr. William Smith was chosen bishop elect for Maryland.

A third movement looking toward the reorganization of the Episcopal Church took place in Connecticut just as the war closed. The Connecticut churches had been largely manned by native clergymen, working under the S. P. G. and ten of these earnest men, several of whom had been loyalists in the war, met at the home of one of their number in December, 1783, and there selected two men, either of whom was to go to England to secure episcopal consecration. One of the two selected, the Rev. Jeremiah Leaming, declined because of his age, but the other, Samuel Seabury, Jr., accepted the charge and the next spring sailed for England. He bore with him letters from the clergy of Connecticut and New York to the Archbishop of Canterbury. Though politely received by the English ecclesiastical authorities they hesitated and then finally refused his request for consecration, on the ground, first, that the oaths of allegiance to the king, in the ordination office, placed there by Parliamentary Act could not be omitted, and second, they felt that before they could consecrate a bishop for Connecticut that state should indicate its consent. Seabury now turned to the non-juring bishops of Scotland, the descendants of the Scotch bishops, who in 1688 had refused to disown James II or to take the oath of allegiance to William of Orange. The church had been disestablished in Scotland because of its participation in the uprisings of 1715 and 1745, but there was no doubt as to the validity of their orders. Seabury's consecration took place on November 14, 1784, in the house of John Skinner, Coadjutor Bishop of Aberdeen, with Bishops Skinner and Kilgour as consecrators. Bishop Seabury returned home at once and on August 3, 1785, held the first convocation of his clergy with no laymen present. Seabury's consecration was not at all pleasing to several of the other church leaders in America, who felt that his course during the Revolution would still further discredit the church in the eyes of the people.

The first step in the formation of a national organization was the calling of a convention to be held in New York in October, 1784, to which eight states sent representatives, there being twenty-six delegates in all, eleven of them laymen. The basis for the discussion of the delegates was a series of resolutions which had been adopted by a Pennsylvania meeting under the leadership of Dr. White and sent to the several states. The Seabury movement could not have resulted in a national church, for reasons already indicated. The New York Convention adopted a general plan for a national organization which called for a general Episcopal Church for the United States, to be governed by clerical and lay representatives from each state; while the liturgy and doctrines of the Church of England were adopted so far as they were consistent with the changed political situation in the United States. This plan was now sent to the several states to be ratified and if adopted they were to elect delegates to a General Convention to convene September 27, 1785, at Philadelphia.

The Philadelphia Convention opened on the appointed day with seven states represented by sixteen clergymen and twenty-four laymen, and William White was chosen to preside. Bishop Seabury's consecration was a serious complication, and although he had been invited to the Philadelphia convention, neither he nor any representatives from the New England states was present. The great work of the convention was the preparation of the "Ecclesiastical Constitution of the Protestant Episcopal Church in the United States of America," which provided for equal lay representation in the governing body. The Prayer Book submitted was never adopted, though it was published, but never widely used. The second session of the constitutional convention met in Philadelphia in June, 1786, and in October at Wilmington, Delaware, when some slight alterations were made in the constitution. Meanwhile other bishops had been elected by the state assemblies, in addition to William Smith of Maryland. These were William White for Pennsylvania, Samuel Provoost for New York and Dr. Griffith for Virginia. Griffith because of ill health and poverty never went to England for consecration, while Smith, as bishop-elect for Maryland, was refused certification on grounds of conduct, but White and Provoost sailed for England in November, 1786, and through the help of John Adams, then minister to the Court of St. James, their consecration took place in Lambeth Palace, February 4, 1787. On their return the two new bishops received a letter from Bishop Seabury expressing anxiety for the unity of the church. Bishop Provoost had been bitterly hostile to Bishop Seabury because of his Toryism, but two years later (1789) Seabury was invited and accepted the invitation to attend the national convention and here the new constitution was adopted. Bishop Seabury was recognized and thus was consummated the union of the Protestant Episcopal Church in the United States.

No religious body was so well fitted to meet the new problems of independent America as the Presbyterians. They had supported the Revolution with almost complete unanimity; they had an American-educated and able leadership, imbued with the American spirit. For these reasons the task of forming a national organization was comparatively simple. Nor had any church grown more rapidly. Between 1758 and 1789 two hundred and thirty new ministers had been ordained and new presbyteries were forming in the west and south. Redstone Presbytery in southwestern Pennsylvania was founded in 1781 while at the close of the war two Kentucky presbyteries were organized, Transylvania and Lexington. The Synod of New York and Philadelphia was the most important Presbyterian body in the country, though there were several other Presbyterian bodies, such as the Associate and Associate Reformed synods, two conservative bodies representing the Covenanters and the Seceders and also the German and Dutch Reformed churches.

In the process of reorganization Dr. Witherspoon, president of the College of New Jersey, was the leading spirit, though Duffield and Ewing of Philadelphia and Rodgers of New York gave powerful assistance. At the meeting of the synod of New York and Philadelphia in 1785 he headed a committee to devise a system of general rules for the government of the synods, presbyteries and churches, which was to report at the next yearly meeting. The next year (1786) the boundaries of the presbyteries were rearranged, so that the number was increased from twelve to sixteen, and these were grouped into four synods, while it was provided that there should be a General Assembly consisting of ministerial and ruling elders, elected annually by the presbyteries. At this session of the synod also a committee was appointed, again headed by Witherspoon, to prepare "a book of discipline and government . . . accommodated to the state of the Presbyterian Church in America." This committee met in September (1786) and prepared and published a draft of their government and discipline, which was distributed through the church, for consideration, in preparation for its discussion the following year. The next year (1787), after full discussion, some alterations were made and again copies of the amended instrument were sent to the presbyteries and churches for further discussion. Finally at the Synod of 1788 the Confession of Faith, somewhat amended in the matter of the civil magistrate's relation to the church, the longer Catechism also somewhat amended, the shorter Catechism, the Directory of Worship and the Form of Government and Discipline, were adopted. Thus by 1788, the year in which the Federal Constitution was being ratified by the states, the Presbyterian Church had adopted a form of government for a great national church.

It has sometimes been suggested that there is an intimate relationship between the constitution of the Presbyterians and the Federal Constitution. The constitution-making period in the Presbyterian Church and in the nation covers the same years, 1785-1788; both constitutions were formulated in the city of Philadelphia, while it is undoubtedly true that such well-informed men as James Madison and James Wilson must have been familiar with the Presbyterian forms of government. But it is also true that the Episcopalians were likewise engaged in constitution-making at the same time, and in the same place, and a like claim might be made for their influence. As a matter of fact, there must have been a large interplay of influence, which we are not now able to trace definitely but which any fair inference is justified in assuming.

The constitution-making period in the Dutch Reformed Church was between the years 1784 and 1792. At the close of the war the governing bodies of the church were given titles which indicated their independence, and in 1788 a committee was appointed to translate and publish the creeds and articles of church government and in doing this it was found neeessary to modify the articles in order to adapt them to the American Church. This work was completed in 1792 and was adopted.

The German Reformed body were slow in breaking their Old World connections, because of the lack of leadership and also because a majority of their ministers were still receiving financial assistance from the Holland authorities. An important step was taken in 1787 in the founding of Franklin College at Lancaster, Pennsylvania, which began as a joint institution under the auspices of both Lutheran and Reformed, and received the name Franklin because Benjamin Franklin had given the largest sum for its establishment. When the American Coetus in 1789 informed the Holland Classis that steps must be taken to form a national organization, the suggestion was ignored, but three years later, no word having come from Holland, a committee was appointed to draw up rules for a national church, which were adopted the next year, when the new synod met at Lancaster. The name chosen was "The Synod of the Reformed Church in the United States." In 1795 the Heidelberg Catechism was reissued and the first edition in English was published in 1810.

When the Revolution began the elder Mühlenberg was supervising seventy Lutheran congregations in Pennsylvania and adjacent colonies, while in other sections there were some thirty other congregations. A semi-synodical organization, known as the Ministerium of Pennsylvania, —which had no formal constitution,—had been formed in 1748 designed to include Lutheran ministers throughout the colonies, while in 1781 a constitution was adopted, providing for clerical representation only. In 1792 a new constitution was adopted and amended in 1796, providing for lay representation in the synodical meetings, an indication that the Lutherans were being influenced by the democratic spirit of the new nation. At the same time the name "German" was attached to their official name which had not previously been used, an indication of a fear that English influence might become dominant. Later the language question caused a bitter fight in the denomination and even today it has not been completely solved. The adoption of this constitution also marks the end of European control of the American Lutheran churches. The movement toward gathering the Lutheran churches into separate state organizations was begun in 1786 with the formation of the Ministerium of New York; was continued in 1803 by the formation of the Synod of North Carolina, in 1818 by the Synod of Ohio and in 1820 by the Synod of Maryland and that of Tennessee. In the latter year the first General Synod, uniting four state synods, was organized, which was the only general Lutheran body in America to the Civil War.

The small body of American Moravians were hampered at the close of the war and for a number of years afterward by the domination of the governing board in Germany and by the continuance of the use of the German language in their worship, while the laymen had no voice in the management of the affairs of the church. There was also a lack of well-qualified ministers. For these reasons the Moravians failed to grow, and the Moravian Church is the best example among the churches of the folly of resisting the rising spirit of nationalism in

America as it manifested itself in the years following the Revolution.

The Quakers also continued their connection with the mother church in England and in 1784 there were ten Americans present at the London Yearly Meeting. This relationship, however, did not really affect the independence of the American Friends in their Yearly Meetings, but was largely for the purpose of spiritual encouragement and advice.

At the close of the Revolution the number of Catholics in the United States numbered some twenty-four thousand, the great majority being found in Maryland and Pennsylvania. There were twenty-four clergy, most of them former members of the Society of Jesus, for when the Order was suppressed in 1773 the individual members became diocesan priests. The nominal head of the American Catholic body was the Vicar Apostolic in London, but he was completely inactive and in order to secure their property in America the American ex-Jesuits formed themselves into a legal corporation. The American Catholics, being a small body throughout the colonial period, were naturally favorable to religious toleration and had become thoroughly imbued with the growing idea of the separation of church and state. They gave almost unanimous support to the War for Independence and a number of their leaders had taken a conspicuous part in the Revolutionary cause in Maryland, especially the Carroll family.

With the close of the war the Vicar Apostolic of London declared that he would no longer exercise jurisdiction in the United States, and the American priests began at once a movement, largely led by John Carroll, to form an American Roman Catholic organization. John Carroll was a member of the well-known Maryland Carrolls, and was born in 1735 in Prince George county. His education was received in a Jesuit school in Cecil county, Maryland, and was later sent to St. Omer's College in France. After studying in several Jesuit institutions he became a priest of that order at the age of twenty-eight and for fourteen years was a professor in Jesuit institutions at Liége and Bruges. When his order was suppressed he returned to Maryland where the opening of the Revolution found him.

The first action looking toward a plan of government for the American Catholics was a meeting held at White-marsh, Maryland, June 27, 1783, where a plan was drawn up and submitted to the priests of Maryland and Pennsylvania. Later in the same year two other meetings were held and a committee was named to petition the Pope to appoint the Rev. John Lewis as "Superior" with power to confirm, bless chalices and impart faculties to the priests in the mission. The petition was referred to the "Congregatio de Propaganda Fide," the organization in Rome having in charge the missionary activities of the church. Instead of appointing Lewis, John Carroll, to his surprise, was appointed Superior, the reason being the great age of Lewis and the influence exercised by Franklin, the American minister in Paris. Franklin had become involved in a scheme to subordinate the American Catholic Church to the French, but the American Congress, by refusing to act in a matter of religion, fortunately caused the scheme to fail.

With Carroll's appointment (June 6, 1784) the English jurisdiction over the American Church ceased. Carroll's power as Superior was limited and though at first inclined to decline such a doubtful honor he was finally led to accept. Accompanying his letter of acceptance he enclosed a description of religious conditions in the United States, in which he gives the number of Catholics in the country as 15,800 in Maryland, 1,500 in New York, 7,000 in Pennsylvania, and 200 in Virginia. There were nineteen priests in Maryland and five in Pennsylvania. The authorities in Rome replying to this letter, informed Carroll of the intention of the Pope to appoint him as first bishop, which was done November 6, 1789, after he had been selected for that office by the American priests as a special concession from the Pope. They were also allowed, in this case, to name the seat of the first American See, and Baltimore was the choice. On August 15, 1790, Carroll was consecrated in the chapel of Lulworth Castle, England, by the Vicar Apostolic of London. With Carroll's return to America in December, 1790, the American Catholics had secured as their first bishop a leader admirably fitted for the peculiar task which America presented.

Strange to say, New England Congregationalism seemed to be little affected by the nationalizing tendencies and centralizing influences of the period, in spite of the fact that federalism was more strongly intrenched in New England than perhaps in any other section of the country. The Congregational leaders, such as Nathaniel Emmons and Jonathan Edwards the younger, were emphasizing the pure democracy of Congregationalism, and

in Massachusetts particularly the tendency was to reassert
the old emphasis upon the independence of each congregation. Emmons had trained in his home more than one
hundred young men for the ministry, and no one exercised greater influence in Congregationalism. In 1803 in
his fight to oppose the establishment of state associations
in Massachusetts he stated:

Association leads to Consociation; Consociation leads to
Presbyterianism; Presbyterianism leads to Episcopacy; Episcopacy leads to Roman Catholicism; and Roman Catholicism
is an ultimate fact.

Even in Connecticut the decentralizing tendency was
abroad and in 1784 the law establishing the state association was repealed. This failure on the part of Congregationalism effectively to unite in these years of national
expansion proved a blow to the growth of the denomination. Later there arose an impulse to unite into voluntary
missionary societies, but such organizations were no
match for the more highly developed denominational
machinery of the Presbyterians and Methodists and even
of the Baptists.

The Baptists in the period of the Revolution and during the years following had developed a distinct national
spirit and to a certain degree a national organization.
This had come about in spite of Baptist theory of the
complete independence of each congregation, due to their
leadership in the fight for religious liberty and the separation of church and state. In order to carry on this fight
effectively an organization that was strong enough to
bring pressure to bear upon the new state governments

was found necessary. Thus there arose the Warren Association, made up of the Baptist churches in New England. In Virginia a General Committee of Baptists was in existence from 1784 to 1799 which was made up of delegates from the several Baptist Associations. This General Committee was responsible for effecting a union between the Regular and Separate Baptists in Virginia, and carried on correspondence with Baptist churches all over the United States. In a sense this committee represented the Baptists in the United States and in that capacity sent an address to the newly elected president, and President Washington in his reply addressed the Baptists all over the nation. This was also a period of great activity in the organization of Baptist associations and between 1774 and 1789 nineteen were organized and the movement continued as Baptist people moved westward into the new regions beyond the Alleghanies.

✛✛✛✛✛✛✛✛✛✛✛✛✛✛✛✛✛✛✛✛✛✛✛✛✛✛✛✛✛✛✛✛✛✛✛✛✛

Chapter XIV

THE WESTERN MOVEMENT OF POPULATION AND THE RISE OF THE POPULAR CHURCHES

THE treaty which closed the Revolution fixed the western boundary of the United States at the Mississippi River, but in this vast expanse of territory there was only a very narrow line of settlements, with many breaks between, scattered along the eastern seaboard from Maine to Georgia. In the first general census taken in 1790 it was found that there were in round numbers 4,000,000 people in the United States, and the enumeration revealed that population was moving rapidly westward in three distinct streams. One stream made up largely of New England people, was pushing out along the valley of the Mohawk, a second passed through southern Pennsylvania and Maryland, while a third was observed going westward through the Valley of Virginia and by way of the passes over the Blue Ridge into Kentucky and Tennessee. These were largely Virginians and North Carolinians. The census also showed that five per cent of the total population were already living west of the mountains, in southwestern Pennsylvania, in western Virginia, and in the present states of Kentucky and Tennessee.

This western movement, noted in the first census, continued with increasing momentum for the next four decades. Previous to 1795 the largest percentage of population was going into the region south of the Ohio. The general economic distress along the eastern seaboard following the Revolution set in motion this westward movement. In the northern and middle states the movement was soon checked by the return of better times, due to the restoration of credit and the opening of the West Indian trade, which called for such products as fish, lumber, horses, wheat, flour and other foodstuffs, the staple products of these states. As a result wages were good and work plentiful and the discontent which always produces emigration largely disappeared. But in the South hard times continued, for the people here were neither ship-owners nor shipbuilders, while the products of the South were similar to those of the West Indies. For these reasons emigration from Virginia, Maryland, and the Carolinas continued over the passes of the Blue Ridge which soon furnished to Kentucky and Tennessee a population sufficient for their admission into the Union, Kentucky in 1792, Tennessee in 1796.

When the Ordinance of 1787 was adopted, which created a government for the territory north of the Ohio River, known as the Old Northwest, a population began to move into that region. In the year previous to the adoption of the famous ordinance a land company, called the Ohio Company, had been organized in one of the taverns of Boston by a group of New Englanders. This company purchased a large section of land in what is now southeastern Ohio, and there in 1788 at the mouth of the Muskingum their first settlement was formed and called Marietta. The first settlers were New Englanders and were typical representatives of the New England movement westward.

The great movement of population into the region north of the Ohio, however, did not begin until after General Wayne's victory over the Miami Confederacy at the Battle of Fallen Timbers, August 20, 1794, and the signing of the Treaty of Greenville the next year. This treaty opened up more than half of Ohio and a narrow strip in southeastern Indiana to settlement. The second census revealed that in the ten years from 1790 to 1800 an immense movement of population had taken place; Kentucky now had a population of 220,955; Tennessee, 105,602; Ohio, 45,365; while Indiana had more than five thousand and Mississippi territory, the region south of Tennessee, contained more than eight thousand. The town of Lexington, Kentucky, boasted 1,750 souls, Cincinnati, 500, while Pittsburgh claimed more than 1,500. The early movement westward was made up largely of native Americans, for the non-English strains, except the Scotch-Irish, had largely disappeared except in Pennsylvania as there had been little immigration in the previous twenty years.

The third census (1810) showed that emigration had gone steadily forward, especially from Massachusetts and Connecticut in New England, and from New York, Pennsylvania, Virginia and the Carolinas. The Ohio River was the great highway westward, people floating down the river in great flatboats, filling up all southern Ohio, which had already been admitted to statehood (1802), raising Indiana to a territory of the second grade, over-running Tennessee and Kentucky and pushing southward into northern Alabama. The New England element had also filled more than half of the "Western Reserve" along the south shore of Lake Erie while their Marietta settlements were greatly extended and other New Englanders were now to be found here and there scattered through central and southern Ohio.

But the greatest movement of population westward was yet to come. This began with the passage of the embargo (1808) and continued with little interruption throughout the War of 1812, until indeed the return of good times in the East, which did not come until about 1820. Nothing like it had ever been seen before. The roads westward swarmed with wagons, cattle, sheep and horses. Through one Pennsylvania village lying on the road to Pittsburgh, toward the end of 1811, two hundred and thirty-six wagons and six hundred Merino sheep had passed on the way to Ohio in one day. Old settlers in central New York declared that they had never seen "so many teams, and sleighs loaded with women, children and household goods" on their way to Ohio, as in the winter of 1814. All winter long the movement westward continued and throughout the next summer, all journeying to Ohio, which was then but another name for the West. During the month of July, 1814, six wagons with seventy persons, all from Massachusetts, passed through Newburgh bound for the West, while from Lancaster, Pennsylvania, came the report that a hundred families had passed through that town in one week; at Zanesville, Ohio, fifty wagons crossed the Muskingum in one day. "All

America," said a European observer in 1817, "seems to be breaking up and moving westward."

Towns sprang up in the new country almost overnight, while the older states were beginning to become alarmed at the great loss of population. In North Carolina in 1815 the assembly appointed a committee to investigate the matter, as did also Virginia. It is estimated that in 1816, 42,000 settlers came to Indiana alone, while the increase in population in the five states of the Old Northwest from 1810 to 1830 was sixfold. In 1816 Indiana was admitted to the Union with a population of 63,897 and two years later a census in Illinois placed the population at 40,258. Again as in 1814 even winter weather failed to stop the movement westward. Some of the settlers went on foot, drawing their small belongings in carts while during this winter (1817) a train of sixty wagons carrying one hundred and twenty souls, men, women and children, journeyed to Indiana, carrying their minister with them, where they planned to buy a township. These are but examples of the many thousands who set their faces westward during the years between 1808 and 1820.

The fourth census (1820) was startling to the eastern states. New York had become the most populous state in the Union, crowding out Virginia from that distinction, and had added 413,000 people. Ohio came next in the total increase of population, adding 351,000, and now ranked fifth among the states in the Union, while Kentucky was sixth, having added a population of 158,000. In 1821 the total number of states in the Union numbered twenty-five, and of the twelve new states, ten were west of the Alleghanies. These were critical years in the history of the American churches, for the future of the nation as well as the future of religion in America was largely to be determined by the way in which organized religion met the problem of the new West. And the churches which met this problem most adequately were the ones destined to become the great American churches.

THE PRESBYTERIANS

Of all the American churches at the opening of the national era, the Presbyterian was the most strategically located for an immediate advance into the West. The Scotch-Irish constituted the last great wave of emigration previous to the Revolution, and by 1760 Scotch-Irish Presbyterian churches were to be found scattered along from "the frontiers of New England to the frontiers of South Carolina." In 1766 the Rev. Charles Beatty and Mr. Duffield were appointed by the Synod of New York and Philadelphia to visit the frontier inhabitants in western Pennsylvania; they reported the following year that they had found on the frontiers "numbers of people earnestly desirous of forming themselves into congregations, and declaring their willingness to exert their utmost to have the gospel among them." Year by year other ministers were appointed to spend longer or shorter periods "over the Alleghany Mountains." In 1772 the synod instructed the Donegal Presbytery, then the farthest west of the presbyteries, "to send either Mr. Craighead or Mr. King to Monongahela and other places adjacent, to supply as long as they can," while in 1775 a Mr. Forster was appointed to supply six Sabbaths in the frontier parts of

Pennsylvania. Thus occasional ministers visited the region over the mountains for a number of years before regular ministers removed to the West. Between 1776 and 1781 there came to be four regular ministers in the southwestern corner of Pennsylvania, among them John McMillan, and in the latter year the Redstone Presbytery was formed, the first west of the mountains. Each of the four early preachers had two churches under their charge from eight to twelve miles apart, though there were fifty places calling for ministers and needing aid. Frequently in responding to these calls the ministers would travel many miles, often with no road to follow, and many times were compelled to be away from their families for days together, while the danger from Indian raids filled the absent minister with constant alarm for their safety. It was not until Wayne's victory at Fallen Timbers (1794) that dread of Indian forays was removed.

Meanwhile Presbyterian people were finding their way from Virginia and North Carolina into Kentucky and Tennessee. The father of Kentucky Presbyterianism was David Rice. Rice, a native of Hanover county, Virginia, had been the pastor of three Presbyterian congregations in Virginia, and like many another of that time was the father of a large family of children. In 1783 Rice decided to visit Kentucky with the idea, if the country pleased him, of removing thither in order to secure cheap land for his "rising family." After his return to Virginia he received a call, signed by three hundred men, inviting him to return to Kentucky and officiate as a minister among them. The next year he took up his residence in Kentucky, settling on a farm near Danville where he became the minister of three congregations, Danville, Cane Run and the Forks of Dick River. The next year a church was built for him in Danville, the first Presbyterian church in the present state of Kentucky. Rice was also instrumental in forming several other churches such as that at New Providence on Salt River, organized in 1785, where a log house was erected to serve the double purpose of school and church. Five years later this building gave place to a large hewn log building, which again in 1803 was enlarged, and sometime within the next twenty years gave way to a brick building "substantially built and handsomely and commodiously finished."

By 1785 there were as many as twelve Presbyterian congregations in Kentucky and steps were taken to form a presbytery. The Synod of New York and Philadelphia at its meeting this year authorized the dividing of the Abingdon Presbytery and the formation of the Transylvania, which was to include the district of Kentucky and the settlements on the Cumberland. The first meeting of the new presbytery was held in the courthouse in Danville, in October, over which David Rice presided as Moderator. "But the blighting curse of schism," to quote one of the early Presbyterian chroniclers, "was soon to retard the healthy and triumphant march of evangelical truth." The perpetrator of this unfortunate split was the Rev. Adam Rankin, the second Presbyterian minister to come to Kentucky, who had in 1784 become the minister at Lexington. The presbytery finally found it necessary (1792) to expel Rankin on account of his virulent opposition to Watts' Psalmody and his general "pugnacious propensities." The following year Rankin was admitted to the ministry of the Associate Reformed Presbyterian Church and proceeded to organize some congregations from among his followers. Eventually there came to be several of these congregations in Kentucky, but by 1818 most of them had disappeared.

Meanwhile other congregations and presbyteries in the new West were in process of formation and in 1802 when the Synod of Kentucky was organized it consisted of three presbyteries, Transylvania, West Lexington and Washington. The same year a separate presbytery was formed of the churches on the Cumberland, consisting of six ministers, among them James McGready and William McGee whose names had become well known throughout the whole western country as leaders in the Great Revival.

Of great significance to the growth of Presbyterianism in the West was the adoption of the "Plan of Union" of 1801 by which the Congregationalists and the Presbyterians agreed to combine their forces in the great work of carrying religion to the new settlements. Since the adoption of the Saybrook platform in 1708 among Connecticut Congregationalists, particularly, the trend toward Presbyterianism had been noticeable, so that the names Congregational and Presbyterian were used more or less interchangeably. After the Great Awakening there was a considerable intermingling of the two bodies, evidenced by the coming of Jonathan Edwards to Princeton, while from 1766 to 1775 the Synod of New York and Philadelphia and the associations of Connecticut sent representatives to meet together in an annual convention to oppose the establishment of an American episcopate. These meetings were interrupted by the Revolution, but soon after peace was signed steps were again taken to bring about closer coöperation between the two bodies. In 1791 an agreement was reached by which the General Assembly of the Presbyterian Church and the General Association of Connecticut should each be represented in the other body by delegates and after 1794 these representatives were given the right to vote in the meetings. Within a few years following the Congregational state organizations of Massachusetts, New Hampshire and Vermont entered into similar agreements with the Presbyterian General Assembly.

The Plan of Union was proposed by Jonathan Edwards the younger in the Connecticut General Association in 1800 where he was sitting as a delegate of the Presbyterian General Assembly. The next year the Plan was adopted by both bodies. It provided a scheme whereby Congregational and Presbyterian settlers in a new community might combine to form a single congregation, and might call a minister of either denomination. If the majority of the members were Presbyterian they could conduct their discipline according to that church even if their minister were a Congregationalist, and vice versa. In case of disagreement between pastor and church the matter could be referred to the presbytery or association of which the pastor was a member or, if this was not agreeable, to a committee consisting of equal representatives of each group. Appeals were to be taken to the presbytery in case the minister was a Presbyterian, but if a Congregationalist the male members of the church were to be the final court. Later the other New England state associations approved the plan.

The plan as formulated evidently called for the organization of Congregational associations as well as presbyteries in the regions where it was to operate, but as a matter of fact it worked in almost every instance to the advantage of the Presbyterians. It was in the region north of the Ohio River that the Plan of Union largely operated, and in central-western New York, Ohio, Illinois and Michigan many churches which began as Congregational became Presbyterian; indeed, it has been estimated by a careful student of the operations of the Plan of Union that more than "two thousand churches, which were in origin and usages Congregational" were transformed into Presbyterian churches. The founding of the First Presbyterian Church in Chicago furnishes an interesting example. The first minister, Jeremiah Porter, was a New Englander, educated as a Congregationalist in a Congregational college and was ordained by a Congregational association, while a large majority of the first members—indeed, twenty-six of the original twenty-seven—were Congregationalists, and yet the church was organized as Presbyterian. Another example is that of the church at Jacksonville, Illinois. Here there was a mingling of Presbyterians, largely from Kentucky, and New England Congregationalists. Illinois College was founded by a group of Yale graduates, known as the Yale Band, but the first church to be established was the Presbyterian, though the Congregational influence was so strong in Jacksonville that soon afterwards a Congregational church was also organized—one of the few to come into existence in the region where the two churches were coöperating.

That the Presbyterians were more tenacious than Congregationalists of their denominational standards there can be no doubt, and they were likewise more assertive of their denominational spirit. There was undoubtedly also a feeling, largely held among Congregationalists, at this time that their form of organization was not suited to new and unformed communities, a fact which led the American Home Missionary Society (organized in 1826), though Congregational in origin, to advise all young men going out as missionaries to the West to receive Presbyterian ordination.

As might be expected the first schools and colleges in the new West were those established either by Congregationalists or Presbyterians. In February, 1785, a school was opened in the house of the Rev. David Rice at Danville; this had been provided for by the Virginia legislature five years previously when eight thousand acres of land had been set aside for the purpose, while in 1783 an endowment of twelve thousand acres had been added for the new Transylvania Seminary. In 1788 the seminary was moved to Lexington, where, according to Davidson the prejudiced historian of the Presbyterians of Kentucky, it fell into the hands of the liberal element and the Rev. Harry Toulmin, a Baptist minister of English birth, "a known disciple of Priestley," became the head and the Presbyterians lost control. The Transylvania Presbytery, foreseeing this result, took steps in the spring of 1794 to found a school of their own which would be under their direction, with the provision that half the trustees should always be ministers of the presbytery. "Father" Rice was sent to the legislature to secure the charter and "The Kentucky Academy" was launched, the legislature granting it six thousand acres of land as an endowment. The ministers of the presbytery collected a thousand pounds in Kentucky, while the commissioners to the next General Assembly were authorized to collect money in the East, where they secured nearly $10,000, among the donors being George Washington and John Adams.

Meanwhile the Presbyterians had opened a grammar school at Pisgah, near Lexington, and in the fall of 1797 an academy began operations at the same place. Transylvania Seminary in Lexington had failed to prosper under the management of the liberals, and the citizens of Lexington now proposed that the two schools be united, promising that the majority of the trustees should be Presbyterians. This was done by act of legislature in December, 1798, under the imposing title of "Transylvania University," and medical and law schools were made a part of the university, besides the usual college and academy. For a time the university prospered, but gradually, as vacancies occurred in the trustees, these were filled by "prominent political characters" until finally the Presbyterians found themselves in a hopeless minority. The crisis came in 1818 when the Rev. Horace Holley was chosen president. Holley was a graduate of Yale and was evidently a man of attractive personality, and although he was suspected of holding liberal views his administration began auspiciously, even "the intractable Presbyterians were reduced to silence." It was soon reported, however, that the president was holding up to ridicule the doctrine of human depravity and denied the "real personality of the devil" or that the world was created in six days. This was too much for the Presbyterians and

steps were taken by the Kentucky Synod to establish a
school in which orthodox teaching would be assured.
After some delay a charter for Centre College was secured
and the college opened at Danville in 1823. President
Holley's popularity meanwhile had waned and he was
forced to resign in 1826, becoming the head of a college
at New Orleans, where his health soon broke and he died
at sea while journeying northward in search of health.

While the Presbyterians south of the Ohio were busy
founding schools their brethren in western Pennsylvania
and Ohio were likewise engaged. The first Presbyterian
ministers in western Pennsylvania conducted schools in
connection with their churches, one of which was that
of the Rev. John McMillan in the Redstone country, who
like William Tennent conducted a "log" college. Among
his early pupils was James McGready. An academy was
established at Canonsburg in 1794 partly under Presbyterian patronage, which in 1802 became Jefferson College.
The Congregationalists also early founded academies in
the Northwest Territory, that at Marietta being established
in 1790 and later developing into Marietta College.

The Presbyterians and Congregationalists made the
largest contributions to the educational and cultural life
of the frontier, though they did not succeed in gaining
large numbers for their churches. Both the Baptists and
Methodists far surpassed them in this respect. The census
of 1820 placed the population of Kentucky at 563,317
while the church population for the same year was but
46,730, or one in twelve. Of the total church membership the Baptists and Methodists had about equal numbers, 21,000 each; the Presbyterians had but 2,700 and

the Cumberland Presbyterians another 1,000 while all others numbered 500. These figures are typical of conditions generally on the frontier. The average Presbyterian clergyman ministered as a rule to not more than three churches, and usually to but two, while he spent some weeks of each year on preaching tours through the new settlements under the direction of the presbytery. In most cases, however, it would seem that the initiative in the formation of new churches came from laymen, and ministers were not settled until there were enough Presbyterian members in a given community to provide for his support. Then too the Presbyterians were a particularly rigid body in both doctrine and polity, and every innovation to meet the peculiar needs or problems of a new country were always strongly opposed.

THE BAPTISTS

Among the early emigrants across the Alleghany Mountains into Kentucky and Tennessee were numerous Baptists from Virginia and North Carolina. Generally speaking they belonged to the class, economically, which would be attracted by the lure of cheap land. The pure democracy of Baptist church government would also tend to attract them to the freer life and the greater democracy of the frontier. Their preachers came from the people, and were self-supporting, and were themselves, indeed, farmers on the lookout for better land. Thus the Baptists were particularly well suited in their ideas of government, in their economic status, and in their form of church government to become the ideal western immigrants.

{312}

John Taylor was a typical Baptist preacher of the frontier, and has left us a fascinating picture of the work of a backwoods Baptist preacher in his *History of Ten Churches*. Taylor was a Virginia Baptist preacher who in 1779 went out to Kentucky and finally removed his household to the new country in 1781. By that time there were several Baptist preachers in Kentucky and in June, 1781, the first Baptist church west of the Alleghanies was formed, known as the Severn's Valley Church, which is still in existence and whose early records may still be seen. An interesting example of Baptist migration into the West is that of the Gilbert's Creek Church in Kentucky. This church came out to Kentucky in a body, with their pastor, Lewis Craig. Its organization was kept up in the march over the mountains, the pastor preached as they camped along the way, while several baptisms were performed in the clear mountain streams. On their march westward they heard the news of the surrender of Cornwallis at Yorktown and made the hills ring with the firing of their rifles in their glad rejoicings. Finally reaching the place of their new settlement in December, 1781, they gathered for worship "around the same old Bible they had used back in Spottsylvania," in Virginia.

By 1785 six Baptist churches in Kentucky sent "messengers" to the house of Lewis Craig and there formed the first Baptist association west of the mountains, called the Elkhorn Association. In October of that same year four other little backwoods churches, in the settlements to the west, formed the second western association, called the Salem, while two years later the South Kentucky Association was organized by the Separate Baptists; the two earlier associations being Regular Baptists. In 1801 this distinction was abolished when the two bodies agreed on terms of union.

In like manner the western migrations had brought Baptist people into eastern Tennessee, where at Boon's Creek a church was formed in 1781. These were Baptists from the Sandy Creek Association in North Carolina and by 1786 seven churches had been organized and the Holston Association was formed. In the Cumberland settlements in central Tennessee Baptists were among the first settlers; in fact, in most instances Baptists were first on the ground in the western settlements, for their preachers came with the settlers and the formation of a church was a comparatively simple matter.

The typical Baptist preacher on the frontier was a settler who worked on his land five or six days each week, except when called upon to hold week-day meetings or funerals. He was generally without much formal education, for there was a deep-seated prejudice against educated and salaried ministers, though some of the preachers received some support, which in the early days was paid in kind. There were two types of frontier Baptist preachers, *licensed* and *ordained*, and sometimes there were several ministers in a congregation, though generally one was designated as the pastor of the flock. Licensing a preacher was the first step in the making of a minister after he had been permitted to "exercise his gifts" by vote of the church. When chosen to take charge of a regular congregation he was then ordained. Frontier Baptists generally accepted a mild form of Calvinism, and there was little doctrinal discord among them though

out-and-out Arminianism was strongly condemned. The
initiative in the formation of a frontier Baptist church
came generally from a licensed or ordained farmer-
preacher settled in a new community. Sometimes there
were several preachers living in the vicinity and all would
take a hand in the organization, as John Taylor tells us
was the case of the Clear Creek Church in Kentucky.

The churches once organized held business meetings
once each month with the minister as moderator, and a
large share of the business had to do with the disciplining
of members. A random turning of the pages of any of the
old record books of the early frontier churches will soon
convince one that the church was a large factor in maintaining order in these raw communities. Discipline was
meted out to members for drinking, fighting, harmful
gossip, lying, stealing, immoral relation between the
sexes, gambling and horse racing. Even business dealings
and intimate family affairs, such as the relation between
parents and children, were considered matters for church
discipline. In the region south of the Ohio particularly
all the churches had slave members and the churches
watched over the slaves with as much care as over the
white members, and in some cases the slave members
were permitted a voice in church matters.

Practically all the early frontier Baptist churches were
named after creeks, runs, valleys or rivers, which simply
means that the frontier settlements were located along
the streams and that the first geographic names which
became familiar to the settlers were those of rivers or
creeks. Thus every one of the first churches constituting
the Elkhorn Association took its name from a stream:

Gilbert's Creek, Tate's Creek, South Elkhorn, Clear Creek, Big Crossing and Limestone. Of the seven churches constituting the Illinois Association in 1807 five were named for streams or valleys: Mississippi Bottom, Silver Creek, Wood River, Kain Spring and Richland Creek. The first Baptist places of worship were the rude cabins of the settlers, which as a rule served for the first several years after a church was formed, for the membership of the early churches was small. Numerous churches were formed with no more than six to ten members, and probably the average was not more than twenty. The first meeting-houses were of round logs, to be followed in a few years, if the church prospered, with a house of hewn logs with a fireplace and chimney built of brick. Such a building Thomas Lincoln helped to build on Pigeon Creek, Indiana, in 1819. The period of the better meeting-houses, frame or brick, came fifteen or twenty years after the formation of the average congregation.

THE METHODISTS

The most successful of the American churches in following the population as it moved westward, especially in the earlier years, were the Methodists. Both in organization and in doctrine they were well suited to the frontier. The circuit system had been devised by Wesley for his English societies, but once introduced into America by Francis Asbury it proved especially adaptable to the needs of a new country where settlements were scattered and far between. All the early Methodist preachers were itinerants, that is, they had no one place or congregation to which they ministered, but traveled circuits varying in size according to the number of settlements. Thus, if the country was new, the circuits were very large, requiring from four to five weeks for the circuit rider to make the rounds. At convenient places he established "classes" over which "class leaders" were appointed, and on the average circuit there were twenty to thirty such classes. The circuit rider preached almost every day, with the possible exception of Monday, nor was he particular where he preached; a log cabin, the barroom of a tavern and out under the trees were all alike to him. Nor did he delay his visits until Methodists moved into a community; his task was not so much to find Methodists among the settlers as to make Methodists of the raw material which he found on the frontier. Often he made his appearance before the cabin of a settler was completed, or before the mud in the stick chimney was dry.

The doctrine preached by the Methodist circuit riders was also well adapted to meet the hearty acceptance of the frontiersmen. It was a gospel of free will and free grace, as opposed to the doctrines of limited grace and predestination preached by the Calvinistic Presbyterians, or even the milder Calvinism of the Baptists. The frontier Methodist preachers brought home to the pioneers the fact that they were the masters of their own destiny, an emphasis which fitted in exactly with the new democracy rising in the West, for both emphasized the actual equality among all men.

The Methodist system of lay or "local" preachers was likewise one which lent itself easily to the spread of Methodism in a new country. A young man who gave any evidence of ability in public speaking was urged by the class leader and by the circuit preacher to "exercise his gifts," and if he proved useful, when the presiding elder came around to hold the "quarterly meeting conference" the young man was recommended to receive an "exhorter's license." Some of these lay preachers joined the "conference" and became regular traveling preachers, but many of them remained lay preachers, preaching frequently in the vicinity of their homes and were often instrumental in organizing classes in new settlements. These men, like the Baptist farmer-preachers, had little learning but were full of zeal and earnestness. It was, indeed, two local preachers, Francis Clark and John Durham, both from Virginia, who were responsible for founding the first Methodist classes in Kentucky.

It was in 1782 that the first regularly appointed circuit rider was sent over the mountains, to the Yadkin country, and the next year both Yadkin and Holston are listed among the Methodist circuits. In 1784 the Redstone circuit in southwestern Pennsylvania appears and by 1789 there were ten Methodist circuits in the new West, four in Tennessee, three in Kentucky and three along the waters of the upper Ohio. The number of circuits increased as population grew; the circuit preachers followed the moving population across the Ohio, with the close of the Indian wars, so that by the end of the century there were more than two thousand Methodists in Kentucky and Tennessee, while in the Northwest Territory there were four circuits and also one—the Natchez—in the region of the lower Mississippi.

The administration of the church in every section of the United States was placed upon the shoulders of Bishop

Francis Asbury. Nor was he an absentee supervisor, directing the work from a comfortable seat east of the mountains. Again and again he crossed the Alleghanies from 1788 to 1800, holding conferences of the preachers, assigning them to their circuits, preaching and advising. In 1790 he passed over the mountains from western North Carolina into eastern Tennessee, where he found the preachers "indifferently clad, with emaciated bodies." Returning to the East, he again in the same year recrossed the mountains into Kentucky, "over mountains, steep hills, deep rivers, and muddy creeks, and thick growth of reeds for miles together."

There was early objection to Asbury's supreme appointing power which resulted in 1792 in a serious schism. The leader of the malcontents was James O'Kelly, a prominent Virginia preacher of strong character and with a following numbering several thousands. Those who withdrew called themselves "Republican Methodists" and there were a number of adherents among the Kentucky and Tennessee Methodists. It is, indeed, passing strange that the highly centralized Methodist system of government could win its way in the new West, the most democratic section of the nation. The Methodists, however, preached a democratic gospel while they were under a monarchial form of church government, on the other hand, the Presbyterians and Baptists had a more democratic form of church government but preached a monarchial gospel. The arbitrary Methodist system, however, was greatly tempered by the fact that the early bishops moved about the country, from north to south, from east to west; stayed in the rude cabins on the frontier, preached at camp-meetings and received the same salary as the humblest circuit rider.

The name "Western Conference" was applied to the great region west of the Alleghany Mountains from 1800 to 1812. In 1800 all the western circuits were gathered into one district and placed under the supervision of William McKendree, who for a number of years, until his election as a bishop in 1808, was the major-general of the Methodist forces on the frontier. When the century began there were 2,622 white Methodists and 179 colored in the whole western country, in 1812 there were 29,093 white and 1,648 colored, while the circuits had increased from nine to sixty-nine. In 1830, instead of one conference west of the Alleghanies, there were eight, while the membership had grown from thirty thousand to more than 175,000, and among these were nearly two thousand Indians and more than fifteen thousand negroes.

THE CATHOLICS

Among the settlers in the new West there was early a sprinkling of Roman Catholics, mostly from Maryland, who were occasionally visited by itinerant priests. The old French settlements along the Mississippi and about the Great Lakes were supplied with priests by Bishop Carroll, among them being the Rev. Benedict Joseph Flaget who was sent in 1792 to Vincennes on the Wabash. He found there "a very poor log building, open to the weather and almost tottering. The congregation, if possible, in a still more miserable condition. Out of seven hundred souls, only twelve could be induced to approach holy communion during the Christmas festivities." In like manner Kaskaskia and Cahokia, in Illinois, and Detroit were supplied with faithful missionary priests. The first priest ordained for Kentucky was the Rev. Stephen T. Baden and with his coming the Catholic Church had its real beginnings in this region. Other priests also came, among them Charles Nerinckx, a native of Belgium, who was active in forming churches and created a sisterhood, while the Dominicans established a convent and a college.

By 1808 the Catholic growth in the West had increased to such an extent that it was thought necessary to erect a new diocese, known as that of Bardstown (Kentucky), which included besides Kentucky and Tennessee all the Northwest Territory. Benedict Joseph Flaget, who for several years had been the priest at Vincennes, was named the first bishop. He came down the Ohio in a flatboat and reached his diocese in June, 1811. Four years later he reported nineteen churches in Kentucky and ten priests; he estimated the number of Catholics in Kentucky at ten thousand; the number of Catholics in Ohio at fifty families without a priest; a hundred and thirty Catholic families in Indiana; three Catholic parishes in Illinois with a hundred and twenty families, while in Detroit there were some two thousand Catholics. By 1817 the work of supervising this vast diocese had become so burdensome that Bishop Flaget asked for a coadjutor and the Rev. John Baptist David was appointed in July of that year. In 1815 the diocese of Louisiana and the Floridas was erected, and in 1829 the diocese of Cincinnati.

Chapter XV

THE SECOND AWAKENING AND THE FRONTIER
SCHISMS

THE famous Marquis of Pescara once said to the papal legate, "It is impossible for men to serve Mars and Christ at the same time." "It is possible for individuals," suggests J. Franklin Jameson, "but it is difficult for a whole generation." It will not be surprising, then, to learn that the decade and a half following the close of the American Revolution was one of spiritual deadness among all the American churches. A historian of the Episcopalians has characterized the period from the close of the war to 1812 as one of suspended animation. Nor was this true of the Episcopalian body alone. It was, indeed, "the period of the lowest ebb-tide of vitality in the history of American Christianity." At this period deistic influence was particularly strong, described by the orthodox as "the spirit of half belief or unbelief." This influence had come from both England and France and there were soon numerous Jacobin clubs and societies of the Illuminati throughout the country, devoting their energy to ridicule of Christianity and to the bringing in of the *Age of Reason*.

Lyman Beecher, who was a student at Yale College in

1795, describes in his interesting *Reminiscences* the religious conditions in the college at that time. He says:

"The College was in a most ungodly state. The college church was almost extinct. Most of the students were skeptical, and rowdies were plenty. Wine and liquors were kept in many rooms; intemperance, profanity, gambling, and licentiousness were common." Tom Paine was the great vogue among the young men, and boys came to college boasting of their infidelity and addressing one another as Voltaire, Rousseau, d'Alembert, etc.

So low were the fortunes of the Protestant Episcopal Church at this period that even some of the bishops looked for it to die out with the old colonial families. So hopeless did Bishop Provoost of New York consider the religious situation that he resigned his office, while Bishop Madison of Virginia, we are told, shared the conviction of Chief Justice Marshall, himself a devout churchman, that the church was "too far gone ever to be revived." William Meade, later Bishop of Virginia, tells us that when he offered himself for ordination at Williamsburg in 1811, universal surprise was expressed that a college-bred man should apply for orders. And on the way to the dilapidated Williamsburg church, where the ordination services were to be performed, they met a party of students with dogs and guns, all of whom passed the church scornfully by, having recently debated the question "whether Christianity had been beneficial or injurious to mankind." In 1813 when a special convention was called in Virginia to elect a successor to Bishop Madison, who had died the previous year, only seven clergymen and eighteen laymen were present.

In the Presbyterian Church there was likewise reason for concern. The college at Princeton, which but a generation before was noted for its evangelical fervor, had in 1782 but two students who professed themselves Christians. In 1798 the General Assembly thus describes religious conditions in the country:

We perceive with pain and fearful apprehension a general dereliction of religious principles and practice among our fellow-citizens, a visible and prevailing impiety and contempt for the laws and institutions of religion, and an abounding infidelity, which in many instances tends to atheism itself. The profligacy and corruption of the public morals have advanced with a progress proportionate to our declension in religion. Profaneness, pride, luxury, injustice, intemperance, lewdness, and every species of debauchery and loose indulgence greatly abound.

The Baptists had been so busy fighting for the separation of church and state that they too, in the words of Robert Semple the old historian of the Virginia Baptists, "suffered a very wintry season. With some exceptions," says he, "the declension was general throughout the state. The love of many waxed cold. Some of the watchmen fell, others stumbled, and many slumbered at their posts." The Methodists also suffered a decline and for a number of years reported a steady decrease in membership.

If moral and religious conditions were at low ebb along the eastern seaboard they were even more deplorable in the new West. The pioneer Baptist preacher, John Taylor, who visited Kentucky for the first time in 1779, was distressed by the low state of religion which he found there, while David Rice, the first settled Presbyterian minister in Kentucky, states that when he came to the West (1783) he "found scarcely one man and but few women who supported a creditable profession of religion. Some were grossly ignorant of the first principles of religion. Some were given to quarrelling and fighting, some to profane swearing, some to intemperance, and perhaps most of them totally negligent of the forms of religion in their own houses." Peter Cartwright tells us that Logan county, Kentucky, was called "Rogues' Harbor" and was the refuge for escaped murderers, horse thieves, highway robbers and counterfeiters. People from the East who visited the West were shocked by the swearing, fighting, gouging, Sabbath-breaking and general lawlessness which prevailed.

"However great the apathy which had fallen upon the spirit of American religion," to quote the words of a recent interpreter of this period, "it would surely recover, as the nation itself gradually recovered from the ravages and injuries of war. A nation inspired by the sense of a career of future greatness can seldom fail to develop active religious life in some form, and it was certain that America would sometime become religious, even if it were not so in the years immediately after the Revolution." Nor was a revival of religion in America to be long delayed.

Times were, indeed, ripe for a renewed emphasis upon vital religion throughout the nation. The movement in this direction was first noticed in the East. Almost imperceptibly people began to take a larger interest in matters of religion and in numerous New England communities especially churches were strengthened by the addition of new members, while new churches were established. The revival in New England was, no doubt, partly due to the introduction of Methodism, with its strong evangelistic emphasis. In 1789 Bishop Asbury appointed Jesse Lee, a tall Virginian, to the first Methodist circuit in New England, and he preached his first sermon in the New England metropolis standing on a deal table on Boston Common in 1790. Six years later the New England Conference was formed with three thousand members, while a network of circuits soon covered all the New England states.

The changing attitude is well illustrated by what was taking place at Yale College. Timothy Dwight, the grandson of Jonathan Edwards, became the president in 1795, and under his administration the whole moral and religious atmosphere of the college was changed for the better. He met the students on their own ground and in a series of frank discussions both in the classroom and in the college chapel treated such subjects as "The Nature and Danger of Infidel Philosophy," "Is the Bible the Word of God?" while he preached a notable series of sermons in the college chapel on "Theology explained and defended," in which he grappled with the principles of deism and materialism. Soon he had won the admiration of the students and in 1802 a revival began in which a third of the student body professed conversion, to be followed at frequent intervals by other awakenings. Dartmouth, Williams and Amherst colleges experienced similar religious awakenings while the movement spread

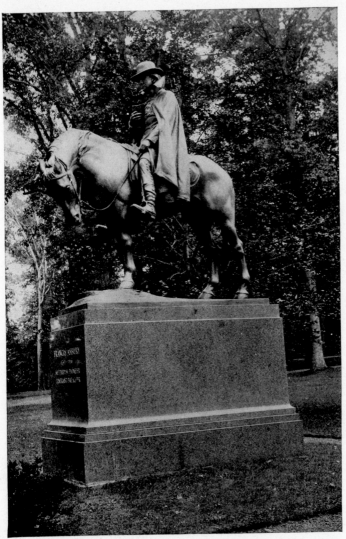

STATUE OF FRANCIS ASBURY, BY HENRY AUGUSTUS LUKEMAN
(1872-   ), ON THE CAMPUS OF DREW THEOLOGICAL
SEMINARY, MADISON, NEW JERSEY

into the middle states and into the South, especially among the Presbyterians.

The spread of infidelity was effectively checked and out of the renewed interest in religion came the beginnings of home missionary effort as well as the foreign missionary enterprise. The founding of numerous academies and colleges, was another result, and it also furnished the impulse for the founding of the first theological seminaries for the special training of ministers. The first two decades of the nineteenth century saw likewise the founding of numerous interdenominational societies and philanthropic organizations, as well as the beginning of religious journalism, all of which was largely the result of the new emphasis upon religion which characterized this period. So important were these new organizations that they deserve special consideration in a separate chapter.

The western phase of the second awakening was far different from the quiet spirit of revival which largely characterized its eastern progress. In the East there were no prominent leaders or evangelists, nor was there great excitement engendered. On the other hand, the revival in the West was attended by such excitement and by such strange manifestations as were never before seen in America.

The outstanding leader at the beginning of the revival in the west was James McGready, a Presbyterian minister of Scotch-Irish parentage. Born in Pennsylvania, he moved with his parents at an early age to Guilford county, North Carolina, where as a youth he was particularly careful about his religious duties and early determined to study for the ministry. Accordingly he became one of John McMillan's first students at his Log College in western Pennsylvania and after the completion of his studies was licensed to preach by the Redstone Presbytery. He preached within the bounds of that presbytery for a time, but later went to the Carolinas where under his preaching a revival was soon begun. He has been described as exceedingly uncouth in his personal appearance, with small piercing eyes, coarse tremulous voice, and so unusual was his general ugliness as to attract attention.

He was accused in South Carolina of "running people distracted" and of diverting them from their occupations, and there soon developed fierce opposition to him and his preaching. Indeed, the opposition became so extreme that his pulpit was torn out of the church and burned, while a threatening letter was sent him written in blood. This opposition led him to visit the West in 1796, where after a short time he became the pastor of three Presbyterian churches in Logan county, Kentucky: Gasper River, Muddy River and Red River. It was here under his zealous and persuasive preaching that the great western revival began which came to be known as the Logan county, or Cumberland, revival.

Through 1797, 1798 and 1799 the religious interest increased, while several other Presbyterian and Methodist preachers united their efforts with those of McGready to carry the revival throughout the whole region. It was in the summer of 1800, however, that the Cumberland revival reached its culmination. In June of that year unusual excitement had attended a meeting held on Red River, which had been encouraged by a Methodist preacher,

John McGee, who, overcome by his feeling, "shouted and exhorted with all possible energy." Numbers professed conversion, but the unusual excitement which attended the meeting filled some of the Presbyterian ministers present with amazement and others with resentment. The news of this meeting soon spread far and wide so that at subsequent meetings even greater crowds assembled to see the strange sights. It was at this period that people began to come to the meetings prepared to spend several days on the ground, bringing their provisions with them —which is undoubtedly the origin of the camp-meeting. Other meetings with similar results were held at Gasper River, Muddy River and at a Methodist Quarterly Meeting in August at Edward's Chapel. This latter meeting lasted four days and nights and more than a hundred conversions were reported.

The revival now spread rapidly throughout Kentucky and Tennessee, into North and South Carolina, western Virginia and Pennsylvania and into the settled regions north of the Ohio River. Sacramental services were the occasions for some of the largest gatherings. In these meetings the Presbyterians and Methodists commonly united; the Baptists also held joint preaching with the others, but since they generally held to "close communion," would not unite in the communion services.

People traveled long distances to see for themselves what was going on at the Logan county meetings. Among the visitors was Barton W. Stone, the minister of two little Presbyterian churches in Bourbon county, Kentucky, who in the spring of 1801 journeyed to Logan county to investigate the religious situation. He soon returned fully convinced that the work was genuine and deeply affected by what he had seen. Immediately a revival broke out under his preaching at Cain Ridge, one of his churches, and the happenings in Logan county were duplicated in Bourbon county. Perhaps the greatest of all the single phases of the western revival was what has come to be known as the Cain Ridge meeting. This was a sacramental meeting held in August, 1801, attended by a crowd variously estimated at from 10,000 to 25,000. There are numerous descriptions by eyewitnesses of this great meeting. One such eyewitness states:

I attended with 18 Presbyterian ministers; and Baptist and Methodist preachers, I do not know how many; all being either preaching or exhorting the distressed with more harmony than could be expected. The governor of our State was with us and encouraging the work. The number of people computed from 10, to 21,000 and the communicants 828. The whole people were serious, all the conversation was of a religious nature, or calling in question the divinity of the work. Great numbers were on the ground from Friday until the Thursday following, night and day without intermission, engaged in some religious act of worship. They are commonly collected in small circles of 10 or 12, close adjoining another circle and all engaged in singing Watt's and Hart's hymns; and then a minister steps upon a stump or log, and begins an exhortation or sermon, when, as many as can hear collect around him. On Sabbath I saw above 100 candles burning at once and I saw 100 persons at once on the ground crying for mercy, of all ages from 8 to 60 years. . . . When a person is struck down he is carried by others out of the congregation, when some minister converses with and prays for him; afterwards a few gather around and sing a hymn suitable to the case. The whole number brought to the ground, under convictions, were about 1,000, not less. The sensible, the weak, etc., learned and unlearned, the rich and poor, are the subjects of it.

Camp-meetings played a particularly important part in the western revival and they were soon being held in every section of the West. The camp-meetings at night were particularly impressive, for everything in the immediate surroundings combined to furnish those elements which would greatly affect the imagination. "The glare of the blazing camp-fires falling on a dense assemblage . . . and reflected back from long ranges of tents upon every side; hundreds of candles and lamps suspended among the trees, together with numerous torches flashing to and fro, throwing an uncertain light upon the tremulous foliage, and giving an appearance of dim and indefinite extent to the depth of the forest; the solemn chanting of hymns swelling and falling on the night wind; the impassioned exhortations; the earnest prayers; the sobs, shrieks, or shouts, bursting from persons under intense agitation of mind; the sudden spasms which seize upon scores, and unexpectedly dashed them to the ground; all conspired to invest the scene with terrific interest, and to work up the feelings to the highest pitch of excitement." Meetings of this sort were held in many places as the revival spread. Through Kentucky and Tennessee the movement continued powerful, while from North Carolina and Georgia came reports of the progress of the revival. In 1803 a revival began among the Presbyterians on the upper Ohio and spread through all the churches of the Ohio Presbytery. Ministers from Kentucky crossed the river and carried the revival to the Ohio settlements, and by 1803 it had reached as far north as the Western Reserve.

There were some among the Presbyterians especially who opposed the revival from the start. Stone tells of an attempt of some of the opponents to put a stop to a camp-meeting in Paris, Kentucky, where for the first time a minister arose and opposed the work. This preacher proposed that the people go to a nearby town to worship in the church. Some of them responded to this suggestion and repaired to the church where the opposing minister, we are told, addressed the people in "iceberg style" and labored hard to "Calvinize" them. The meeting, however, was turned into a particularly warm revival by Stone, who began to pray at the close of the sermon. On this turn of affairs some of the opposing preachers jumped out of a window back of the pulpit and left the meeting to the revivalists.

The revival produced several peculiar bodily exercises, such as falling, jerking, rolling, running, dancing and barking. Perhaps the most common was the falling exercise which befell all classes "the saints and sinners of every age and of every grade." The subject would generally "with piercing scream, fall like a log on the floor or ground" and appear as dead, sometimes lying thus for hours at a time. All the eyewitnesses testify to the commonness of this occurrence. The jerking exercise affected different persons in different ways. Frequently one of the limbs only would be affected, sometimes the whole body, and often the head alone. It often happened that "sinners" were taken, cursing and swearing as they jerked. "Sometimes the head would be twisted right and left, to a half round, with such velocity, that not a feature could be discovered." Cartwright tells us the more the exercise was resisted "the more they jerked," and the only way to stop it was to pray earnestly. "To see," he further says, "proud young gentlemen and young ladies, dressed in their silks, jewelry, and prunella, from top to toe, take the jerks would often excite my risibilities. The first jerk or so, you would see their fine bonnets, caps and combs fly; and so sudden would be the jerking of the head that their long loose hair would crack almost as loud as a wagoner's whip." The other exercises were little more than variations of these already described.

The influence of the revival upon western society was both good and evil, with good predominating. The immediate effect upon western morals was undoubtedly good. "Father" Rice, whose attitude toward the revival was particularly sane, stated in a sermon before the Synod of Kentucky in 1803: "A considerable number of persons appear to me to be greatly reformed in their morals. This is the case within the sphere of my particular acquaintance. Yea, some neighborhoods, noted for their vicious and profligate manners are now as much noted for their piety and good order. Drunkards, profane swearers, liars, quarrelsome persons, etc., are remarkably reformed." Another witness writing to an eastern correspondent thus describes the general effect of the revival:

On my way I was informed by settlers on the road that the character of Kentucky travelers was entirely changed, and that they were as remarkable for sobriety as they had formerly been for dissoluteness and immorality. And indeed I found

Kentucky to appearances the most moral place I had ever been. A profane expression was hardly ever heard. A religious awe seemed to pervade the country. Upon the whole, I think the revival in Kentucky the most extraordinary that has ever visited the church of Christ; and all things considered, it was peculiarly adapted to the circumstances of the country into which it came.

In 1802 another witness wrote that the "revival has confounded infidelity, awed vice into silence, and brought numbers beyond calculation under serious impression." On the other hand, a more recent student concludes that there is reason to think "that the habits of impulsive social action, developed and fostered in the early years of the century by the Kentucky revivals, and imitated at intervals ever since, have played their unworthy part in rendering that section of our country peculiarly susceptible to highly emotional outbreaks of prejudice, passion and even criminality."

The effect upon denominational growth was particularly marked. Though the revival was largely Presbyterian in its beginnings, the Methodist and Baptists reaped the largest results in church membership. In two years during the time when the revival was at its height the Western Conference of the Methodists alone added more than six thousand members. The Baptists also greatly increased their numbers. Between 1800 and 1803 more than ten thousand were added to the Baptist churches in Kentucky alone, and there were like increases pretty generally throughout all the western Baptist associations. The Presbyterians also added large numbers to their churches, but as a whole the revival was to prove detrimental to Presbyterian interests in the West, due to the serious schisms which occurred as a result of the extravagances, disorders and heresy disputes which soon arose.

Two serious schisms occurred in the Presbyterian Church in the early years of the nineteenth century, the first centering in the Cumberland region, resulting in the formation of the Cumberland Presbyterian Church, the second centering in north central Kentucky which came to be known as the New Light schism. These were the two great centers of the Kentucky revival and produced the two outstanding revival leaders, James McGready and Barton W. Stone. In both sections serious opposition arose to the revival and to the "fervor, noise and disorder" which accompanied it. In the Cumberland country the ministers were evenly divided, five favorable and five against; in northern Kentucky six ministers were strongly revivalistic while the remainder opposed the "noise and false exercises," among whom was "Father" Rice, and thus there came to be two distinct parties among western Presbyterians.

The Cumberland schism was precipitated when the Cumberland Presbytery, which had been formed in 1802, began to license and then ordain certain men who lacked the required educational qualification for the Presbyterian ministry. This had been done to meet the increased demand for preaching which the revival had created. As early as 1801 the Transylvania Presbytery had given permission to four laymen to exhort and catechize in vacant congregations. When the Cumberland Presbytery was formed additional catechists were licensed, until there came to be seventeen, characterized by the strict Presbyterian party as "illiterate exhorters with Arminian sentiments." These exhorters traveled through the vacant congregations, which they called "circuits," in imitation of the Methodists, while the presbytery directed the churches to contribute toward their support. Meanwhile strong opposition to these innovations was developing among the opponents of the revival, and at the meeting of the Kentucky Synod in 1805, after a committee had found the records of the Transylvania Presbytery "defective, discordant and obscure; and abounding in evidences of the flagrant violation of the Rules of Discipline," the synod proceeded to appoint a special commission with full synodical power to visit the Transylvania Presbytery and to make an examination into its affairs.

This precipitated a crisis which soon brought about a schism. The commission summoned the members of the presbytery before it, but some of them refused to appear on the ground of its unconstitutionality. The commission also made accusations of heresy against three of the ministers, stating that they held doctrines contrary to those contained in the Confession of Faith, while others were cited to the next meeting of the synod. Twelve ministers were summoned to stand an examination as to their qualifications for the ministry, to which they refused to comply, while certain churches, presided over by untrained ministers, were declared vacant and the Cumberland Presbytery was dissolved.

When the commission had finished its work the revivalist members immediately formed themselves into a Council, which at once made an appeal to the Transylvania Presbytery to act as a mediator. This was without avail. Next an appeal was made to the General Assembly of 1809 praying for redress, but this too was defeated. Nothing seemed to be left to the revivalists but to form themselves into an independent presbytery, and this was done largely through the efforts of Finis Ewing and Samuel King in February, 1810, and there was created the Cumberland Presbyterian Church. By 1829 the church had grown to considerable proportions, there being at that time eighteen presbyteries, and in that year a General Assembly was formed. The rapid growth of the new church was due to the fact that it adopted the camp-meeting as well as the circuit system, while its warm evangelical preaching of a radically modified Calvinism made a large appeal to the frontier people of the section where it ministered.

Equally unfortunate was the New Light schism which began at about the same time in north central Kentucky. Barton W. Stone, the outstanding leader of the revival in that region, had from the beginning of his ministry been troubled over the doctrines of election and predestination, doctrines which stand at the very center of strict Calvinism. At his ordination he had told some of the ministers of his doubts and had said to them that he was only willing to accept the Confession of Faith as far as he felt it consistent with the Word of God. Four other Presbyterian ministers who were intimately associated with him in the revival were all likewise troubled concerning the Calvinistic doctrines. These men were Richard McNemar, John Thompson, John Dunlavy and John Marshall. In their preaching they laid chief emphasis upon God's love for the "whole world" and upon the ability of all sinners to accept the means of salvation —doctrines flatly antagonistic to the Calvinistic system— which soon brought down upon them the censures of their orthodox brethren. At the meeting of the Synod of Kentucky in 1803 charges were brought against McNemar and Thompson for preaching erroneous doctrines and from the first it was apparent that the decision would go against them. Before matters could go farther the five preachers under suspicion held a conference and decided to withdraw from the jurisdiction of the synod, though not from the Presbyterian Church. After attempts to reclaim them on the part of a committee of the synod had failed, the synod suspended the five ministers and declared their pulpits vacant.

The five suspended ministers, together with several others who joined them, now proceeded to organize a new presbytery which they called the Springfield Presbytery, and for the course of a year carried on their work under this name. By the end of a year it became apparent to them that they were forming a new denomination, a thing that was furthest from their desire. Already they had published an *Apology* in which they maintained that all creeds and confessions ought to be rejected and that the Bible alone should be the bond of Christian fellowship. They now decided to dissolve the Springfield Presbytery, which was announced in what was termed, in a semi-humorous vein "The Last Will and Testament of the Springfield Presbytery." This was accompanied by an address in which they explained the reasons for this action. Their chief motive, they state, was their desire to promote the unity of Christian people, which they felt could not be done under the present organization of the churches. They adopted the name "The Christian Church," a name without sectarian bias, while they rejected all forms of organization, such as presbyteries, synods, conferences, sessions, etc., which did not have a Scriptural basis. The movement thus inaugurated spread rapidly through Kentucy and extended northward into Ohio, while Stone spent his time traveling extensively, preaching and organizing churches. The movement was retarded, however, by the defection of McNemar and Dunlavy to the Shakers, and by the return of Thompson and Marshall to the Presbyterians.

Shakerism was introduced into the West in the midst of the great revival, by three missionaries who had been sent out from their communities in the East. This peculiar communistic sect had originated in England in the middle of the eighteenth century and was brought to America in 1774 when Ann Lee, or "Mother Ann" as she was called, with a small group of followers migrated to New York where several small communities were formed. The Shakers repudiated marriage as the root of all evil and claimed that theirs was the only true church having all the apostolic gifts. In their worship they adopted a peculiar form of dancing and handclapping, in which they expressed their joy in the Lord and from which they received their name of "Shakers." The three missionaries who now visited Kentucky were soon successful in winning a number of converts, both ministers and people, and eventually two Shaker communities were established in Ohio, two in Kentucky and one in Indiana. The orthodox churches in the West were soon united in their opposition to Shakerism. Cartwright tells us that the "Shaker priests" were successful in sweeping scores of "members of different churches away from their steadfastness into the muddy pools of Shakerism."

For some time the question of the mode of baptism disturbed the leaders of the New Light movement, but eventually immersion was accepted as the Scriptural form. The acceptance of immersion gave Stone and his helpers access to the Baptists and in numerous instances Baptist churches came over entirely into the Stonite movement, rejecting their confessions and associations and, as Stone expressed it, becoming "one with us in the great work of Christian union."

Hardly had the New Light movement gotten under way in Kentucky and southern Ohio before a similar movement had begun in western Pennsylvania and Virginia, under the leadership of Thomas Campbell and his more brilliant son Alexander. The Campbells were Scotch-Irish Anti-Burgher Presbyterians, the most conservative of all the Presbyterian bodies. The father was a minister of an Anti-Burgher church in County Armagh, Ireland, dividing his time between his church and a school which he conducted. Though belonging to this very conservative body the Campbells were in contact with more liberal groups arising in both Scotland and Ireland, such as the "Old Scotch Independents," the "Tabernacle Churches" which arose through the evangelistic activity of Rowland Hill and the Haldanes.

In 1807, on the advice of his physician, the elder Campbell came to America to seek his health, leaving his family behind, and his school in charge of his son Alexander. Landing in Philadelphia he found the Anti-Burgher Synod in session in that city, and on presenting his credentials was admitted and sent to the Presbytery of Chartiers in southwestern Pennsylvania. The Associate Synod, or the Anti-Burgher Synod in America, was even more conservative than was the parent body in Scotland and had, in 1796, passed an act prohibiting "occasional communion," or communion with other bodies of Christians. To this narrow ruling Thomas Campbell could not subscribe, and it was his custom to invite all Presbyterian parties who were without pastoral care to join his members in partaking of the sacrament. This gave offense to some of his brethren in the ministry and proceedings were soon begun against him in the presbytery. The condemnation voted by the presbytery caused him to appeal to the synod, and in his letter to that body he set forth certain opinions which indicate his trend away from narrow creeds and theological formulas, and makes the Scripture a basis of Christian unity. Though the synod set aside the judgment of the presbytery, yet an atmosphere of hostility and criticism remained, and rather than try to work under such strained relations he decided to sever his connection with the Seceder body and become a *free lance* in the western religious world.

Thomas Campbell now began to hold meetings wherever opportunity offered, in barns, groves and houses, and soon a considerable number of persons had placed themselves under his spiritual care. After a time these friends met and agreed upon a basis of coöperation calling themselves "The Christian Association of Washington." It was at this time that Campbell, in an address, stated a principle which was to become a "watchword" among his followers: "Where the Scriptures speak, we speak; where they are silent, we are silent," and in August, 1809, the association adopted a "Declaration and Address," prepared by Campbell, setting forth the purposes of the association. This has been termed the most important document in the entire history of the Disciples body although, like Stone, Campbell had no desire to form a new sect but hoped that all Christian people might unite upon the broad platform of the Scriptures.

Just as the Declaration and Address was issuing from the press the son, Alexander Campbell, arrived in America and he at once heartily accepted the principles laid down in the address. The next turn in events (1810) was the application of the elder Campbell to the (Regular) Presbyterian Synod of Pittsburgh to be taken into that body, together with the association. When this was refused the Christian Association organized themselves into the Brush Run Church (May 4, 1811) in which Thomas Campbell was appointed elder and Alexander was licensed to preach, while four deacons were chosen. Soon after the church was formed the question of baptism arose for discussion, and finally it was decided that upon the principles which they had adopted there was no place for infant baptism, and accordingly immersion was accepted as the only form of baptism allowed in the Scriptures. When the Redstone Baptist Association learned that the Brush Run Church had adopted the practice of immersion they were elated, and urged that it join their association. After full discussion, among themselves, and

THEOLOGICAL SEMINARY AT ANDOVER

From a picture in possession of the Massachusetts Historical Society

after it was pointed out to the Baptists that their views were not entirely in harmony regarding the Lord's Supper or even regarding baptism, the Brush Run Church finally (1813) decided to unite with the Baptist body.

From 1813 to 1830 the Campbells and their followers were nominally Baptists. And from this time forward Thomas Campbell began to retire into the background, while his brilliant son became more and more the active leader of the movement. Up to about 1820 Alexander Campbell was chiefly occupied in establishing and conducting a seminary at Bethany, in western Virginia, but from 1820 to 1830 he became increasingly active in propagating his peculiar views, especially among the Baptists. Soon a party had formed, made up of his followers, called the "Reformers," advocating the "restoration of the ancient order of things." In 1823 he established a paper, *The Christian Baptist,* to promote his teachings, while he began to travel more and more extensively throughout western Pennsylvania and Virginia, Ohio and Kentucky, preaching and debating wherever he had opportunity. Campbell was an especially able debater, and both in his debates and in the pages of his paper attacked all human innovations which had crept into the churches, such as Sunday schools, Missionary societies, synods, conferences, bishops, reverends, etc. Soon groups of Reformers were to be found in almost every Baptist congregation in the West, and by 1826 the Reformers began to separate from the Baptist churches to form congregations of their own. It has been estimated that in Kentucky alone more than ten thousand Baptist members withdrew to form *Disciple* congregations. Thus the movement which had begun as a protest against the numerous sects of Christians, instead of uniting them had only succeeded in adding one more to the number.

By the year 1827 the followers of Stone began to come in frequent contact with the followers of Campbell and as they came to know more and more about one another, it became increasingly apparent that they had much in common. The churches of both groups were organized on a strictly congregational basis, and the only way to promote union between the two bodies was for individual congregations to unite. It 1832 two men, one representing the "Disciples" the other the "Christians," were sent out among the churches to bring about union in Kentucky, while similar coalitions took place between the two groups in the other states where they were numerous. There was an element among the "Christians" who did not welcome the union, however, and after uniting with the "Republican Methodists" they formed what became known as the "Christian Connection Church," which in 1929 voted to unite with the Congregational Church. Since the union of the "Christians" and the "Disciples" the two names have been used interchangeably since there is no central body with authority to adopt an official name for the denomination.

While the Presbyterians and Baptists were suffering serious losses because of controversy and schism, the Methodists likewise were facing disruption. There is abundant evidence to show that although Francis Asbury was thoroughly devoted to the cause of advancing Christianity, he was also extremely arbitrary in his administration of the church. He demanded absolute obedience and was seldom willing to take advice from others. He has been characterized as "a born conservative and a born autocrat," and it is not at all strange that such arbitrary procedure should provoke rebellion. The O'Kelly schism of 1792 has already been mentioned, but in 1830 a far more serious split resulted from a ten-year agitation to secure the election of presiding elders and the admission of laymen into the conferences. This movement had its largest following in Maryland, while Baltimore was the center of agitation. Those favoring these changes called themselves "Reformers" while their opponents termed them "radicals," and when the General Conference of 1828 refused to pass favorably upon their petition they began to withdraw in considerable numbers and in 1830 formed themselves into the Methodist Protestant Church. It may seem strange that this movement in the direction of greater democracy did not gain headway on the frontier but was confined so largely to the East. Perhaps the chief reason the new west did not rebel against the Methodist arbitrary system is because of the personal popularity of such men as McKendree, who became a bishop in 1808, and the fact that in their lives the leaders of frontier Methodism showed themselves as simple and democratic as the people among whom they worked.

Another religious body which came into existence in the early years of the nineteenth century was the United Brethren in Christ. Though not in its origin a frontier schism, it was soon engaged in important work among the early German settlers in the West. The founder of this body was Philip William Otterbein, who came out to America in 1752 as a missionary to the German Reformed people in Pennsylvania. He, like most of the other German missionaries, was Pietistic in his emphasis, and preached the necessity of an inner spiritual experience, and so strongly did he bear down upon this emphasis that he offended some of his people as well as his colleagues. At about the same time he came in contact with a Mennonite preacher, Martin Boehm, who was preaching in the same general region and emphasizing the same doctrines. Otterbein, in 1774, accepted a call to an independent Reformed church in Baltimore, and with Baltimore as the center continued his evangelistic tours among the German-speaking people of the surrounding states at the same time keeping in touch with Boehm. Meanwhile Otterbein had come into close personal touch with Francis Asbury, and when in 1784 Asbury was ordained in Baltimore as General Superintendent of the Methodist Episcopal Church, he requested that Otterbein assist in the ordination. Gradually there came to be a number of preachers associated with Otterbein and Boehm who were evangelistic in their emphasis, and they began to meet in informal conferences in 1789. It is quite probable that if the Methodists had made any adequate provision for work among the German-speaking people Otterbein and those coöperating with him might have united with the Methodists, but unfortunately this was not the case. In 1800 Otterbein, Boehm and eleven others felt it necessary to form a new church, which they called the "United Brethren in Christ." The name was derived from the greeting "We are brethren" which Otterbein extended to Boehm after hearing him preach for the first time. The new church was organized along Methodistic lines and, like the Methodists, was Arminian in doctrine. In the first decade of the nineteenth century the United Brethren had crossed the Alleghany Mountains and soon established their work in Ohio, Indiana and Illinois.

Another German Methodistic body which arose in the early nineteenth century was the Evangelical Association, now called the Evangelical Church. Under Jacob Albright, a Pennsylvania German and a former exhorter in the Methodist Church, this body was formed in 1803, and as the Germans moved westward spread into the central and northwestern states.

A schism which belongs to this period, but which has no relationship with the frontier, was that which resulted from the Trinitarian and Anti-Trinitarian controversy in New England. The beginnings of this controversy have already been noted, and occurred in the years immediately following the Great Colonial Awakening. King's Chapel, the oldest Episcopal church in New England, was the first to become openly Unitarian. This church had lost its rector and many of its members in the migration of leading Tory families to Nova Scotia, following the British evacuation of Boston in 1776. James Freeman, a young graduate of Harvard College, acted as lay reader in the absence of a minister, was finally chosen pastor and accepted lay ordination. For some time Freeman had been troubled about the doctrine of the Trinity and had conducted discussions among his members on the subject of Christian doctrine. These discussions led finally to action, on the part of the congregation, to strike out of the order of service all references to the Trinity.

This action was taken in 1785, and thus King's Chapel became the first American Unitarian church.

Of greater importance to the progress of Unitarianism in New England was the election in 1805 of an avowed Unitarian, Henry Ware, to the Hollis Professorship of Theology at Harvard. For a number of years Congregational ministers in and about Boston had been gradually accepting Anti-Trinitarian views, but there had been no open break. The election of Ware, however, aroused resentment among the orthodox and three years later Andover Theological Seminary was established as a protest at the defection of Harvard. The orthodoxy of Andover was protected by a provision that each professor was to sign periodically a statement of the seminary creed. The very year Ware was elected to his professorship *The Panoplist*, under the editorship of a young lawyer, Jeremiah Everts, began publication in the defense of orthodoxy. A clean-cut alignment now began to appear between the two parties. Of the sixteen pre-Revolutionary Congregational churches in Boston, fourteen were tending toward Unitarianism, while the movement was spreading to the smaller towns in the vicinity. It was not, however, until 1815 and after that the actual separation took place. Two influences contributed directly to the separation. One was the review of Belsham's "American Unitarianism" in the *Panoplist*, a pamphlet which had formerly circulated only among Unitarians. It was an English publication and described the progress of the liberal movement in Massachusetts, frankly discussing the actual situation and giving names and churches. The other event was a sermon preached by William Ellery Channing at the installation of Jared Sparks (1819) as the minister of a Unitarian church in Baltimore. The sermon was an arraignment of the orthodoxy of the time, which aroused the resentment of the great body of orthodox ministers, made Channing the recognized leader of the American Unitarians, and from this time forward the liberal churches began to assume their true position.

After separation had finally taken place it was found that the largest percentage of the people of wealth and position in and about Boston had gone into the Unitarian churches. Although calling themselves liberals in theology, this class was at the same time the most conservative element in New England society in every other respect, especially in their economic and political ideas. In 1820 the State Supreme Court of Massachusetts established in the Dedham case a ruling which gave to the Unitarians a large share of the property in dispute. It provided "that an orthodox majority of church members might be overruled in questions affecting church property by the 'society' or parish, in which the actual communicants might be and frequently were in the minority." This decision was a blow to the orthodox party, but it served to arouse them thoroughly to action, and within a few years a whole series of new orthodox churches was formed. To these new pulpits were called an especially able group of preachers, who, while accepting the substance of the old theology, were yet able to restate it in such a way as to give it a popular appeal. Of these new pulpits none was more influential than that of Hanover Street Church where Lyman Beecher, the most able of the orthodox ministers, was the pastor.

Chapter XVI

THE ERA OF ORGANIZATION AND THE RISE OF MODERN MISSIONS

THE first years under the Federal Constitution are frequently characterized as the period of nationality. This period marked the temporary decline of state powers and sectional interests, for in these early years of the nation's life the people had caught the vision of national need and were uniting in common national tasks. The great Chief Justice John Marshall was rendering his nationalistic decisions, and the principle of nationality was generally dominant. The churches likewise were imbued with the thought of national need and were uniting to carry on the great common Christian tasks. "Both church and nation felt themselves called at the same period to grapple with the same problem," that of securing harmonious coöperation among the states and among the churches. Coupled with the dominant idea of national need was the new religious energy and zeal which had been engendered by the great revival which had swept over the country in the closing years of the eighteenth and the opening years of the nineteenth century. While the revival resulted in several unfortunate schisms, yet in the early years of the century, especially, there had been a large growth of interdenominational good will, which soon manifested itself in concrete form by the formation of numerous interdenominational societies.

Naturally the revival greatly increased the desire of Christian people to spread the gospel among all classes, and especially among the many new settlements forming in the West, and among the American Indians. The early missionary societies which had been formed in England and Scotland, such as the S. P. G. and the S. P. C. K., were organized to work primarily among the colonists of the far-flung British Empire. Beginning with the latter eighteenth century, however, emphasis began to be laid upon work for the so-called heathen, and in 1792 the English Baptists organized a society and sent William Carey to India. Three years later the London Missionary Society was formed by Presbyterians, Congregationalists and some adherents of the Church of England, while similar societies were springing up in the Netherlands and Scotland. A like movement began at about the same time in America influenced by their English brethren, and numerous missionary societies were formed in the New England and middle states, and among Congregationalists, Presbyterians, Baptists, Dutch Reformed and finally the Methodists.

At first these societies were local in their scope and were primarily concerned with the conversion of the heathen in America—the Indians—and were generally interdenominational. Thus the New York Missionary Society, formed in 1796, was made up of representatives of Presbyterians, Dutch Reformed and Baptists and its immediate object was to carry the gospel to the southern

Indians. In 1803 this organization received about $5,000 for its work and soon there were several auxiliary societies formed in other sections of the state and work among the New York Indians was enlarged. In New England there were numerous Congregational societies, the earliest being the Missionary Society of Connecticut, organized by the General Association in 1798. The purpose of this society was "to Christianize the heathen in North America, and to support and promote Christian knowledge in the new settlements within the United States." In 1800 it sent its first missionary, David Bacon, "afoot and alone, with no more luggage than he could carry on his person," to the region south and west of Lake Erie, where he was instructed to visit the wild tribes of that region, "learn their feelings with respect to Christianity, and, so far as he had opportunity, to teach them its doctrines and duties." The Connecticut society was the strongest of the early societies and was supported by numerous auxiliaries, and by 1807 it had a permanent fund of $15,000. Within the next few years at least eight such societies had been formed in the New England states, all of them with numerous smaller local societies as auxiliaries. Thus the Massachusetts Missionary Society was supported by the "Boston Female Society for promoting the Diffusion of Christian Knowledge"; "the Cent Institution" supported by Boston women, who promised to pay a cent a week for the purchase of Bibles, Psalms and hymn books, primers, catechisms, etc. Similar organizations were to be found in Rhode Island where Samuel Hopkins was the prime mover; in New Hampshire; in Maine and in Vermont.

Of great importance in the spreading of missionary

propaganda was the missionary periodical which now came into existence. *The Connecticut Evangelical Magazine* was the official organ of the Connecticut Missionary Society beginning in 1800, and for fourteen years, as the magazine quaintly states, communicated "instruction upon the great truths and doctrines of religion" in order "to comfort and edify the people of God and to interest the pious mind by exhibiting displays of the grace and mercy of God." Such were the objects of its work, "rather than to amuse the specialist and entertain the curious." *The Massachusetts Missionary Magazine* began operations in 1803 and from the beginning produced a profit for the Massachusetts Missionary Society. In 1805 *The Panoplist* was launched as a private enterprise for the purpose of combating Unitarianism, which in that year had gained its first great victory in the election of its candidate to the Hollis Professorship of Divinity in Harvard College. Three years later it was combined with the *Massachusetts Missionary Magazine* and has continued since 1820 as the *Missionary Herald.* The New Hampshire Society published *The Religious Repository* though it proved short-lived, while the Vermont Society supported as its official organ the *Vermont Evangelical Magazine* which continued its operation until 1815. By the latter date all the Congregational magazines had disappeared except the *Panoplist and Missionary Magazine.*

Organized missionary effort among American Presbyterians began with the incorporation of the General Assembly in 1799 with the power of holding property for pious and charitable purposes, and three years later a standing committee on missions was appointed to supervise the work of missionaries. Previous to this, missions had been supported by individual churches, presbyteries and synods. Several of the synods and presbyteries also organized as missionary societies, as did the Synod of Pittsburgh in 1802 when it formed the Western Missionary Society "to carry the gospel to the Indians and interim inhabitants." Early Presbyterian mission activities had four objectives: frontier communities, settled regions without churches, Indians and negroes. From 1805 to 1809 *The General Assembly's Missionary Magazine or Evangelical Intelligencer* was published as their missionary organ. The Dutch churches also began to manifest interest in missions about the same time, and in 1800 were supporting six missionaries in Upper Canada.

The Baptists, before the formation of formal missionary societies, were missionary in purpose, and missionaries had been sent out by individual churches and associations as early as 1778, when the Warren Association of the New England Churches sent workers to the northern section of the country. With the opening of the new century (1802) the Massachusetts Baptist Missionary Society was launched, which was soon publishing a magazine. Within a few years Baptist societies were to be found in Maine, Pennsylvania, New York, all with their supporting organizations of the usual type. At about the same time the Friends also manifested a new interest in Indian missions which were carried on under the supervision of committees appointed by the Yearly Meetings.

The Methodists were several years behind the other churches in their formal missionary organization, the reason being that Methodism had from the beginning

been missionary in character. During the latter years of
Asbury's life he had collected money wherever he could,
to supply the wants of the frontier preachers and their
families. The sums collected were also used to extend
the work of the church among the poor and the destitute.
The early American Methodists, however, had done little
for the Indians, and it was largely the aroused interest
in Indian work which led to the formation of the Methodist Missionary Society in 1819. This interest was first
awakened through the work of John Stewart, a freeborn mulatto who after his conversion at a camp-meeting
in Ohio felt the call to preach to the Indians. Stewart began his work among the Wyandots at Upper Sandusky,
Ohio, in 1816, was licensed as a local preacher of the
Methodist Church two years later, and the next year his
work was taken over by the Ohio Conference and regular
missionaries appointed. Meanwhile steps were being taken
in New York to form a Methodist Missionary Society,
the reasons for which were thus summarized by Nathan
Bangs, one of the organizing committee and the first historian of Methodist missions: First, other denominations
had organized missionary societies and so zealous were
they that many Methodist people were contributing to
them; second, it was evident that although the Methodist
system is missionary in character yet there were many
places, such as new and destitute settlements, which were
incapable of supporting the gospel; third, work among
the Indians was opening up; fourth, it might become the
duty of Methodists to help "others in extending the Redeemer's kingdom in foreign nations"; and finally it was
evident that such an organization could probably raise

much more money and consequently do more good than under the present arrangement.

While the early American interest in missions was confined principally to work among the new settlements and the Indians, yet there was to be found at the same time a growing interest in the great "heathen world" outside America. New geographical and anthropological knowledge was arousing the interest of an increasing number of American readers, while the work of early English missionaries was eagerly followed by the readers of the numerous American missionary magazines. Missionaries sent out by the London Missionary Society frequently made the voyage to the East by way of America. Such was the case of Robert Morrison, who sailed for China in 1807 by way of the United States. Here he met Presbyterian, Reformed and Baptist missionary leaders who not only gave him assistance while here, but after he reached China continued to assist his mission. American interest in foreign missions, however, was brought to a head by the dramatic appeal of a group of students in Andover Theological Seminary in 1810.

The leader of this group was Samuel J. Mills, who had become interested in foreign missions through the efforts of Samuel Hopkins, the minister of the First Congregational Church at Newport, Rhode Island, to send two young negroes as missionaries to Africa. Mills came to Williams College aflame with zeal to take the gospel to the non-Christian lands, and through his influence a group of students banded themselves together into a secret society, each pledging to devote his life to missionary service. On graduation from Williams College most of the group entered Andover Theological Seminary where three others joined them, Adoniram Judson, Samuell Newell and Samuel Nott, Jr. The burning desire of this group to engage in missionary work led them to petition the General Association of Massachusetts (1810) to inaugurate a foreign mission and offered themselves to go as missionaries. The time, evidently, was ripe for such an appeal, for immediately steps were taken by the association to carry out their desire, and the American Board of Commissioners for Foreign Missions was formed (June, 1810). Immediately liberal donations began to flow to the board; four wealthy supporters gave $7,000; $4,000 came from auxiliary societies, while in 1811 a legacy of $30,000 came to them. Thus means were seemingly providentially provided for the sending out of the young missionaries, and in February, 1812, in Salem, Massachusetts, five young men were ordained and soon set sail for India.

Even more dramatic was the beginning of foreign mission organization among the Baptists. On the long voyage to India, two of the missionaries sent out by the American Board, Judson and Rice, though sailing on different vessels, were converted to Baptist principles through diligent study of the Scriptures, and on landing they and their wives were immersed, in the Baptist Church at Calcutta. The announcement of these dramatic conversions to Baptist views, and the fact that the converts offered themselves as ready to serve as Baptist missionaries seemed a providential happening to many leading Baptists in America. Rice returned to the United States to urge the appeal on their immediate attention, while Judson remained in Burma to establish the first Baptist mission. Luther Rice now entered upon his task of awakening American Baptists to their missionary responsibility and to his appeal there was an immediate response. His first work was an extended tour through the United States, establishing missionary societies in all the important Baptist centers. In May, 1814, there gathered in Philadelphia thirty-three delegates representing eleven states, and out of this gathering came the "General Missionary Convention of the Baptist Denomination of the United States of America for Foreign Missions." This event was notable, not alone because it was the first Baptist foreign missionary society, but it was the first general organization of the Baptists in the United States.

Rice now became the field marshal of Baptist Missions, and from this time until the end of his life in 1836 he traveled throughout the country furthering that cause together with education. At the meeting of the General Baptist Society in 1817 plans were laid for the beginning of home missions in the West, under the conviction that "western as well as eastern regions are given to the Son of God for an inheritance," and in that year John M. Peck and James E. Welch were sent to the Missouri territory. Though the General Society soon discontinued their support, Peck remained in the West and devoted the remainder of his life to the missions and to education. After 1820 the Massachusetts Baptist Missionary Society gave him some support, though much of his work was carried on through local societies which he established. No other man in the early history of Illinois exercised a larger influence than did Peck, and it is stated that he

ORDINATION OF THE FIRST AMERICAN FOREIGN MISSIONARIES

From an engraving in possession of the American Board of Commissioners for Foreign Missions, Boston, Mass. Reproduced by Harper & Brothers, 1852

did more than any other single individual to induce
tlers to come to Illinois through his publications, *Gui*
for Emigrants (1831) and *Gazetteer of Illinois* (1834

Baptist work among the Indians began the same ye
Peck came to Missouri when Isaac McCoy was appointe
a missionary to the Indians of Indiana and Illinois. I
1820 McCoy opened a mission at Fort Wayne where h
conducted a school, for English and French Indians and
negroes. Two years later he established a mission in southern Michigan to which he gave the name Carey, and here
he and his wife labored for four years amidst privations
and sickness, though with great success. In 1823 a United
States exploring expedition, under the command of Major
S. H. Long, visited the mission and he has left us a
glowing account of McCoy's work in his journal. Though
the mission had been established but seven months at the
time of Long's visit, yet he found "a large and comfortable dwelling house,—a schoolhouse, a blacksmith's
shop, and other out houses—a large garden, pasture
ground enclosed with a good fence, together with a large
field of plowed ground planted with corn." The school
contained about forty pupils, half of them the children of
Indian parents, the others mixed breed. The girls were
taught, besides the usual subjects, needlework, knitting
and spinning, while the boys, besides the general branches
of education, were taught the art of agriculture. The
government appropriated $1,000 a year for the support
of the mission, which was to be expended to provide a
teacher and a blacksmith, while additional support came
from the Baptist Missionary Society of Washington City.

From the year 1820 onward mission work among the

Indians received great impetus through the announced policy of the Federal government of distributing annually a subsidy of several thousands of dollars among the missionary societies already engaged or prepared to engage in missionary work. This led to a rapid expansion of Indian mission activity among all the churches, and real progress was made toward civilization especially among the southern Indians. An excellent illustration of this growth is presented by the Indian work of the American Board of Commissioners for Foreign Missions. In 1817 their first missionary was sent to the Cherokee nation on the Tennessee, which by 1830 had grown to eight stations, the most important being Brainerd. At the latter station in 1822 the mission property was valued at $17,300 and consisted of four large buildings, including a mission house, two schoolhouses, a saw and grist mill and ten outbuildings, while the mission farm was stocked with five yoke of oxen, thirty cows, one hundred young cattle, three hundred swine, twelve sheep and three horses with four colts, besides blacksmith and farm tools. In 1830 the board was supporting the following Indian missions: to the Cherokees one on the Tennessee and another on the Arkansas, Chickasaw, Choctaw, Osage mission on the Neosho, Osage mission on the Missouri, Green Bay mission, mission at Mackinaw, mission at Maumee, mission among the New York Indians, and a mission in the Northwest. Similar expansion took place among the Presbyterians, Friends, Baptists, Methodists, Roman Catholics. The Methodists, for instance, in 1830 were maintaining Indian missions in Ohio, Tennessee and Mississippi and reported that year an Indian membership of 4,501.

The American Board of Commissioners for Foreign Missions was Congregational in its origin, but in 1812 it became interdenominational by the election of Presbyterians to its board, and four years later Dutch Reformed representatives were added. During the first thirty years of its existence the board sent out 694 missionaries and among the most notable of its early achievements was the Christianization of the Hawaiian Islands, which was begun in 1820, and five years later the Ten Commandments were made the basis for the laws of the islands. Early mission work among the frontier settlements, as has been noted, was carried on by numerous local societies, among the several denominations, while the Indian missions were conducted under the early foreign mission boards. The first home missionary organization, on a national scale, was the American Home Missionary Society, formed in 1826, which like the American Board for Foreign Missions was interdenominational in character.

The American Home Missionary Society became the principal agent in carrying out the Plan of Union of 1801. At first the society was largely Presbyterian in membership, but later the numerous Congregational local societies became auxiliary, and a large proportion of the missionaries sent to the West were young men from Congregational colleges and seminaries. The society did an immense work in spreading Christian institutions throughout the West, while it supported weak churches in every section of the country. Nine years after its formation (1835) the society was employing 719 agents and missionaries, four hundred and eighty-one of these were settled pastors or employed as "stated supplies" in single congregations; one hundred and eighty-five were placed over two or three congregations, while fifty were employed in larger districts. Twenty years later (1855) the society was employing one thousand and thirty-two missionaries working in twenty-seven different states and territories. The other American churches soon organized their own home missionary societies to carry on work in the West. The societies of the Protestant Episcopal (1828) and the Methodist (1819) churches at first served the double purpose of foreign and home missions, while the Baptists organized their national Home Missionary Society in 1832.

An example of the spirit of sacrifice and devotion to the cause of missions is illustrated by the "Illinois Band," a group of eleven students at Yale Divinity School, who in 1828 banded together and pledged themselves to seek service in Illinois as teachers and ministers. All but one of the number went to Illinois immediately on graduation, sent by the American Home Missionary Society, where some became ministers and others established Illinois College. One of the band, Julian M. Sturtevant, became the first instructor in the college while Theron Baldwin, another of the band, after helping to found the college, assisted in forming the Society for the Promotion of Collegiate and Theological Education in the West, and as secretary of this organization came to be known as "The Father of Western Colleges." Some years later Asa Turner, one of the Illinois Band, after a period as minister in Quincy, moved across the Mississippi into the "Black Hawk Purchase" which became in 1838 a part of the territory of Iowa. After establishing a Congregational church at Denmark, he was joined by a Yale friend, Reuben Gaylord, who organized a number of churches, while in 1843 a band of eleven young men from Andover Theological Seminary came to the territory. They were all ordained in Turner's little church at Denmark and then scattered through the territory to plant churches and found schools. Out of their work came Iowa College, first established at Davenport, later moved to Grinnell, and now known as Grinnell College.

Interest in missions, both foreign and home, gave rise also to many kindred organizations. The increased demand for missionaries led to the establishment of schools where they could be adequately trained. To aid in this important work Education Societies began to be formed, and a national organization known as the American Education Society was organized in 1815. This society had for its purpose the aiding of "all pious young men, of suitable talents, who appear to be called to preach Christ, and who belong to any of the evangelical denominations." In 1818 the Protestant Episcopalians established their own Education Society as did later the Baptists, Methodists and others.

To this period also belong the establishment of the first theological seminaries, as well as the first colleges among Baptists and Methodists. From 1808 to 1840 at least twenty-five theological seminaries were established by Congregationalists, Presbyterians, Baptists, Dutch Reformed, German Reformed and Unitarians. The first to be founded was Andover in 1808, which came about as a result of the seating of an avowed Unitarian in the professorship of Divinity at Harvard in 1805. In 1810 the

Dutch Reformed Church established their seminary at New Brunswick; two years later the Presbyterian seminary at Princeton was opened, to be followed in rapid succession by Bangor (Maine) in 1816; by an Episcopalian Seminary in New York, 1817; Auburn in 1821; Yale Divinity School in 1822; Union Seminary in Virginia (Presbyterian) in 1824; in 1825, the Baptist Seminary at Newton, Massachusetts, and the German Reformed Seminary at York, Pennsylvania; and in 1826 the Lutheran Seminary at Gettysburg. Other seminaries were founded in the thirties and forties including several Catholic seminaries for the training of priests, while the first Methodist Seminary was that at Concord, New Hampshire, established in 1847, and later removed to Boston. It is significant that all of the early theological seminaries were to be found in the East.

Of greater importance from the standpoint of general education in the West was the founding of numerous colleges during these same years. The establishment of the small denominational college generally came about in the process of settlement. This is particularly well illustrated in the states of Ohio, Indiana, Illinois, and Missouri. Indeed, almost any section of the United States will furnish illustrations of this process. Harvard College, for instance, was established while Massachusetts was in process of settlement, while Yale, Dartmouth, Williams, and William and Mary were frontier colleges at the time of their founding. And the history of these older institutions furnished inspiration to the founders of the colleges in the Ohio and Mississippi valleys. These colleges were manned almost entirely by ministers. The presidents were always clergymen, as were also a large proportion of the faculties.

As has been noted, the earliest colleges west of the Alleghanies were those established by Congregationalists and Presbyterians, but by 1830 Baptists and Methodists were giving increasing attention to education. In 1832 a Baptist institution was opened at Granville, Ohio, which in 1847 assumed the dignity of a college, later becoming Denison University. John M. Peck's school, first established at Rock Spring, Illinois, was moved to Upper Alton in 1832 and in 1835 became Shurtleff College. The Baptists were also busy forming State Conventions, and State Education Societies, and the slogan "every state its own Baptist college" was soon coming true in the establishment of Baptist institutions in most of the older states as well as in the newer communities of the West. The oldest of these state institutions was Colby College, Maine, which opened under Baptist patronage in 1820. The first permanent institution of college grade founded by the American Methodists was Wesleyan University, at Middletown, Connecticut, which was chartered in 1831; the next year Randolph-Macon College in Virginia was founded, while Dickinson College became a Methodist institution in 1833, although it had been chartered fifty years before. Allegheny College dates from 1834. The oldest Methodist college west of the Alleghanies is that at Lebanon, Illinois, which opened as Lebanon Seminary in 1828 and became McKendree College in 1834. Three years later (1837) the Indiana Conference founded at Greencastle, Indiana, Asbury University, which later became DePauw University.

The religious destitution of the frontier, the lack of Bibles and religious literature in the cabins of the early settlers, prompted the establishment of organizations in the East to print and distribute Christian literature. When Samuel J. Mills made his first missionary tours of the United States in 1812-1813 and again in 1814-1815 in which he covered nearly ten thousand miles, he reported these conditions in a pamphlet published in 1815. At Kaskaskia, then the capital of Illinois Territory, he found but five Bibles in one hundred families, and there was an amazing lack even in the older sections of the country. It was such conditions as these which led to the founding of the American Bible Society in New York in 1816, although there had been local Bible Societies for several years previous. The national Bible organization in 1829-1830 made a systematic drive to place a Bible in every home, throughout the country, while efforts were made to supply foreign immigrants with copies of the Bible as they entered the ports of the United States. In 1825 a kindred organization was formed in New York known as the American Tract Society. Like the American Bible Society this organization sought the support of Christians of all denominations, and its board of publication was composed of ministers representing the several orthodox churches. Among the larger publications of the Tract Society were the *Evangelical Family Library* of fifteen volumes and the *Religious Library* consisting of twenty-five volumes. The society published a paper called the *Christian Messenger* which soon had a large circulation throughout the country, while its agents of one kind or another were sent into every section of the nation, visiting towns and villages and supplying the poor with books and tracts. In 1855 the Tract Society had 659 colporteurs at work, 126 of whom were laboring among the Germans and immigrants; they visited in that year 639,193 families, 64,686 being Roman Catholic.

Besides this interdenominational distribution of literature throughout the country, most of the larger churches were soon engaged in publishing and distributing their own literature. The oldest of these denominational publishing houses was the Methodist Book Concern, established in New York in 1789, and every Methodist circuit rider became its agent distributing its publications throughout the network of the circuits. The American Baptist Publication Society (1840) grew out of the Baptist Tract Society organized in 1824, while the Presbyterians, Episcopalians, Friends, Lutherans and others likewise had their tract, Bible and publication societies. It would be difficult to overestimate the influence for good of this tremendous output of Christian literature which found its way into every nook and corner of the land.

The Methodists seem to have been the first to introduce Sunday schools into the United States as early as 1786, the movement having already gained considerable impetus in England. By 1816 Sunday schools had been formed in various parts of the country and soon societies were organized in the larger cities, as New York and Philadelphia, for the publication of little books, for the instruction of children, such as spelling and hymn books, and catechisms. Finally in 1824 there was begun a movement resulting in the organization of the American Sunday School Union, composed of an association of men of all denominations, the board of managers being laymen, the greater part of them living in Philadelphia. Its two-fold object was to promote the establishment of Sunday schools and prepare and publish suitable books and manuals for Sunday school use, and also for libraries, which were intended to furnish children with suitable home reading. In 1839 the society resolved to establish a Sunday school in every neighborhood without one, in the West. Three years later it adopted the same resolution in regard to the southern states, and great efforts were put forth to carry out these resolves; large sums of money were collected and many new Sunday schools were established, while the society employed agents and missionaries to travel through the country visiting the Sunday schools and establishing new ones.

While the vast majority of Christian people of every denomination throughout the country were giving enthusiastic support to these many new societies, there was developing in the West an opposition which gained considerable headway, particularly among the Baptists. At first the Baptists in the West gave hearty support to the cause of missions, and when John M. Peck came to Illinois he was well received by the Illinois Baptist Association and the cause of missions recommended to the churches. But soon it became evident that opposition was developing, especially among the old frontier Baptist farmer-preachers, and by 1825 anti-mission sentiment was to be found in almost every section of the West. The anti-missions resolutions adopted by the Apple Creek Baptist Association of Illinois in 1830 are typical. They declare that "We as an association do not hesitate to say, that we declare an unfellowship with foreign and domestic mission and bible societies, Sunday schools, and tract societies, and all other missionary institutions." Further they emphatically state, "No missionary preacher is to have the privilege of preaching at our association," and they "advise the churches to protest against Masonic and missionary institutions, and not to contribute to any such beggarly institutions." In 1832 the Sugar Creek Association in Indiana placed in their constitution the following: "Any Church suffering their members to unite with any of the Mission Conventions, Colleges, Tracts, Bible, Temperance, etc., Societies, and failing to deal with their members, shall be considered of such a violation of the principles of the union, that the Association when put into possession of a knowledge of such facts shall punish such churches as being not of us."

In certain sections of the West the anti-mission movement made almost a clean sweep of the Baptist churches, and by 1846 there were more than 68,000 Anti-Mission Baptists in the United States, by far the largest majority being found in the West. A good share of the responsibility for the rise of this movement is due to the activity and influence of three men, John Taylor, the old pioneer Baptist preacher of Kentucky, Daniel Parker, likewise a Baptist preacher, first in Tennessee and later in Illinois and Indiana, and Alexander Campbell, who has been mentioned before as the leader of the "reform" party among the western Baptists from 1820 to 1830.

John Taylor struck the first blow at missions in 1819 when he published a pamphlet called "Thoughts on Missions." The assumption on the part of the missionaries that there had been no religious work done in the West previous to their coming aroused the old veteran's ire and he says: "To hear and read their reports it would seem as if the whole country was almost a blank as to religion" and that there was not a preacher in the country which deserved the name except missionaries. The arch-enemy of missions in the West, however, was Daniel Parker. In 1820 he published a pamphlet of twenty-eight pages called "A Public Address to the Baptist Society" in which he vigorously opposed the cause of missions, and four years later published another pamphlet in which he set forth his two-seed doctrine, which purports to furnish a theological basis for anti-missionism. The third arch-opponent of missions was Alexander Campbell, who between the years 1820-1830 was particularly active in preaching, debating and conducting his paper the *Christian Baptist*, and after 1829 the *Millennial Harbinger*. Campbell professed to be favorable to missions, and to the spread of the gospel, but he objected to all societies which did not have a Scriptural basis and authorization.

One of the chief reasons for Baptist opposition to the cause of mission and other societies was their objection to the centralization of authority. One of the fundamental principles of the Baptists is the complete independence of the congregation, and the formation of societies, with their officers and paid secretaries, with authority to send men here and there, seemed to some a complete violation of Baptist principles. Taylor states: "I consider these great men, [the missionary secretaries], are verging close on an aristocracy, with an object to sap the foundation of Baptist republican government." Baptist objection to a paid ministry constituted another reason for their opposition. Taylor considered Rice a "modern Tetzel, and the Pope's old orator of that name was equally innocent with Luther Rice and his motive about the same," while Parker compares the missionaries to the money changers whom Christ drove from the temple, and he expects Christ will do the same thing for these modern traders in sheep and oxen. Undoubtedly also jealousy of the better educated missionaries on the part of the frontier preachers played its part in their opposition, while their contention that missionary societies were unscriptural was strongly stressed. This was the chief argument used by Campbell, and the columns of his paper were filled with bitter attacks upon all man-made societies. Parker in his pamphlet states that God did not send Jonah to Nineveh through a missionary society, nor was he "sent to a seminary of learning to prepare him to preach to these Gentiles; but was under the tuition of God, and was in no case under the direction of any body of men whatever, neither did he look back to a society formed to raise money for his support."

The doctrinal basis of anti-missionism was hyper-Calvinistic. It stated that God in His sovereign power did not need any human means to bring His elect to repentance. Nor was there need to preach to the non-elect, for all the preaching in the world could not bring them to repentance. Indeed, Parker held that sending the gospel to the non-elect, or to the devil's bona-fide children, as he called them, or giving them the Bible were acts of such gross and supreme folly that no Christian should be engaged in them. Campbell, had become Arminian in his theology and did not accept this doctrine, but opposed missionary societies as being an unscriptural means of carrying the gospel. Later he gave up his opposition, and in 1849 became the first president of the Missionary Society of the Disciples, though this move was strongly opposed by others, who got their best arguments against the society from the columns of the *Christian Baptist.*

Chapter XVII

RELIGION IN THE RESTLESS THIRTIES AND FORTIES

THE period from the adoption of the Federal Constitution to 1830 is usually called the era of nationalism; with equal appropriateness that from 1830 to the opening of the Civil War may be termed the era of sectionalism. This holds true both in politics and in religion. In both church and state the spirit of nationalism gradually gave way to that of sectionalism. Especially was this true after the question of slavery began to occupy the center of stage, until the country was divided into two distinct sections, each with its peculiar political and economic demands. So likewise was the trend in church affairs resulting in divisions and subdivisions of the churches, while each denomination began to emphasize its own peculiar interest. Loyalty to a denomination comes now to be the great emphasis, just as loyalty to the South or the North becomes the catchword in politics. The period is characterized by quarrels and contentions and slanders among the churches. Protestants are arrayed against Catholics; the famous Plan of Union of 1801 between Presbyterians and Congregationalists is first rejected by conservative Presbyterians and then by the Congregationalists; the great popular churches divide over slavery and then contend with unchristian bitterness for the border, while acrimonious conflicts are waged within the Lutheran, Episcopalian and German Reformed churches, and even the newly formed liberals, the Unitarians, find it impossible to agree among themselves.

New winds were blowing over the American people in the thirties and forties. A new democracy had arisen, manifesting its power by the elevation of Andrew Jackson to the presidency of the United States. Rapid changes were taking place in the economic life of the people; indeed, an industrial revolution was under way comparable to that which had taken place in England a century before. New streams of population were pouring into the country, especially from Ireland and southern Germany, profoundly disturbing the whole economic, political and social equilibrium of the nation. And withal it was a period of immense optimism. This had come about with the elevation of the common people to place and power. Opportunity was the key word of this new era. "Few boys of that generation escaped being told that they might become president. Few were not told that in the matter of money the future was in their hands." To the American of the thirties and forties his country was a land of boundless opportunity, nor did he for a moment doubt his own ability to take full advantage of it. Naturally an individualistic attitude dominated the period, while emotionalism everywhere prevailed. We must not be surprised, then, to find in this period a great variety of new interests arising; new and strange sects;

NEWTON THEOLOGICAL INSTITUTION

From a picture in possession of the Massachusetts Historical Society

new movements in thought; reforms of one kind or another; many of them the result of individual vagaries.

The first of the great American churches to be torn by internal strife was the Presbyterian. The controversy which finally culminated in the schism of 1837-1838 came about largely as a result of the working of the Plan of Union, and the operations of the American Home Missionary Society, which after 1826 became the chief agent in carrying out its provisions. Plan of Union churches had been formed numerously through central New York, in Ohio, Michigan, Indiana, Illinois and Wisconsin. In all of these churches there were large and influential New England groups, with their Congregational background, and influenced by the new theological currents coming out of New England. On the other hand, there was the large body of Presbyterians with their rigid Scotch-Irish background, who looked upon any change in the Calvinistic system as dangerous heresy. It was the presence of these two divergent elements in the church which was the fundamental cause of division.

The rift between these two elements began in New England, occasioned by a sermon preached by Dr. Nathaniel W. Taylor, of Yale Divinity School, at the Commencement of 1828. Taylor belonged to the new school of theological thought, farthest removed from the old strict Calvinism, while he was particularly severe on the doctrine of original sin. The following year the young and brilliant Presbyterian minister at Morristown, New Jersey, Albert Barnes, in a sermon before his congregation announced his agreement with the position of Taylor, admitting, however, that such a position was out of harmony with the Westminster Confession. The next year when Barnes was called to be the minister of the First Presbyterian Church of Philadelphia, the mother church of the denomination in America, his installation was opposed by conservative members of the presbytery. From this time on for a period of six years, Barnes was the storm center in the Presbyterian Church. The fact that his church was generally the meeting place of the General Assembly caused the controversy to assume a national significance. Year by year his case came before the General Assembly in one form or another, while in 1836 a new charge of heresy was lodged against him by Dr. George Junkin, a representative of the rigid Scotch-Irish group, and Barnes was suspended from his pulpit by action of the Philadelphia Synod, though the next General Assembly reversed the decision.

Another heresy trial of the period was that of Dr. Lyman Beecher, president of Lane Theological Seminary. Beecher had come from a brilliant pastorate of a Congregational church in Boston to take charge of the new seminary in Cincinnati, a Plan of Union project. Charges of heresy, slander and hypocrisy were placed against him in 1835 by Dr. Joshua L. Wilson, one of the "war horses" of western Presbyterianism, but his acquittal by the synod, though Old School in its sympathy, was soon obtained by a large majority. Two years before two of the professors of Illinois College and the president, Edward Beecher, were arraigned before the Presbytery of Illinois for teaching the "New Haven doctrines" and when they were acquitted their accuser appealed to the synod, though the case was not pushed further. All of these young men were Yale graduates and were working under the Plan of Union. The conservatives, by this time, were thoroughly aroused to the dangers of heretical teachings on the part of the "Congregationalized" Presbyterians generally and the slightest tendency in the direction of liberalism in religion on their part was sure to result in protest if not in accusation of heresy from the orthodox brethren.

Matters were now drifting rapidly toward a division in the church. In 1836 Union Theological Seminary in New York had been founded by the liberal, or New School, wing, independent of the control of the General Assembly. This was undoubtedly one of the factors which threw the Princeton Seminary influence toward the Old School position, and made their ultimate victory possible two years later. Of fundamental importance in the whole controversy was the Home Missionary Society, the agency through which the Plan of Union largely functioned. The Old School party contended that the Plan of Union churches established through the Home Missionary Society were not real Presbyterian churches. These churches, they contended, were lax in discipline; did not possess full presbyterial organization and were heretical in their doctrinal position, while a growing number of Old School leaders felt that abolitionism was gaining too strong a hold among the New School brethren. The rigid Old School party now began to advocate, more and more, the establishment of their own denominational societies, and the repudiation of the agreement with the interdenominational Home Missionary Society and the American Board. This program they hoped to carry through the

General Assembly of 1836. This they were unable to accomplish, however, as that assembly contained a New School majority, who carried through their own program with a high hand. This New School victory greatly alarmed the Old School party and led them to take steps, at once, to divide the church.

The crisis came in the General Assembly of 1837. In this assembly the Old School party, now joined by the moderates, or Princeton Seminary group, were in a decided majority, and having met previous to the convening of the assembly, were well organized with a fully laid program. No religious body ever took such heroic measures to rid the church of what was considered heresy as did the Presbyterian body in 1837. Without hesitating a moment, four synods, and eventually 533 churches and more than 100,000 members, were read out of the church by a strictly party vote. This having been accomplished the assembly then proceeded to separate the church from the voluntary and interdenominational societies and adopted the Western Missionary Society as the assembly's Foreign Mission Board, while it declared their own Boards of Education and Domestic Missions to be their only agents in those respective fields.

The New School party were taken completely by surprise, while many belonging to the Old School were indignant at the high-handed manner in which the church had been divided. In August, 1837, the New School body held a convention at Auburn, New York, where it was determined to stand by the Plan of Union and to make an attempt, at the next General Assembly, to regain their place in the church. They also drew up a document maintaining their doctrinal soundness. Their plan, however, to regain their place in the church was completely unsuccessful, for when the New School delegates presented their credentials to the assembly of 1838 the moderator refused to recognize them. There was nothing left now for the New School delegates to do but to withdraw, and steps were immediately taken to organize a separate church. After the formation of the New School body into a church, other synods and presbyteries outside the exscinded synods joined them, so that eventually the New School represented four-ninths of the ministry and membership of the old church. In many instances synods, presbyteries and churches were divided. The New School strength lay largely at the north, though the Synod of Eastern Tennessee and a few southern presbyteries adhered to them, but the overwhelming majority of southern presbyteries were Old School.

The part played by slavery in this famous controversy is difficult to determine. There is no doubt, however, but that anti-slavery sentiment was much stronger among the New School party than in the Old School, and there were undoubtedly numerous Old School leaders who were immensely relieved to have the church rid of the radical New England influence. The great slavery controversy in its bearing upon all of the American churches will be fully traced in the following chapter.

The epidemic of controversy which characterized the years under discussion in the American churches manifested itself among the Episcopalians in a bitter contest between the High Church and Low Church parties. The outstanding influences in the early years of American

Episcopalianism were decidedly Low Church, under the leadership of Bishop William White, but beginning with the consecration in 1811 of John Henry Hobart (1775-1830) as Bishop of New York, the High Church party obtained an especially aggressive leadership, and a new period in the history of American Episcopalianism was begun.

By the close of the War of 1812 the Episcopal Church was no longer looked upon with suspicion by patriotic Americans, for "churchmen" had fought on the American side in the war, while in New England they naturally aligned themselves with the party fighting for the abolition of the privileges of the standing order. Thus they were identified with the rising popular party under the leadership of Thomas Jefferson. A new and energetic leadership within the church was also arising. Besides Bishop Hobart, three other bishops stand out in this period of renewed life and advance in the church: Alexander V. Griswold, Bishop of the Eastern Diocese (New England), Richard Channing Moore of Virginia, and Philander Chase the founder of the church in the great region west of the Alleghanies. Each of these leaders had distinctive characteristics. Hobart was the high churchman *par excellence*, Griswold was as emphatically low church, Moore was warmly evangelical, while Chase was the ideal leader of the pioneer forces of the church.

If the period to 1812 was one of suspended animation, that from 1812 to 1835 may be as truthfully characterized as one of almost feverish activity. If the old leaders lacked energy, the new leaders burned themselves out with their excess of toil. The work of Hobart is particularly significant. When he came to the New York diocese there were twenty-eight clergymen, at his death in 1830 the number had grown to one hundred and twenty-seven. He was the "embodiment of positive assertion and aggressive action." With his coming the Episcopal Church in New York ceased to exist on sufferance and became "self-conscious, self-confident and aggressive." He took openly and proudly the high church position, at the time when that position was unpopular in his own church and especially unpopular in the country. His church he considered the one channel of saving grace; to him the sacraments were the only vehicles of that grace, and valid only when administered by a priesthood ordained in proper apostolic succession. He would have nothing to do with interdenominational societies, fearing if he united with others he would thereby weaken the claims he made for his own church. But he organized numerous societies within the church, such as the Episcopal Tract Society, the Sunday School Society, the Bible Society and a Missionary Society, and missionaries were sent to the Indians in western New York to whom he gave personal supervision.

The opposite of Hobart in his churchmanship was Bishop Griswold, who from 1811 to 1843 administered the affairs of the Episcopal Church in New England. Low churchman and a strong preacher he was a man of deep and simple piety, with an abundance of "moderation, good sense and careful equipoise." During his long episcopate he saw his original diocese divided and subdivided, as the number of churches grew, until at his death there were five dioceses in the original territory over which he presided at the beginning of his episcopate.

When Bishop Moore was consecrated Bishop of Virginia in 1814 there were not more than five active ministers in Virginia; at his death in 1841 there were nearly a hundred ministers and one hundred and seventy churches. These three bishops were typical of the church of their time.

Bishop Chase was of pure New England stock and a graduate of Dartmouth College, where as a student he was brought into the Episcopal Church through the study of the Prayer Book. Soon after graduation he was ordained and became an eager and restless missionary and remained a frontiersman until the end of his life. His first parish was on the New York frontier. Thence he went to New Orleans, where he formed the first Episcopal church in that newly acquired region. Returning to New England in shattered health he stayed only long enough to regain his strength and then was off again, on horseback, in the middle of winter, for the Western Reserve of Ohio. Here he went about from house to house and from settlement to settlement gathering together the people of his church. Finally in 1818, largely through his pioneering work, there had come to be five clergymen in the state of Ohio, and in that year these five with nine laymen met and organized a diocese and elected Chase their bishop.

The number of Episcopalians on the frontier were few, and the people of the other denominations generally hostile, but none knew better than this frontier bishop how to overcome their prejudice. Perhaps the greatest monument to Bishop Chase's work is Kenyon College which was established on a beautiful ridge in the midst of a primeval forest in central Ohio in 1824. After Chase had determined to establish a college, he journeyed to England to raise money and in spite of opposition from other bishops in America he succeeded in his enterprise and came home with twenty thousand dollars, largely obtained through the help of Lord Gambier and Lord Kenyon, and appropriately to the town which grew up about Kenyon College he gave the name Gambier. In 1831 Chase resigned both his bishopric and the presidency of the college, due to disagreements which arose in his administration. For three years he combined farming with missionary labor in Michigan, but in 1835 a new diocese was formed in Illinois, and the three clergymen who constituted it called upon Chase to be their bishop. Here he duplicated his work in Ohio, even journeying to England in search of funds to found Jubilee College, while generous help was also received from American churchmen. Meanwhile two other western dioceses had been organized in 1829, Kentucky and Tennessee, and in 1835 the General Convention adopted the policy of sending out missionary bishops into the new country without waiting for any call for them, and in that year the first missionary bishop was elected in the person of Jackson Kemper and largely through his apostolic labor his church was established in Indiana, Iowa, Minnesota and Wisconsin.

The Protestant Episcopal Church was expanding in spite of internal dissension. By about 1835 a line of cleavage had been run through the church, separating the two radically opposite parties, the high churchmen on the one hand and the evangelicals, or low churchmen, on the other. When Chase began his work in Ohio in 1817 he called "together his neighbors and his companions for the preaching of the Word, and the Prayers. When Breck and his companions laid down their packs under an elm-tree in Minnesota, in 1850," they erected "a rustic cross," built "a rude altar of rough stones," and began "their work by the celebration of the Eucharist Feast." Thus is illustrated the radically different emphases of these two church parties.

The high church party adopted the name "Anglo-Catholic" by which they meant a half-way position between Roman Catholicism and Protestantism, but which many could not distinguish from Romish Catholicism. They stood for the authority of the church as opposed to the right of individual judgment. Through the influence of such leaders as Bishop Hobart, year by year this exaltation of the church was winning converts among the people and gradually the Protestant Episcopal Church "was becoming more sharply differentiated, not only from the world, but from the current forms of American Christianity." This movement, already under way, was tremendously augmented by the influence of the "Oxford Movement" which began in 1833, at Oriel College, Oxford, by a group of young men who formed an "Association for vindicating the rights of the Church and Restoring the Knowledge of Sound Principles." In a series of able tracts, largely from the pen of John Henry Newman, the *Via Media* between Protestantism and Romanism was set forth. Their influence in America soon swelled the high church movement into a flood, and from 1835 onward to the Civil War was a period of strife within the church. Those opposing the movement feared that the high church party were making of the Protestant Episcopal Church a training-school for Rome, while able defenders set forth the Anglo-Catholic position. Each side formed their own societies to propagate their own views, and a pamphlet warfare was fiercely waged. Election of bishops brought on bitter party contests and the marvel is that the church did not split into fragments.

The church leader most responsible for preventing such an unfortunate result was William A. Mühlenberg who called himself an Evangelical Catholic. Mühlenberg, the great grandson of Henry M. Mühlenberg, had come to New York in 1847 as rector of a free church, the Church of the Holy Communion, built by his sister, having previously established the first Protestant Episcopal Church school in connection with his church at Flushing, Long Island. He later established the first order of deaconesses in the Episcopal Church and was the founder of St. Luke's Hospital, opened in 1856. This broad-spirited man consistently stood for "a broader and more comprehensive ecclesiastical system" and for a larger freedom of opinion within the church. He felt that the high and low church parties both had a legitimate place within the church. At the General Convention of 1853 these views were put in the form of a memorial and presented to that body where they were accepted by both parties and a reconciliation became an accomplished fact. The church parties, however, did not disappear, but from this time forward the "evangelical" party declined in influence until some thirty years later when the Reformed Episcopal Church was formed by a secession made up of discontented evangelicals.

The American Lutherans contributed their full share to the controversy of the period. A bitter dispute arose between two parties within the church, one advocating Americanizing the Lutheran Church and a liberal interpretation of the Confession, while a growing conservative party insisted upon the continued use of the German language and a strict adherence, not only to the Augsburg Confession, but to the symbolical books associated with it. The outstanding leader of the liberals was Samuel S. Schmucker who in 1826 had been the prime mover in the founding of the Lutheran Theological Seminary at Gettysburg and six years later of Pennsylvania College. Here he spent the remainder of his life as professor of theology and exercised widespread influence as a liberalizing force. In this respect he was the successor of Henry M. Mühlenberg, who had advocated the use of the English language and whose general outlook was particularly sane. Schmucker maintained that American Lutheranism had come out of a background of wholesome evangelism and he advocated the reincarnation on American soil of that spirit "which had characterized the school of Francke." On the other hand, he opposed that type of Lutheranism which had its background "in the sixteenth and seventeenth century confessional orthodoxy."

Dr. Schmucker might have swung American Lutheranism to his way of thinking if it had not been for the great wave of German immigration which set in about 1830 and continued until well past the Civil War. Up until the former year American Lutheranism had just kept pace with the growth of population in the country, but between 1830 and 1870 Lutheran increase was three times that of the general population. In the decade just previous to the Civil War nearly a million Germans came to America. Many of these German immigrants were Roman Catholics and a larger share were hostile to all religion, but perhaps the majority were Lutherans. The coming of this vast body of new fellow religionists placed a heavy burden upon the American Lutherans, but in many instances these new immigrants brought their own ministers with them and also their Old World conservatism and orthodoxy.

It was during these years that a number of extremely conservative Lutheran synods were formed: the Missouri Synod in 1846; the Buffalo Synod in 1845; the Iowa Synod in 1854. The recognized leader among these extremely conservative Lutherans was C. F. W. Walther who had come out as a young pastor with a number of immigrants from Saxony in 1839. These immigrants had left Saxony largely because of the growing rationalism in the state church and were strict Lutherans of the extreme orthodox type. After a period of uncertainty, during which one group advocated their return to Germany, Walther succeeded in restoring confidence among the colonists, and eventually gave them a new idea of the church, which characterizes the Missouri Lutherans to this day. He became the pastor of their church in St. Louis and in 1844 began the publication of *Der Lutheraner* which became a powerful influence in maintaining Lutheran orthodoxy as it was interpreted by Walther. He advocated the establishment of parochial schools and the acceptance of all the symbolical books as "the pure and uncorrupted explanation and statement of the Divine

Word," and led in the establishment of colleges and seminaries for the training of its ministry.

The decade and a half just previous to the Civil War saw also the beginning of a large immigration of Norwegians and Swedes. Illinois early attracted this immigration and in 1853 the Norwegians organized an American Synod. The Swedes at first united with the General Synod and received help from eastern Lutheran bodies and were even assisted by the American Home Missionary Society, but in 1860 under the leadership of Lars Paul Esbjörn they withdrew from that body and formed the Augustana Synod and organized their own college at Rock Island, Illinois. Both of these Lutheran bodies helped swell the volume of Lutheran conservatism in the country and played their part in the controversy of the period.

While this Lutheran immigration was resulting in the formation of these several new bodies, it was at the same time exerting an increasing influence in the older Lutheran organizations. In 1820 a General Synod had been organized which had come out of the growing sense of need of closer coöperation, as the church expanded westward and southward. Schmucker for many years was the leading influence in this general body, and worked consistently for "American Lutheranism" and also for a closer coöperation among the American churches. In 1838 he issued an appeal for the reunion of the churches on "the apostolic basis" and was one of the strongest advocates of the "Evangelical Alliance," organized in 1846. By the middle of the century, however, the conservative wing in the General Synod had become the larger party and

Schmucker's influence steadily declined and more conservative leaders came into the ascendancy. In these years numerous Lutheran periodicals began publication advocating one side or the other of the issue, while within the synods controversy went on often resulting in lasting divisions and in the formation of new synods.

Somewhat similar to the controversy among the American Lutherans was that which went on within the German Reformed Church. The language controversy was particularly severe in Philadelphia, resulting in the withdrawal of those advocating the use of the English language and the formation of congregations of their own. But far more important was the controversy which arose over the so-called "Mercersburg theology."

The first theological seminary of the German Reformed body was established at Carlisle, Pennsylvania, in 1825, but ten years later it was removed to Mercersburg, and the same year Marshall College was founded in the same place. In 1840 Dr. John W. Nevin, a Presbyterian of Scotch-Irish ancestry, was chosen to a professorship in the Mercersburg Seminary, and in 1844 Dr. Philip Schaff, a young Swiss scholar, was elected professor of historical and exegetical theology. Both Nevin and Schaff were scholars of high rank and were thoroughly familiar with the new German theological currents. It was not long until the more conservative ministers began to find cause for alarm in the teachings of these two brilliant professors and the "Mercersburg theology" was attacked in the church papers and in some instances there were withdrawals from the church. Both Nevin and Schaff were particularly active in their scholarship and a series of scholarly books came from them during this period of controversy that have been equaled by few if any among American scholars.

Of greatest importance from the standpoint of the rapid growth of Roman Catholicism in the United States from 1830 to the Civil War was the Irish and German immigration. The Irish had been coming to America for years previous to 1845, but after that date two causes account for its rapid increase: one was the greatly improved means of ocean transit, the other was the potato-rot famine in 1845-1846. By this time the potato had become the great Irish staple. In the former year a blight, which destroyed the potato plant overnight, swept over the island and the next year (1846) again the crop was destroyed. This brought on a famine, most devastating and terrible in its consequences, and resulted in a mighty wave of Irish emigration to America which has continued more or less down to the present time. These Irish immigrants were mostly peasant farmers with slender resources, which were soon exhausted after their arrival in an American port and they were a hundred per cent Roman Catholics. This meant that they must settle down where they landed, and Boston, New York, Philadelphia and Baltimore early became centers of Irish Roman Catholic influence.

As has been noted in connection with Lutheran growth, emigration from southern Germany was particularly large after the unsuccessful revolutions of 1830 and 1848. These immigrants were better financed than were the Irish and settled mostly in the newer sections of the country north of the Ohio or beyond the Mississippi;

Missouri and Wisconsin becoming great centers of German influence, though many Germans came to Cincinnati, and to the other cities along the Ohio, such as Evansville and Madison, Indiana. Perhaps a third of these Germans were Roman Catholic.

The large Catholic emigration to the United States prompted the organization of missionary societies among European Catholics to aid their coreligionists in the United States. The two most important of these societies were the Lyon (France) Propaganda, organized in 1822, and the Leopold Society of Austria, formed in 1829. In 1828 the Lyon Propaganda sent to the United States more than a hundred thousand francs and in 1846, 660,-207 francs were distributed among the twenty-one bishoprics and missions in America. From the time of its organization to 1850 this society alone sent nearly nine millions of francs to the United States. Other European societies also sent large sums, amounting in some years to as much as 1,000,000 francs.

Of considerable importance to American Roman Catholicism was the resuscitation (1805) of the Jesuits, who had been suppressed by the Pope in 1773. Of even greater importance in many respects was the founding of the Order of Sisters of Charity at about the same time, and the beginning of the work of religious women of other orders, such as the Ursulines, Carmelites and Sacred Heart, with their numerous schools, convents and religious houses. By 1835 every large city in the United States contained houses of these orders. Meanwhile, year by year new dioceses were established; Charleston, South Carolina, in 1820; Richmond in 1821; Cincinnati in 1823;

Mobile in 1824; St. Louis in 1826; Detroit, 1832; and between 1834 and 1847, Vincennes, Dubuque, Little Rock, Nashville, Natchez, Pittsburgh, Milwaukee, Chicago, Hartford, Oregon City, Albany, Buffalo, Cleveland and Galveston. Thus by 1850 practically every considerable city in the United States had become the head of a diocese.

The two outstanding American Catholic leaders in the period from 1820 to the Civil War were Bishop John England who became, in the former year, the first Bishop of Charleston (1820-1842), and Bishop John Hughes of the diocese of New York. These two great Irish Catholic bishops were men of decided character and great ability, bold, fearless and independent. Bishop England's diocese covered a territory eight hundred miles in length and from two to three hundred miles inland. He traveled through this vast territory continuously in his carriage, administering the sacraments, preaching, and instructing; made frequent trips to Rome where he was known as the "steam bishop," and in the midst of all these activities found time to prepare catechisms, establish "Book Societies," deliver lectures and write books. About the name of Bishop John Hughes two great Roman Catholic controversies center, that of "Trusteeism" and the "Common School question."

The struggle over trusteeism began in 1785 in New York City when the "Trustees of the Roman Catholic Church in the City of New York" purchased a site for a church and were incorporated. The trustees claimed the right to appoint and dismiss their pastors, as well as to administer the property. This was opposed from the start by the Catholic authorities, but it was not until Bishop Hughes took charge of the diocese that the matter was finally settled. Due to the long controversy between the trustees and the bishop, five of the eight New York churches became bankrupt, and when they were sold at a sheriff's sale, were bid in by Bishop Hughes on his own right, and by skillful management and an appeal to European Catholics for aid he finally succeeded in paying off the large debts. In Philadelphia a similar struggle over trusteeism occurred. In 1831 Bishop Kendrick of Philadelphia issued an interdict against St. Mary's Church, forbidding all sacred functions until the trustees were willing to disclaim their pretensions to authority. This severe measure was finally successful and the trustees gave way.

The Public School question likewise centered in New York, and arose in 1823 when "The New York Public School Society," an organization formed in 1805 for the education of poor and neglected children, objected to the distribution of public school funds to church schools. This practice had been going on for a number of years and several denominations had been securing funds annually from the state. On the protest of the Public School Society the Protestant churches gave way, but the Roman Catholics, headed by Bishop Hughes, continued to insist upon state appropriations for their schools and other benevolent work. In 1840 Bishop Hughes brought the school matter to a head by appearing before the corporation of the city in behalf of the Catholic schools and later a petition was presented asking that seven Catholic schools be permitted to share in the public school fund.

This was finally denied by the corporation. The Catholics then took the matter to the legislature, where the Catholic petition was again defeated, though the lower house favored their demands. This discussion created great excitement throughout the country and was one of the factors which led to the Know-Nothing, or Native American, movement which swept over the nation in the forties and fifties.

The Native American party began in 1837 primarily to emphasize the necessity of limiting immigration and advocating the passage of more stringent immigration and naturalization laws, and demanded that a residence of twenty-one years be made a condition for obtaining citizenship. A few years later, however, it became frankly an anti-Catholic movement. In 1845 an organization of Native Americans was formed claiming a membership of 100,000, while in 1850 it became a secret organization under the name, known only by its members, as "The Supreme Order of the Star-Spangled Banner," which later came to be known as the Know-Nothing party. To be admitted to the lodges of this organization the candidate had to be a native-born American citizen, reared under Protestant influence, and neither himself, his wife, nor his parents Roman Catholics. In the initiation of members the president thus addressed the candidates: "In every city, town and hamlet, the danger has been seen and the alarm sounded. And hence true men have devised this order as a means . . . of advancing America and the American interest on the one side, and on the other of checking the stride of the foreigner or alien, of thwarting the machinations and subverting the deadly plans of the Jesuit and the Papist." The Know-Nothing movement was unjust and ill-timed, while such methods as it pursued are always under suspicion, and can only lead to disorders and rioting and a vast increase of ill-feeling.

In spite of such attempts to resist the growth and influence of Catholicism in the United States, their numbers were increasing by leaps and bounds. In 1830 there were in round numbers, 600,000 Catholics in the United States; twenty years later (1850) they were numbered at 3,500,000, while on the outbreak of the Civil War they had increased another million.

So far in this chapter the controversies and outstanding happenings among some of the larger American churches have been considered. The strange and unusual religious movements which so crowd this restless period will now be treated. A bare catalogue of these many movements with their founders would more than fill a page, and would include names of men and women long since forgotten, but who at the time of their activity were household words in many sections of the United States. It will be possible to discuss only a few of the more important of these movements, such as Mormonism, the Millerite Movement, Spiritualism and some of the more successful communistic experiments. Along with the many strange religious phenomena which characterize the period, there also arose numerous other reform movements, such as temperance and other humanitarian societies of one kind or another. These movements, although differing radically among themselves, sprang usually from a common background of revivalism, influenced by disturbed economic conditions.

From the beginning of the century to 1845 was a period of revivalistic emphasis throughout the country, but if there was one section where the revival emphasis was stronger than anywhere else and the excitability of the people greater, it was in central-western New York, which came to be known as the "burnt-over district" because of the repeated revival waves which swept over this region. These counties had been settled by New Englanders, the first wave being of "rather unsavory fame," though they were followed by an intelligent and industrious class from eastern New York and New England. The mingling of these two classes gave a peculiar psychological character to the people, producing, on the one hand, sane and progressive social movements, and, on the other, tendencies toward fanaticism. Added to this was the tendency, which seems to be in New England blood, toward "eccentricity of opinion and extremity of temper," which has made of New England a "fertile seed-plot" for fads and extravagances. In this territory originated the anti-Masonic agitation in 1826; a few years later it became one of two chief centers of the Millerite craze; here lived the Fox sisters who were responsible for the beginnings of the spiritualistic movement; while the greatest of all, in its permanent influence, Mormonism, likewise originated in this region. This region also produced the greatest revivalist of the time in Charles G. Finney, who, though a native of Connecticut, was taken in childhood by his parents to Oneida county, New York, and later moved farther westward into the country about Lake Ontario. John Humphrey Noyes, one of Finney's converts, became the founder of a new religious cult, which established one of the most successful of the communistic communities—the Oneida Community—in this same region.

"Mormonism sprouted in the revival-singed soil of Seneca county, western New York, among an uncouth and unstable people pitifully eager for signs and wonders." Joseph Smith, the founder, was born of superstitious parents, seers of visions and believers in miraculous cures, who had come from Vermont to western New York. The father was a digger for hidden treasures and was accustomed to use a sort of divining rod to locate proper places to dig wells. At the age of fourteen Joseph Jr. professed conversion, joined the Methodists and soon began to tell of his visions. When eighteen years of age (September, 1823) he professed that the angel Moroni appeared to him and told him that the Bible of the western continent lay buried in a hill near by, but it was not until 1827 that he claims to have dug up a stone box in which was a book made up of thin gold plates, covered with characters which he states was the "reformed Egyptian tongue." With the golden book, according to Smith's account, was found a pair of supernatural spectacles by the aid of which the characters could be read. Smith being unable to read or write well, employed at different times four helpers, among them his wife, to whom he dictated from behind a curtain the Book of Mormon, which was printed in 1830 at Palmyra, accompanied by the sworn statement of three witnesses as to the manner in which the golden plates were found and translated. Soon after this the golden plates disappeared, being taken away, according to Smith, by the angel who had told him of their existence.

The Book of Mormon professes to be a history of America from its settlement by a company of "Jaredites," a people who had been dispersed at the Tower of Babel. These first settlers eventually destroyed one another. Later a company from Jerusalem settled on the coast of Chile, and these after a period of years fell to quarreling among themselves, one group becoming known as the "Lamanites," an idle and warlike people with dark skins, the American Indians; the other were the "Nephites," or God's chosen people. Between these two peoples wars ensued for many centuries. The Nephites finally fell away from the true faith and were nearly destroyed in 384 A.D. in a battle in Ontario county, New York, only Mormon and his son Moroni and a few others escaping. Mormon collected the sixteen books of records of his people into one volume with some personal recollections and buried them in a hill where, he was told, a true prophet would eventually find them. This was Smith's account of his wonderful discovery. The Anti-Mormons, however, had another version of how the Book of Mormon was written. They claimed that an ex-minister, Solomon Spaulding, had written a fanciful account of the origin of the American Indians which he called "The Manuscript Found." This he read to a number of people, who asserted that the Book of Mormon corresponded closely to Spaulding's manuscript, and that Smith must have, somehow, obtained either Spaulding's original manuscript or a copy of it.

But whatever the origin of the Book of Mormon, Smith and his new revelation were soon accepted as genuine by numerous followers and a church was formed at Fayette, in Seneca county, in April, 1830, and in October the first missionaries were sent out by Smith. One of the first and most important of the converts was Sidney Rigdon, originally a Baptist preacher, who had recently joined the followers of Alexander Campbell. Rigdon was soon a recognized leader among the Mormons and began at once to write down new revelations. But Smith was too well known in the region where the first churches were organized, and his past kept coming up to plague him and his followers. A number of lawsuits and other troubles finally decided Smith and Rigdon to remove to Kirtland, Ohio. This was the Mormon headquarters from 1831 to 1837. Here Smith established a general store, a tannery and a saw mill, and a large stone temple was built and dedicated in 1836. It was here that Brigham Young, a painter and glazier from Vermont, joined the Mormons and within a short time became one of the "Twelve Apostles." Lawsuits against Smith and Rigdon for violating the law against unchartered banks finally led them to leave Ohio for Missouri, where they joined a group of other Mormons who had previously settled in Jackson county. Mormon migration to Missouri now became large, and "Far West" in Caldwell county became their center. Trouble soon arose between the Mormons and the Missourians and after Smith had urged his followers in a Fourth of July sermon to wage a war of extermination against those who opposed them, a civil war actually began. The state militia was called out and in October "Far West" surrendered and 15,000 Mormons crossed the Mississippi into Illinois.

From 1840 to 1846 Nauvoo, Illinois, was the Mormon "New Jerusalem." The Illinois politicians of both parties welcomed the Mormons hoping to secure their vote in the presidential election of that year, and a charter was easily obtained for Nauvoo, making the town practically independent of state control. The town grew rapidly; a university was established, the Nauvoo Legion, a military organization, was formed and Smith was commissioned "lieutenant general" by the governor of the state. The downfall of this flourishing community came soon after Joseph Smith received a revelation (July, 1843) authorizing polygamy. Although not officially published at the time, it became known in the town and a party was soon formed opposing Smith and his new revelation, and a paper called the *Expositor* was begun to expose Smith's immoralities. The editors of the paper were arrested and their printing office destroyed, and a general uprising against the Mormons and Smith ensued. The militia was called out, the Nauvoo Legion surrendered and Smith and his brother were placed in prison at Carthage, on the charge of treason. Here on the night of the twenty-seventh of June, 1844, a mob, with the evident collusion of the militia, broke into the prison and shot the two brothers. Two years later the Mormons left Nauvoo, and in January, 1847, the march across the plains to their new place of refuge was organized, and before the close of the year 1848 five thousand were located in the valley of the Great Salt Lake, in what is now the state of Utah.

The story of the economic and political development

of the "State of Deseret," as Utah was called by the Mormons; the introduction of large scale irrigation; the success with which Brigham Young defied Federal authority, are a part of the general political and social history of the United States. The missionary policy of the Mormon Church was responsible for making many converts outside the United States, and an Emigration Fund was established in 1850 to assist emigrants to come to Utah. From the beginning a large proportion of the converts have come from outside the United States.

During the same years in which Joseph Smith Jr. was gathering his Mormon Church, another religious movement was sweeping over the eastern and middle states, under the preaching of an honest and earnest New England farmer of Baptist background, William Miller. The doctrine which won so many followers from among all the churches, and which so profoundly stirred many communities in different sections of the country, was the setting of the exact time when Christ should return to the earth and make an end of the world. All the evangelists of the time had been preaching the second coming of Christ, but none of them had fixed the exact date of that coming. This is just what Miller did, by the study of certain passages from the books of Daniel and Revelation. The year of the second coming he fixed at 1843, and the day around the twenty-first of March.

It was in August, 1831, that Miller began his great mission to warn the people of the United States of the approaching end of all things. At first he preached his simple message among the villages near his home whenever and wherever opportunity offered. In 1839 he was invited to preach in the Chardon Street Baptist Church of Boston and his message now became of more than local importance. He soon was invited to speak in many of the larger churches, in the cities of the East, and calls began to come from many sections of the country for preachers and literature setting forth the great message. Soon Second-Advent journals began publication: *The Signs of the Times* in Boston, *The Midnight Cry* in New York, the *Philadelphia Alarm* and others were soon spreading the new gospel.

The number of Miller's followers at the height of the movement has been variously estimated at from 50,000 to 1,000,000, the former number being perhaps more nearly correct. At first there was no attempt to gather them into a single organization, and most of them retained their membership in their respective churches. But as the "craze" increased, and as preachers of less sanity began to advocate the new doctrine, clashes between them and the orthodox naturally resulted. Excitement grew as the time approached for the supposed end of the world. Great meetings were held in churches, tents, public buildings, and in the fields and groves, and finally when the year 1843 dawned the emotions of the believers were at white heat. In some instances insanity resulted, while under the stress of their emotions people fell to the floor and professed seeing visions and hearing heavenly voices. With the coming of the eventful year Miller thus addressed his followers:

This year, . . . O glorious year! the trump of jubilee will be blown, the exiled children will return, the pilgrims reach their home, from earth and heaven the scattered remnants come and meet in the middle air . . . fathers before the flood, Noah and his sons—Abraham and his, the Jew and the Gentile,—This year! the long looked-for year of years! the best! it has come!

As March 21 dawned people in many places went out into the open fields or climbed to hilltops to await the coming of the Lord, but the day passed and nothing unusual occurred. Then Miller reminded his followers that he had never definitely fixed the exact day, but it might occur any time within the next year. The awful day was surely coming, and for another year the believers waited in nervous suspense. But the year passed and March 21, 1844, came, but still things went along as usual. Miller was now almost prostrated with disappointment and dismay at the failure of his careful calculations. But some of his followers revised the figures and fixed another date, in the fall of the same year, for the coming of the Lord, and again there was excitement and preparation among the believers; stores were closed, homes were broken up, while the minds of the most credulous gave way, and even murders were committed under the excitement. Again the new day of prophecy dawned, October 22, 1844. Some people sought the graveyards as an appropriate place from which to ascend; others climbed to the housetops; some arrayed themselves in their best clothes, but it was all to no avail; Christ did not appear in the clouds and the day passed.

This ended the prophecy of the exact day, but still the leaders did not give up their belief in the eventual second coming. But the old authority was gone, and with it went the old accord. In 1845 a loose organization was perfected of all Adventists but in 1846 the Seventh Day Adventists separated from the main body on the question of the observance of the Jewish Sabbath; in 1861 the Advent Christian Association was organized, separating over the question of immortality of the soul, while other divisions came in 1864 with the formation of the Life and Advents Union; in 1866, the Church of God was formed and in 1888 a number of small adventists bodies organized an association called the Churches of God in Jesus Christ.

In this era of religious chaos the rise of Spiritualism must not be overlooked. In 1855 it was claimed that there were nearly two million people who were believers in spiritualism in the United States. As early as 1837 spiritualistic phenomena began in the several Shaker communities but the occurrences which created the great stir in the country began in a little house in western New York in 1847, not far from Palmyra where the Book of Mormon was first printed. The Fox sisters, Margaret and Kate, lived in this house with their parents; and in the above year they began to be disturbed by rapping noises, which were discovered to be directed by some intelligence. Within two years the Fox sisters had succeeded in convincing Horace Greeley and other leaders that there was "something in it" and spiritualism was not six years old when a petition was presented to Congress signed by fifteen thousand signatures, most of them of educated people, asking for a Federal investigation of the spiritualists claims. About this time one of the sisters confessed to a committee of physicians that the raps had been produced by "cracking the joints" of the knees. But other such phenomena occurring at different places over the country could not be accounted for by fraud, and table-tipping, rappings, and automatic writing continued to attract the attention not only of the ignorant and credulous, but of such men and women as Bancroft, Cooper, Bryant, N. P. Willis, Poe, Theodore Parker and Harriet Beecher Stowe. In 1857 a list of sixty-seven books and magazines on spiritualism were listed in the *Practical Christian* and belief in spiritualism was undoubtedly widespread throughout the country. The chief apostle and clairvoyant was Andrew Jackson Davis, while Robert Dale Owen and many original communists, phrenologists and mesmerists and innovators of one kind or another came into the spiritualist associations.

Of the Communistic experiments with which this period is crowded only three can be briefly mentioned: the Rappite Community, first at New Harmony, Indiana, and later removed to Economy, Pennsylvania; the Oneida Community under the leadership of John Humphrey Noyes; and the Brook Farm Community made up of New England transcendentalists. George Rapp, a native of Würtemberg, was the founder of the New Harmony community, on the lower Wabash in Indiana, in the year 1814. Rapp, a peasant farmer of strong character became the leader of a group of Pietists who refused to remain within the state church and for that reason were subject to persecution. Because of this he and some three hundred of his followers determined to seek a land where they could enjoy religious freedom. The migration to America began in 1803, settling first in western Pennsylvania. Here within a few years they established a prosperous community, and were raising large crops of corn, wheat, oats, potatoes, flax and hemp and other products. But the community was twelve miles from a navigable stream and the country was not suited to fruit raising. For these reasons and also because they desired a warmer climate they removed to the lower Wabash. Here they founded New Harmony, which soon became the largest town in Indiana Territory. Soon the Rappite fertile fields were yielding abundant crops; log, frame and brick buildings were erected, and orchards and vineyards planted. Everybody worked. An entire block was given over to manufacturing purposes, and here were woolen, grist and saw mills; and soon great flatboats of Rappite products were floating down the great river to New Orleans and other markets. New Harmony "became a garden of neatness" with its gable-roofed buildings and vine-covered hills, its stately church and fruitful orchards.

Nor was the life of the Rappites out of harmony with the beauty and neatness of their community. Simplicity, neighborly love, self-sacrifice, prayer and worship, with their regular and persevering labor made up their lives. Father Rapp required confession to him of all transgression, nor were quarrels allowed to remain uncompromised. Regular religious services were conducted on Sunday and on Thursday, and four religious holidays observed throughout the year. Celibacy was practiced by all in the community and even hostile critics have found nothing to indicate any irregularities.

Because of the prevalence of malaria in the Wabash valley the Rappites sold out their large holdings in 1824

Brigham Young's Wives in the Great Mormon Tabernacle
From *Harper's Weekly*, September 26, 1874

to Robert Owen, the English social reformer, for $150,000 and moved to the banks of the Ohio, seventeen miles below Pittsburgh. The new community was called Economy. Here a prosperous town was soon established, duplicating what had already been done at New Harmony. In 1827 there were five hundred and twenty-two members in the community; in 1844 it had dwindled to three hundred and eighty-five. Some years since, when only three members remained, a Pittsburgh syndicate purchased the town and all it contained for several millions of dollars.

Equally successful economically, but far different in respect to the relation of the sexes, was the Oneida Community established in 1847 by John Humphrey Noyes. Noyes, a graduate of Dartmouth College, studied for the ministry at both Andover and Yale. Previous to his entering college he had come under the influence of the great evangelist, Charles G. Finney, and had professed conversion. While at Yale he made a profession of perfection, and because of his peculiar doctrines was asked to leave the school and his license to preach was revoked by the New Haven Association. He soon became a leader of a movement in which perfectionism was the central doctrine. Indeed, at this period perfectionists were many, especially in those regions over which numerous revival waves had passed, which as has been noted was particularly true of central and western New York. Noyes finally came to hold that direct divine guidance was above Scripture and that true Christians are not subject to sin. As might be expected such teachings soon led to the wildest excesses on the part of many who accepted these views. For a period of about ten years (1836-1847) Noyes was gradually gathering together a group of people at Putney, Vermont, into a community, which he called a "Bible School," where he taught an entirely new ethical and doctrinal system. The basis of this new system was sexual promiscuity. The new society which he hoped to establish was to have everything in common including a community of women.

In 1848 this system was put into operation at Oneida, New York, where for thirty years he and his followers followed the practice of "complex marriage." In 1879, the practice was given up, due to aroused public opinion. Economically the community was a success, based largely on the manufacturing of traps for the catching of fur-bearing animals. When a visitor suggested that the making of traps for the killing of animals was a strange way to bring in a "terrestrial kingdom of heaven" he was told by a communist that the earth was under a curse of which vermin are a consequence and that by destroying them they were helping to bring nearer that time when the earth might be perfect. Soon other manufacturing was going on, such as silk-making machinery, traveling bags, sewing and embroidery silks, hardware, and eventually the famous Community silver. When in 1881 the community was transformed into a stock company an issue of $600,000 was made.

The best known of all the Community experiments in the United States, and one of the most dismal failures, was that at Brook Farm in eastern Massachusetts. This was an outgrowth of a schism which took place in American Unitarianism in 1832 when Ralph Waldo

Emerson, then the pastor of Second Church in Boston, preached a sermon in which he proposed a radical change in the observance of the Lord's Supper. When the church refused to agree to this proposed change, Emerson resigned and retired "to his literary seclusion at Concord" where he brought forth books and pamphlets in which he set forth his objections to all fixed forms of belief and rejected all restrictions upon the freedom of intellectual action. Soon Emerson became the intellectual leader of a number of New England Unitarians who became known as Transcendentalists. A Transcendental Club was formed in Boston in 1836, made up of a group of brilliant idealists, such as James Freeman Clarke, A. Bronson Alcott, Margaret Fuller, Elizabeth Peabody and Theodore Parker. This group formed the Brook Farm Association in 1841 for the purpose of bringing cultivated and thoughtful people together, and a farm was purchased where speculation was to be put into practice. But the members proved far better speculators than farmers, and after seven years the experiment came to an unhappy end and the farm was sold.

The chief revival movements of these years may be appropriately gathered about the name of Charles G. Finney. Finney was a New Englander born in Connecticut, but brought up in the "burnt-over" district in western New York. While still a young man he revolted against the strict Calvinism of the Presbyterians, and soon after his quiet conversion in 1820 resolved to preach a gospel of "free and full salvation." Largely self-taught, his admission to the ministry was opposed by some of the members of the presbytery, but in 1824 he was finally licensed to preach and from this time until his death he was a flaming evangelist. Beginning his ministry in Jefferson county, New York, he began to preach a type of gospel that aroused the whole community and soon brought down upon him the censures of his brethren in the ministry. Very soon he gave up a settled ministry and began to hold meetings in various sections of the country; in New York State, Pennsylvania, Ohio and throughout New England. His most remarkable revivals were those in Rochester, New York, where in the thirties, forties and fifties great campaigns were conducted and nearly three thousand converts were secured. Boston and New York City were also favorite areas for his activity, while campaigns were conducted in Scotland and England. In 1834 Broadway Tabernacle was built in New York, with the understanding that Finney was to be the pastor, but the next year he was called to the new school organized in Oberlin, Ohio, and later became its president. Here he divided his time between the college and revival campaigns throughout the country.

Finney's doctrine and revival methods were not long in arousing opposition, and the more staid Presbyterians and Congregationalists determined to curtail his activities. Dr. Lyman Beecher was particularly active in his opposition to Finney and his type of revivalism, but Finney went on to the end. After 1843 Finney, during a revival at Oberlin, began to advocate a doctrine of Christian perfection, denying, however, that there was any relationship between his doctrine and that of Noyes. Thus from its beginning Oberlin became widely known as a revival center, while in many instances reform movements of one kind or another followed in the wake of the revivals. It is significant that in those regions where the revivals had been most successful, the temperance and anti-slavery movements found largest support.

Many of these strange religious movements were the unhealthy offspring of the revivals of the thirties, forties and fifties. But along with the rise of Mormonism, Adventism, Perfectionism and all the other "isms," the great Protestant churches were adding tens of thousands of sane Christians to their membership, were busy planting new churches in the ever advancing frontiers, founding colleges, expanding their missionary work to the Indians, especially in the Northwest, while their mission work beyond the seas was receiving increasing attention.

✛✛✛✛✛✛✛✛✛✛✛✛✛✛✛✛✛✛✛✛✛✛✛✛✛✛✛✛✛✛✛✛✛✛✛✛

Chapter XVIII

SLAVERY CONTROVERSY AND SLAVERY SCHISMS

NOWHERE else in the world has negro slavery exercised such a large influence upon the Christian Church as in the United States. All of the great American churches grew up in more or less intimate contact with the institution of slavery and all of them were of necessity greatly affected by it. The most important of the many schisms which have occurred among the American churches were those growing out of negro slavery, while some of the most difficult problems facing the churches today are due to the negro and the bitter contests which have arisen in the churches because of him.

Indian slavery early arose in New England and grew out of the ordinary course of the Indian wars. The sanctioning of Indian slavery led to a ready sanction of negro slavery. The New England Calvinist considered himself God's elect and that to him God had given the heathen for an inheritance, and by enslaving the Indians and trading them for negroes he was doing nothing more than entering into his heritage. As long as this type of theology prevailed in New England the New England churches could not be expected to raise any protest against the institution. And it is a significant fact that it was not until their Calvinism was radically modified that New England's opposition to slavery began. Many of the most influential Congregational ministers were slave owners, as were John Davenport of New Haven, Ezra Styles, president of Yale, and even Jonathan Edwards. It is also true that Congregational ministers were early interested in the conversion of slaves, as was Cotton Mather, and several of the New England churches had negro members and gave instruction to them, but there was no settled policy developed nor organized work among them.

As is well known, New England and especially Rhode Island became the center of the slave trade during the eighteenth century. The first English slave voyage was that of John Hawkins in 1562, when this famous English captain secured a cargo of slaves on the west coast of Africa and sold them to the Spanish colonies in the West Indies, then the only slave market. About a hundred years later (1672) the Royal African Company was organized, with the Duke of York at its head, which eventually came to trade primarily in slaves. For twenty-five years this company had a monopoly of the trade and prospered greatly, but after 1697 private traders were permitted to share in the trade of the Guinea coast by paying the company a percentage on the value of its cargoes. It was during this period that the New England slave trade arose and by the middle of the eighteenth century the company was driven out of existence by the private traders. Hand in hand with the New England slave trade went rum making, for the best article of trade on the African coast was rum. By 1730 Rhode Island alone was sending eighteen or more vessels each year to Africa to trade in slaves, carrying at least eighteen hundred hogsheads of rum. The most respected of New England's citizens invested in the early slave voyages; the well-known Boston merchant, Peter Faneuil, owning an interest in the famous slave ship *Jolly Bachelor*. The ethics of the slave trade are well illustrated by the following instructions of the notorious privateer, Peter Potter: "Make ye Cheaf Trade with the Blacks and Little or none with the White people if possible to be avoided. Worter ye Rum as much as possible and sell as much by the short measure as you can. Also order them in the Bots to worter thear Rum, as the proof will Rise by the Rum standing in ye Son."

Slaves, though never numerous in New England, were to be found in every New England colony. Massachusetts had the largest number, there being nearly six thousand at the opening of the Revolution. The most effective influence in colonial New England against slavery and especially the slave trade was that exercised by Dr. Samuel Hopkins, who became the minister of the First Congregational Church at Newport, Rhode Island, in 1769. Although he had himself been a slaveholder, what he saw in Newport soon made him a bitter foe of the institution and he began preaching against the evils of the slave trade. He saw the so-called best people, his friends, the wealthiest men in the town engaged in the slave trade and he determined, no matter what it might cost him, to obey his conscience and denounce the whole slave business. In 1770 he preached a sermon against kidnaping, purchasing and retaining slaves. The people of Newport were astonished and one wealthy family left the church, but most of his members were surprised that they had not long before seen the evil of the system. Hopkins went from house to house urging people to free their slaves, while his anti-slavery influence was soon widespread throughout New England. His most influential anti-slavery publication appeared in 1776 called "Dialogue Concerning the Slavery of the Africans," while the same year he published an address to slave owners. Opposition to slavery became common among Congregational ministers in the period of the Revolution and their influence was almost unanimously exerted in the direction of emancipation, and they were undoubtedly a large factor in bringing about the emancipation acts which were passed by the New England and middle states, during and immediately following the war.

The only colonial church which had a definite program as far as religious work among slaves and other negroes was concerned was the Anglican. This work was carried on by the Society for the Propagation of the Gospel, which from its organization (1701) looked upon "the instruction and conversion of the negroes as a principal branch of their care; esteeming it a great reproach to the Christian name, that so many thousands of persons should continue [pagans] under a Christian government and living in Christian families as they lay before under, in their own heathen countries." Although the Established Church was the most active in work among the slaves, nowhere do we find it denouncing the institution itself. The Scotch-Irish Presbyterians were largely non-slaveholders in the colonial period, due largely to their location and economic condition. Some of their preachers, however, such as Samuel Davies, preached to the negroes in Virginia. The early Baptists likewise did not generally belong to the slaveholding class and therefore had little intimate contact with the institution.

The largest anti-slavery influence wielded by any religious body in the colonial period was that exerted by the Quakers. Protests against both the slave trade and the holding of slaves began in the latter seventeenth century and continued until the institution was completely outlawed in every Friends' Yearly Meeting in the United States. George Fox in his visit to America in 1671-1672 urged slaveholders to "deal mildly and gently with their negroes, and not use cruelty toward them . . . and that after certain years of servitude they would make them free." Slavery was recognized by the charter of Pennsylvania, yet there were provisions in the charter that slaves should be freed under certain conditions after fourteen years of service. From the beginning the question of slavery was discussed in the Friends' meetings, but the matter was handled very cautiously. The most aggressive in its anti-slavery position was the Quarterly Meeting of Chester, Pennsylvania, where as early as 1711 a minute was passed discouraging the enslavement of any more negroes. Year by year from this time on the Chester Quarterly Meeting and the Philadelphia Yearly Meeting discussed the question, particularly of buying and selling slaves. Indeed, it was not until after the middle of the century that the matter of holding slaves began to be seriously considered and this forward step was largely due to the agitation carried on by several individuals, among them Benjamin Lay, William Southby, Ralph Sandaford, but particularly Anthony Benezet and John Woolman.

Anthony Benezet, the son of a Huguenot refugee, came to Philadelphia as a teacher and about 1750 became especially interested in the cause of the slave. His significance in the anti-slavery agitation among the Quakers is that he used every form of publication, such as newspapers, almanacs, pamphlets and books, to spread his ideas. Clarkson, the great English anti-slavery apostle, states that his interest in the cause of the slave was first aroused by reading one of Benezet's booklets. But the greatest of all the Quaker anti-slavery advocates and the one chiefly responsible for the final disappearance of slavery from among the American Quakers was John Woolman. After 1743 Woolman gave his time as an itinerant preacher among the Quakers, visiting Friends' meetings in every section of the colonies, urging upon them the iniquity of slave-keeping. He also wrote an influential tract called "Considerations on Keeping Negroes Recommended to the Professors of Christianity of every Denomination," while he has left in his *Journal* one of the most beautiful and simple revelations of a great human soul.

The Philadelphia Yearly Meeting between 1758 and 1776, by a series of regulations passed from year to year, provided for the complete elimination of slaveholders. In 1775 the Yearly Meeting directed that "such members as continued to hold slaves be testified against as other transgressors are by the Rules of our Discipline of other immoral, unjust and reproachful conduct," which meant exclusion of slaveholders from the society. In the other

Yearly Meetings similar action was taken in the years following: in New England Yearly Meeting in 1783; the New York in 1784; while the Maryland, the Virginia and the North Carolina Yearly Meetings had completed the work by 1787. The work of freeing the slaves met many handicaps in the southern Yearly Meetings. In North Carolina a law was enacted by the state legislature forbidding the manumission of slaves "except for meritorious services" which were to be adjudged and allowed by the court. Acting under this law forty slaves which had been freed by the Quakers were seized and sold. The Friends took the case to court and finally won their case on the ground that the law under which the freed negroes had been seized was *ex-post facto*. The anti-slavery action in the Yearly Meetings led to a large migration of southern Friends to Ohio, Indiana and Illinois, especially from Virginia and North Carolina.

During the latter eighteenth century two forces were at work, among English-speaking people particularly, which were to exercise large influence in affecting public opinion in regard to the institution of slavery. One such influence was the great humanitarian impulse which grew largely out of the evangelical revival and resulted in such enterprises as the founding of the colony of Georgia for debtors, in the prison reform movement, and in the amelioration of the penal code. As a whole, people were becoming more sympathetic and humanitarian in their attitude toward the unfortunate and the downtrodden. This was the chief influence back of the crusade led by Thomas Clarkson and William Wilberforce in England against the slave trade, which eventually resulted in the abolition of slavery throughout British dominions. A second influence was the diffusion of liberal ideas, which constituted the philosophy of the American Revolution. Such statements as that all men are created equal, and that all have a right to life, liberty and the pursuit of happiness, and that "all men are by nature free and independent," were commonly made and believed, and found expression in the Declaration of Independence and the Virginia Declaration of Rights. These ideas were propounded not only by the French political philosophers of the eighteenth century, but by such English leaders as John Wesley, Adam Smith in his *Wealth of Nations,* by Edmund Burke, Charles James Fox and William Pitt; while in America they were proclaimed and believed by all the Revolutionary leaders.

Under such influences the first anti-slavery society was formed in America, the Philadelphia Society (1775) of which Franklin was the president; all the states north of Delaware and Maryland provided for the immediate or gradual emancipation of slavery; the anti-slavery clause was written into the Ordinance of 1787, while the southern states prohibited the further importation of slaves. Indeed, at the close of the War for Independence the leadership of the new nation was practically a unit in its opposition to the institution of slavery. Jefferson, though a large slaveholder, denounced slavery as endangering the very principle of liberty on which the nation was founded. Patrick Henry declared: "I will not, I cannot justify it! I believe a time will come when an opportunity will be offered to abolish this lamentable evil," while Washington wrote in 1786 that it was one of his chief desires that some plan might be devised "by which slavery may be abolished by slow, sure and imperceptible degrees."

This widespread anti-slavery sentiment also found expression in the formation of numerous anti-slavery societies, especially in the border states, as Kentucky, Tennessee, Ohio, Maryland and North Carolina, which were supported in many instances by slaveholders themselves. Indeed, these early societies were to be found in every state of the Union except New England, a few of the extreme southern states and Indiana. A national organization was formed in 1794 called "The American Convention of Delegates from Abolition Societies," which after 1818 became the "American Convention for Promoting the Abolition of Slavery and Improving the Condition of the African Race." In the conventions half of the delegates came from southern states lying nearest the border. Every phase of the slavery question was freely discussed in these societies, while they were active in supporting anti-slavery publications and addressing petitions to state legislatures and to Congress.

As might be expected, during this period in which anti-slavery opinion was commonly held throughout the nation the American churches were likewise active in passing strong anti-slavery resolutions, and in some cases even made the attempt, though unsuccessful in most instances, to rid their churches of slaveholding members. From the Revolutionary period onward both Methodists and Baptists were particularly active in carrying on religious work among negroes and in 1795 there were 17,644 negro Baptists in the states south of Maryland, while in 1800 there were 15,688 negro Methodists throughout the country.

At the Christmas Conference in 1784 when the Methodist Episcopal Church was formed, a rule was adopted providing that every slaveholding member must within a year execute a legal instrument agreeing to free his slaves, while the preachers were required to keep a record of all such transactions in their circuits. All members were required to comply with this ruling within a year or withdraw from the church. This was the most extreme anti-slavery legislation enacted by the Methodist Episcopal Church until the outbreak of the Civil War. It was soon found, however, to be too extreme, for in less than six months it was necessary to suspend the rule. The following year (1785) Bishop Coke, because of his anti-slavery utterances, almost met physical violence in Virginia, and Asbury soon learned, to his sorrow, that any mention in the South of anti-slavery views might lead to evil consequences for the church. In 1796 a new rule was adopted and an attempt made to restrict slavery within the church. It provided that official members must agree to emancipate their slaves, while slave sellers were to be expelled. Preachers were to surrender their positions at once if they refused to free their slaves where it was legal to do so. Under these provisions there is evidence that a considerable number of slaves were emancipated, but year by year it became increasingly difficult to carry out its provisions, especially after the southern states, one by one, passed legislation prohibiting their emancipation.

In 1789 the General Committee of Virginia Baptists, representing all the Baptist churches in the state, passed

a resolution declaring that "slavery is a violent depriva-
tion of the rights of nature and inconsistent with a republican government and therefore recommend it to our
brethren to make use of every legal means to extirpate
this horrid evil from the land." The same year the Philadelphia Baptist Association gave its endorsement to
societies working for abolition of slaves and recommended
that Baptist churches form societies of their own. But
perhaps the most active anti-slavery sentiment in this
early period is to be found among the Baptists of Kentucky and a little later in Illinois. From the beginning
the most influential leaders in Kentucky neither desired
nor expected slavery to continue long in their state and
among these early anti-slavery leaders were several
Presbyterian, Methodist and Baptist preachers. In the
Constitutional Convention of 1792, of the six ministerial
members who voted against slavery three were Baptists.
The slavery issue was also early introduced into the Baptist associations, and in 1807 an anti-slavery association
was formed, called the Friends of Humanity Association,
which adopted a set of anti-slavery regulations, known
as Tarrant's Rules, rigidly excluding all slaveholders from
their churches.

A much larger anti-slavery movement among Baptists
was that in Illinois, organized under the guidance of
James Lemen who claimed that Thomas Jefferson had
financed his removal from Virginia to Illinois to help in
the anti-slavery struggle. Eventually several Friends to
Humanity Associations were formed in Illinois and Missouri and the Baptists played a considerable part in the
critical slavery controversy in Illinois before 1818, and also

THE COLONIAL SLAVE TRADE
The choicest pieces of her cargo were sold at auction
Harper's Magazine, January, 1895

a few years later when the slavery issue was again before the people of the state.

The Presbyterians, like the Methodists and Baptists, went on record during this first period of general anti-slavery agitation, against the institution of slavery. As early as 1787 the Synod of New York and Philadelphia passed resolutions approving the "general principles in favor of universal liberty, that prevail in America; and of the interest which many of the states have in promoting the abolition of slavery" and recommending that slave-holding members give their slaves "such education as may prepare them for the better enjoyment of freedom." The resolution on slavery passed by the General Assembly in 1818 takes the strongest anti-slavery position of any Presbyterian declaration. Members are urged to use "honest, earnest and unwearied endeavors to correct the errors of former times, and as speedily as possible to ef-face this blot on our holy religion, and to obtain the complete abolition of slavery through Christendom, and if possible throughout the world."

An organization which had the hearty endorsement of the churches from its organization in 1816 was "The American Society for the colonization of the Free People of Color of the United States." The immediate plan of this organization was to carry the free negroes out of the country and colonize them in Africa. But it was generally thought that the net influence of colonization would be in the direction of the ultimate abolition of the institution of slavery. Interest in this movement was large, particularly between 1820 and 1830, when the first settlement was made in Liberia, and this society absorbed most of the public interest in the negro whether slave or free and was one of the causes which accounts for the dying out of the early abolition societies.

By 1830 the first period of anti-slavery agitation had come to an end, and a new and more aggressive movement was about to begin. The anti-slavery sentiment in the churches was now quiescent and their voice was no longer heard in protest. This first anti-slavery movement had been largely negative. Its leaders were, no doubt, sincere in their desire to promote the ultimate abolition of slavery, but to most of them abolition was a theory to be held rather than a fact to be accomplished. Thus slave owners could and did belong to these early anti-slavery societies, while slave-owning church members were found willing to vote for resolutions calling for the abolition of slavery.

The passing of the first phase of the anti-slavery movement was due, first, to the revolution in southern agriculture which was taking place between 1790 and 1830. The rise of a new cotton market in England, due to the invention of spinning and weaving machinery, created an increased demand for cotton, while Whitney's cotton gin (1792) made possible the profitable growing of the short staple cotton in the upland South. A few figures showing the rapid increase in southern cotton production will tell the story. Between 1791 and 1795, 5,200,000 pounds of cotton was produced; between 1826 and 1830, 307,244,400 pounds; in 1820 cotton constituted twenty-two per cent of the nation's exports, in 1860 fifty-seven per cent. In 1790 good negroes might be purchased for $300; the same negro in 1830 would bring $1,200, and in 1860 $1,500 to

$2,000. In other words, slavery was vastly more important economically both to the South and to the nation between 1830 and 1860 than it was between 1775 and 1830. Cotton had become the most important American product; it made up more than half of our exports; and by 1830 southern leaders were convinced that the welfare of the nation depended upon cotton culture.

A second factor which brought a change in the whole slavery situation in America was the rise of a new and aggressive anti-slavery leadership, especially in New England, and in those sections which had been settled by New England people. Under the lash of such extreme abolition propagandists as William Lloyd Garrison with his *Liberator*; of Wendell Phillips with his eloquent appeal for the downtrodden slave; of John G. Whittier and his numerous anti-slavery poems, and many others who joined in the new crusade, thousands of converts were soon made to the new gospel of freedom. This new gospel of abolitionism was very different from the older negative anti-slavery doctrine and called for immediate action. Once more anti-slavery societies were numerously formed, and in 1833 the American Anti-Slavery Society was organized. In contrast to the older anti-slavery societies, these new organizations were to be found most numerously in New England and the central states, and were also numerous and active in northern Ohio and southern Michigan. Thus at the very time the institution of slavery was becoming more important to the economic life of the South, a bold and aggressive abolition movement began in the North. With this background we are prepared to understand the conflict over slavery which now began in the great democratic churches and which eventually brought schism and bitterness.

The new anti-slavery movement found ready support among church people, and it was not long until the question of slavery became a church issue of prime importance. The anti-slavery societies at their meetings took frequent action regarding the relation of the churches to the anti-slavery movement. In 1837 the New England Anti-Slavery Society passed a resolution urging the necessity "of excommunication of slaveholders, and a solemn consideration of the question whether the churches remaining obdurate, it is not the duty of the advocates of truth and righteousness to come out from among them and be separate." Two years later at the national anti-slavery convention it was decided to push the slave question in the churches, to abolitionize them if possible, and if not successful to secede from them. Soon anti-slavery societies sprang up in the churches, and champions of the cause came forward, while Baptist associations and Methodist conferences and other religious bodies, particularly in New England, began to pass strong anti-slavery resolutions. Thus the Maine Baptist Association declared in 1836: "of all the systems of iniquity that ever cursed the world, the slave system is the most abominable." In 1835 both the New England and the New Hampshire conferences of the Methodist Episcopal Church formed anti-slavery societies, while such ministers as Orange Scott and LeRoy Sunderland were tireless in their anti-slavery agitation.

This radical anti-slavery agitation in the churches at the North was met by pro-slavery defenders at the South.

The southern ministers were not long in finding arguments based on the Scriptures which confirmed them in their pro-slavery position. Thus the clergy at Richmond, Virginia, passed resolutions depreciating the unwarrantable and highly improper interference of the people of any other state with the domestic relations of master and slaves, and they quoted the example of Christ and his apostles in not interfering with the question of slavery as one which should be followed by all ministers of the gospel. Ministers of such prominence as Dr. Furman (Baptist) of South Carolina in 1833 proclaimed that "the right of holding slaves is clearly established in the Holy Scriptures both by precept and example," while similar views were widely held by southern ministers of all denominations. Between these two extreme radical groups especially among the Methodists and Baptists were the moderates who tried to keep peace between them.

It will be necessary from this place forward to trace separately the steps leading to schism in the great democratic churches. Naturally those churches were most affected by the slavery controversy which were the most evenly distributed throughout the nation North and South. This was particularly true of the Baptists, the Methodists and the Presbyterians. The Congregationalists were generally anti-slavery, but they were largely confined to the northern states with practically no slaveholding membership.

One of the fundamental principles of the Baptist denomination is the independence of the congregation, but these independent congregations may unite in certain voluntary organizations, such as associations, state conventions and missionary societies. The oldest and most prominent general Baptist organization in the United States, at the period of the slavery controversy, was the "General Convention of the Baptist Denomination in the United States for Foreign Missions." This had been formed in 1814 with headquarters in Boston but drew its support from Baptist churches throughout the country. A Baptist Home Missionary Society had also been formed in 1832, likewise supported by Baptist churches both north and south. Both societies met triennially in the same place which was known as the Triennial Convention.

At the meeting of the Triennial Convention in 1841, which met at Baltimore, slavery was a prominent issue and both sides were fully alive to it. At this convention certain southern associations sent up protests against the anti-slavery activities of their northern brethren. One such protest came from the Savannah River Association, stating that the conduct of Baptist abolitionists is "censurable and meddlesome" and demand of their northern brethren whether "they can acknowledge these fanatics as their co-workers," while they informed the convention of the impossibility of further coöperation of Georgia Baptists unless the abolitionists on the Board of Managers of the convention were dismissed. Particularly obnoxious to the Southerners was the Rev. Elon Galusha, vice-president of the Board of Foreign Missions, who was an active abolitionist, and the southern delegates came to the meeting determined that he should be removed. This they accomplished through the coöperation of the northern moderates, and the Rev. Richard Fuller of South Carolina was named in his place. The meeting came to an end without further disturbance, for the moderates of both sections were in control, and an understanding was reached that slavery was a subject which should not be discussed by the convention. The southern delegates went home with the feeling that their views had triumphed, which was thus expressed by one of them: "And now if we of the South and they of the North, whose sympathies are with us, shall be mild, I am satisfied that abolitionists will go down among Baptists." "All the leading men," states another southern delegate, "are sound to the core on this vexed question."

But abolitionism did not "go down among Baptists" as the southern delegates had hoped. Rather the years from 1841 to 1844, the latter the year of the next meeting of the Triennial Convention, were filled with increased anti-slavery agitation among northern Baptists, particularly in New England. Anti-slavery Baptists were growing rapidly in numbers and influence. In May, 1843, an American and Foreign Free Baptist Missionary Society was projected in Tremont Temple, Boston, where a pledge was signed by all friends of the movement promising to separate themselves "from all connection with religious societies that are supported in common with slave-holders," if the coming Triennial Convention did not take steps to throw off their partnership with slave-holders. Thus secession was threatened by northern abolitionists as well as southern radicals.

In 1844 the Triennial Convention met in Philadelphia, with 456 delegates present, only ninety-two of whom were from slaveholding states. But again the moderates were in control and Francis Wayland, president of Brown University, was chosen president and Dr. J. B. Taylor, of Virginia, secretary. Dr. Richard Fuller, the leader of the southern moderates, took a prominent part in the discussions on slavery and declared that he was not convinced that slavery was a sin but he regarded it as a great evil. It was the opinion of the majority that slavery did not concern the convention, and a resolution to this effect was finally passed, which declared: "that in coöperating together as members of this convention in the work of Foreign Missions, we disclaim all sanction either expressed or implied, whether of slavery or anti-slavery, but as individuals we are perfectly free both to express and to promote our own views on these subjects in a Christian manner and spirit." This simply laid the whole matter on the table. The Home Missionary Society met also at Phladelphia at the same time and they too discussed slavery pro and con and came to the same conclusion and passed the same type of resolutions as did the General Convention. Thus the solution of the vexed problem was again avoided and left to the boards of the two societies finally to determine the issue.

The slavery question came up for final decision first before the Home Board. The Georgia Baptist Convention in April, 1844, instructed its executive committee to recommend for appointment as a missionary Mr. James E. Reeves, at the same time stating that he was a slaveholder. This was intended to be a test case, the letter accompanying the application stating: "We wish his appointment so much the more as it will stop the mouths of gainsayers. . . . There are good brethren among us, who notwithstanding the transactions of your society at Philadelphia, are hard to believe that you will appoint a slave-holder a missionary, even when the funds are supplied by those who wish his appointment." A decision on this question was not reached by the board until October, but meanwhile the question was discussed by associations and churches, North and South. The Michigan *Christian Herald* stated: "The religious sentiment of the North and West are fast setting against the vile system of American slavery," while the Wisconsin Baptist Association proclaimed that "The great ecclesiastical bodies and church organizations which are in communion with slavery, 'sanction and sanctify' the sum of all villainies, and present the greatest obstacle in the way of emancipation." Southern sentiment favored continued coöperation with the society if the board would act fairly with the South and appoint southern as readily as northern men as missionaries. When the board finally reached its decision it declared that the application to appoint Reeves introduced the subject of slavery, in direct contravention of the letter and purpose of the constitution, and they therefore were not at liberty to entertain the application of Reeves. The net result of this decision was the withdrawal of the southern associations from the old Board of Home Missions and the formation of a Board of Domestic Missions supported by Baptists at the South.

Of greater importance was the decision of the Foreign Board regarding the question of the appointment of slaveholding missionaries. In the fall of 1844 a member of the Alabama Baptist Convention raised the question:

"Is it proper for us in the South to send any more money to our brethren at the North for missionary and other benevolent purposes before the subject of slavery be rightly understood by both parties?" This question led the Alabama Convention to pass a series of resolutions, the second of which demands that the authorities in control of the bodies receiving funds from the Baptist churches state whether or not "slaveholders are eligible and entitled equally with non-slaveholders to all the privileges and immunities of their several unions." To this question the board gave answer on December 17, 1844, and declared that in thirty years no slaveholder had applied to be a missionary and since the board does not send out servants it could not send out slaves. Further they state: "If, however, any one should offer himself as a missionary, having slaves, and should insist on retaining them as his property, we could not appoint him. One thing is certain, we can never be a party to any arrangement which would imply approbation of slavery."

Under the conditions prevailing such a decision could lead to nothing short of the withdrawal of the southern Baptists from participation with their northern brethren in the cause of missions, and steps looking toward separation were soon taken. The Virginia Baptist Foreign Missionary Society led the way, withdrawing from further connection with the Boston Board and recommended a southern convention, while southern churches and associations generally passed resolutions favoring this move. The convention met at Augusta, Georgia, May 8, 1845, with three hundred and seventy-seven delegates present, representing eight slaveholding states. The following day it was resolved in the interest of "peace and harmony and in order to accomplish the greatest amount of good" to separate from their northern brethren and organize their own society. Dr. Fuller, however, stated that this action "did not divide the Baptist Church: that could not be separated, it was independent and republican, having no general head, and only associated for a general purpose." The next day a constitution was presented for the "Southern Baptist Convention," the purpose of which was to promote foreign and domestic missions. Thus did the great Baptist denomination divide over the slavery issue, and one of the great spiritual ties binding the Federal Union was broken.

In the Methodist Episcopal Church, as among the Baptists, the moderates led by the bishops, the general secretaries and editors of the official church papers, were in control during the thirties and early forties. The bishops as they traveled from conference to conference tried to discourage discussion of slavery, while two of the bishops in 1835 united in a pastoral letter to New England Methodists pointing out the evils which had already resulted from slavery discussion and warning them of even greater disasters if the discussion were continued. At the General Conference which met in Cincinnati in 1836 abolitionism was roundly condemned, when two delegates from the New Hampshire Conference attended and addressed a meeting of a local anti-slavery society. The address of the bishops to the church in 1836 counseled their brethren that abolitionism be not discussed and pointed out the fact that the church was opposed to radical movements. But instead of allaying discussion the action of this General Conference simply furnished ammunition for explosions in the annual and quarterly conferences. In the anti-slavery conferences the preachers were determined that an expression of their strong anti-slavery views should be placed on record, while the presiding bishops were equally determined that this should not be done. At the New England Conference in 1837 the presiding bishop was told that several petitions were to be presented bearing on the slavery question and they wished these to be referred to a committee for action. The bishop refused to hear the petitions on the ground that the General Conference had condemned abolitionism. He thus appealed to the conference: "Will you, brethren, hazard the unity of the Methodist Episcopal Church . . . by agitating those fearfully exciting topics, and that too in opposition to the solemn decision and deliberate conclusion of the General Conference? . . . Are you willing to contribute to the destruction of our beautiful and excellent form of civil and political government, after it has cost the labor, treasure and blood of our fathers to establish it? . . . I would that it [slavery] were obliterated from the earth; but in view of the terrible consequences that are likely to follow the agitation of those exciting topics, at the present I cannot consent to be participant in any sense or degree, in those measures which are advocated by modern abolitionists."

In many instances the advice of the General Conference of 1836 against abolitionism was followed and for ten years in the Philadelphia Conference every young minister applying for admission was asked the question "Are you an abolitionist?" and if the reply was in the affirmative he was not admitted. The Ohio, Baltimore, New York, Pittsburgh, Michigan and other conferences passed resolutions expressing regret at the proceedings of abolitionists, while many abolition leaders among the preachers suffered the heavy hand of discipline because of their activities. But the struggle went on, and gradually new converts were made to the cause of abolitionism among both ministers and laymen. As the General Conference of 1840 approached, discussion as to its probable action became rife and the radicals began to hint at possible withdrawal from the church if the oppressive measures which had silenced them in the annual conferences should be continued. When the General Conference met the great question before it was the matter of the power of a president of a quarterly or annual conference in declining to put a question or receive a petition. The conference went on record as recognizing this right to exercise gag rule, and the whole contention of the abolitionists was thus denied and the radicals seemed to be defeated at every point.

Following the General Conference of 1840 abolitionism throughout the United States, both in and out of the church, fell upon evil days. Among the Garrisonian party there was internal strife, and a new anti-slavery society was formed. The Methodist abolition leaders were discouraged and inactive. Sunderland had withdrawn from the church and repudiated orthodox Christianity, while Scott stated in 1842 there was no choice "but to submit pretty much to things as they are or secede." And this is exactly what took place the following year. A group of radical leaders gathered in Albany and there decided definitely to withdraw from the Methodist Episcopal Church, giving as reasons the attitude of the old church on the question of slavery, its aristocratic government, and its uncharitable attitude toward the dissenting brethren. A second meeting convened at Andover, Massachusetts, in February, 1843, and in May of the same year the Wesleyan Methodist Connection was organized at Utica, New York, with six thousand members. The new church prohibited slavery and intoxicating liquors, provided for lay representation in the conferences and allowed conferences to elect their own presidents. Though the secession was ridiculed and its principles misrepresented, yet it had an immediate effect upon the Methodist Episcopal Church in developing and crystallizing the latent anti-slavery spirit in the church. The official papers became more outspoken on the question of slavery, and several Methodist conventions were held which took radical anti-slavery ground; all of which greatly alarmed the Methodists of the slaveholding states.

The crisis in the controversy was reached in the General Conference of 1844, when one hundred and eighty delegates, representing thirty-three annual conferences and the best talent of the church, met in New York in May. From the beginning of the month's session slavery was the burning issue, and an appeal of a slaveholding minister, who had been suspended from the Baltimore Conference for refusing to free his slaves, brought the question to the center of the stage. Eventually, after long debate in which the whole slave issue was reviewed, the conference voted, overwhelmingly, to uphold the decision of the Baltimore Conference. This decision revealed the anti-slavery temper of the majority of the conference and presaged their decision on the more important question as to what was to be done with Bishop James O. Andrew of Georgia, who by a second marriage had become the possessor of a few household slaves and thus became the first Methodist slaveholding bishop.

What was to be done with a slaveholding bishop? Some of the anti-slavery brethren said either let him rid himself of his slaves or resign. Southern delegates stated that the bishop had violated no rule of the church; northern delegates contended that he might be tried under the general phrase "improper conduct." The Southerners claimed that the bishops were beyond any such interference as the conference contemplated; as the bishops were a coördinate body with the General Conference. The debate lasted eleven days but was carried on in the best of temper. Compromises were proposed; delay for another four years was suggested, but all to no avail, and when finally the vote was taken on the resolution asking the bishop to desist from his episcopal labors until he should rid himself of his slaves, it was carried by a large majority, one hundred and eleven yeas to sixty nays.

The conference occupied itself in the closing days of the session drawing up a Plan of Separation, suggested by Dr. William Capers of South Carolina. A committee of nine was appointed to bring in a plan for separating the church if the southern churches found it necessary to divide. The Plan as reported and adopted provided a method of establishing a boundary between the two parts of the church if separation was to take place; "it allowed ministers to choose without blame the church to which they would adhere"; recommended modification of the constitution to permit a division of the property of the Book Concerns, and suggested certain rules for the division and transfer of property. It was, indeed, a most generous and Christian provision, "enacted," as Norwood suggests, "in a fit of Christian generosity during the dying hours of the General Conference." Perhaps the drawing up of the Plan was a bid to the South to withdraw. At any rate the day after the General Conference adjourned the southern delegates met and there determined to call a convention of the southern churches to meet in Louisville, Kentucky, on May 1, 1845, and issued an address to the ministers and members of the southern states and territories setting forth the situation as they saw it.

The southern annual conferences one by one took favorable action on the question of the division of the church and appointed delegates to the Louisville Convention. The convention met at the appointed time and place and was completely harmonious. On the second day it voted by an overwhelming majority to separate, and then and there steps were taken to form a new church. The Plan of Separation was their *Magna Charta*, while the church in every respect was modeled closely after that of the Methodist Episcopal, even keeping the name Methodist Episcopal Church with "South" added.

While these steps were being taken by the southern brethren, opinion in the North was fast crystallizing in opposition to the Plan of Separation, which had been so generously offered in 1844. The very men who had urged its adoption were now demanding its repudiation. It was characterized as unconstitutional; it was urged that the South had violated the Plan, while others claimed that it was entirely unnecessary. Perhaps it was too much to expect of human nature, even among a body of Christian ministers, that they should stand by their generous proposals especially after they had been so bitterly assailed by southern partisans. Sad to relate, at the General Conference of 1848 the Methodist Episcopal Church repudiated the Plan of Separation by a large majority and refused to receive the fraternal delegate sent to them from the Methodist Episcopal Church, South.

From 1848 to the opening of the Civil War was a period of growing bitterness between the two branches of American Methodism. One cause was the border conflict, since both churches immediately made plans to retain the border, and conflicts were thus inevitable in Maryland, Kentucky, western Virginia and Missouri, where the two churches met. Misunderstanding and conflict resulted also from the attempt of the Southern Church to gain its share of the Book Concern properties. Leaders in the North took the view that they were under no obligation to divide the property and funds, and no steps were taken to satisfy the demands of the Southern Church. Finally two suits were brought in the Federal courts, one in New York involving the New York branch of the Book Concern, the other in Ohio involving the Western Book Concern at Cincinnati. The New York suit was decided in favor of the South, while the Ohio suit was decided for the North. The South appealed the Cincinnati case and it was brought before the Supreme Court of the United States in 1854, where a unanimous decision was handed down in favor of the South. Eventually a settlement was reached and the property was divided to the satisfaction of the South.

In tracing the slavery controversy among the Presbyterians the New School body will first be considered. At the time of the schism (1837-1838) the two Presbyterian bodies were nearly equal in size, but the Old School was from the beginning in far better condition for future growth. The Old School had been granted the general property by the courts, while the New School was further weakened by the withdrawal of churches which became Congregational. The large New England element in the New School body would presage a larger interest in the anti-slavery cause and explains the legislation which finally brought schism in 1857.

Slavery discussion occupied much of the time of every New School General Assembly and at every session numerous petitions and memorials on slavery were presented, and there seems never to have been any attempt to stop discussion. The General Assembly of 1846 adopted by an overwhelming majority a declaration stating that they considered slavery a wrong and urging the churches to put away the evil. In 1847 there was a secession of some radical anti-slavery churches in Ohio which formed the Synod of the Free Presbyterian Church, but this movement developed only in the Middle West, and in 1862 when it reunited with the New School embraced five presbyteries and forty-three ministers. In 1849 the General Assembly again sternly condemned slavery and stated that "It is the duty of all Christians . . . as speedily as possible to efface this blot on our holy religion" but adds this statement, "where freeing is impossible, there are other duties of instruction and preaching to attend to." Meanwhile abolition sentiment was growing in the church and in 1853 the assembly ordered that a census be taken to determine the number of slaveholders in the church, the number of slaves held by them, to what extent the slaves are held by unavoidable necessity, and what provision is made for their religious well-being.

In seeming open defiance of the action of the Assembly of 1853 the Presbytery of Lexington, Kentucky, reported that a number of its ministers, elders and members held slaves "from principle" and "of choice," believing it to be right. Twenty-seven anti-slavery memorials were presented to the General Assembly of 1857 and after days of discussion the assembly adopted resolutions exhorting "all our people to eschew" such doctrines as that "slavery is an ordinance of God" and that in the United States it is "Scriptural and right." They express pain at the action of the Presbytery of Lexington, and declare that such doctrines and practices cannot be tolerated in the Presbyterian Church. The southern delegates protested the passage of this measure, but in spite of their protest it passed by an overwhelming majority. The southern delegates then issued a call to all Presbyterians for a convention to constitute a General Assembly in which slavery would not be introduced. This movement resulted in the formation of the United Synod of the South, made up of six synods, twenty-one presbyteries and about fifteen thousand communicants.

Of greater importance, but more difficult to understand was the position taken by the Old School body in regard to the all-absorbing question of slavery. Year after year its assemblies adopted the policy of laying all memorials on slavery on the table without debate, but this policy aroused vigorous protest on the part of a growing number of anti-slavery advocates. In 1844 twenty memorials on slavery were presented, and at the Assembly of 1845 so large was the number of petitions and memorials that definite action on the subject was necessary. A special committee was appointed to consider these memorials and prepare a report on slavery, of which Dr. N. L. Rice was made chairman, a man characterized as the ablest "fencewalker" in the church. The report submitted to the assembly and passed by a large majority denied every demand of the anti-slavery delegates and virtually accepted slavery as a legitimate Christian institution, since Jesus did not denounce it. In 1849 in response to protests against its action of 1845 the General Assembly resolved "that in view of the civil and domestic nature of this institution, and the competency of our secular Legislatures alone to remove it . . . it is considered peculiarly improper and inexpedient for this General Assembly to attempt to propose measures in the work of emancipation," and thus like Pontius Pilate they washed their hands of the whole matter.

The conservative party represented by Dr. N. L. Rice determined the policy of the Old School body, as far as slavery was concerned, to the opening of the Civil War. In his letters on slavery Rice thus sets forth the position of his church:

The Presbyterian Church has stood at an equal remove from the extremes of Abolitionism and Pro-slaveryism. She has refused to pervert God's word to make it either denounce or sanction slavery. She has regarded it as a great evil, but as an evil inherited, an evil of long standing, and so interwoven with the very texture of society, that, like a chronic disease, it must require much time, and patience, and kind treatment, to eradicate it. She is fully persuaded, that for the evils under which mankind suffer, the Gospel is the great and only remedy. Refusing, therefore, to mingle in heterogeneous conventions, and to sanction their vague and unmeaning resolutions, she goes forward on her sublime mission, preaching the Gospel alike to master and slave, saying openly and boldly all the apostles said, and refusing to say a word more. And today she stands ready to compare notes, as to results, with her traducers.

Thus the necessity of defending its middle position drove the Old School Presbyterian Church to take a position almost if not quite pro-slavery. And in taking this position the Old School leaders felt that they were set apart from others, who could not see how profoundly Christian it was. They felt that their church was the last great spiritual influence binding the Union together, and pride in this fact we find expressed again and again.

As might be expected the Old School Presbyterians furnished the most able defenders of slavery on Scriptural and moral grounds. Dr. J. H. Thornwell, of South Carolina, in a sermon preached in 1850 at a dedication of a negro church, defined slavery as an obligation to labor for another determined by the providence of God. The master, he stated, has a right to the labor of the slave, but not to the man. Slavery is inconsistent to the perfect state, yet it is a natural evil which God has visited upon society. Class distinctions is an evil of the same kind, but in our world absolute equality would lead to stagnation. Though founded on a curse, slavery may not be inconsistent with the spirit of the gospel, as that spirit operates among "rebels and sinners," in a degraded world, and under a dispensation of grace. The Christian beholds in his slave, not a tool, not a chattel, not a brute or a thing, but an immortal spirit assigned to a peculiar position in this world of wretchedness and sin. Not greatly unlike Thornwell's position was that held by Dr. Charles Hodge of Princeton Theological Seminary as set forth in several articles in the *Biblical Repertory*, of which he was the editor.

There was, however, considerable anti-slavery sentiment in the Old School church, especially in Ohio, led by Dr. E. D. MacMaster. MacMaster was the son of a minister of the Associate Reformed Presbyterian Church which had excluded slaveholders in 1831. As early as 1845 MacMaster and Rice had differed on the slavery issue and when MacMaster became a professor in the New Albany Theological Seminary (1849-1857) the seminary became involved in the dispute. The seminary was finally moved to Chicago where it took the name McCormick Theological Seminary because of a gift of $100,000 by Cyrus McCormick. McCormick was pro-slavery in his sentiment and was a member of the church in Chicago of which Dr. Rice was the minister.

The position of Alexander Campbell on the question of slavery well illustrates the changes which were taking place among southern church leaders between 1830 and

1850. Campbell had been a member of the Virginia Constitutional Convention of 1830 and had been one of the anti-slavery leaders. In 1832 he declared in his *Millennial Harbinger* that slavery was an economic evil in Virginia; in 1845 he had come to the conclusion that the relation of master and slave was not unchristian.

After the great popular churches had reached a definite position on the question of slavery there was a rapid increase along all lines of church activity in both North and South. "Revivals, educational movements, and missionary zeal were the fruits of the reformation." Within ten years after the great split the Southern Baptists were as numerous as the united church had been in 1844, and contributed within the first thirteen years after the division seven times as much for home missions as they had given in the same number of years preceding. The same activity characterized the Methodists, South and within ten years they had added a net increase of 150,000. Especially were the Southern Methodists active in work among the Indians and negroes. The old restraint in the matter of their attitude toward slavery which existed before 1844 was now completely thrown off, and the churches in both sections became aggressive and denominationally conscious, to an exaggerated degree.

While the slavery controversy was at its height the Presbyterian and Methodist churches were busy establishing the first Protestant missions in the Pacific Northwest. Attention of Christian people was drawn to the Oregon country by an appeal made to General William Clarke of St. Louis on the part of four Indian chiefs who had journeyed all the way from the Oregon country, asking

that they be given the "white man's Book from Heaven."
The appeal caught the imagination of the Methodists and
in 1833 Jason Lee was appointed to head a mission to the
Oregon country, and in September, 1834, he preached his
first sermon at Fort Vancouver. Lee soon saw the larger
aspects of his task and became active in securing funds
and bringing settlers to Oregon and within a period
of ten years Methodism was firmly established, especially
in the Willamette valley. The leader of Presbyterian
work in the Northwest was Marcus Whitman who was
sent by the American Board to the Oregon country in
1836. Near the present site of the city of Walla Walla,
Whitman and his wife with one associate and his wife
labored among the Indians and soon a prosperous mission was established. In 1842 Whitman made his famous
ride to Boston and Washington. There has been much
controversy in regard to Whitman's motives in making
this long journey, crossing the Rockies in the midst of
winter. Years afterward it was claimed by those closely
associated with him, that he had two purposes, one to
urge upon the Federal government the necessity of doing
something to save Oregon to the United States, the other
to persuade the board to rescind the order closing the
Oregon mission. Lee died in 1845 after he had been removed by the Methodist Board from the superintendency
of the mission, and Whitman and his wife with twelve
others were brutally murdered in 1847 by the Indians
whom they were trying to serve, but the labor of these
two pioneers was not in vain.

At the same time that Protestant missions were being
established in the Northwest, the first Catholic mission-

aries also began their work in the region. Father DeSmet was successful in founding missions at various places, especially in the Willamette valley. The Catholics were more successful in their Indian work than were the Protestants and it is claimed that in six years six thousand Indians had embraced the Catholic faith.

Chapter XIX

THE CHURCHES NORTH AND SOUTH AND THE CIVIL WAR

IN THE last formal speech made by John C. Calhoun in the United States Senate, in the great debate over the Compromise of 1850, he stated: "The cords which bind the states together are not only many but various in character. Some are spiritual or ecclesiastical; some political, others social." Of these cords the strongest are those of a religious nature, and they have begun to snap. In the powerful Methodist Episcopal Church, "The numerous and strong ties which held it together are all broke and its unity gone." Instead of one church there are now two hostile bodies. "The next cord that snapped was that of the Baptists, one of the largest and most respectable of the denominations." That of the Presbyterians is not entirely snapped, but some of its strands have given away. The Episcopal Church "is the only one of the four great Protestant denominations which remains unbroken and entire." It was the explosive force of slavery agitation which broke these cords, and, he stated, if the agitation goes on every cord will snap, political and social as well as ecclesiastical, and then there will be nothing to hold the states together except force. The snapping of the ecclesiastical cords had undoubtedly a large influence in creating the final breach between North and South. Indeed, there are good arguments to support the claim that the split in the churches was not only the first break between the sections, but the chief cause of the final break.

The long agitation carried on in the great churches over the slavery issue prepared them to take a definite stand when the Civil War began. And no war in modern times, not even excepting the Great War, received such unanimous support from the churches. Baptists, Catholics, Methodists, Lutherans, Congregationalists, Moravians, German and Dutch Reformed, Old and New School Presbyterians vied with one another in their determination to give support to the Federal government. Only in the Protestant Episcopal and Old School Presbyterian churches were there protests against the passage of patriotic resolutions, and in these churches the protestors represented but a small minority.

The General Assembly of the Old School Presbyterian Church at its session in 1861 adopted resolutions acknowledging and declaring their obligation to promote and perpetuate "the integrity of these United States, and to strengthen, uphold and encourage the Federal Government in the exercise of all its functions under our noble Constitution." These resolutions were introduced by Dr. Gardiner Spring, of the Brick Presbyterian Church in New York, who throughout the slavery controversy had been on the side of the extreme conservatives and whose utterances on the slavery issue had mostly been in the form of denunciations of abolitionism. In 1862 the resolutions on the "State of the Country" were introduced in the assembly by Dr. R. J. Breckenridge, of Kentucky, and as might be expected were much more outspoken in their denunciation of disloyalty, affirming: "This whole treason, rebellion, anarchy, fraud, and violence is utterly contrary to the dictates of natural religion and morality, and is plainly condemned by the revealed will of God," while he exhorts all "who love God or fear his wrath to turn a deaf ear to all councils and suggestions that tend towards a reaction favorable to disloyalty, schism, or disturbance either in the Church or in the country."

The Methodists were particularly proud of their one hundred per cent loyalty, though at the opening of the war there had been a considerable loss of members from the border conferences to the Church South. At the General Conference of 1864 held in Philadelphia a Special committee was formed to prepare an address to the President of the United States and a deputation of five members were sent to bear the address to Washington. The address stated that the Methodist Church had sent thousands of its members and many of its ministers into the Union armies to maintain the cause of God and humanity, and they pledged to the President all appropriate means to suppress the cruel and wicked rebellion. To this President Lincoln made the following reply:

Gentlemen: In response to your address, allow me to attest the accuracy of its historical statements, indorse the sentiment it expresses, and thank you in the nation's name for the sure promise it gives.

Nobly sustained as the Government has been by all the

Churches, I would utter nothing which might in the least appear invidious against any. Yet without this, it may fairly be said that the Methodist Episcopal Church, not less devoted than the best, is by its greater numbers the most important of all. It is no fault in others that the Methodist Episcopal Church sent more soldiers to the field, more nurses to the hospitals, and more prayers to heaven than any! God bless the Methodist Episcopal Church! Bless all the Churches! And blessed be God, who in this our trial giveth us the Churches.

(Signed) A. LINCOLN

The patriotic resolutions passed by the Ohio Baptist Convention in 1862 were typical of many others enacted by their numerous associations and conventions. They avowed it to be their right and duty as Christian citizens to tender sympathy and support to those intrusted with the government and they promised to uphold the armies "in their endeavors to crush the wicked rebellion" and to "offer up" their "prayers and supplications daily" in this behalf. They heartily approved the proclamation of the President declaring liberty to the slaves, and promised support in carrying out that proclamation "till our beloved country shall be purged of the accursed blot" which they declared to be "both the cause of the war and the chief means in our enemy's hands of carrying it on."

During the first year of the war the church periodicals were very critical of the administration because of its failure to take immediate steps to free the slaves which fell into the hands of the Union forces. When General Frémont issued his proclamation freeing the slaves in the department of the Missouri in August, 1861, he, and General Benjamin F. Butler, who had declared the slaves

{ 451 }

within his lines contraband of war, were hailed by the church press as "the day stars to our Nation." When President Lincoln recalled Frémont's unwise order, one editor of a church paper in the Northwest states: "Never had a brave man such difficulties thrown in his path as Frémont . . . yet he has held to his way. . . . The people are incensed." It is one of the ironies of history that these two Union generals, Frémont and Butler, probably the two most incompetent and corrupt commanders of high rank in the Union army, should have received such high praise at the hands of the northern church people.

During the summer of 1861 delegates from the Old School synods and presbyteries in the Confederate States met in Augusta, Georgia, and there formed the Presbyterian Church in the Confederate States of America, and elected as its first moderator Benjamin M. Palmer of South Carolina, who from the beginning had been one of the most ardent and eloquent advocates of secession. In a long address setting forth the cause of their separation they declare that the only condition upon which the two churches could have remained together was "the rigorous exclusion of the questions and passions of the forum from its halls of debate." Their attitude toward slavery is thus summarized: "We venture to assert that if men had drawn their conclusions only from the Bible, it no more would have entered into any human head to denounce slavery as a sin, than to denounce monarchy, aristocracy or poverty." To the next General Assembly (1862) the committee on the State of Religion report that Presbyterian congregations without exception in the southern states evince "the most cordial sympathy with the people of the Confederate States" to maintain their rights against the despotic power which is attempting to crush them. And they are convinced that "this struggle is not alone for civil rights, and property and home, but for religion, for the Church, for the gospel." In 1864 the United Synod of the South, which had separated from the New School in 1857, united with the Presbyterian Church in the Confederate States and thus by the end of the war southern Presbyterianism was completely united.

The Southern Baptist Convention in 1861 adopted a series of resolutions on the State of the Country, prepared by Dr. Richard Fuller, of South Carolina. After recounting the steps taken by the South in separating from the Federal Union, in which, he states, they but desired a fair and amicable adjustment but which the government at Washington insultingly repelled, and since the United States government insists "upon letting loose hordes of armed soldiers to pillage and desolate the entire South," and since the northern churches and pastors, whom he had hoped would interpose and protest against the appeal to the sword, are "breathing out slaughter and clamoring for sanguinary hostilities," therefore be it resolved that the formation of the Confederate States of America be approved; that the Divine direction be invoked upon those who rule over them and that the Confederate States and also the Kingdom of Jesus Christ may prosper; that the President of the Confederacy and the Confederate Congress be assured of their sympathy and confidence; that every principle of religion and patriotism calls them to resist invasion; and that prayer be offered for those from their families who are in the armies "to cover their heads in the day of battle, and give victory to their arms." They would also pray for their enemies, "trusting that their pitiless purposes may be frustrated" and that blessing and prosperity may be restored under the two governments. Baptists throughout the South are called upon to observe certain fast days, and are enjoined to follow the example of Baptists during the Revolution and War of 1812 in which they "bated no jot or heart or hope for the Redeemer's cause."

Of all the American churches none handled the delicate situation created by the war more tactfully than did the Protestant Episcopal. Although there were ardent patriots on both sides among the bishops, yet there was an absence of bitterness which speaks well for their Christianity. After the secession of the cotton states a convention, made up of delegates from those states, was held at Montgomery, Alabama, July 3, 1861, and there it was unanimously determined that the formation of the government of the Confederate States made necessary an independent organization of the dioceses within the seceded states. After drawing up a draft of a constitution, the convention adjourned to meet in October at Columbia, South Carolina, where the Protestant Episcopal Church in the Confederate States was formed. Bishop Polk of Louisiana was the most ardent of the southern bishops for the southern cause, and was the first to urge the necessity for a separate organization. Soon after the war opened, Bishop Polk, who had been educated at West Point, was made a major-general in the Confederate army, and was killed during the course of the war.

The Protestant Episcopal Church in the United States

had never recognized the withdrawal of their southern brethren, and at the General Convention of 1862 the roll call included the names of the southern dioceses. At the next convention three years later (1865), again the roll call included the southern deputies. Such courtesy and deference was shown to the southern bishops who attended the convention that their hesitation was soon overcome and thus most fortunately unity was restored to the church with the end of the war, and all traces of strife and bitterness soon vanished. This easy solution of the problem of separation was made possible by the fact that the Protestant Episcopalians had never taken sides on the slavery issue and there was therefore no pre-war bitterness to overcome.

The need of chaplains in the army was early recognized by the War Department and at the opening of the war a general order was issued allowing to each regiment one chaplain, specifying that he must be a regularly ordained minister. Later Congress passed an act ratifying this order of the War Department. It was soon called to the attention of President Lincoln that chaplains were also needed for hospitals, and in May, 1862, Congress authorized the appointment of chaplains for each permanent hospital. The war had not progressed long, however, before complaint was made that some very unworthy men were occupying the position of chaplain. To safeguard the office Congress passed an act (July 17, 1862) requiring that only a regularly ordained minister of good standing in his denomination, who had recommendations for his appointment from an authorized ecclesiastical body or from not less than five accredited ministers belonging to his denomination, should receive appointment to the office. All the churches coöperated in providing chaplains to the army and navy; the Methodists alone furnishing nearly five hundred. Frequently a regimental church was formed which held regular services, and if the chaplain was an evangelical a long stay in camp was likely to be improved by holding a revival meeting among the soldiers. In a New York regiment a revival meeting was kept up for thirty nights in succession in a tent furnished by the commanding general and more than a hundred soldiers professed conversion. The chaplains often kept in touch with friends in the North and made appeals for literature, provisions and comforts for their men, and also acted as distributing agents of the American Bible and Tract Societies.

The religion in the Confederate armies was even more conspicuous than in the armies of the Union. Both Generals Lee and Jackson were men of strong religious conviction and gave great encouragement to the work of the chaplains among their soldiers. One Confederate officer testified that "I seldom heard an oath in the Confederate camps, and I had every opportunity, from second lieutenant to the command of the regiment. Our camps often resounded at night with hymns and spiritual songs; arrests for drunkenness were very rare." In the year 1863-1864 a great revival swept through the army of northern Virginia and thousands professed conversion. The Baptists, Methodists, Presbyterians and Episcopalians were all active in their cooperation in religious work in the Confederate army. The Episcopalians furnished nearly a hundred chaplains, the Southern Methodists more than two hundred while Baptists, Catholics and Presbyterians sent their full quotas. The following quotation from the diary of a chaplain in the Confederate army will give some idea of the feverish interest in religion prevailing among the southern soldiers:

May 17, 1863, 10 A.M., I preached in the Presbyterian Church: house crowded with officers and soldiers; serious attention. At three o'clock, I preached in Bates' brigade: a very good time; revival in the brigade. May 19th, I preached in Johnson's brigade: thirty to forty mourners; glorious work in this command. May 20th. I preached in General Polk's brigade: many mourners; several conversions. May 21st, I preached in General Wood's brigade: forty to fifty mourners; fifteen or twenty conversions. May 22nd, I spoke in General Riddle's brigade: a great work here; already more than one hundred conversions in this command.

At the battle of Chickamauga this chaplain remained on the battlefield eleven days, "nursing the sick, ministering to the wounded, and praying for the dying. The sight was awful. Thousands of men killed and wounded. They lay thick all around, shot in every possible manner, and the wounded dying every day."

The churches coöperated in supporting a number of organizations which were working among the soldiers and sailors. Most important of these were the Christian Commission, the American Bible and Tract Societies, and the several Freedmen's Societies which came into existence during the course of the war. The Christian Commission was formed in New York in 1861 to supply comforts and supplies to the armies not furnished by the Federal government. It received its support largely through the churches, and made its appeals through ministers and church papers, as the commission published no organ of its own. During the four years of the war it received more than $2,500,000 in cash, besides stores and clothing of many kinds. At the Thanksgiving Day services in 1863, $83,400 were received by the commission. Those who carried on the work of the commission in the camps and on the field were called *delegates* and were voluntary workers drawn largely from the churches. Hundreds of ministers volunteered their services to the commission for short periods of time and rendered valuable service, circulating good publications in the armies, encouraging and helping soldiers to communicate with their friends, giving aid to surgeons, and comfort to sick and dying soldiers.

The American Bible Society was particularly active during the war, distributing Testaments and Bibles to both Union and Confederate armies. In 1864 the society received $429,464.12 and distributed during the year 994,473 copies of the Bible. The Christian Commission alone distributed more than a half million copies in the Union armies and navies, while 50,000 copies were sent to the Confederate army under General J. E. Johnston and 50,000 to the army under General Bragg, besides 100,000 copies sent to the Board of Colportage of North Carolina. The Tract Societies were also unusually active during the years of the war, printing and distributing among the soldiers many thousands of tracts.

As the war progressed and as the Union armies pushed farther and farther into the South the number of negroes dependent upon the care and protection of military com-

THE CHRISTIAN COMMISSION IN THE FIELD
Reproduced from *Harper's Weekly*, August 20, 1864

manders increased. To care for this situation several of the commanding generals organized departments of Negro Affairs. Among the duties of those placed in charge of this work was to take a census of the negroes in the region, provide food, clothing and medicines where needed; see that all the able-bodied had employment, while there was an effort also to establish schools. Early in the war the attention of religious organizations at the North was called to the growing need among freedmen, and by the end of 1861 the American Missionary Association had several representatives in the field. By the beginning of 1862 Freedmen's Relief Associations began to spring up in every section of the North, from Maine to Missouri. These societies received a large share of their support through the churches, but toward the end of the war the denominations began to form their own Freedmen's Societies. Thus the United Presbyterians of Ohio formed a Freedman's Society in 1863; while the same year the Baptists, the United Brethren and the Reformed Presbyterians formed their own societies. The Protestant Episcopalians formed a Freedmen's Aid Society at their General Convention in 1865 and the same year the Congregationalists began their large work among the negroes and called upon their churches for a quarter of a million annually. The Methodist Episcopal Church continued to coöperate with the local Freedmen's Societies until 1866 when they too formed their Freedmen's Aid Society. Work among negroes soon became one of the great benevolent enterprises of the church.

A phase of religious activity on the part of most of

the Protestant churches at the North, which left some unfortunate consequences, was their attempt to push into the South during the progress of the war. As a natural result of war, many localities throughout the Confederacy were soon without ministers and were thus deprived of regular Christian worship. After the capture of New Orleans in 1862 more than two score churches in that city were left without ministers. In the five Methodist churches in the city there was not a single minister habitually officiating and the same condition was true of the five Presbyterian churches. In Baton Rouge, Newbern, Vicksburg, Natchez, Pensacola and Memphis and in many other places throughout the South, large and small, like conditions prevailed. This situation was soon brought to the attention of the northern church officials. The chaplains with the armies of invasion wrote numerous letters to the northern church papers describing these conditions. Sometimes the chaplains used the vacant southern churches for their services and in that case the civilian congregation was invited to attend the services with the soldiers. Under such conditions it was but natural that there should be a movement started in the North to send missionaries into the South to take over these abandoned fields.

Before such work could begin it was necessary to gain the consent of the Federal government and the protection of Union commanders secured. As early as 1862 an order was obtained from the War Department signed by Secretary Stanton directing the commanding generals of the several departments in the South to place at the disposal of certain designated bishops "all houses of worship belonging to the Methodist Episcopal Church, South, in which a loyal minister, who has not been appointed by a loyal Bishop of said church does not officiate." The order further stated that the government considers it a matter of great importance in order to restore tranquillity to a community "that Christian ministers should by example and precept, support and foster the loyal sentiment of the people." The commanders were instructed to supply the bishops designated (Bishop Ames in the departments of Missouri, the Tennessee and the Gulf) "with transportation and subsistence when it can be done without prejudice to the service" and are to afford them "courtesy, assistance and protection." Later other northern Methodist bishops were given jurisdiction over Methodist churches in other southern military departments.

In 1864 similar orders were issued concerning the Baptist churches in the South, the military commanders being directed to turn over to the American Baptist Home Missionary Society all churches of the Baptist Church South "in which a loyal minister of said Church does not now officiate." Like orders were issued regarding the United Presbyterian Church and the Associate Reformed Presbyterian Church as well as both Old School and New School bodies. In every instance these orders were issued at the solicitation of some church official. The order issued to the United Brethren gives permission "to teachers and missionaries" to enter southern military departments, while in the case of the Presbyterians the agencies designed to work in the South were the Domestic Missionary Society and the Presbyterian Committee of

Home Missions, these orders having been solicited by the secretaries of these societies.

Thus the way for considerable missionary activity at the South on the part of the northern churches was opened. In 1864 the Missionary Board of the Methodist Episcopal Church made an appropriation of $35,000 for this work and missionaries were soon to be found in numerous places. In Norfolk and Portsmouth, Virginia, all churches were placed under the provost marshal who was to see that the pulpits were filled by loyal ministers, and orders were issued requiring that the churches be opened to all officers and soldiers "white or colored" at the usual hour of worship and "at other times if desired."

This action on the part of northern churches in going into the South at this time and under these circumstances aroused great indignation on the part of the Southerners. The Presbytery of Louisville in 1864 passed resolutions of protest against the Board of Domestic Missions procuring the order from the War Department and called upon the General Assembly to "at once disavow the said act, so that the church may be saved from the sin, the reproach, and ruin which this thing is calculated to bring upon her." In 1864 a convention of southern Methodist ministers from states within the Federal lines met at Louisville to protest against this activity. They stated that they did not believe that the President of the United States approved of this action, and characterized the procedure as "unjust, unnecessary and subversive alike of good order and the rights of a numerous body of Christians."

These southern ministers were right in their surmise

that President Lincoln did not approve of such interference with the churches. The President's attitude in regard to the military interferences with the churches is brought out in connection with the famous McPheeters case of St. Louis. Dr. Samuel B. McPheeters was the minister of an important Presbyterian church in St. Louis and in December, 1862, the commanding general of the department of the Missouri deposed McPheeters from his pulpit and ordered both him and his wife to leave the state within ten days. This was done because of the refusal of McPheeters to declare his loyalty to the United States, and also on the ground that his influence greatly encouraged the enemies of the government, while his wife had openly avowed that she was a rebel. McPheeters wrote a long letter of protest to the Attorney-General of the United States, which led to a long discussion covering more than a year, into which the President was eventually drawn. The President writing to the commanding general at St. Louis in January, 1863, stated: "I add that the United States Government must not, as by this order undertake to run the Churches. When an individual, in a Church or out of it, becomes dangerous to the public, he must be checked; but let the Churches, as such, take care of themselves. It will not do for the United States to appoint Trustees, Supervisors, or other agents for the Churches." Later in a letter to McPheeters President Lincoln wrote: "I have never interfered, nor thought of interfering as to who shall or who shall not preach in any Church, nor have I knowingly or believingly tolerated any one else to so interfere by my authority."

Up to this time the President had not heard of the orders issued by the War Department giving military commanders the right to seize churches and turn them over to the loyal agents of the northern bodies. His attention was brought to the situation by a Missouri Methodist preacher, the Rev. John Hagan, claiming to represent the loyal members of the Methodist Episcopal Church, South in Missouri. When he heard of the orders he wrote at once to Secretary Stanton, stating: "After having made these declarations [in reference to the McPheeters case] in good faith and in writing you can conceive of my embarrassment at now having brought to me what purports to be a formal order of the War Department, bearing date November 30, 1863, giving Bishop Ames control and possession of all the Methodist Churches in certain Southern military departments where pastors have not been appointed by a loyal bishop or bishops . . . and ordering the military to aid him against any resistance which may be made to his taking such possession and control. What is to be done about it?" The Secretary of War wrote at once, modifying the order, exempting all loyal states from its operations, but even then the President feared it was liable to abuses, but he stated, "it is not easy to withdraw it entirely and at once."

Writing in March, 1864, to the military commander at Memphis, who had interfered with the churches in that city, the President stated: "If the military have need of the church building, let them keep it, otherwise let them get out of it, and leave it and its owners alone, except for causes that justify the arrest of any one." Still the church squabble continued in Memphis and two months later the President again wrote the military commander: "I am now told that . . . the military put one set of men out of and another set of men into the building. This, if true is most extraordinary. I say again, if there be no military need of the building leave it alone, neither putting one set in or out of it, except on finding some one preaching or practicing treason, in which case lay hands on him, just as if he were doing the same thing in any other building, or in the street or highway." Such vigorous words well illustrate the clearsightedness with which the President saw the situation, and also indicate how much his patience was taxed by these petty squabbles.

It is difficult to find justification for the action of the northern churches in entering the South in the midst of the war, and starting their work in regions where the southern churches were at their mercy. The argument that this would help strengthen the Union cause was frequently used, while the northern church leaders stated that they were simply performing their Christian duty of taking the gospel where it was not preached, that they were following Christ's injunction by going "into all the South and preach the Gospel to every creature." In both North and South patriotism became the chief theme of the pulpit and the church press, and too often the Christian ideal of forgiveness and the Golden Rule gave way to a bitter vindictiveness.

During the course of the war the United States government asked certain church leaders to go abroad as unofficial representatives to explain the Federal policies to European peoples, who were prone to be critical. In 1863

Henry Ward Beecher, who had already won great fame, both for his eloquence and for his advocacy of the cause of the slaves, was sent to England. In the face of much irritating heckling he toured England and through his efforts helped change public opinion in that country toward the United States. Archbishop John Hughes, of New York, was likewise sent to France in 1861 where through interviews with members of the ministry, high Catholic officials and finally with Napoleon III, he succeeded in placing before them the true situation of affairs in America. Dr. John McClintock, a Methodist minister, was from 1861 to 1863 the pastor of the American Church in Paris and both in France and in England exercised no little influence in favor of the cause of the Union, especially through articles which he sent to both French and English papers.

Bishop Matthew Simpson, of the Methodist Episcopal Church, was a close personal friend of President Lincoln's and was one of the most eloquent preachers in the country. Through his patriotic lecture entitled "Our Country" delivered in every section of the North during the war, Bishop Simpson often produced telling effects. *Harper's Weekly,* describing the effects of this lecture in Pittsburgh, in October, 1864, stated: "Toward the close [of the address] an eye witness says: 'Laying his hand on the torn and ball-riddled colors of the Seventy-third Ohio, he spoke of the battle fields where they had been baptized in blood, and described their beauty as some patch of azure, filled with stars, that an angel had snatched from the heavenly canopy to set the stripes in blood.' With this description began a scene that Demosthenes

A Negro Camp-Meeting in the South

Reproduced from *Harper's Weekly*, August 10, 1872

might have envied. All over the vast assembly handker-
chiefs and hats were waved, and before the speaker sat
down the whole throng arose as if by magic influence and
screamed, and shouted, and saluted, and stamped, and
clapped, and wept, and laughed in wild excitement.
Colonel Moody sprang to the top of a bench and called
for 'The Star-Spangled Banner,' which was sung or rather
shouted, until the audience dispersed." This moving lecture was delivered in the Academy of Music in New
York on November 3, 1864, where it played an influential part in the winding up of the presidential campaign.

The Civil War period saw the rise of charities on a
larger scale than had ever before existed in the United
States. Increased giving is noted to Home and Foreign
Missions, to Bible and Tract Societies and for the aid
of the poor and the homeless. Men of wealth vied with
one another in their giving, to every good cause. The
American Home Missionary Society at the close of the
war was maintaining eight hundred missionaries, two
hundred fewer than five years before, but the Baptist
Home Missionary Society doubled both its numbers of
missionaries and its receipts. All the benevolent enterprises of the Methodist Episcopal Church showed a steady
increase throughout the years of the war. The Protestant
Episcopal, the Old and New School Presbyterians maintained their activities at least on the pre-war level and the
general complaint in all the churches was for more men
rather than for more money. In 1864 the receipts of the
American Board of Commissioners for Foreign Missions
showed that the receipts of the society had increased
more than fifty per cent since the opening of the war and

that old deficits were wiped out and a surplus created. In 1860 the Methodist Episcopal Church reported $270,-000 for home and foreign missions; in 1865, $607,000. In the New School Presbyterian Church the amount contributed for foreign missions in 1860 was $80,000, in 1865, $112,000; in the Old School Church the figures were $137,000 in 1860 and $180,000 in 1865, while missionary giving in the Baptist denomination increased from $88,000 to $153,000. In 1865 twenty-six missionary societies, home and foreign, gave $3,000,000 to the cause.

But in spite of all this increased giving the cause of vital religion and morals undoubtedly suffered as a result of the war. Membership in the churches generally showed a decrease for the war years, while many a minister could subscribe to the following complaint: "The sound of the drum calling for volunteers, the training of soldiers, companies leaving for the seat of war, are but scenes of every day's occurrence. Amid the excitement consequent upon such a state of things, you can readily understand the difficulty of sustaining the institutions of religion. In fact the pastor and his church are continually in danger of having their feelings more deeply interested in the fearful conflict between the North and the South than in their own growth in grace, or in the winning of soldiers for Christ." From Albany, New York (1862), came the report: "Of the general state of religion in this city and neighborhood, I regret to say that our worst fears in regard to the effects of the war are realized. Ever since the calamitous conditions of the country became the all-engrossing subject of thought and conversation, the higher interests of Christ's kingdom have been thrown proportionately in the background. The additions to most of our churches have been few; the interest in our week-day meetings has diminished; the preaching of the gospel has not excited the accustomed power; in short, the humiliating confession must be made that the church and world seem to a great extent, to have fallen into a common slumber. And the saddest thing is that our condition in this respect seems to be but too faithful a representation of the conditions of nearly the whole church."

Toward the end of the war religious conditions began to show some improvement in various sections of the country. From Massachusetts, Michigan, New Jersey and other states came reports of revivals, while in many cities new branches of the Young Men's Christian Association were being formed and new churches were being erected. The high tension of feeling brought on by the opening of the war; the terrible bloodshed of the first great battles; the hospitals filled with wounded and dying men; all this had stunned men's finer feelings and as a result religion suffered. But as the war progressed a readjustment came and the spirit of religion again asserted itself. But the brutalizing effects of the four bloody years, the resulting increase of drunkenness and human selfishness generally, were to exercise their blighting influence upon the life of the nation for years to come.

Chapter XX

THE CHURCHES IN THE PERIOD OF RECONSTRUCTION

THE Civil War was considered by church people in both North and South as primarily a moral and religious struggle, and it appealed more strongly to religious zeal than any war in modern times. The great northern churches, which had given an almost unanimous support to the government during the stress of war, felt that they not only had a right, but that it was their duty, to take a hand in the solution of reconstruction problems. Hence in the period following the war we find the influence of the churches in politics considerably on the increase. As has been suggested, loyalty to the government had become almost a part of the creed of the great body of northern church members. In Missouri every minister admitted to orders in the Methodist Episcopal Church had been compelled to take the oath of allegiance to the United States, and throughout the North Methodists and Baptists especially were considered as practically one hundred per cent Republican. The missionaries who had gone into the South during and following the war realized that the success of their work there depended upon the continued triumph of the Republican party, and especially of that wing of the party which supported radical reconstruction.

In the struggle between President Andrew Johnson and Congress over the policy of reconstruction church people of the North generally supported Congress. A Baptist editor, in October, 1865, gave this solemn warning, "Let the military be withdrawn, and the Union men will be slaughtered like sheep by these unhung traitors." A southern missionary writing to a church paper in 1866 stated that if President Johnson's policy succeeded "Union men, missionaries and the teachers of the freedmen" would be in danger, and every church and schoolhouse established in the South would be destroyed, and asserted: "If Congress fail we fail: if Congress succeeds we succeed." The Methodists especially were accused of political activity and were active in their hostility to President Johnson whom they accused of moral corruption and drunkenness. Gideon Welles, Secretary of the Navy in both the Lincoln and Johnson cabinets, in his *Diary*, accuses Bishop Simpson of having "brought his clerical and church influence to bear" in order to bring about the conviction of the President. The Methodist Episcopal General Conference which met in Chicago in May 1868, during the progress of President Johnson's trial, set aside an hour of prayer that the country might be delivered from the "corrupt influences" which were being exerted to prevent the conviction of Johnson, while the African Methodist Episcopal Church at their conference session in Washington likewise prayed for the President's conviction.

The missionary work begun in the South by the northern churches during the war was carried forward with increasing momentum during the period of reconstruction. The Freedmen's Aid Societies soon had numerous negro schools in every section of the South. The Presbyterian and Congregational societies were particularly active in their educational work, resulting in the intellectual and moral uplift of the freedmen rather than in winning members to their own churches. On the other hand, the Methodist Episcopal Church, through their Freedmen's Aid Society, soon had not only many schools in operation but also by 1869 had formed ten new annual conferences in the late slaveholding states, working among both negroes and whites. They were much more successful, however, in winning negroes than whites and by 1871 their negro membership was twice that of the white.

The southern churches, though in a greatly disorganized condition, recognized their obligation to their ex-slaves and were making plans to meet that obligation. Thus the Alabama Baptist Convention in 1865 stated: "The condition of our colored population appeals strongly to the sympathy of every Christian heart and demands, at the hands of all who love the Saviour, renewed exertions for their moral and religious improvement," and recommend the establishment of negro Sunday schools and that means be provided for more adequate preaching of the gospel to them. The Protestant Episcopal Church took like action the same year, the Bishop of North Carolina pointing out in his pastoral letter the ignorance and inexperience of the colored people, and warned his members of the danger of the negro

{ 472 }

falling into mischievous hands; he urged the formation of negro congregations in the towns and that means be provided for the religious training of negro children. Likewise the Methodist Episcopal Church, South recognized their obligation to the negroes and by 1866 had outlined a plan for their colored members. They were to be formed into separate charges with their own quarterly conferences; colored persons were to be licensed to preach, and where conditions justified, colored districts were to be organized, and later to be formed into Annual Conferences, and when there came to be two or more Annual Conferences they were to be assisted in forming a separate church. Thus in 1870 the Colored Methodist Episcopal Church was organized, consisting of the negro members who had remained in the Methodist Episcopal Church, South.

But the efforts of the southern churches for the negro were more or less in vain. The negroes were now free and many of them, if for no other reason than to put their freedom to the test, were anxious to separate themselves from the churches of their former masters. In many cases the negroes were suspicious of the intention of the southern churches, in which they had formerly worshiped under the eye of their white masters, with the result that the negro membership of the old southern churches rapidly decreased. The negro membership of the Southern Presbyterian Church decreased seventy per cent within a few years following the war, the majority going into the independent negro churches. In 1860 the Methodist Episcopal Church, South had 207,000 negro members; by 1866 only a few more than 78,000 remained.

Organization of negro Baptist churches went on rapidly throughout the South during the years 1865-1870, frequently aided by the whites. Thus in Montgomery, Alabama, the white Baptists of that city assisted the negro Baptists in the organization of their church and in the erection of a building. The ease with which a Baptist church could be organized largely accounts for the great number formed among negroes, though the practice of baptism by immersion likewise attracted negroes to that church. The independent negro Methodist churches also grew with amazing rapidity during the years following the war. The African Methodist Episcopal Church, which had been formed in Philadelphia in 1816, and until the Civil War had existed only among northern negroes, by 1880 had nearly 400,000 members, mostly in the South. The African Methodist Episcopal Zion Church, organized in New York in 1820, in ten years during this period grew from 26,746 members to nearly 200,000.

At the close of the war the negroes were enthusiastic for education and religion. The Freedmen's Bureau organized by the Federal government emphasized negro education while northern benevolent and missionary agencies coöperated. Frequently negro schools were taught by negro preachers, and especially was this true of the northern negro ministers who had come into the South with the close of the war. Naturally the freedmen had strange ideas regarding freedom, many thinking it meant freedom from work, and thousands forsook the plantations and flocked into the towns and cities. Idleness among the negroes gave them plenty of opportunity to exercise their religious desires and it is reported that

Negro Baptism at Tullulah, La.

Reproduced from a photograph in possession of the author

baptizings were as popular as were operas among the whites.

Unfortunately the negro churches and schools soon began to be used by unscrupulous politicians for their own ends. Religion and politics were naturally blended in the mind of the negro at this period. He could see no distinction between his political and religious interests and emotions. His religion was tinged with political thought and his political thought shaped by religious conviction. He could not understand why he should not bring his politics into the church, or why the Union League or the Lincoln Legion should not hold their meetings there. Unprincipled carpetbaggers, both white and colored, frequently took advantage of this situation and used negro churches for the political organization and control of the negro. One such carpetbagger in Florida is thus described: "He preached to the blacks in their churches, kissed their babies and told them that Jesus Christ was a Republican." Numerous negro ministers were elected to office during the period of negro rule, along with a long list of dishonest and corrupt carpetbaggers. It is to be regretted that the independent negro churches should have had their rise in the South in this particular period of our history, but it was seemingly inevitable that independent negro churches should have been formed.

As far as his church organization is concerned the negro has been largely an imitator of his white brother. According to the latest religious census (1926) there were in the United States twenty-four exclusively colored denominations, with more than 36,000 churches and more than four and a half millions of members. Besides, there were more than six hundred thousand colored members in thirty white denominations, making a total of more than five million negro church members in the United States. Of this number the negro Baptists alone make up more than half, while the number of negro Methodists total 1,500,000. Thus there are nearly ten times as many negro Baptists and Methodists as there are negro members of all other denominations.

As might be expected, the negro churches have displayed shortcomings. Frequently in their churches worship is subordinated to amusement, due largely to the poverty of the race in social institutions. Too frequently also, the negro church has tolerated lax morals among both ministry and membership especially in financial and sexual matters, facts which negro leaders themselves admit, though investigation shows that in this respect slow gains are perceptible. The negro church is still used by unprincipled leaders for political purposes, especially in the large northern cities such as Chicago, to which vast numbers of southern negroes have recently come. Sometimes the negro church has opposed the best colored leaders, a fact most unfortunate to the best interests of the colored race, while until very recent years the negro churches have not lived up to their opportunities in dealing with the fundamental social problems either in the cities or in rural communities. While these unfortunate facts cannot be disputed, yet the negro churches have played a large if not the largest part in the moral, social and educational advancement of the negro race in the United States.

Lowering of the standards of conduct in both public

and private life was one of the unfortunate consequences of the Civil War. The country's wealth was increasing with an alarming rapidity in the midst of political and social confusion while the war brought to prominence a class of rough, unscrupulous men, with low standards of personal conduct, who too frequently were permitted to gain leadership in both business and politics. Out of such a general background came an era of wholesale corruption in politics which affected every section of the nation and every department of government. The use of money in buying elections was but one of the many forms of political corruption. Votes were bought and sold in more than one state capital as commonly as meat in the market; governors' signatures to bills intended to create private fortunes were purchased with sums which reached into the tens of thousands. New York City was being robbed of millions by the famous "Boss" Tweed ring, while at the national capital well-known Congressmen and leaders of national prominence were involved in transactions which brought to them eventual disgrace and humiliation.

Corruption in business was even more common, if possible, than in government. Defalcations, wildcat stock selling, oil speculations, fraudulent railroad projects were some of the ways in which dishonest adventurers robbed the unwary. Unscrupulous methods of destroying business competitors were common, well illustrated by the "war" carried on between Cornelius Vanderbilt on the one side and Daniel Drew and Jay Gould on the other for the control of the Erie Railroad. Even while this disgraceful affair was in progress, Vanderbilt "maintained an air of high respectability" and was giving large sums of money to found Vanderbilt University, while Daniel Drew professed a deep interest in religion, having a few years before promised large gifts for the establishment of Drew Theological Seminary. Even the business of the church did not entirely escape the corruption of the time and serious frauds were uncovered in the conduct of the great publishing business of the Methodist Episcopal Church. A few years later the Augustinian Fathers, of Lawrence, Massachusetts, having borrowed large sums from parishioners for the erection of church edifices, through extravagance and bad management became hopelessly insolvent, causing serious loss and scandal.

The liquor evil, which had been considerably checked in the forties and fifties by the Washingtonian movement and the adoption of temperance legislation by a number of the states, attained greatly increased proportions during and following the Civil War. The Federal tax on liquors, which had been enacted as a war measure for the purpose of revenue, was continued after the war and gave to both liquor drinking and the liquor business an added respectability. The amount of capital invested in the liquor business grew from $29,000,000 in 1860 to more than $190,000,000 in 1880. This situation brought into existence the Prohibition party in 1869, and in 1874 a convention of Christian women met in Cleveland, Ohio, and formed The Woman's Christian Temperance Union; five years later Frances E. Willard became its president. This organization from the start was closely allied with the churches and was soon a powerful influence in the temperance cause.

Immigration was one of the factors which accounts for the rapid growth of the liquor traffic and for the important part the liquor interests soon began to play in politics. In 1873 the editor of a brewer's journal pointed out that the foreign-born citizens and their children were strong enough at that time to turn the scale in favor of one or the other political parties. He claimed that in some states the German vote alone could do it, and urged the liberal people to unite to give the deathblow to puritanical tyranny. "The future," he stated, "is ours! The enormous influx of immigration will in a few years overreach the puritanical element in every state in the Union."

From 1865 to 1884 more than seven millions of immigrants entered the ports of the United States, nearly fifty per cent of whom came from Ireland and Germany. This immigration was mostly Catholic, Lutheran or rationalist and its influence upon American Protestantism is most important. The Germans, both Lutheran and Catholic, brought with them the "continental Sabbath," and in many places used the day as one of general merrymaking, which soon became a cause for alarm among the evangelical churches. Ministers throughout the seventies denounced the growing tendency to forsake the Puritan sabbath and warned their people that the very foundations of the Republic were being undermined. In 1872 when the Germans of Chicago opened their Turner Hall they boldly announced that they were giving to Chicago "the honor and fellicity of an European Sabbath," while a Baptist editor described Chicago on Sunday as a "Berlin in the morning and a Paris in the afternoon." By the eighties, however, even strict Sabbaterians began to admit that the maintenance of the Puritan Sabbath was impossible and began to adjust themselves to the change.

The increase of foreign-speaking people and the rapid growth of cities following the Civil War created new problems for the American churches. Both Methodists and Baptists had begun working among the Germans in the eighteen-forties and after 1865 this work was greatly increased. The Baptist Home Mission Society reported in 1867 that they had forty-nine ordained "foreigners" who were laboring among Germans, Hollanders, French, Welsh, Norwegians, Swedes and Danes, while foreign language departments were opened at three Baptist theological seminaries for the training of ministers for this work. Similar work was carried on by the Methodists, Presbyterians, Congregationalists and other denominations. Strong city churches began to establish missions in needy sections where foreign populations were predominant. Thus in 1870 the First Baptist Church of Chicago was working among the Welsh, Swedes, Danes, and Germans while it maintained missions in four different localities in that city. During these years home mission work in the cities assumed large proportions and was carried on most effectively by all the larger denominations.

Serious efforts to meet the new religious problems presented by the rapidly growing cities were made by laymen in such interdenominational organizations as the Young Men's Christian Association. The rise of the Y. M. C. A. was largely a city affair. The first organization of the kind was formed in London in 1844, where under the leadership of George Williams a little group of young men engaged in the draper's trade banded together for "the improvement of the spiritual condition of young men engaged in the drapery and other trades." The purpose was soon widened to include young men generally and by 1851 there were twenty-four such organizations in Great Britain. In that year the first organization was formed in Boston. In 1861 two hundred organizations had been formed in the United States and during the Civil War the Y. M. C. A.'s in the northern cities were active in caring for the soldiers and sailors and in supporting the Christian Commission. In 1869 a business man made a trip through Ohio, New York, and Pennsylvania where he found the Y. M. C. A. in nearly every city enjoying the full confidence and sympathy of the churches. Full membership in the Y. M. C. A. was granted to members in regular standing of an evangelical church.

Dwight L. Moody, the most effectual evangelist of the post-war period, was a layman and began his career as a religious worker in the city of Chicago. He came to Chicago in 1856 where he joined Plymouth Church and was soon renting four pews which were filled each Sunday by young men whom he invited as his guests. Soon he had organized a Sunday school in one of the neediest sections of the city, persuading an influential Chicago merchant to become its superintendent. In 1860 he gave up business and devoted himself to city missionary work and during the Civil War to labors among the soldiers. Between 1865 to 1869 he served as the president of the Chicago Y. M. C. A. and collected funds for the erection of the first Y. M. C. A. building in the country. In 1871 he was joined by a remarkable evangelistic singer, Ira D. Sankey, whose singing added greatly to the effectiveness of Moody's preaching. From this time until his death Moody was occupied in revivalistic efforts. He made three extensive trips to England and Scotland where amazing results were accomplished, such as had not been witnessed since the days of Whitefield and Wesley. Moody and Sankey held great meetings in every leading city in the United States and Moody was undoubtedly the outstanding evangelist in the English-speaking world. His sermons were simple but full of conviction and point. He had intense sympathy for and insight into the individual and great practical skill and tact. His singular largeness and sweetness of spirit and his consuming passion for mending souls gave him a unique place as a religious worker.

Recent revivalists have been largely imitators of Moody and Sankey, though there are many indications that the Moody type of evangelism is losing its appeal. Modern psychology has given considerable attention to the study of conversion and the revival, especially since the publication of Starbuck's *Psychology of Religion* and William James' *Varieties of Religious Experience*.

During and following the Civil War population continued to move westward. Kansas was admitted to the Union in 1861, and two years following the close of the war Nebraska became a state. During the sixties and seventies the great mining boom brought an increasing number of people into the Rocky Mountain region, which

Mr. Moody Preaching at the Hippodrome

Reproduced from *Harper's Weekly*, March 11, 1876

by 1876 was sufficient to raise Colorado to statehood and led to the organization of the territories of Nevado, Arizona, Idaho, Montana, Wyoming, New Mexico and Dakota. The building of railroads west from Chicago, Omaha and Kansas City offered inducements for the rapid settlement of the prairie states, while streams of covered wagons brought large numbers into western Kansas, Nebraska, the Dakotas and regions farther westward.

The churches were fully alive to the opportunities as well as the problems presented by the rapid occupation of the trans-Missouri regions and were eager for the conquest of these new areas. The Baptist Home Missionary Society obtained a pledge from the Union and Central Pacific railroads to deed to them land sufficient for a meeting-house and parsonage in every city and town along their extended routes and in some cases they obtained whole blocks. The Methodists organized a Church Extension Society in 1864 as the task of erecting new churches in the new states and territories was too great for the Missionary Society. This society not only assisted in the erection of churches by direct gifts but established a loan fund, which stimulated the erection of thousands of churches. From 1868 to 1884 "Chaplain" C. C. McCabe was the assistant secretary of the Church Extension Society. One day while riding on the train he saw in the newspaper that at a "freethinkers'" convention, Robert G. Ingersoll in an eloquent speech before the convention had stated that "the churches were dying out all over the land." At the next station McCabe got off the train and sent this telegram to Ingersoll:

Dear Robert: 'All hail the power of Jesus name'—we are building more than one Methodist Church for every day in the year, and propose to make it two a day! C. C. McCABE

This incident caught the imagination of Methodists throughout the land and Chaplain McCabe went from ocean to ocean singing:

> The infidels, a motley band,
> In council met and said:
> "The churches die all through the land,
> The last will soon be dead."
> When suddenly a message came,
> It filled them with dismay:
> "All hail the power of Jesus' name!"
> We're building two a day.

One of the unfortunate consequences of the pushing of settlers into the trans-Missouri region and the building of the transcontinental railroads was the unrest produced among the western Indians. At the close of 1865 at least twenty-five thousand troops were on the frontiers of Minnesota, the Dakotas, Kansas, and in Arizona and New Mexico holding the restless Indians in check, keeping open the mail routes, guarding the telegraph line from Omaha to Carson City and protecting the settlers thronging westward. This general situation was particularly hard on Indian missions, for many missionaries were compelled to flee for their lives, and religious and economic conditions among the Indians were rapidly going from bad to worse. Meanwhile a rising humanitarian sentiment in the country found expression in memorials and petitions to Congress from religious and philanthropic organizations asking that the policy of the Federal government be changed to meet the urgent needs of the critical Indian situation. In April, 1869, an act was passed providing a fund of two million dollars for immediate Indian relief, while a board of Indian Commissioners was to be appointed, made up of ten intelligent and philanthropic men who were to have joint authority with the Secretary of the Interior in administering this fund. This board was in hearty sympathy with the efforts of missionary organizations, and served as an intermediary between the government and the religious bodies working among the Indians. "The Peace Policy" as this new plan of dealing with the Indians was termed, has produced on the whole good results, though for the first few years after its inauguration Indian wars continued.

The government now spends about $4,000,000 yearly for Indian education, and has established several types of schools, all, however, laying large emphasis upon industrial training. Besides the work carried on by the government, sixteen Protestant denominations and the Roman Catholics are engaged in educational and religious work among them. Religious instruction and services are not only conducted in the mission schools, but in many of the government reservation and non-reservation schools parts of the buildings are assigned to the workers from the several churches, who hold Sunday services and conduct week-day religious instruction. Under this influence the American Indian has made rapid progress from a barbarian to a civilized man, especially when one considers "that it has only been within the last half century that intensive training along educational lines has been given by missionary societies."

In 1904 the Indian population of South Dakota was about 20,000, and of this number four thousand were communicants of the Protestant Episcopal Church and in that year contributed more than $8,000 to the support of their churches. One Indian congregation in Arizona had a membership (1904) of 525 and is one of the churches formed by Charles Cook. In 1870 Cook was the pastor of a German church in Chicago, when he heard an army officer describe the condition of the Pima Indians. He resigned his church and started to Arizona without pledge of support from any organization and for ten years supported himself as a trader. He learned the Indian language and gradually won the confidence of the Indians. In 1904 there were more than a thousand Christian Indians under his care, and his work required nine helpers, six of whom were Indians.

In 1923 reports of the United States Indian office showed that there were 650 missionaries engaged in missionary work among the Indians; of these 410 were Protestant and 240 Catholic. There were 41,072 Protestant and 52,316 Catholic church-going Indians attending 991 churches. Not included in these statistics are the five civilized tribes of Oklahoma, which are largely Protestant.

By 1869 the causes for the division between Old and New School Presbyterians had largely disappeared and in that year a reunion of the two bodies was happily consummated, and the next year (1870) the first united assembly met in Albert Barnes' church in Philadelphia.

Thus the northern Presbyterians were united just in time to meet the increased demands of the new west. Previous to the reunion both churches had maintained societies for promoting church building and at the reunion both these organizations were merged into the Board of Church Erection. The Presbyterian Board of Home Missions was active in sending ministers into Kansas, Nebraska and the Dakotas and on westward, while the Board of Church Erection aided in the building of churches in the new communities.

The years following the Civil War constitute an era of denominational awakening among Congregationalists. This movement was inaugurated before the war when a group of Congregational leaders began to express impatience with the Plan of Union and the willingness of Congregationalists to subordinate the well-being of their own denomination to plans of coöperation in which other churches reaped a large share of the advantage. This feeling finally culminated in the unanimous rejection of the Plan of Union at a national convention of Congregationalists which met at Albany in 1852. This meeting also mapped out a comprehensive plan of Congregational advance, and in 1853 the American Congregational Union was formed, to unite the energies of the church throughout the country. Among the functions of this new organization was to coöperate in the building of meeting-houses and parsonages. Out of the Albany convention also came numerous new enterprises, among them the establishment of Chicago Theological Seminary (1855). Following the war Congregationalism advanced into the new prairie and mountain states and continued its educational tradition by establishing colleges—Washburn College in Kansas in 1865, Carleton in Minnesota in 1867, Colorado College in 1874, and others in Nebraska, South Dakota and Washington.

A strong competitor of the Methodists and Baptists in the new West was the Disciples who in 1883 established a Church Extension Fund to be loaned to churches needing help. A few years later a Board of Church Extension was created and located at Kansas City. By 1904 this board had aided in the erection of more than eight hundred churches and one of the policies instituted was the purchasing of strategic sites for future church building purposes and by 1904 the board was holding such sites in fifty-six cities and towns in the United States.

The churches which benefited most largely from the post-war immigration were the Catholic and Lutheran. In 1890 the Roman Catholics in the United States embraced immigrants from nearly all the countries of western Europe, and had a membership of 6,231,417. There were thirteen archdioceses and more than sixty dioceses with property valued at nearly $120,000,000. In this year the Catholic population in New England exceeded the Protestant communicants by more than two hundred thousand, and all the great cities throughout the country had become centers of Catholic influence and power.

Of greatest importance to American Lutheranism was the large Scandinavian immigration which entered the United States in the reconstruction years. From 1870 to 1910 one and three-quarter million Northmen came to American shores, one-half of whom were Swedes, while Norway furnished one-third and Denmark a sixth of the total. Minnesota became their chief home which by 1900 had a Scandinavian population of more than a million. Wisconsin, the Dakotas, Illinois, Michigan, Iowa and Kansas also received large numbers. This great body of sturdy people were potential materials for the Lutheran Church in America, but unfortunately the American Lutheran bodies were unable to meet fully the problems presented by their coming and a large majority were lost to the church. It has been estimated that only seven per cent of the Danes joined any church; not more than twenty per cent of the Swedes and less than thirty per cent of the Norwegians.

This failure on the part of American Lutheranism to embrace fully its great opportunity was due in part to the fact that from 1860 to 1870 was a period of disruption among the American Lutherans. The first rupture came in 1860 when the Swedes and Norwegians withdrew from the General Synod and formed the Augustana Synod. The second break came in 1862 as a result of the war, when the southern Lutherans withdrew and formed the United Synod of the South, which embraced more than twenty thousand members. Meanwhile strained relations continued between the conservative element in the church and the more liberal group, finally culminating in 1867 in the withdrawal of the conservative element and the organization of the General Council of the Evangelical Church in America, which soon became a larger body than the General Synod.

The first national organization of Jewish congregations was formed in 1873, called the Union of American Hebrew Congregations, and in 1875 established Hebrew

Union College in Cincinnati. Many German Jews had come to America in the great migrations of 1830 and 1848; this soon produced a new and aggressive leadership, out of which came largely the Jewish Union and Reform movement. The leader in this movement was Isaac M. Wise, who was rabbi of congregations first in Albany and later in Cincinnati. He was prime mover in the Union movement and became the first president of the Hebrew Union College. The Reformed Jews accept the moral laws of the Mosaic code only and reject all ceremonial and rabbinical regulations which they deem not suitable to modern life. This interprets the Messianic hope as the dawning of a new era rather than the coming of a person, while it emphasizes the universal aspects of Judaism rather than the restoration of the Jewish state and the return to Palestine. The great majority of Jewish congregations in the United States, however, have remained orthodox, and the number of orthodox Jews have been greatly increased by the large Jewish immigration from Russia and Poland which began in 1882 and has continued to the present time. In 1877 there were 278 Jewish congregations in the United States and a Jewish population of 230,000. By 1890 the Jewish population and also the Jewish congregations had doubled; in 1926 there were 3,118 congregations and a total population of more than four millions. In polity each Jewish congregation is independent and there are no conferences, synods or hierarchy which in any way controls the ritual or customs of the congregation. At the present time there are three federations of synagogues, one representing the reformed, the second the conservative and the third the orthodox.

At the end of the Civil War the great churches in the United States were thoroughly orthodox and conservative, but there were at work certain influences which were soon to bring about far-reaching changes in religious thinking. One such influence was that exercised by Horace Bushnell, a Congregational minister at Hartford, Connecticut. Without attempting to set up a complete theological system, and with little thought of combating any of the old theological positions, Bushnell in his sermons and writing became the inspirer of new religious thought and experience. His work was largely that of emancipating American Christianity from unchristian conceptions. This is well illustrated by his little book *Christian Nurture* which first appeared in 1846, and in its final form in 1861. American revivalism had largely ignored the law of Christian growth and in this book he sharply criticized the practice of the revivalistic churches in their insistence upon a conscious emotional experience and maintained "that the child is to grow up a Christian and never know himself as being otherwise." This would be possible, he maintained, if the life in the home was truly Christian and if the child was given his proper place in the church. This volume was one of the strong influences which turned the attention of the churches toward the more adequate training of youth. Bushnell also repudiated the old mechanical theories of the atonement then in vogue, and advanced what was known as the "moral influence theory," by which he tried to show that the atoning work of Christ falls under the law of self-sacrifice. Of all the preachers of his time in America, Bushnell was the most successful in restating the truths of religion in terms of human life and experience.

At first he was attacked by his ministerial brethren as a dangerous heretic and his association attempted to bring him to trial before the consociation. Pulpits were closed against him, but his own church stood by him and finally withdrew from the consociation. Ill health caused him to resign his church at Hartford in 1861, but for fifteen years thereafter he continued his writing; his influence steadily grew with the years, and at his death he was recognized as the foremost citizen of Hartford as well as the chief inspiration of the new liberalizing movement in religion and theology. The more widely acclaimed ministries of Henry Ward Beecher and Phillips Brooks were largely inspired by the essentials of Bushnell's message which through them reached Christian people in every section of the nation.

It was in this period also that the church began to be disturbed by the principle of evolution which had been announced by Charles Darwin, because it seemed to conflict with the Biblical account of creation. Most Christian people in the United States at this time were literalists as far as the Scriptures were concerned and to many earnest people evolution seemed to strike at the very foundation of Christian belief. There soon arose, however, several able defenders of the position that evolution is not necessarily subversive of religion. John Fiske was one of the most successful popularizers of these ideas, and in a series of widely read volumes performed a useful service for both science and religion. Henry Drummond's

Natural Law in the Spiritual World and his *Ascent of Man* also exercised a wide influence, especially on young men, and were widely read in America. Another influential Christian evolutionist was Lyman Abbott, the successor of Beecher at Plymouth Church, Brooklyn, who proclaimed that creation is "a process not a product," and that "'God is not merely a Great First Cause, but' the one Great Cause from whom all forms of nature and of life continuously proceed." As the editor of the *Independent* and a lecturer, he performed a great service to multitudes of people who were perplexed as to the relations of science and religion.

The church was also divided during the latter quarter of the nineteenth century into liberal and conservative groups by controversy over what was called the "higher criticism." In 1881 a revision of the New Testament was published, the aim of the combined English and American committee being to "adapt the King James' version to the present state of the English language without changing the idiom and vocabulary," at the same time utilizing the further knowledge which Biblical scholarship through three hundred years had made available. Four years later the revised version of the Old Testament appeared. In 1901 an American revision was published containing the readings preferred by the American committee, and since that time other translations have appeared, some of them "based upon the new knowledge of the differences between classical and hellenistic Greek."

The revisions of the Bible naturally led to discussions of creedal revisions which became especially intense among the Presbyterians, resulting in a decided reaction toward conservatism. The question of the inspiration of the Bible and the errancy or inerrancy of the Scriptures were warmly discussed in every section of the church, and resulted in a number of unfortunate heresy trials. The trial which attracted most attention was that of Professor Charles A. Briggs, a distinguished Hebrew scholar in Union Theological Seminary. Some members of the New York Presbytery took exception to some of his views. The case was finally brought to the General Assembly in 1893, which by a large majority found him guilty of the violation of his ordination vows and suspended him "from the office of a minister in the Presbyterian Church." Soon after this Briggs withdrew from the Presbyterian Church and took orders in the Protestant Episcopal Church. About the same time another distinguished Presbyterian scholar, Henry Preserved Smith, of Lane Theological Seminary was brought to trial on a similar charge, the inerrancy of the original manuscript of the Scriptures, and was also convicted. A few years later Professor A. C. McGiffert of Union Theological Seminary was accused of heresy, the accusation based upon certain statements in his book *Christianity in the Apostolic Age*. The General Assembly referred the case to the Presbytery of New York, of which the accused was a member, but rather than cause further disturbance in the church, McGiffert announced his withdrawal from the Presbyterian ministry. Altogether these famous heresy trials served no other purpose than to rid the church of its most distinguished scholars and create differences and divisions which still persist.

Chapter XXI

THE AMERICAN CHURCHES IN THE AGE OF BIG BUSINESS

AMONG the first names to be enrolled in the peerage of
the new industrial age, which began with the close of
the Civil War, are Jay Cooke and J. Pierpont Morgan
"of the financial seigniory"; Andrew Carnegie "of the
steel demesne"; James J. Hill, Jay Gould, William H.
Vanderbilt, Collis P. Huntington and Edward H. Harri-
man, railroad barons; John D. Rockefeller of the "oil
estate"; Philip D. Armour and Gustavus F. Swift "of
the province of beef and pork"; and Cyrus McCormick of
the farm machinery appanage. Of this group all except
Andrew Carnegie, who seems to have been tinged with
skepticism, were members of the church in regular standing. Cooke and Rockefeller were particularly active in
their denominations. Cooke was a tither and gave liberally
to charitable and benevolent causes, was generous in his
support of church enterprises, and for many years taught
a Sunday school class. Armour, Hill and Morgan gave
liberally to the church, while McCormick and Vanderbilt gave large endowments to church educational institutions which bear their names.

The outstanding factor in the development of the

United States since the Civil War has been the tendency toward the consolidation of political and economic institutions. In politics this tendency is illustrated by the steadily growing power of the Federal government at the expense of the states; in business, by the rise of great corporations and the consolidation of management, at the expense of the individual operator. This is well illustrated by the history of the American railroads. Previous and during the Civil War the railroads were short lines controlled by numerous independent companies; in 1900 there were more than 198,000 miles of track in the United States directed by a few powerful corporations. Before the Civil War there were fifty telegraph companies operating in the United States and more than four hundred coal mines under independent management. Today great corporations such as the United Steel Corporation, the American Telephone and Telegraph Company, the great oil corporations, the American Tobacco Company are but typical of American business organization. In 1919 the great corporations employed eighty-six per cent of the wage-earners and produced more than eighty-seven per cent of the total value of the products.

Naturally in this period of the development of big business there was an accompanying emphasis upon efficiency, system and organization, while responsibility was delegated to committees and boards. The successful business man became the symbol of modern America and his ideals and methods began to permeate every phase of American interest and life. Nor was the church long in feeling his influence and in responding to it. The admission of laymen to the General Conference of the Methodist Episcopal Church in 1872 is an indication of the rising influence of laymen, while the appointment of wealthy business men to church boards became increasingly common in all the churches. Better business methods in the conduct of the individual church became a matter of discussion in the church assemblies. At the Illinois Christian Convention in 1868, an annual interdenominational meeting at Bloomington, the great subject of discussion was Christian efficiency, and complaints began to be heard that business meetings were taking the place of prayer meetings and that the churches were being controlled by little groups of individuals, constituting committees who were applying modern business methods to the affairs of the "kingdom." In city churches particularly men with business ability were more and more sought after to serve as church officials.

Laymen's organizations in the church soon appeared, at first confined to local churches. Among the earliest were the Social Unions. The first Baptist social union was formed in Tremont Temple, Boston, in 1864, but ten years later such organizations were to be found in many of the larger churches, and in 1874 a convention was called of delegates from all the Baptist social unions of the country to meet in Brooklyn to discuss the place of laymen in the denominational movements, their responsibility to the churches, the education of the ministry, the endowment of colleges and other subjects of interest to the denomination as a whole. This movement eventually developed into the Baptist Congress which met annually from 1881 to 1912 and performed a most valuable service to the church in that it brought together the best minds of the denomination, both lay and clerical. At these meetings it was frequently urged that the great business enterprises of the churches be under the control of laymen, and from this time on the treasurers of the Baptist national societies, almost without exception, were outstanding business men. One of the results of the introduction of lay representation into the General Conference of the Methodist Episcopal Church was the increased energy and interest displayed by them. Dwight L. Moody reported in 1868, after an extensive tour of Christian conventions throughout the country, that "churches that had been closed against laymen were freely thrown open, pastors taking seats with the listeners, and laymen speaking from pulpits and burning hearts."

Not only was the business administration of churches falling more and more into the hands of laymen, but to a larger degree was this true in the denominational colleges. Men of wealth began to make princely gifts to educational institutions. George Peabody gave $3,000,000 to stimulate education in the South; Matthew Vassar gave $800,000 to found a woman's college, to be followed in rapid succession by the establishment of Wellesley, Smith and Bryn Mawr. The Crozer family gave $275,000, besides buildings and houses for the professors, to the Theological Seminary which bears their name, while DePauw, Colgate, Cornell, Stanford, John D. Rockefeller and finally the Duke family gave their millions to establish new or more richly endow already established institutions. As a result every college president in the country dreamed of finding some merchant prince, oil magnate or railroad baron who might endow his institution. Places on the boards of trustees formerly held by ministers began to be filled more and more by wealthy laymen, and in many instances wealthy men who were without church affiliation were urged to accept such positions. The business and administration end of the colleges began to receive greater attention. Even presidents of small colleges no longer had time to teach, as had been commonly the case previous to 1890, but more and more gave their entire attention to administration. Instead of a part-time secretary, college presidents now were served by one, two and even three secretaries and a new official, the assistant to the president, made his appearance, until in some instances the budget for administration in denominational colleges equaled that devoted to teaching.

Still another influence of growing wealth was the building of costly churches and larger giving to all benevolent enterprises. In the great cities the larger denominations built Gothic temples and supplied them with rich furnishings and costly organs, while thousands of dollars were expended each year for trained musicians. Even the churches which had been known as the churches of the poor vied with one another and with the so-called aristocratic churches in their expenditures for church buildings, hospitals and other church institutions. Previously Baptists and Methodists had been proud to call themselves the poor man's church; they now began to boast of their wealth, to talk of the "sanctification" of wealth, and to speak of it as "consecrated power."

As the great denominations came more and more to be dominated and controlled by business methods and by men of wealth, and as the services became more formal, complaints were raised that "heart religion" was disappearing. Beginning about 1880 and continuing until the close of the century the so-called "holiness" question agitated the Methodist Episcopal and the Methodist Episcopal Church, South, and the other churches of the Methodist family. Churches were divided over the issue, and soon a distinct line of cleavage divided whole conferences into "holiness" and "anti-holiness" groups. The "holiness" advocates claimed that they were simply holding to the doctrine of Christian perfection as preached by John Wesley and that they were trying to get the church to return to the true Wesleyan position. On the other hand, the bishops and the intellectual leaders of the church disparaged the whole movement, especially the tendency to form associations and hold separate meetings, with their own preachers and evangelists. The result was that the "holiness" people felt increasingly ill at ease in the regular churches and soon were leaving the older bodies in increasing numbers and forming independent organizations. This separatist movement gained considerable momentum as the liberal tendencies in the Methodist theological seminaries and colleges showed themselves more openly in the latter nineties, while the tendencies of the Methodist churches away from the old revivalistic emphasis further convinced the "holiness" leaders that the only hope for their movement lay in their complete withdrawal.

Between 1880 and 1926 at least twenty-five of these pentecostal bodies came into existence, most numerously in the Central West where their chief feeders, the Methodistic bodies, are most numerous. The groups which formed these sects were largely the poor and uneducated classes in both country and city. Though largely rural, where their work is carried on either in the open country or in small towns among the unschooled and under-privileged, yet bodies such as the Church of the Nazarene have a considerable number of city churches where their work is confined to the working classes and the small-salaried people. Many of the people whom they attract would be repelled by the larger denominations, and these small sects have therefore rendered a real service to many lowly and needy people.

Belonging in a peculiar sense to this period of big business and prosperity is the Christian Science Church which has been described as the "outgrowth of a well-fed and prosperous society," and as the religion of the comfortable.

The recognized founder of this new religion was a remarkable woman, Mrs. Mary Baker G. Eddy, a native of New Hampshire who from childhood had been afflicted by a strange nervous malady. After the failure of every attempt on the part of regular physicians to afford her relief, she at last heard of a certain "Dr." P. P. Quimby who was achieving some marvelous cures in Portland, Maine, by methods of mental healing. She placed herself under the care of Quimby and at once found relief if not an entire cure. She now became a pupil of Quimby's and was permitted by him to copy his manuscripts, which she used for a number of years in carrying on mental healing, and which eventually became the nucleus of the Christian Science textbook called *Science and Health*. Mrs. Eddy and her followers have denied any relationship between Quimby's teachings and writings and *Science and Health*, but to any impartial investigator, who compares the Quimby manuscripts (published 1921) with Mrs. Eddy's writings, such a dependence becomes at once more than a conjecture. To admit any dependence, however, upon Quimby would, of course, undermine any claim on the part of Christian Science to a divine origin.

Organized Christian Science began in the city of Lynn, Massachusetts, where Mrs. Eddy had carried on her teachings and had finally organized her followers into The Christian Science Association. Here she had but meager success and the enterprise was on the verge of collapse when in 1882 she decided to move to Boston. "She was canny enough to see," says a recent biographer, "that it was in the large cities that her Science could be most profitably promoted." Here the First Church of Christ Scientist was organized and with Boston as the center the teachings of Christian Science spread with fair rapidity, winning its largest following, however, in the larger cities. Mrs. Eddy lived to a great age, but although retiring more and more from public view, the control of her great organization was never for a moment out of her hands. Mrs. Eddy at the time of her death in 1910 had accumulated a large fortune, largely through the sale of her book *Science and Health* and the numerous Christian Science publications.

Christian Science teaches that matter has no real existence, nor has evil, sickness, sin or even death. These are all illusions of mortal mind. Upon these principles Mrs. Eddy based her system of healing, by simply affirming

THE CHAPEL AT THE UNIVERSITY OF CHICAGO

"Another influence of growing wealth was the building of costly churches"

that disease does not exist. Without discussing the absurdity of her "philosophic sophistries," it may be stated with truth that "the therapeutic psychology which formed a part of her system" has conferred an almost inestimable boon upon many of those brought under its influence.

Organized labor was one of the inevitable accompaniments of capitalism. Having before them the examples of the great corporations, such as those presented by the railroads, the telegraph lines, the great oil and steel combinations, it was inevitable that the wage-earners should organize to protect their interests. The history of labor organizations in the United States properly begins with the formation of the Knights of Labor in Philadelphia in 1869. This organization included all branches of labor, and aimed to improve the economic, moral, social and intellectual condition of its members. By 1885 it had become a powerful body with more than 700,000 members. After 1890 the Knights of Labor declined while its place was largely taken by the American Federation of Labor. By this latter date about five hundred newspapers, devoted to the cause of labor, were published in the United States, and the formation of organizations among the farmers, especially in the Middle West, indicates the growing tendency of the less powerful classes to unite.

The latter seventies and eighties was a period of industrial strife throughout the United States. Chicago particularly was the center of disturbance, and there on May 1, 1886, occurred the famous Haymarket riot. But this was only the climax of a long series of labor disturbances. During the year 1886 there were nearly 1,600 controversies involving more than 600,000 men and causing an estimated financial loss of $34,000,000. In 1892 came the violent strike at the Carnegie Steel Company's works at Homestead, Pennsylvania; this came about because of the reduction of wages and the refusal of the company to recognize the Steel Workers' Union. Two years later the most disastrous of the strikes was precipitated among the employees of the Pullman Palace Car Company of Chicago when the company made a twenty-five per cent reduction in wages. Eventually the American Railway Union and all the railroads entering Chicago were involved and the property loss, together with the loss in wages, totaled more than $80,000,000.

Such was the immediate economic background out of which came the beginnings of the emphasis among the American churches upon the social teachings of Jesus. The bitter contests between capital and labor, coupled with the fact that the churches and church institutions were the recipients of large gifts from capitalists and seemed to be largely under their control, brought the frequent accusation that they were the agents and tools of capital. There was just enough truth in this accusation to cause church leaders to squirm under it and the fear began to be expressed that the laboring classes were being permanently alienated from the church. Other factors contributing to this emphasis were the developing interest in the study of sociology in the universities, the unprecedented immigration to the United States of these years, and the growing interest in socialism on the part of a few thoughtful Christian ministers. In 1889 a small group calling themselves Christian Socialists met together in Boston and in their declaration asserted that "the control of business is rapidly concentrating in the hands of a dangerous plutocracy" and that "the teachings of Jesus Christ lead directly to some specific form or forms of socialism." Among the forerunners in this new religious emphasis were Washington Gladden, Josiah Strong, Professors Richard T. Ely, David Jayne Hill and E. Benjamin Andrews. Gladden was a Congregational minister in Columbus, Ohio, and although opposed to socialism "flayed the plutocracy in scorching words," and in a succession of volumes—*Workingmen and their Employers*, 1876; *Applied Christianity*, 1887; *Tools and Men*, 1893—exercised a determining influence upon the rising generation of young ministers. Strong, in a series of books, popularized the conception of the Kingdom of God as a social ideal, while Ely, Hill and Andrews were university professors, all of whom, between 1888 and 1895, published important books discussing the social aspects of Christianity.

A few years later the University of Chicago became an important center for the presentation and application of the social teachings of Jesus, under the leadership of Shailer Mathews, A. W. Small and Charles R. Henderson, while at the same time Graham Taylor was appointed professor of Christian Sociology in the Chicago Theological Seminary. Others who contributed to the movement in its earlier years were George D. Herron, of Grinnell College, Walter Rauschenbusch, of Rochester Theological Seminary, Francis G. Peabody, of Harvard, and Harry F. Ward. Ward began his career as pastor of a church in the stockyards district of Chicago where he became the champion of social Christianity in its practical application, which work he later carried on as a professor in the Boston University School of Theology and at Union Theological Seminary. By the end of the century courses in Christian Sociology or Social Service were being offered in many of the theological seminaries, while college settlements had been established in most of the large American cities, where students of sociology might receive practical training in dealing with the problems of society. As Beard suggests, "Whatever the dominant force behind this effort to cross the social divide, it exerted, beyond all question, a direct and immediate influence on American thinking about industrial questions and on the course of social practice."

In the years since the beginning of the twentieth century interest in social Christianity has steadily grown, and practically all of the religious bodies have adopted social creeds, as well as establishing social service commissions to put these social creeds into practice. In 1908 the Federal Council of the Churches of Christ in America adopted the "Social Creed of the Churches," an exceedingly able declaration which has exercised large influence upon the social thinking of all the Protestant churches.

There were many thoughtful people in the United States in 1914 who sincerely believed that such a calamity as a world war was an utter impossibility. In the first place, they stated, modern warfare was so costly that even the resources of the richest nations would so soon be exhausted that once a war was begun it could last but a few months at most. Added to this economic reason was the progress the peace movement had made since the first Hague conference in 1899, and the formation of the permanent court of arbitration. From 1900 to 1914 the United States entered into many international agreements and this had aroused a larger public interest in diplomacy than ever before. Presidents Roosevelt and Taft, as well as Secretaries Hay and Root had given enthusiastic support to the general practice of settling international disputes by judicial process, while "the education of public sentiment in the direction of universal peace was organized on a colossal scale" through the great gifts of Andrew Carnegie and others like-minded. The churches gave hearty support to all these movements, organized peace societies and associations, and a feeling of optimism regarding world peace generally prevailed.

Many a minister who preached on the subject of Peace on Fourth of July Sunday in 1914 had completely revised his whole attitude toward peace and war by the middle of August, and by the time the United States entered the World War in 1917 was ready to proclaim as holy the cause of the Allies. No men and women labored more faithfully and tirelessly in the interests of war efficiency than did those who made up the membership of the Christian churches. The ministers as a whole supported every government policy that looked toward the winning of the war. They urged men to join the armed forces of the United States; opened their churches to the Red Cross and other war-time organizations; helped gather contributions to the numerous funds; preached sermons from outlines sent them by the government propaganda agencies, and too often believed and circulated the stories of enemy atrocities. Ministers went to training camps as chaplains, or volunteered to go as workers, to help carry on the great task which the government had placed upon the Young Men's Christian Association, in the camps both in the United States and overseas. All the great churches created War Commissions to direct the special war-time activities of the churches, while a General War-Time Commission was created by the Federal Council, made up of one hundred members representing not less than thirty-five denominations. This body raised and spent more than $300,000 during the course of the war, while its chief work consisted in helping the government secure efficient men to serve as chaplains. The Roman Catholics also, through their National War Council, were active in war work.

The unqualified support which the churches gave to the war program was largely gained because of the widespread belief among Christian people generally that they were engaged in "a war to end war." "The steady stream of atrocity stories, the suppression of all evidences of better feeling on the part of any section of the German people, the disheartening effects of the pronunciamento of the German intellectuals, the honest and sincere revulsion of feeling against a nation, the action of whose leaders had plunged mankind into these unspeakable horrors—all worked to make righteous anger seem a Christian duty." As often happens in such crises individual ministers were often more extreme in their denunciation of the enemy than were the average citizens, though in the great church bodies, such as the General Assemblies, Conventions and Conferences and especially in the pronouncements of the Federal Council, the Christian note was never entirely absent.

This latter pronouncement called attention to the fact that the Federal Council represented Christian citizens, upon whom rested a double responsibility. They owed it to their country and to their descendants to preserve freedom and democracy, but above all they must be loyal to their divine Lord. All that is done and planned in the nation's name must be brought "to the test of the mind of Christ." Some of their number believed that it is forbidden the disciples of Christ to engage in war under any circumstances; others believed that Christ enjoins that the sacred rights of humanity be defended, but all were one in devotion and loyalty to the country. Among the special duties enjoined upon members of the Church of Christ was to purge their hearts "of arrogance and selfishness"; to keep before themselves and allies the ends for which they fought; to testify to fellow Christians everywhere, especially those from whom they were estranged, their consciousness of unbroken unity in Christ; to be diligent in works of relief and mercy; to care for the young men in the armies and navies that they might be strong to resist temptation; to protect the rights of conscience against every attempt to invade them; to keep an open mind and a forward look that the war may teach lessons that may not be forgotten when peace comes; and above all to call men to obedience to the will of God, who through Christ invites men "to share with Him His ministry of reconciliation."

William Adams Brown, the secretary of the War-Time Commission of the churches, who has most adequately appraised the work of the churches during the war and the effect of the war upon them, has stated that the war did three things for the churches. It first of all showed them the inadequacy of their organization; second, it revealed unexpected spiritual resources; and third, it inspired them with an extravagant hope. Out of the first came a stronger movement in the direction of Christian unity, which has already resulted in uniting divided bodies and in other hopeful unification movements. Second, the war revealed a tremendous latent idealism in the heart of the American people, out of which came "undreamed-of capacity" for self-sacrifice, which has shown itself since the war in a determined effort on the part of a growing body of people to bring in a warless world. And third, the extravagant hope engendered was responsible for the inauguration of the Interchurch World Movement, which grew out of a splendid vision of a united "American Protestantism in a single campaign for money, men and spiritual power." The sudden let-down on the coming of peace and the fact that several of the great denominations, particularly the Methodists, Baptists, and Presbyterians, were already committed to definite plans for denominational advance, at least partly accounts for the dismal failure of this great interchurch plan. But the same forces in the nation which defeated the League of Nations were also largely responsible for the defeat of this "League of the Churches" and furnish the present opposition to the movement for international peace.

The abnormal emotions engendered by the war, and following the war, the natural reaction from internationalism to a strong nationalism, together with the decline of the war-time idealism, were factors in the formation of such organizations as the Ku Klux Klan with its anti-Catholic, anti-Jew, anti-alien and anti-negro program. Throughout the South and the Middle West, in the post-war years, the Klan became a powerful organization, drawing many members of Protestant churches into its membership, while in not a few instances Protestant ministers became Klan organizers and welcomed the order into their churches. The anti-Catholic propaganda especially carried on by the Klan aroused active resistance on the part of American Catholics; in numerous communities this caused the formation of new political alignments and aroused new antagonisms and hatreds.

During this period of post-war reaction the Fundamentalist movement also gained a greater momentum. Indeed, students of society have recognized the Ku Klux Klan and Fundamentalism as identical types of reactionism. The so-called Fundamentalist movement began in 1910 with the publication of a series of little books entitled *The Fundamentals: A Testimony to the Truth*, which professed to set forth the five fundamental Christian truths. More than 2,500,000 copies of the twelve volumes were published and circulated with money furnished by two wealthy laymen. The doctrines set forth as fundamental were the Virgin birth of Christ, the physical resurrection, the inerrancy of the Scriptures in every respect, the substitutionary theory of the atonement, and the imminent, physical Second Coming of Christ. Those who supported these views did not hesitate to denounce as "no Christian" any who denied them. In a broader sense Fundamentalism may be defined as an organized attempt to preserve the authoritarian position of historic Protestantism, against the rising tide of "modernism"; while Modernism may be defined as the "use of the methods of modern science to find, state and use the permanent and central values of inherited orthodoxy in meeting the needs of a modern world."

The controversy between these two types of Christianity became particularly active during the early post-war period and affected every evangelical denomination. The issues in the several churches were not always the same but the attitudes engendered were in every case similar. The Baptist and Presbyterian churches were the ones most affected by the controversy, though in the Disciples body and among the Methodists the issues were clearly drawn. For several successive years in the Northern Baptist Convention and in the General Assembly of the Presbyterian Church in the United States the Fundamentalist-Modernist controversy occupied the center of the stage, though in both churches the extreme fundamentalists were eventually defeated.

The two most widely advertised events in the controversy were the attempt on the part of the Presbytery of Philadelphia to bring Harry Emerson Fosdick to trial for heresy and the trial of John T. Scopes, a teacher in the public schools of Dayton, Tennessee, accused of teaching evolution in violation of the Tennessee Anti-Evolution law which had been passed by the legislature of that state in 1925. Fosdick was a Baptist minister and a professor in Union Theological Seminary in New York, and had been invited by the First Presbyterian Church of New York to be its pastor. This invitation he had accepted with the understanding that he be permitted to remain a Baptist. Fosdick was soon recognized as the most influential modernist in the country and his preaching soon aroused the fundamentalists among the Presbyterians, especially after he had affirmed that "Creedal subscription to ancient confessions of faith is a practice dangerous to the welfare of the Church and to the integrity of the individual conscience." When the matter came to the General Assembly in 1924 that body saw fit to invite Dr. Fosdick either to enter the ministry of the Presbyterian Church or vacate his Presbyterian pulpit. He chose the latter alternative and has since become the minister of a new independent church in New York, adjacent to Union Theological Seminary.

The trial of John T. Scopes attracted world-wide attention. William Jennings Bryan, who had by that time given up all his political ambitions and was devoting himself to furthering the cause of fundamentalists in the Presbyterian Church, assisted the prosecution, while representatives of the modernist views and well-known scientists went to the little Tennessee town to assist in the defense. The trial was decided against the defendant, for expert testimony was excluded and the broad issues involved were not faced.

The attempt of the fundamentalists to control Princeton Theological Seminary finally resulted in the withdrawal of the conservative members of the faculty and the formation of a new institution in the City of Philadelphia. This fundamentalist institution has taken the name Westminster Seminary and began operation in the fall of 1929 with some fifty students. From the beginning of the controversy Moody Bible Institute in Chicago and the Bible Institute of Los Angeles, California, have been centers of fundamentalism, both of which are largely under Presbyterian influence and control.

In recent years a more extreme type of modernism has been gaining some prominence within certain churches and especially in university centers. Its apostles call it the new humanism as distinct from the old humanism which was the term often applied to the classical revival of the Renaissance. The new humanist is an individual "who seeks and finds the divine in man and who doubts or denies the existence of any God other than the God resident in the human will-to-goodness." A recent interpreter has declared that the religion of humanism is a natural reaction to the experiences through which the present generation has passed, especially the experiences of the war. That it has grown out of "a certain healthy impatience and indignation with too easy cures for the pains of the world." The humanist is not willing to trust any other cure for the world's evil and pain than "the will-to-goodness" in the soul of man.

A movement of growing importance among all the Protestant churches is that which aims at raising the educational standards of Sunday schools, and emphasizing the other educational functions of the church. The movement began with the opening of the century when the Protestant churches first realized the danger arising from the omission of religious teaching in the public schools. This meant that the religious training of American children must depend upon the Sunday schools, together with what training might be received in the home. For the first time the educational incompetence of the average Sunday school began to be fully realized. In 1903 the Religious Education Association was formed, and in 1922 several religious educational agencies were merged into the International Council of Religious Education, the purpose of which was to bring about educational coöperation among the Protestant churches. Many of the larger churches have installed directors of Religious Education, while standards of Sunday school work have been raised and week-day and vacation church schools are now commonly conducted in many places. Denominational colleges and theological seminaries have installed professors of Religious Education for the purpose of training competent workers in this new field.

In recounting the history of religion in America it has been necessary to say much concerning disagreements and divisions among the Christian churches. Revivals, slavery and secession, doctrine, church rites and practices, and church government have been the causes of many of these divisions. The Great Awakening in the colonial period divided churches in New England into the New Lights and the Old Lights. In the middle colonies the Presbyterians were split into the Old School and New School, the latter favoring the revival, the former opposing it. Out of the great Western Revival came the Cumberland Presbyterian Church and the Church of the Disciples, while the United Brethren and the Evangelical churches came about through the influence exerted by Methodism on the German Reformed and Lutheran churches. The leaders and most of the original members of these two German revivalistic churches were drawn largely from the older German churches which were opposed to the revival methods. Slavery and secession caused serious schisms in the great democratic churches. Doctrinal differences divided Congregationalism and the Society of Friends and have played their part in numerous other schisms. Differences regarding the administering of the sacraments and other rites have caused division among Baptists, Episcopalians, Dunkers and Disciples. Disputes over church administration and government have divided the Methodists as well as other churches. Considered in the light of our day, many of these divisions seem to have been unjustifiable, but at the time they occurred the leaders in the disputes and separations were undoubtedly sincere and loyal to what they considered the highest good. They were men of conviction and we can respect their motives, although we may at the same time deplore the divisions they were so largely responsible for creating.

Though there have been many divisions in the American churches there have always been forces working toward Christian unity. The greatest of all the colonial preachers, George Whitefield, felt equally at home among Congregationalists, Presbyterians, Reformed, Baptists and Quakers. From 1801 to 1837 the Congregationalists and Presbyterians worked together on the frontier under the Plan of Union, while the American Board of Commissioners for Foreign Missions and the American Home Missionary Society were interdenominational bodies. The American Bible Society since its organization in 1816 has been supported by all of the Protestant denominations, while its work in supplying Bibles to every race and tongue in the world has been equally helpful to all the churches. The greatest of all modern revivalists, Dwight L. Moody, did not have a denominational hair in his head, while the revival movements since his day have been more and more undenominational in character and have had a considerable unifying influence.

The years following the Civil War were fruitful in the formation and development of interdenominational organizations among young people, such as the Young Men's and Young Women's Christian Associations and the Student Volunteer Movement, which from its beginning has been closely allied with the Y. M. C. A.'s and Y. W. C. A.'s in the colleges. The Student Volunteer Movement was inspired by Dwight L. Moody as early as 1868. Thirty years later it produced the World's Student Christian Federation, to unite the various student movements in all lands, to foster closer relations among them, to collect information regarding religious conditions among students everywhere, and to promote a deeper spiritual life among students, as well as to enlist students in the cause of extending Christianity. The inspirer of this organization was John R. Mott, who for many years was the secretary of the International Young Men's Christian Association. Aside from the organizations which he has fostered, Mr. Mott himself has exercised a large influence for Christian unity.

Of great significance in the progress of Christian unity was the formation in 1881 of the Christian Endeavor Society, founded by Francis E. Clark in Portland, Maine. Within a quarter of a century there were fifty thousand Christian Endeavor Societies in several denominations. It soon became international in scope, and through its local, national and international gatherings it has brought together tens of thousands of young people, representing many denominations, to discuss the problems of Christian service.

No single force has been more influential in developing interdenominational understanding and coöperation than has the cause of missions. The absurdity of Christian competition in foreign fields brought about the formation in 1893 of the Foreign Missions Conference of North America, which includes all the Protestant missionary societies and boards in the United States and Canada. This body functions through a Committee on Reference and Council, which maintains a permanent staff, while the conference meets once each year to discuss common problems. In 1908 the Home Missions Council was formed, made up of thirty-six Home Missionary Boards, and this performs a similar service for home missions. Coöperation has worked admirably in certain foreign fields especially. In China there are more than twenty educational institutions under interdenominational control, while in all the important mission fields numerous coöperative enterprises are in operation. In the Philippine Islands an Evangelical Union of the Philippines was early formed, made up of Baptists, Congregationalists, Disciples, Methodists, Presbyterians and United Brethren. The union has prevented duplication of work and has served to unite Christian forces in the great common cause. Most of the mission boards working in Latin-American countries have worked out a plan of coöperation, their agent being the Committee on Coöperation in Latin America, which maintains an office and a permanent

CHRISTIAN SCIENCE CHURCH, BOSTON

Reproduced from drawing of Francis E. Getty by Foster Brothers
of Arlington and Boston. Used by permission

staff in New York. The growing accord which is evident among the churches in the mission fields cannot but strengthen the ties of union among the churches in America.

The first step in the direction of church federation was the formation, in London in 1846, of the Evangelical Alliance. This body was made up of fifty different evangelical bodies in Europe and America, and branches were soon established in nine European countries and in the United States. A prime mover in this organization was Dr. S. S. Schmucker of the Gettysburg Theological Seminary who has been called the Father of the Evangelical Alliance. The object of the alliance was to promote evangelical union, in order to increase the effectiveness of Christian work, to promote the cause of religious freedom, and to further the cause of Christ everywhere. From the foundation of the branch alliance in the United States (1867) to the end of the century it furthered many coöperative enterprises. By the end of the century, however, its influence was waning and in 1901 it gave way to a Federation of Churches and Christian Workers, which in turn was replaced in 1908 by the Federal Council of the Churches of Christ in America.

Theodore Roosevelt, in the year 1900, in addressing a meeting of representatives of the churches of New York at which the New York State Federation of Churches was formed, said, "There are plenty of targets that we need to hit without firing into each other." One of the great weaknesses of American Protestantism is its inability to speak with a united voice on matters of great moral and religious concern. The Federal Council of the

Churches of Christ in America is a step in the direction of uniting the member denominations that compose the council in such a way that they may be able to speak with one voice on matters of general moral, social and religious concern. The Federal Council proved its usefulness during the World War, and its work of mercy and relief since the war has more than justified its existence.

The problem of church unity in the United States has two distinct phases. One is the task of securing unity within each denomination; the second is that of bringing about unity between different communions. At first glance it might seem an easier task to achieve the former than the latter, but as a matter of fact neither is easy of accomplishment. The first obvious task, of course, is to bring about unity within each denominational family. It would seem that before there can be unity between Presbyterians and Methodists in the United States, the Methodists in the United States, the Methodist Episcopal Church and the Methodist Episcopal Church, South must be brought together; and just as certainly the first task to be accomplished by the Presbyterians is to heal the schism between the Presbyterian Church in the United States and the Presbyterian Church in the United States of America. The process by which the Canadian Presbyterians, Methodists and Congregationalists finally united to form the United Church of Canada (1925) would seem to be that which must be followed in the United States if equally happy results are to be achieved. All three bodies had previously secured internal unity, while theological and other differences had largely disappeared.

Real progress has been made in recent years in the direction of achieving denominational unity. The Presbyterian bodies in America have experienced many divisions and reunions. In 1858 the two branches of the Scottish dissenting churches, the Reformed and the Associate Reformed, united to form the present United Presbyterian Church. In 1905 the majority of the Cumberland Presbyterian Church and the Presbyterian Church in the U. S. A. effected organic union and in 1920 the Welsh Calvinistic Methodist Church was also received into the Presbyterian Church. The work of healing the schism between the two great bodies of Episcopal Methodism went forward hopefully, especially from 1916 to 1926. A joint commission was appointed and a plan for unification was proposed and approved by the General Conference of the Methodist Episcopal Church in 1924, but two years later it was rejected by the General Conference of the Methodist Episcopal Church, South. Perhaps the best example of progress toward denominational unity is that furnished by the formation of the United Lutheran Church accomplished in 1918. The occasion was that of the celebration of the quadricentennial of the Reformation in 1917. A joint committee representing the General Synod, the General Council and the United Synod of the South was appointed to coöperate in the preparations. Out of this committee came the proposal to unite the American Lutheran bodies as far as possible into the United Lutheran Church in America. With almost complete unanimity the three English Lutheran bodies adopted the proposal and in November,

1918, the first convention of the new United Lutheran Church met in the city of New York.

There have been many attempts to bring denominations together in the United States, but few have been successful. The Protestant Episcopal Church has actively championed the cause of church union since 1886. In that year a petition signed by a thousand clergymen and thirty-two bishops was presented to the General Convention of the Protestant Episcopal Church asking that a definite proposal be made for Christian reunion. This resulted in the issuing of what came to be known as the Quadrilateral, proposing a union of religious bodies on the basis of the Holy Scriptures, the Nicene Creed, the Two Sacraments and the Historic Episcopate. Since that time these proposals have been discussed at various conferences and conventions, but the insistence on the part of the Episcopalians that episcopacy is essential to the being of the church has proved, so far, a hindrance to union with non-episcopal bodies.

Since the Great War an exceptional number of movements looking in the direction of unification within denominational families and between communions have been inaugurated. The experience of coöperation during the World War; the growing evidence of the need of uniting Christian forces to meet the new problems arising in a rapidly changing world; the example of successful union presented by the United Church of Canada, are some of the factors which account for this encouraging activity. Three Lutheran bodies—the Ohio Synod, the Iowa Synod and the Buffalo Synod—have voted to unite; negotiations are under way looking toward the union of several Presbyterian bodies; the Universalists and Unitarians have adopted resolutions favoring union. A union which has been but recently consummated is that between the Congregational and Christian (New Light) churches. This unites two bodies which where similar in polity, on the basis of the acceptance of Christianity "as primarily a way of life, not upon uniformity of theological opinion or upon practice of ordinances." In February, 1929, commissioners from the Reformed Church in the United States, the Church of the United Brethren in Christ and the Evangelical Synod of America adopted a basis of union, which was submitted to the governing bodies of the three churches. These three churches are about equal in membership, have a common German background and are similar in doctrinal emphasis.

A proposal to unite the Methodist Episcopal Church and the Presbyterian Church in the U. S. A., was made at the Methodist General Conference in 1928. The proposal was heartily received by the Presbyterian General Assembly and referred to a standing committee on Church Coöperation and Union. Commissioners representing the two churches met in Pittsburgh in February, 1929, where sub-committees were appointed to consider the chief problems of unification. Such a union between large churches may not be immediately achieved, but meanwhile there is every indication among all the Protestant churches, great and small, that the day of contented separation is fully passed and there is undoubtedly a growing will to, as well as an enlarging expectation of, union.

✝✝✝✝✝✝✝✝✝✝✝✝✝✝✝✝✝✝✝✝✝✝✝✝ ✝✝✝✝✝✝✝✝✝✝✝✝

BIBLIOGRAPHY

GENERAL

BACON, L. W., *A History of American Christianity*. American Church History Series, Vol. XIII. New York, 1897.

DORCHESTER, DANIEL., *Christianity in the United States*. New York and Cincinnati, 1890.

MODE, P. G., *Sourcesbook and Bibliographical Guide for American Church History*. Menasha, Wis., 1920.

ROWE, HENRY K., *The History of Religion in the United States*. New York, 1924.

WEIGLE, LUTHER A., *American Idealism*. The Pageant of America Series, Vol. X. New Haven, 1928.

CHAPTER II

BAIRD, CHARLES W., *The Huguenot Emigration to America*. (2 vols). New York, 1895.

BRAITHWAITE, WILLIAM C., *The Beginnings of Quakerism*. London, 1912.

CHEYNEY, EDWARD P., *European Background of American History, 1300–1600*. The American Nation Series, Vol. I. New York, 1904.

EGGLESTON, EDWARD, *Beginnings of a Nation*. New York, 1896. Particularly good for the new sects arising in England.

FAUST, A. B., *The German Element in the United States* (2 vols). New York, 1928.

HALL, T. C., *The Religious Background of American Culture*. Boston, 1930.

{ 524 }

HANNA, CHARLES A., *The Scotch-Irish or the Scot in North Britain, North Ireland and North America* (2 vols). New York, 1902.

LECKY, W. E. H., *England in the Eighteenth Century* (2 vols). 1878-1890.

LINDSAY, THOMAS M., *A History of the Reformation* (2 vols). New York, 1910.

WALPOLE, C. G., *The Kingdom of Ireland*. London, 1885.

WEISS, CHARLES, *History of the French Protestant Refugees*. London, 1854.

CHAPTER III

ANDERSON, JAMES S. M., *History of the Church of England in the Colonies and Foreign Dependencies of the British Empire* (3 vols). London, 1845.

GOODWIN, EDWARD L., *The Colonial Church in Virginia*. Milwaukee, 1927.

HAWKS, FRANCIS L., *Contributions to the Ecclesiastical History of the United States of America: Rise and Progress of the Protestant Episcopal Church in Virginia*. New York, 1836.

JERNEGAN, M. W., *The American Colonies, 1492–1750*. Epochs of American History. New York, 1929.

McCONNELL, S. D., *History of the American Episcopal Church* (10th ed). Milwaukee and London, 1916.

PERRY, WILLIAM S., *The History of the American Episcopal Church, 1587–1883* (2 vols). Vol I—*The Planting and Growth of the American Colonial Church*. Boston, 1885.

——*Historical Collections relating to the American Colonial Church*. Vol I—*Virginia*; Vol II—*Pennsylvania*; Vol III—*Massachusetts*; Vol IV—*Maryland and Delaware*. 1870-1878.

TIFFANY, CHARLES C., *A History of the Protestant Episcopal*

Church in the United States of America. American Church History Series, Vol. VII. New York, 1895.

WERTENBAKER, THOMAS J., *The First Americans, 1607–1690. A History of American Life*, Vol II. New York, 1927.

WILBERFORCE, SAMUEL, *A History of the Protestant Episcopal Church in America*. London, 1844.

CHAPTER IV

ADAMS, J. T., *The Founding of New England*. Boston, 1921.

DEXTER, H. M., *The Congregationalism of the Last Three Hundred Years*. New York, 1880.

MATHER, COTTON, *Magnalia Christi Americana: or the Ecclesiastical History of New England* (2 vol). Hartford, 1820.

MORISON, S. E., *Builders of the Bay Colony*, Boston, 1930.

MURDOCK, K. B., *Increase Mather*. Cambridge, 1925.

PARRINGTON, V. L., *The Colonial Mind, 1620–1800*. Vol. I of his *Main Currents in American Thought*. New York, 1927.

PRATT, W. S., *The Music of the Pilgrims*. Boston, 1921.

SEWALL, SAMUEL, Diary, Mark Van Doren, editor (abridged). 1927. Complete Diary published as Vols. V-VIII, Series 5, Massachusetts Historical Society. Collection 1878-1882.

WALKER, WILLISTAN, *History of the Congregational Churches in the United States*. American Church History. Series, Vol. III. New York, 1894.

WERTENBAKER, T. J., *The First Americans, 1607–1690. A History of American Life*, Vol. II. New York, 1927.

WINTHROP, JOHN, *History of New England* (2 vols). J. K. Hosmer, editor. New York, 1908.

CHAPTER V

AUGUR, HELEN, *An American Jezebel: The Life of Anne Hutchinson*. New York, 1930.

BACKUS, ISAAC, *A History of New England with Particular*

Reference to the Denomination of Christians called Baptists (2 vols.). (2nd ed.) Newton, Mass., 1871.

GREENE, E. B., *The Foundations of American Nationality.* New York, 1922.

NEWMAN, A. H., *A History of the Baptist Churches in the United States*, American Church History Series, Vol. II. New York, 1898.

O'GORMAN, THOMAS, *A History of the Roman Catholic Church in the United States,* American Church History Series, Vol. IX. New York, 1895.

STRAUS, OSCAR S., *Roger Wlliams the Pioneer of Religious Liberty.* New York, 1894.

VEDDER, HENRY C., *A Short History of the Baptists.* Philadelphia, 1907.

WILLIAMS, ROGER, *The Bloudy Tenent of Persecution*, etc. London, 1848.

CHAPTER VI

BOWDEN, *History of Friends in America.* London, Vol. I, 1850; Vol. II, 1854.

CHALKLEY, THOMAS, *Journal.* London, 1851.

COLENBRANDER, H. T., *The Dutch Element in American History.* American Historical Association Reports, 1909, pp. 193-201.

CORWIN, E. T., *A History of the Reformed Dutch Church.* American Church History. Series, Vol. VIII. New York, 1895.

——*Manual of the Reformed Protestant Dutch Church* (3rd ed.). 1879.

FOX, GEORGE, *The Journal of* (2 vols). Philadelphia, 1911.

JAMESON, J. F., *Narratives of New Netherland*, In *Original Narratives of Early American History.* New York, 1909.

Jones, Rufus M., *The Faith and Practice of the Quakers*. London, and New York, n.d.

——*The Quakers in the American Colonies*. London, 1911.

Putnam, Ruth, *The Dutch Element in the United States*. American Historical Association Reports, 1909, pp. 205-218.

Thomas, R. M., *A History of the Society of Friends*, American Church History Series, Vol. XII. New York, 1894.

Van Pelt, Daniel, *Pictures of Early Dutch Life in New York City*. 1893.

Chapter VII

Bente, F., *American Lutheranism* (2 vols). St. Louis, 1919.

Brumbaugh, Martin G., *A History of the German Baptist Brethren in Europe and America*. Elgin, Ill., 1899.

De Schweinitz, Edmund, *The History of the Church of the Unitas Fratrum*. Bethlehem, Pa., 1885.

Dubbs, J. H., *A History of the Reformed Church*, German (American Church History Series, Vol. VIII). New York, 1895.

Faust, A. B., *The German Element in the United States* (2 vols). New York, 1927.

Finck, W. J., *Lutheran Landmarks and Pioneers in America*. Philadelphia, 1913.

Hamilton, J. T., *A History of the Church Known as the Moravian Church or the Unitas Fratrum*. Bethlehem, Pa., 1900.

Harbaugh, Henry, and Heisler, D. Y., *The Fathers of the German Reformed Church in Europe and America* (5 vols). Lancaster and Reading, 1857 ff.

Jacobs, H. E., *Lutherans*. American Church History Series, Vol. IV. New York, 1893.

NEVE, J. L., *A Brief History of the Lutheran Church in America*. Burlington, Iowa, 1916.

REICHEL, WILLIAM C., editor *Memorials of the Moravian Church*. Philadelphia, 1870.

SACHSE, JULIUS E., *The German Sectarians of Pennsylvania, 1708-1742*. Philadelphia, 1899.

SMITH, C. HENRY, *The Mennonites*. Berne, Ind., 1920.

WENTZ, A. R., *The Lutheran Church in American History*. Philadelphia, 1923.

WINGER, OTTO, *History and Doctrine of the Church of the Brethren*. Elgin, Ill., 1920.

CHAPTER VIII

BLAIKIE, ALEXANDER, *A History of Presbyterianism in New England*. Boston, 1881.

BRIGGS, C. A., *American Presbyterianism its Origin and Early History*. New York, 1885.

GILLETT, E. H., *History of the Presbyterian Church in the United States of America*. Vol. I. Philadelphia, 1864.

HANNA, CHARLES A., *The Scotch-Irish or the Scot in North Britain, North Ireland and North America* (2 vols). New York, 1902.

HODGE, CHARLES, *The Constitutional History of the Presbyterian Church in the United States of America*. Part I 1705 to 1741. Philadelphia, 1839.

Records of the Presbyterian Church in the United States of America, etc. Philadelphia, 1904.

THOMPSON, R. E., *A History of the Presbyterian Churches in the United States*. American Church History Series, Vol. VI. New York, 1895.

WEBSTER, RICHARD, *A History of the Presbyterian Church in America from its Origin until the year 1760*. Philadelphia, 1857.

Chapter IX

Allen, A. V. G., *Jonathan Edwards*. Boston, 1890.

Davenport, F. M., *Primitive Traits in Religious Revivals*. New York, 1905.

Edwards, Jonathan, *Thoughts on the Revivial of Religion in New England, to which is prefixed A Narrative of the Surprising Work of God in Northampton, Mass.,* 1735. New York, n.d.

Lunn, Arnold, *John Wesley*. New York, 1929.

Tracy, Joseph, *A History of the Revival of Religion in the time of Edwards and Whitefield*. Boston, 1842.

Tyerman, Luke, *The Life of the Rev. George Whitefield* (2 vols). New York, 1877.

Walker, Williston, *Congregationalists*, American Church History Series, Vol. III, Especially Chapter VIII. New York, 1894.

——*Ten New England Leaders*. Chapters VI, VII, VIII. Chicago, 1901.

Chapter X

Foote, W. H., *Sketches of Virginia*. Philadelphia, 1850.

Gewehr, W. M., *The Great Awakening in Virginia*. Durham, N. C., 1930.

Hodge, Charles, *The Constitutional History of the Presbyterian Church*, (2 vols). Philadelphia, 1851.

Jarratt, Devereux, *Life of Devereux Jarratt*. Baltimore, 1806.

Lee, Jesse, *A Short History of the Methodists in the United States of America*. Baltimore, 1810.

Maclean, John, *History of the College of New Jersey* (2 vols). Philadelphia, 1877.

Maxson, Charles H., *The Great Awakening in the Middle Colonies*. Chicago, 1920.

MURPHY, T., *The Presbytery of the Log College*. Philadelphia, 1889.

SEMPLE, R. B., *A History of the Rise and Progress of the Baptists in Virginia*. Beale, G. W., editor. Richmond, 1810; Philadelphia, 1894.

TRACY, JOSEPH, *The Great Awakening: A History of the Revival of Religion in the Time of Edwards and Whitefield*. Boston, 1842.

CHAPTER XI

BROWN, WILLIAM, *The History of Missions; or of the Propagation of Christianity among the Heathen, since the Reformation* (2 Vols). Philadelphia, 1820.

DESCHWEINITZ, EDMUND, *The Life and Times of David Zeisberger, the Western Pioneer and Apostle of the Indians*. Philadelphia, 1870.

EDWARDS, JONATHAN, *Life of David Brainerd*. 1749.

HARBAUGH, H., *The Life of Reverend Michael Schlatter*. Philadelphia, 1857.

JERNEGAN, MARCUS M., *Slavery and Conversion in the American Colonies*. American Historical Review, Vol. XXI, No. 3, pp. 504-527.

KEITH, GEORGE, *A Journal of Travels from New Hampshire to Caratuck, on the Continent of North America*. Collections of the Protestant Episcopal Historical Society, 1851. New York, 1851.

LOSKIEL, GEORGE HENRY, *History of the Mission of the United Brethren among the Indians in North America*. Translated from the German by Christian I. Latrobe, London, 1794.

LOVE, W. D., *Samson Occom and the Christian Indians of New England*. Boston, 1899.

Massachusetts Historical Collections. Vols. I-III.

MATHER, COTTON, *Magnalia Christi Americana: or the*

Ecclesiastical History of New England (2 vols). Hartford, 1820.

Mayhew, Experience, *Indian Converts.* 1727.

North, Eric M., *Early Methodist Philanthropy.* New York, 1914.

Pascoe, C. F., *Two Hundred Years of the S. P. G. An Historical Account of the Society for the Propagation of the Gospel in Foreign Parts 1701–1900.* Based on a Digest of the Society's Records. London, 1901.

Smith, Baxter, P., *The History of Dartmouth College.* Boston, 1878.

Shepard, Thomas, *The Clear Sunshine of the Gospel Breaking Forth upon the Indians of New England.* Reprinted, New York, 1865.

Tyerman, Luke, *The Life of the Reverend George Whitefield.* (2 vols.). London, 1876.

Wieship, George P., editor, *The New England Company of 1649 and John Eliot.* Boston, 1920.

Woodson, C. G., *The Education of the Negro prior to 1861.* New York, 1915.

Chapter XII

Baldwin, Alice M., *The New England Clergy and the American Revolution.* Durham, N. C., 1928.

Briggs, Charles A., *American Presbyterianism, its Origin and Early History.* Especially Chapter IX. New York, 1885.

Cross, Arthur Lyon, *The Anglican Episcopate and the American Colonies.* New York, 1902.

Humphrey, Edward Frank, *Nationalism and Religion in America, 1774–1789.* Boston, 1924.

Jameson, J. Franklin, *The American Revolution Considered as a Social Movement.* Especially Chapter IV. Princeton, 1926.

Jones, Rufus M., *The Quakers in the American Colonies.*

Especially Chapter IX, "Friends in the American Revolution." London, 1911.

SWEET, W. W., "John Wesley, Tory." *Methodist Quarterly Review*, 1922, pp. 255-268.

THORNTON, JOHN W., *The Pulpit of the American Revolution*. Boston, 1860.

VAN TYNE, CLAUDE H., *The Causes of the War of Independence*. Especially Chapter XIII. Boston, 1922.

WEIGLE, LUTHER A., American Idealism. Vol. X—*The Pageant of America*, especially Chapter V. New Haven, 1928.

CHAPTER XIII

BACKUS, ISAAC, *An Appeal to the Public for Religious Liberty, against the Oppressors of the Present Day*, etc. Boston, 1773.

COBB, SANDFORD H., *Rise of Religious Liberty in America*. New York, 1902.

FORTENBAUGH, ROBERT, *The Development of the Synodical Polity of the Lutheran Church in America, to 1829*, Philadelphia, 1926.

GREENE, M. L., *The Development of Religious Liberty in Connecticut*. Cambridge, 1905.

HODGE, CHARLES, *The Constitutional History of the Presbyterian Church in the United States of America* (2 parts). Philadelphia, 1840.

HUMPHREY, E. F., *Nationalism and Religion in America*. Boston, 1924.

MCILWAINE, H. R., *Struggle of the Protestant Dissenters for Religious Toleration in Virginia*. Johns Hopkins University Studies in History and Political Science, 10th Series, No. 4, Baltimore, 1894.

Minutes of the Warren Association.

O'GORMAN, THOMAS, *A History of the Roman Catholic*

Church in the United States. American Church History Series, Vol. IX. New York, 1895.

STEVENS, ABEL, *History of the Methodist Episcopal Church.* New York, 1864.

TIFFANY, CHARLES C., *A History of the Protestant Episcopal Church in the United States of America.* American Church History Series, Vol. VII. New York, 1895.

CHAPTER XIV

BENEDICT, DAVID, *A General History of the Baptist Denomination in America and other Parts of the World* (2 vols). Boston, 1813.

BISHOP, ROBERT H., *An Outline of the History of the Church in the States of Kentucky during a period of forty years: containing the Memoirs of Rev. David Rice.* Lexington, 1824.

BRUNSON, ALFRED, *A Western Pioneer* (2 vols). Cincinnati, 1872.

CARTWRIGHT, PETER, *Autobiography.* New York, 1856.

DAVIDSON, ROBERT, *History of the Presbyterian Church in the State of Kentucky.* New York, 1847.

DUNNING, ALBERT E., *Congregationalists in America.* Chapter XXI, "Congregationalism in the Northwest." New York, 1894.

FINLEY, J. B., *Sketches of Western Methodism.* Cincinnati, 1854.

GUILDAY, PETER, *Life and Times of John Carroll.* New York, 1922.

McMASTER, J. B., *History of the People of the United States.* Vols. I-IV. New York, 1903.

MATHEWS, LOIS KIMBALL, *The Expansion of New England.* Boston, 1909.

PAXSON, F. L., *History of the American Frontier, 1763–1893.* Boston, 1924.

RUSK, RALPH L., *The Literature of the Middle-Western Frontier* (2 vols). New York, 1925.

SHEA, G. S., *History of the Catholic Church in the United States*. Vol. II, 1763–1815.

SMITH, JOSEPH, *Old Redstone, or Historical Sketches of Western Presbyterianism*. Philadelphia, 1854.

SPENCER, J. H., *A History of Kentucky Baptists* (2 vols). Cincinnati, 1885.

SWEET, W. W., *Religion on the American Frontier*. Vol. I, *The Baptists*. New York, 1931.

—— *The Rise of Methodism in the West*. New York, 1920.

TAYLOR, JOHN, *The History of Ten Churches*. Frankfort, Ky., 1823.

WALKER, WILLISTON, *Congregationalists*. American Church History Series, Vol. III, Chapter IX.

WEBB, BENJ. J., *The Centenary of Catholicity in Kentucky*. Louisville, 1884.

CHAPTER XV

CLEVELAND, C. C., *The Great Revival in the West, 1797–1805*. Chicago, 1916.

DAVIDSON, ROBERT, *History of the Presbyterian Church in the State of Kentucky*. Chapters V–IX. New York, 1847.

DRURY, A. W., *History of the Church of the United Brethren in Christ*. Dayton, Ohio, 1924.

GATES, ERRETT, *The Disciples of Christ*. New York, 1905.

McDONNOLD, BENJAMIN W., *History of the Cumberland Presbyterian Church*. Nashville, 1893.

RICHARDSON, ROBERT, *Memoirs of Alexander Campbell* (2 vols). 1868.

ROGERS, JOHN, *The Biography of Elder Barton Warren Stone*, etc. Cincinnati, 1847.

SPEER, WILLIAM, *The Great Revival of 1800*. 1872.

CHAPTER XVI

ANDERSON, RUFUS, *History of the Missions of the American Board of Commissioners for Foreign Missions in India.* Boston, 1874.

BABCOCK, R., *Memoir of John Mason Peck.* Philadelphia, 1864.

BROWN, A. A., *History of Religious Education in Recent Times.* New York, 1923.

CARROLL, B. H., *Genesis of American Anti-Missionism.* Louisville, 1902.

COX, F. A., *History of the Baptist Missionary Society, 1792–1842* (2 vols). London, 1842.

ELSBREE, O. W., *The Rise of the Missionary Spirit in America, 1790–1815.* Williamsport, Pa., 1928.

GREEN, ASHBEL, *Presbyterian Missions.* Reprinted, New York, 1893.

McCOY, ISAAC, *History of Baptist Indian Missions.* Washington, 1840.

Memorial Volume of the First Fifty Years of the American Board of Commissioners for Foreign Missions. Boston, 1862.

MILLS, SAMUEL J., and SMITH, DANIEL, *Report of a Missionary Tour through that part of the United States which lies west of the Alleghany Mountains performed under the direction of the Massachusetts Missionary Society.* Andover, 1815.

MORSE, JEDEDIAH, *First Annual Report of the American Society for Promoting the Civilization and General Improvement of the Indian Tribes in the United States.* New Haven, 1824.

REID, J. M., *Missions and Missionary Society of the Methodist Episcopal Church* (2 vols). New York, 1879.

SCHERMERHORN, JOHN F., *Report respecting the Indians, inhabiting the western parts of the United States.* Massachusetts Historical Society Collections, Series 2, Vol. II. Boston, 1814.

STRICKLAND, W. P., *History of the American Bible Society from its Organization to the Present Time.* New York, 1849.

SWEET, W. W., *Circuit Rider Days Along the Ohio.* Chapter IV, "The Wyandot Mission." New York, 1923.

——— *Religion on the American Frontier.* Vol. I—*The Baptists,* Chapter IV. New York, 1931.

CHAPTER XVII

FERM, VERGILIUS, *The Crisis in American Lutheran Theology.* New York, 1927.

FISH, CARL R., *The Rise of the Common Man.* Vol. VI— *A History of American Life.* Chapters VII, IX, XII. New York, 1927.

GADDIS, M. E., *Christian Perfectionism in America.* Especially Chapter IX, "Experimentalism and Experimentation: Oberlin and Oneida." MS, Ph.D. Thesis, The University of Chicago, 1929.

GILLETT, E. H., *History of the Presbyterian Church in the United States of America.* Vol. II. Chapters XXXVI, XXXVII, XXXVIII. Philadelphia, 1864.

HARKNESS, R. E. E., *Social Origins of the Millerite Movement.* MS, Ph.D. Thesis, The University of Chicago, 1927.

KAUFFMAN, RUTH, and R. W., *The Latter Day Saints.* London, 1912.

LINN, W. A., *The Story of the Mormons.* New York, 1902.

LOCKWOOD, GEORGE B., *The New Harmony Movement.* New York, 1905.

LOUD, GROVER C., *Evangelized America.* Chapters XI-XIV. New York, 1928.

McCONNELL, S. D., *History of the American Episcopal Church* (10th ed). Chapters VII-X. Milwaukee, 1906.

NIEBUHR, H. R., *The Social Sources of Denominationalism.* Chapters VI and VII. New York, 1929.

NOYES, G. W., *Religious Experience of John Humphrey Noyes.* New York, 1923.

SELDES, GILBERT, *The Stammering Century.* New York, 1928.

SHEA, JOHN G., *History of the Catholic Church in the United States.* Vols. III, IV. New York, 1890.

WEIGLE, LUTHER A., *American Idealism.* Vol. X—*The Pageant of America.* Especially pp. 170-186. New Haven, 1928.

WENTZ, A. R., *The Lutheran Church in American History.* Chapters XIII-XVII. Philadelphia, 1923.

YEAKEL, REUBEN, *History of the Evangelical Association* (2 vols). Cleveland, 1909.

CHAPTER XVIII

BARBER, VERLE L., *The Slavery Controversy and the Presbyterians.* MS, Master's Thesis, The University of Chicago, 1928.

BASHFORD, JAMES W., *The Oregon Missions.* New York, 1918.

BIRNEY, JAMES G., *The American Churches the Bulwarks of American Slavery* (2d ed). Newburyport, 1842.

DE SMET, P. J., *Western Missions and Missionaries.* New York, 1863.

DODD, WILLIAM E., *The Cotton Kingdom.* Chronicles of America Series, Vol. 27. New Haven, 1921.

HART, ALBERT BUSHNELL, *Slavery and Abolition 1831–1841. The American Nation: A History,* Vol. 16. New York, 1906.

McNEILLY, J. H., *Religion and Slavery, A Vindication of the Southern Churches.* Nashville, 1911.

NORWOOD, J. N., *The Schism in the Methodist Episcopal Church, 1844.* Alfred Press, Alfred, N. Y., 1923.

PHILLIPS, U. B., *American Negro Slavery*. New York, 1927.

PILLSBURY, PARKER, *The Forlorn Hope of Slavery*. Boston, 1847.

PUTNAM, MARY B., *The Baptists and Slavery, 1840–1845*. MS, Master's Thesis, The University of Chicago, 1910.

STRINGFELLOW, THORNTON, *Scriptural and Statistical Views in favor of Slavery*. (4th ed). 1856. Pro-slavery views presented by a Southerner.

SWANEY, CHARLES B., *Episcopal Methodism and Slavery*. Boston, 1926.

THOMAS, A. C., *The Attitude of the Society of Friends toward Slavery in the 17th and 18th Centuries*. Papers of the American Society of Church History, Vol. VIII.

CHAPTER XIX

ALEXANDER, GROSS, *A History of the Methodist Episcopal Church, South*. American Church History Series, Vol. II. New York, 1894.

CHESHIRE, JOSEPH B., *The Church in the Confederate States; A History of the Protestant Episcopal Church in the Confederate States*. New York, 1912.

FITE, EMERSON D., *Social and Industrial Conditions in the North during the Civil War*. New York, 1910.

JOHNSON, T. C., *A History of the Presbyterian Church in the United States*. American Church History Series, Vol. 11. New York, 1894.

JONES, J. WM., *Christ in the Camp*. Richmond, 1887.

MCPHERSON, EDWARD, *The Political History of the United States of America during the Great Rebellion*. Especially a Chapter in the Appendix, "The Church and the Rebellion," pp. 461-554. Washington, D. C., 1882.

NICOLAY, J. G., and HAY, JOHN, *Abraham Lincoln: A History*. (10 vols). Vol. VI contains a chapter on Lincoln and the Churches. New York, 1890.

STANTON, R. L., *The Church and the Rebellion*. New York, 1864.

SWEET, W. W., *The Methodist Episcopal Church and the Civil War*. Cincinnati, 1912.

CHAPTER XX

ABEL, ANNIE H., *The History of Events Resulting in Indian Consolidation West of the Mississippi River* (Annual Report Am. Hist. Ass'n, 1906). Washington, 1908.

BRADFORD, GAMALIEL, *D. L. Moody, a Worker in Souls*. New York, 1928.

CHENEY, MARY BUSHNELL, *Life and Letters of Horace Bushnell*. 1880, 1903.

Department of the Interior Bulletins; Office of Indian Affairs, *Indian Missions of the United States* Bulletin 8, 1928; *Education of the Indians,* Bulletin 9, 1927.

DOUGLASS, H. PAUL, *Christian Reconstruction in the South*. Boston, 1909.

DUBOIS, W. E. B., editor *The Negro Church*. Atlanta University Studies, Atlanta, 1903.

EDWARDS, MARTHA L., *A Problem of Church and State in the 1870's*. Mississippi Valley Historical Review, Vol. II, pp. 37-53.

GATES, ERRETT, *The Disciples of Christ. Story of the Churches*. Chapters XII, XIII, XIV. New York, 1905.

LANAHAN, JOHN, *The Era of Frauds in the Methodist Book Concern at New York*. Baltimore, 1896.

LUCCOCK, H. E., and HUTCHINSON, PAUL, *The Story of Methodism*. Especially Chapter XXIV. New York, 1926.

McCONNELL, S. D., *History of the American Episcopal Church* (10th ed). Milwaukee, 1916.

MOODY, W. R., *D. L. Moody*. New York, 1930.

NIEBUHR, H. RICHARD, *The Social Sources of Denominationalism*. Especially Chapters VIII and IX. New York, 1929.

Nevens, Allan, *The Emergence of Modern America, 1865–1878. History of American Life,* Vol. VIII. Especially Chapters VII and XII. New York, 1927.

Phillips, C. H., *History of the Colored Methodist Episcopal Church.* Jackson, Tenn., 1925.

Platt, Ward, *The Frontier.* Missionary Education, New York, 1911.

Sweet, W. H., *History of Methodism in Northwest Kansas.* Kansas Wesleyan University, Salina, Kan., 1920.

Sweet, W. W., "Negro Churches in the South: A Phase of Reconstruction." *Methodist Review,* May-June, 1921, pp. 405-418.

Thompson, Charles L., *The Presbyterians. The Story of the Churches,* Chapters XI, XII. New York, 1903.

Wentz, A. R., *The Lutheran Church in American History.* Part V, Chapters XVIII to XXIII. Philadelphia, 1923.

Woodson, C. G., *The History of the Negro Church.* Washington, 1921.

Chapter XXI

Beard, Charles A., and Mary R., *The Rise of American Civilization* (2 vols). Vol. II. Chapter XXV. New York, 1930.

Brown, William A., *The Church in America.* New York, 1922.

Cole, Stewart Grant, *The Psychology of the Fundamentalist Movement.* MS, Ph.D. Thesis, The University of Chicago, 1929.

Dakin, Edwin F., *Mrs. Eddy: The Biography of a Virginal Mind.* New York, 1929.

Faulkner, Harold U., *American Economic History.* New York, 1924.

Gaddis, Merrill E., *Christian Perfectionism in America.* MS, Ph.D. Thesis, The University of Chicago, 1929.

Garrison, W. E., *Catholicism and the American Mind*. Chicago, 1928.

Gulick, Sidney L., *The Christian Crusade for a Warless World*. New York, 1923.

Johnson, Roy H., *Western Baptists in the Age of Big Business*. MS, Ph.D. Thesis, The University of Chicago, 1929.

Lynd, Robert S., and Helen Merell, *Middletown*. New York, 1930.

Mecklin, J. M., *The Ku Klux Klan*. New York, 1924.

Mathews, Shailer, *The Church and the Changing Order*. New York, 1909.

———*The Faith of Modernism*. New York, 1925.

McNeill, J. T., *Unitive Protestantism*. New York, 1930.

Milmine, Georgine, *The Life of Mary Baker G. Eddy and the History of Christian Science*. New York, 1909.

Moehlman, C. H., *The Catholic-Protestant Mind*. New York, 1930.

Rowe, H. K., *The History of Religion in the United States*. New York, 1924.

Sanford, E. B., *Origin and History of the Federal Council of the Churches of Christ in America*. Hartford, Conn., 1916.

Slosser, G. J., *Christian Unity: Its History and Challenge*. London, 1929.

Smith, G. B., *Religious Thought in the Last Quarter Century*. Chicago, 1927.

Sperry, W. L., *Signs of the Times*. Especially Chapter V. New York, 1929.

Weigle, Luther A., *American Idealism. Pageant of America*, Vol. X, Chapter VII. New Haven, 1928.

APPENDIX

Census of Religious Bodies for 1926 Gathered by the Department of Commerce, Washington, D. C.

In September 1928 the Department of Commerce released the following statistics of Religious Bodies in the United States, which constitute the findings of the Federal Census of Religious Bodies for 1926. There has always been much confusion and uncertainty in religious statistics due to the fact that the term "member" has a variety of uses and also because many of the churches have peculiar statistical methods. There is need of a clearing-house through which the several denominations might check up on their own procedure, and through which also some definite understanding might be reached as to the method of reporting membership and financial data. In the present census each church was requested to report its membership according to the definition of "member" in that organization. Thus in some religious bodies the term member is limited to actual communicants; in others, as in the Roman Catholic Church, it includes all baptized persons; while in still others it covers all enrolled persons.

In the ten years from 1916 to 1926 the number of denominations increased from 200 to 213, while the total church membership grew from 41,926,854 to 54,624,976. Total expenditures in 1926 was $814,371,529 as against $328,809,999 in 1916.

SUMMARY OF MORE IMPORTANT STATISTICS, BY DENOMINATIONS:
1926

Denomination	Churches		Membership	
	1926	1916	1926	1916
All denominations................	231,983	226,718	54,624,976	41,926,854
Adventist Bodies:				
Advent Christian Church........	444	534	29,430	30,597
Seventh-day Adventist Denomination.....................	1,981	2,011	110,998	79,355
Church of God (Adventist)......	58	22	1,686	848
Life and Advent Union..........	7	13	535	658
Churches of God in Christ Jesus (Adventist)...................	86	87	3,528	3,457
African Orthodox Church.........	13	—	1,568	—
African Orthodox Church of New York.........................	3	—	717	—
American Ethical Union..........	6	5	3,801	2,850
American Rescue Workers.........	97	29	1,989	611
Apostolic Over-Coming Holy Church of God..............	16	—	1,047	—
Assemblies of God, General Council	671	118	47,950	6,703
Assyrian Jacobite Apostolic Church	3	15	1,407	748
Baha'is.........................	44	57	1,247	2,884
Baptist Bodies:				
Northern Baptist Convention....	7,611	18,319	1,289,966	11,244,705
Southern Baptist Convention	23,374	23,580	3,524,378	2,708,879
Negro Baptists.................	22,081	21,071	3,196,623	2,938,579
General Six Principle Baptists ...	6	10	293	456
Seventh Day Baptists..........	67	68	7,264	7,980
Free Will Baptists.............	1,024	750	79,592	54,833
United American Free Will Baptist Church (Colored)........	166	169	13,396	13,362
Free Will Baptists (Bullockites)..	2	12	36	184
General Baptists...............	465	517	31,501	33,466
Separate Baptists..............	65	46	4,803	4,254
Regular Baptists...............	349	401	23,091	21,521
United Baptists................	221	254	18,903	22,097
Duck River and Kindred Associations of Baptists (Baptist Church of Christ)...........	98	105	7,340	6,872

SUMMARY OF MORE IMPORTANT STATISTICS, BY DENOMINATIONS: 1926 *(Continued)*

Denomination	Churches		Membership	
	1926	1916	1926	1916
Baptist Bodies—*Continued*				
Primitive Baptists.............	2,267	2,142	81,374	80,311
Colored Primitive Baptists	925	336	43,978	15,144
Two-Seed-in-the-Spirit Predesti-narian Baptists..............	27	48	304	679
Independent Baptist Church of America....................	13	—	222	—
American Baptist Association....	1,431	—	117,858	—
Brethren, German Baptists (Dunkers):				
Church of the Brethren (Conservative Dunkers).......	1,030	997	128,392	105,102
Old German Baptist Brethren....	62	67	3,036	3,399
The Brethren Church (Progressive Dunkers)........	174	201	26,026	24,060
Seventh Day Baptists (German, 1728)......................	4	5	144	136
Church of God, New Dunkers ...	9	13	650	929
Brethren, Plymouth:				
Plymouth Brethren I............	166	161	4,877	3,896
Plymouth Brethren II...........	307	129	13,497	5,928
Plymouth Brethren III..........	24	17	684	476
Plymouth Brethren IV..........	47	72	1,663	1,389
Plymouth Brethren V...........	83	80	2,152	1,820
Plymouth Brethren VI..........	6	10	88	208
Brethren, River:				
Brethren in Christ.............	81	72	4,320	3,805
Old Order or Yorker Brethren ...	10	9	472	432
United Zion's Children.........	28	31	905	1,152
Catholic Apostolic Church........	11	13	3,408	2,768
Christadelphians.................	134	145	3,352	2,922
Christian and Missionary Alliance..	332	163	22,737	9,625
Christian Church (General Convention of the Christian Church)..	1,044	1,263	112,795	118,737
Christian Science Parent Church ...	29	—	582	—
Christian Union.................	137	220	8,791	13,692

SUMMARY OF MORE IMPORTANT STATISTICS, BY DENOMINATIONS:
1926 *(Continued)*

Denomination	Churches		Membership	
	1926	1916	1926	1916
Church of Armenia in America.....	29	34	28,181	27,450
Church of Christ, Holiness........	82	—	4,919	—
Church of Christ, Scientist........	1,913	—	202,098	—
Church of God...................	644	202	23,247	7,784
Church of God (Headquarters, Anderson, Indiana)..............	932	—	38,249	—
Church of God and Saints of Christ	112	92	6,741	3,311
Church of God in Christ (Colored)	733	—	30,263	—
Church of the Nazarene..........	1,444	866	63,558	32,259
Church of Christ................	6,226	5,570	433,714	317,937
Churches of God, Holiness........	29	—	2,278	—
Churches of God in North America (General Eldership).........	428	440	31,596	28,376
Churches of the Living God:				
Church of the Living God, "The Pillar and Ground of Truth"..	81	38	5,844	2,009
Church of the Living God, Christian Workers for Fellowship...	149	154	11,558	9,626
Churches of the New Jerusalem:				
General Convention of the New Jerusalem in the United States of America....................	85	108	5,442	6,352
General Church of the New Jerusalem......................	13	15	996	733
Communistic Societies:				
Amana Society.................	7	7	1,385	1,534
United Society of Believers (Shakers).......................	6	12	192	367
Congregational Churches..........	5,028	[2]5,900	881,696	[2]809,236
Congregational Holiness Church...	25	—	939	—
Disciples of Christ..............	7,648	8,396	1,377,595	1,226,028
Divine Science Church............	22	—	3,466	—
Eastern Orthodox Churches:				
Albanian Orthodox Church......	9	2	1,993	410
Bulgarian Orthodox Church.....	4	4	937	1,992

SUMMARY OF MORE IMPORTANT STATISTICS, BY DENOMINATIONS:
1926 (*Continued*)

Denomination	Churches		Membership	
	1926	1916	1926	1916
Greek Orthodox Church (Hellenic)................	153	87	119,495	119,871
Roumanian Orthodox Church....	34	2	18,853	1,994
Russian Orthodox Church.......	199	169	95,134	99,681
Serbian Orthodox Church.......	17	12	13,775	14,301
Syrian Orthodox Church........	30	25	9,207	11,591
Evangelical Church..............	2,054	} 2,592	206,080	} 210,530
Evangelical Congregational Church	153		20,449	
Evangelical Synod of North America	1,287	1,331	314,518	339,853
Evangelistic Associations:				
Apostolic Christian Church......	53	54	5,709	4,766
Apostolic Faith Mission........	14	24	2,119	2,196
Christian Congregation.........	2	7	150	645
Church of Daniel's Band........	4	6	129	393
Church of God as Organized by Christ......................	19	17	375	227
Hephzibah Faith Missionary Association....................	14	12	495	352
Metropolitan Church Association	40	7	1,113	704
Missionary Church Association..	34	25	2,498	1,554
Missionary Bands of the World ..	11	10	241	218
Pillar of Fire..................	48	21	2,442	1,129
Church of God (Apostolic)......	18	—	492	—
Federated Churches..............	361	—	59,977	—
Free Christian Zion Church of Christ	5	35	187	6,225
Free Church of God in Christ......	19	—	874	
Friends:				
Society of Friends (Orthodox)...	715	805	91,326	92,379
Religious Society of Friends (Hicksite)...................	128	166	16,105	17,170
Orthodox Conservative Friends (Wilburite)..................	41	50	2,966	3,373
Friends (Primitive).............	1	2	25	60
Holiness Church..................	32	33	861	926
Independent Churches.............	257	1,615	34,501	56,757

SUMMARY OF MORE IMPORTANT STATISTICS, BY DENOMINATIONS:
1926 (*Continued*)

Denomination	Churches		Membership	
	1926	1916	1926	1916
Jewish Congregations............	2,953	1,615	4,087,357	²357,135
Latter Day Saints:				
Church of Jesus Christ of Latter Day Saints..................	1,275	965	542,194	403,388
Reorganized Church of Jesus Christ of Latter Day Saints....	592	565	64,367	58,941
Liberal Catholic Church..........	39	—	1,799	—
Liberal Churches................	3	—	358	—
Lithuanian National Catholic.....	⁴1	7	⁴492	7,343
Lutheran Bodies:				
United Lutheran Church in America	3,650	3,559	1,214,340	763,596
Evangelical Lutheran Augustana Synod of North America......	1,180	1,165	311,425	204,417
Evangelical Lutheran Synod of Missouri, Ohio and Other States....................	3,917	—	1,040,275	—
Evangelical Lutheran Joint Synod of Wisconsin and Other States....................	709	—	229,242	—
Slovak Evangelical Lutheran Synod of the United States of America..................	55	—	14,759	—
Norwegian Synod of the American Evangelical Lutheran Church..................	71	—	8,344	—
Norwegian Lutheran Church of America..................	2,554	2,740	496,707	318,650
Evangelical Lutheran Joint Synod of Ohio and Other States....	872	826	247,783	164,968
Lutheran Synod of Buffalo.......	41	42	9,267	6,128
Evangelical Lutheran Church in America (Eielsen Synod)....	15	20	1,087	1,206

SUMMARY OF MORE IMPORTANT STATISTICS, BY DENOMINATIONS:
1926 *(Continued)*

Denomination	Churches		Membership	
	1926	1916	1926	1916
Evangelical Lutheran Synod of Iowa and Other States......	873	977	217,873	130,793
Danish Evangelical Lutheran Church in America........	96	101	18,921	14,544
Icelandic Evangelical Lutheran Synod in North America	14	14	2,186	1,830
Finnish Evangelical Lutheran Church of America, or Suomi Synod....................	185	134	32,071	18,881
Lutheran Free Church..........	393	376	46,366	28,180
United Danish Evangelical Lutheran Church in America...	190	192	29,198	17,324
Finnish Evangelical Lutheran National Church of America ...	70	64	7,788	7,933
Finnish Apostolic Lutheran Church....................	138	47	24,016	6,664
Church of the Lutheran Brethren in America................	26	23	1,700	892
Evangelical Lutheran Jehovah Conference.........	3	6	851	831
Independent Lutheran Congregations.....................	50	—	11,804	—
Mennonite Church:				
Mennonite Church.............	295	307	34,039	34,965
Hutterian Brethren, Mennonites .	6	17	700	982
Conservative Amish Mennonite Church...................	7	13	691	1,066
Old Order Amish Mennonite Church....................	71	88	6,006	7,665
Church of God in Christ (Mennonite)....................	26	21	1,832	1,125
Old Order Mennonite Church (Wisler)..................	19	22	2,227	1,608
Reformed Mennonite Church	31	29	1,117	1,281

SUMMARY OF MORE IMPORTANT STATISTICS, BY DENOMINATIONS:
1926 (*Continued*)

Denomination	Churches		Membership	
	1926	1916	1926	1916
General Conference of the Mennonite Church of North America	136	113	21,582	15,407
Defenseless Mennonites	10	11	1,060	854
Mennonite Brethren in Christ	99	108	5,882	4,737
Mennonite Brethren Church of North America	61	53	6,484	5,127
Krimmer Brueder—Gemeinde	14	13	797	894
Mennonite Kleine Gemeinde	4	3	214	171
Central Conference of Mennonites	29	17	3,124	2,101
Conference of the Defenseless Mennonites of North America	9	15	818	1,171
Stauffer Mennonite Church	4	5	243	209
Unaffiliated Mennonite Churches	5	—	348	—
Methodist Bodies:				
Methodist Episcopal Church	26,130	29,315	4,080,777	3,717,785
Methodist Protestant Church	2,239	2,473	192,171	186,908
Wesleyan Methodist Connection (or Church) of America	619	579	21,910	20,778
Primitive Methodist Church in the United States of America	80	93	11,990	9,353
Methodist Episcopal Church, South	18,096	19,184	2,487,694	2,114,479
Congregational Methodist Church	145	197	9,691	12,503
Free Methodist Church of North America	1,375	1,598	36,374	35,291
New Congregational Methodist Church	26	24	1,229	1,256
Holiness Methodist Church, Lumber River Conference	7	6	459	434
Reformed Methodist Church	14	—	390	—
African Methodist Episcopal Church (Colored)	6,708	6,633	545,814	548,355
African Methodist Episcopal Zion Church (Colored)	2,466	2,716	456,813	257,169

SUMMARY OF MORE IMPORTANT STATISTICS, BY DENOMINATIONS:
1926 (*Continued*)

Denomination	Churches		Membership	
	1926	1916	1926	1916
Colored Methodist Protestant Church (Colored).........	3	26	533	1,967
Union American Methodist Episcopal Church (Colored).....	73	67	10,169	3,624
African Union Methodist Protestant Church (Colored)......	43	58	4,086	3,751
Colored Methodist Episcopal Church (Colored).........	2,518	2,621	202,713	245,749
Reformed Zion Union Apostolic Church (Colored).........	48	47	4,538	3,977
Reformed Methodist Union Episcopal Church (Colored).....	25	27	2,265	2,196
Independent African Methodist Episcopal Church (Colored).	29	—	1,003	—
Moravian Bodies:				
Moravian Church in America....	127	110	31,699	26,373
Evangelical Unity of Bohemian and Moravian Brethren in North America.............	34	23	5,241	1,714
Bohemian and Moravian Brethren Churches.................	3	3	303	320
New Apostolic Church...........	25	20	2,928	3,828
Old Catholic Churches in America:				
Old Catholic Church in America..	9	12	1,888	4,700
American Catholic Church......	11	3	1,367	475
North American Old Roman Catholic Church...............	27	—	14,793	
The (Original) Church of God.....	50	—	1,869	
The Pentecostal Assemblies of the World......................	126	—	7,850	—
Pentecostal Holiness Church.......	252	192	8,096	5,353
Pilgrim Holiness Church..........	441	169	15,040	5,276
Polish National Catholic Church...	89	34	60,974	28,245

SUMMARY OF MORE IMPORTANT STATISTICS, BY DENOMINATIONS:
1926 (*Continued*)

Denomination	Churches		Membership	
	1926	1916	1926	1916
Presbyterian Bodies:				
Presbyterian Church in the United States of America..........	8,947	⁵9,773	1,894,030	⁵1,625,817
Cumberland Presbyterian Church.	1,097	1,313	67,938	72,052
Colored Cumberland Presbyterian Church...................	178	136	10,868	13,077
United Presbyterian Church of North America.............	901	991	171,571	160,726
Presbyterian Church in the United States...................	3,469	3,365	451,043	357,769
Associate Synod of North America (Associate Presbyterian Church)...................	11	12	329	490
Associate Reformed Presbyterian Church...................	143	133	20,410	15,124
Synod of the Reformed Presbyterian Church of North America	89	103	7,166	8,185
Reformed Presbyterian Church in North America, General Synod	13	14	1,929	2,386
Protestant Episcopal Church.......	7,299	7,345	1,859,086	1,092,821
Reformed Bodies:				
Reformed Church in America	717	715	153,739	144,929
Reformed Church in the United States...................	1,709	1,758	361,286	344,374
Christian Reformed Church......	245	226	98,534	38,668
Free Magyar Reformed Church in America.................	11	⁶	3,992	—
Reformed Episcopal Church.......	69	74	8,651	11,050
Roman Catholic Church..........	18,940	17,375	18,605,003	15,721,815
Salvation Army.................	1,052	742	74,768	35,954
Scandinavian Evangelical Bodies:				
Swedish Evangelical Mission Covenant of America..........	357	324	36,838	29,164
Swedish Evangelical Free Church of the United States of America	107	102	8,166	6,208

SUMMARY OF MORE IMPORTANT STATISTICS, BY DENOMINATIONS:
1926 (*Continued*)

Denomination	Churches		Membership	
	1926	1916	1926	1916
Norwegian and Danish Evangelical Free Church, Association of North America..........	41	32	3,781	2,444
Schwenkfelders...................	6	6	1,596	1,127
Social Brethren..................	22	19	1,214	950
Spiritualists:				
National Spiritualists' Association	543	343	41,233	23,197
Progressive Spiritual Church.....	9	11	7,383	5,831
National Spiritual Alliance of the United States of America....	59	—	2,015	—
Temple Society of America........	2	2	164	260
Theosophical Societies:				
Theosophical Society of New York, Independent..........	1	1	55	72
American Theosophical Society ..	223	157	7,448	5,097
Universal Brotherhood and Theosophical Society...........	1	—	50,000	—
Unitarians......................	353	411	60,152	82,515
United Brethren Bodies:				
Church of the United Brethren in Christ....................	2,988	3,481	377,436	348,828
Church of the United Brethren in Christ (Old Constitution)...	372	408	17,872	19,106
United Christian Church........	15	—	577	—
Universalists....................	498	643	54,957	58,566
Vedanta Society.................	3	3	200	190
Volunteers of America...........	133	97	28,756	10,204
Other denominations [7]...........	—	144	—	30,492

[1] Includes Free Baptists.
[2] Includes Evangelical Protestant Church of North America.
[3] Seat holders and contributors only.
[4] Returns incomplete to date.
[5] Includes Welsh Calvinistic Methodist Church.
[6] Figures included in "Other denominations," not comparable with 1926.
[7] Not reported in 1926.

✠✠✠✠✠✠✠✠✠✠✠✠✠✠✠✠✠✠✠✠✠✠✠✠✠✠✠✠✠✠✠✠✠

INDEX

{555}

INDEX

INDEX

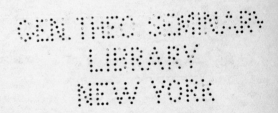

Set up in Linotype Granjon. Format by
A. W. Rushmore. Manufactured by the
Haddon Craftsmen for the Publishers
HARPER & BROTHERS
MCMXXX

✤